OXFORD GREEK AND LATIN COLLEGE COMMENTARIES

Sophocles' *Electra*

OXFORD GREEK AND LATIN COLLEGE COMMENTARIES

THE OXFORD GREEK AND LATIN COLLEGE COMMENTARIES series is designed for students in intermediate or advanced Greek or Latin at colleges and universities. Each volume includes, on the same page, the ancient text, a running vocabulary, and succinct notes focusing on grammar and syntax, distinctive features of style, and essential context. The Greek and Latin texts are based on the most recent Oxford Classical Text (OCT) editions whenever available; otherwise, other authoritative editions are used. Each volume features a comprehensive introduction intended to enhance utility in the classroom and student appreciation of the work at hand.

The series focuses on texts and authors frequently taught at the intermediate or advanced undergraduate level, but it also makes available some central works currently lacking an appropriate commentary. The primary purpose of this series is to offer streamlined commentaries that are up-to-date, user-friendly, and affordable. Each volume presents entire works or substantial selections that can form the basis for an entire semester's coursework. Each commentary's close attention to grammar and syntax is intended to address the needs of readers encountering a work or author for the first time.

Ovid, *Ars Amatoria* Book 3
Commentary by Christopher M. Brunelle

Selected Letters from Pliny the Younger's *Epistulae*
Commentary by Jacqueline Carlon

Aristophanes' *Wasps*
Commentary by Kenneth S. Rothwell, Jr.

Sophocles' *Electra*
Commentary by Hanna M. Roisman

OXFORD GREEK AND LATIN COLLEGE COMMENTARIES

Sophocles' *Electra*

Commentary by
Hanna M. Roisman

OXFORD
UNIVERSITY PRESS

OXFORD
UNIVERSITY PRESS

Oxford University Press is a department of the University of Oxford. It furthers
the University's objective of excellence in research, scholarship, and education
by publishing worldwide. Oxford is a registered trade mark of Oxford University
Press in the UK and certain other countries.

Published in the United States of America by Oxford University Press
198 Madison Avenue, New York, NY 10016, United States of America.

CIP data is on file at the Library of Congress
ISBN 978–0–19–046139–3 (pbk.)
ISBN 978–0–19–005359–8 (hbk.)

1 3 5 7 9 8 6 4 2

Paperback printed by Marquis, Canada
Hardback printed by Bridgeport National Bindery, Inc., United States of America

FOR
Yossi, Elad, Shalev, Helaina, and Diana Roisman
And my granddaughters Talia, Noa, Yael, and Esti Roisman

and
IN MEMORY OF
David P. Mankin

CONTENTS

ACKNOWLEDGMENTS

I WISH TO thank the many students in both Tel Aviv University and Colby College who studied Greek drama with me over the years. Their enthusiasm, original thinking, keen eye for the text, and questioning of accepted views made me repeatedly look at the play with fresh perspectives. I owe special thanks and gratitude to Stephen Esposito, editor of *Oxford Greek and Latin Commentaries*. His encouragement, patience, and insights were invaluable. My friend Cecilia Luschnig was always there for me and I owe much to her kind and unceasing support and learned comments. The patient staff at OUP that guided this book through production deserve my special thanks.

I dedicate the book to my beloved family that makes my life so worthwhile: Yossi, Elad, Helaina, Talia, Yael, Shalev, Diana, Noa, and Esti.

INTRODUCTION

SOPHOCLES AND HIS PLAYS

Not much is known about Sophocles' life. We know that he was born in 496/5 BCE and died in 406/5, in the same year as Euripides.[1] Sophocles showed promise as a child in both wrestling and music, and at age fifteen was selected to lead the chorus that sang the paean at the sacrifice after the Athenian victory at Salamis. He held several political offices in Athens. He served as State Treasurer in 443/2 BCE, and was elected to be a general in the war between Athens and Samos in 441/0 BCE. He was known for his genial personality, which may have helped him win the respect of his fellow citizens. In 411 BCE he was one of the old men appointed to be one of the commissioners (*probouloi*) who decided to put the government of Athens in the hands of the oligarchic Four Hundred. It has also been recorded that Sophocles was unusually pious. He established a shrine to Heracles Informer and was also said to have been the priest of an otherwise unknown hero, Halon, who shared a shrine with Asclepius. Several late sources say that he was worshiped as the hero Dexion. By later antiquity a monument outside of the city wall had been identified as Sophocles' tomb, with an epitaph portraying the poet as "a most holy figure."

Sophocles won his first victory in the yearly dramatic competitions for performances at the City Dionysia (or Great Dionysia) in 469/8 BCE, when he was twenty-seven, defeating Aeschylus, his elder. In the course of his lifetime he is said to have written a total of 113 or 123 dramas. It is impossible now to know which of the two totals is correct, since some plays were known by more than one title, and thus may have been counted more than once.[2] In either case Sophocles wrote more plays than any other poet, including Aeschylus, who is said to have written ninety or Euripides, who according to some sources wrote seventy-five, and others ninety-two. Sophocles won some twenty-first prizes in his sixty-two years as a playwright, while Euripides seems to have won only five prizes. It is noteworthy that Sophocles did not

---

1. I have discussed this material (especially the sections "Theater and Performance" and "Dramatic Treatments of the Myth") elsewhere and have incorporated some of these discussions here. See Roisman (2008), 3–15, 95–111 with the interpretative notes; Roisman and Luschnig (2011), 6–11; Roisman (2017). For a summary of the myth in art see Lloyd (2005), 25–27.

2. For titles of tragedy, see Kaimio (2014).

win the first prize with the trilogy that included *Oedipus Tyrannus*, a tragedy that Aristotle in his *Poetics* (1452a33, 1455a18) regards as a model of plot construction.

From over one hundred plays that Sophocles composed, only seven have survived complete: *Ajax, Electra, Oedipus Tyrannus, Antigone, Women of Trachis, Philoctetes*, and *Oedipus at Colonus*. Of these only two can be dated without doubt: *Philoctetes*, which won first prize in 409 BCE, and *Oedipus at Colonus*, which was produced in 401 BCE after Sophocles' death by his grandson Sophocles II. All the surviving dramas feature intense characters remarkable for their fierce and inflexible determination, worthy of awe, respect, and also sympathy, but who remain isolated literally or figuratively from other people, seldom expressing remorse.[3]

THEATER AND PERFORMANCE

We learn from ancient sources that *Electra*, like most of the extant Greek tragedies, was performed at the City Dionysia of Athens, a religious festival held in late March in honor of Dionysus, god of wine and vegetation. This was the largest and most magnificent of Athens' annual state-sponsored religious festivals. By the time the *Electra* was performed, the Dionysia had become a major Greek festival with an international audience.[4]

The tragic competition lasted three days of the five-day festival. On each of the three days a different playwright mounted three tragedies, followed by a satyr play. The three tragedies, or trilogy, could tell a single story based on sequential events in a particular myth, or different ones, as most probably did. Sophocles, unlike Aeschylus, opted for the latter. The satyr play was a raucous production, rife with obscenity, which provided relief from the emotional intensity of the tragedies.[5]

Like the rest of the festival, the tragedies were sponsored by the state and their production overseen by the *archon eponymos*, the chief official after whom the calendar year was called. This official selected the year's tragedians from among the contestants and assigned each the *choregos* (literally chorus leader, in effect financer and producer)[6] who would mount his plays and, later in the century, the actors who would perform in them. From the mid-fifth century on, the state paid the lead actors and the tragedians. While the playwrights were not quite state employees, they were not independent of the state, either.

Being state sponsored, the plays had a strong didactic element. They familiarized the public with the myths that comprised their cultural heritage and engaged them in considering the myths' meanings and implications. The involvement of the state seems to have ensured that the issues treated in the plays were of public interest, and probably defined the outer

3. Knox [1964] (1983), 28–44. For a literary biography of Sophocles see Lefkowitz (2014)
4. On the Dionysia, see Csapo and Slater (1995), 103–21, 287.
5. On the satyr plays, see Sutton (1980).
6. On the institution of the *choregoi* see Wilson (2000).

boundaries to the questioning and criticism found in many of the plays.[7] It did not, however, have the stultifying effect one might expect.

The plays were produced before huge audiences of between 15,000 and 20,000 spectators. The first few rows of the theater were occupied by the elite,[8] but most of the audience consisted of the ordinary citizens of Athens—by definition adult males—though women and children were also permitted to attend the tragic performances.[9] From the middle of the fifth century, tickets were subsidized for those who could not afford them.

The plays were part of the formal competitions that were held at the festival. They were judged by a panel formed through a combination of selection and lot.[10] Although the judges were probably chosen from among the educated elite, they were often swayed, even intimidated, by the reactions of the audiences[11]—making it likely that the winning playwrights were appreciated by the ordinary folk as well as the upper tiers.

Classical Greek drama was thus also popular drama, in the best sense of the term: drama that was written not for the elite, but for the entire *polis*, and that moved the ordinary Athenians of the time, addressed their concerns, and was fairly congruous with their thinking and worldview.

The plays were performed in the open-air Theater of Dionysus, on the southeast slopes of the Acropolis. The performances began in the early morning and continued, with breaks, through the day. The performing area, located on a leveled space at the bottom of the hillside, consisted of a large orchestra,[12] or dancing place, for the Chorus and a narrow, elevated platform that served as a stage for the actors and was connected to the orchestra by several steps in the center.

Behind the playing area stood a stage building, about twelve meters long and four meters high. It was termed a *skēnē*, after its origin as a tent or hut. When *Electra* was produced, it was probably still a temporary wooden structure that could be dismantled after the festival. Most of the action took place in the outdoor space in front of the *skēnē*, with offstage actions occurring inside the structure, which also served as a changing room and storage space. The *skēnē* represented whatever edifice the play referred to (e.g., palace, temple, cottage, tent, cave). It had a doorway in the middle and possibly two smaller doors, one at each side, for the actors to pass between the outdoor and indoor spaces. On either side of the orchestra,

---

7. See Griffin (1999a) on the impact of the historical events and democratic ideology of fifth-century Athens on the tragic drama.

8. See also Csapo and Slater (1995), 289–90.

9. On women in the audience, see Csapo and Slater 1995), 286–87, 290–93; Taplin (1978), 193–94.

10. Pickard-Cambridge (1988), 96–98. For the problematics of the lottery and the decision procedure, see Csapo and Slater (1995), 158–60.

11. Pickard-Cambridge (1988), 97–98.

12. Wiles (1997), 44–52 maintains the orchestra was circular; others that it was rectangular or trapezoidal.

running up to the stage building, were two broad aisles, referred to as *eisodoi* or *parodoi*, which served as entrances for the Chorus and characters arriving from the outside.

The seating area was large enough to seat all the 15,000 to 20,000 spectators. Stage furniture was minimal. According to Aristotle (*Poetics* 1449a16), Sophocles introduced scene painting (*skēnographia*), done on cloth or wooden panels. Since most of the audience sat too far away to see the details, we can assume that the painting depicted little more than the type of location (e.g., urban, rural, seashore) and the type of edifice the stage building represented.

Greek tragedies can be described as verse musicals. The entire script was in verse of various types. Most was in iambic trimeter, conventionally the meter of speech, which served as the basis for the spoken dialogues and monologues (see the following "Meter and Prosody"). The rest consisted of recitative (declamatory chanting) and of song in a variety of lyric meters (see Lyric Meters), accompanied by double-reed flutes and dancing. Every Greek tragedy featured a chorus, initially of twelve members, later fifteen, who danced and sang, whether alone or in dialogues (termed *kommoi*) with the other characters.

The structure of Greek tragedy is fairly predictable.[13] It typically begins with a *prologos* (prologue), which sets the scene and provides the background to the action. In *Electra*, it is the conversation between the Tutor and Orestes. The prologue comes to an end with the entrance of the Chorus, singing their entry song, or *parodos*, which provides additional background information and strikes the play's key emotional chord.[14] In *Electra*, this is pathos for the suffering heroine. The rest of the play consists of between three and five *epeisodia* (episodes, acts, or scenes), separated by *stasima* (sg. *stasimon*), antiphonal odes sung by the Chorus. In *Electra*, there are four *epeisodia* (lines 251–471, 516–822, 871–1057, 1098–1383), and three *stasima* (472–515, 1058–97, 1384–97). The *epeisodia* consist mainly of spoken dialogue between characters or recitatives between a character and the Chorus, but also contain lyrical passages, lamentations, or incidental songs by the Chorus. The Choral antiphonal odes are composed in variety of lyrical meters and are sung. The action is brought to a height and the tensions resolved in the last episode, termed the *exodos*. The play generally ends with a brief choral song.[15]

The tragedians also tended to observe conventions of plot and character. Most of the plots were based on well-known myths. The main characters were larger-than-life mythical figures: usually great warriors or members of ruling houses. The plays were thus invested with a primal quality that is inherent in myth.

13. For the main features of Greek tragic performance see Dugdale (2014a).

14. For general overview of the Chorus and its function in Greek tragedy, see Ley (2014), Vol. I: 220–204. For discussion of the choral innovations Sophocles introduces in his *Electra* and compared to the role and function of his other choruses, see Esposito (1996), 96–100.

15. For a detailed breakdown of the play's parts, see Dugdale (2014b), Vol. III: 1278–79; Sale (1973), 11–24.

The Chorus consisted of characters from all walks of life; in *Electra*, they were well-born Argive women. Speaking with one voice, the Chorus provided information, commented on the action, and sometimes participated in the action as well. It generally expressed the normative view—which may or may not have been the playwright's. The action, as Aristotle would observe a century later, was usually compacted into a single day and restricted to a single place. These conventions meant that the dramatized action was generally the culmination of events before the play started, action that the playwright had to relate to the audience without boring them. Violence was generally not displayed on stage, but usually recounted by the Chorus or a messenger. In *Electra*, the revenge murder is overheard from inside the palace.

Classical Greek tragedy was formal, stylized, nonrealistic, and removed from the everyday. Both the actors and Chorus wore masks that completely covered their heads in front and back, with openings only for the eyes and mouth. The tragic costume consisted of a tunic and two mantles, one long and one short, and was worn by nearly all the characters. The masks and costumes identified the plays as tragedies, as opposed to comedies, and as dramas, as opposed to "real life." Along with the minimalist scenery and props, the formal structure, and the mythic background, they announced that the events portrayed took place in another realm, beyond the mundane.

Early Greek tragedies were performed with two speaking actors and one or two non-speaking mutes. Aristotle credits Sophocles with adding a third speaking actor (*Poetics* 1449a17). The lead actor was termed the *protagonist*, the second the *deuteragonist*, and the third the *tritagonist*. All the actors were male. Since the tragedies routinely had more characters than actors, actors played multiple roles. The masks were obviously an asset here.

THE MYTH

Sophocles' *Electra* presents a chapter in the gruesome history of the House of Atreus: Orestes' return to Argos, his reunion with his sister Electra, their plans to avenge Agamemnon's murder, and the culminating act of matricide. While the dramatic events of the play stand alone, the Athenian audience would have been familiar with the mythical background of a story beginning when Agamemnon's earliest ancestor, Tantalus, earned a punishment in Hades for his hubristic attempts to deceive the gods. Tantalus' son Pelops carried out his own pair of treacheries. Needing to win a chariot race against King Oenomaus in order to marry the king's daughter Hippodamia, Pelops bribed Myrtilus, Oenomaus' charioteer, to remove a linchpin from a wheel of his master's chariot, as a result of which Oenomaus was killed in the race. Then, instead of granting Myrtilus the promised reward of lying with Hippodamia, Pelops threw the charioteer into the sea. Before dying, Myrtilus cursed Pelops' descendants. The sons of Pelops and Hippodamia, Thyestes and Atreus, eventually quarreled over the kingship of Argos. After Atreus became king, he discovered that his wife Aerope had betrayed him with his brother Thyestes. In a vile act of revenge, Atreus invited Thyestes to a supposedly reconciliatory feast that included the cooked pieces of Thyestes' own two sons. When Thyestes realized what he had eaten, he called down his own curse on the House of Atreus. This curse was actualized in a succession of disasters. On his way to fight in the Trojan War, Agamemnon sacrificed his daughter Iphigenia to recompense the goddess Artemis for a wrong he had inadvertently committed. Then upon his return from Troy ten years later, Agamemnon himself was murdered by his wife, Clytemnestra, and her lover, Aegisthus.

While Sophocles' *Electra* focuses on this final manifestation of the curse, the family background informs the play. Not only would the audience have been familiar with the general outlines of the story, but Sophocles also reminds them by specific references. In the very first speech, the Tutor refers to the palace of Pelops' sons (10); the grieving Electra invokes the spirit of Niobe, Pelops' sister, whose own hubris caused the death of her fourteen children (150); immediately after the matricide, the Chorus state, "the curses are doing their work! Those who lie underground are alive" (1418–19); the Chorus end the play by addressing the children of Atreus. However, like the other ancient tragedians, Sophocles provided his audience only with the specific mythical information necessary for understanding the dramatized events. Like them, he was highly selective about the details he chose to include. He does not, for example, explicitly mention Pelops' treacheries, the fact that Agamemnon and Aegisthus are first cousins, the cannibalistic feast or its cause, or any of the reasons that Aegisthus might have for hating Agamemnon.

Although there has always been speculation about which details of the myth the audience might have known, the general outlines would have been familiar. The story had a long history. The earliest and fullest extant account of the section of the myth covered in the play, the revenge killing, is found in Homer's *Odyssey*, where the gods were discussing the murder of Aegisthus by Orestes. The discussion involved the dilemma facing Telemachus, who was being eaten out of house and home by his mother's suitors on the assumption that Odysseus was never going to return. Orestes' actions could serve as an example for Telemachus, who must take some kind of action against the men courting his mother. In the *Odyssey* Aegisthus is drawn as a villain, a seducer, and a murderer who killed Agamemnon in a cowardly ambush (*Odyssey* 3.193–98, 256–61, 4.524–37).

One of the most problematic issues in the various treatments of Agamemnon's murder concerns Clytemnestra's character and culpability. In the *Odyssey*, her character is not developed. The surviving fragments of the sixth-century *Oresteia* by the first great lyric poet of the West, Stesichorus of Himera in Sicily (640–555 BCE) describe Clytemnestra's anxious dream anticipating the revenge (*PMG* 219), indicating her guilt-driven fear of retribution.[16] The dream is also included in the treatments of the myth by Aeschylus (*Cho.* 32–41, 523–53) and Sophocles (*El.* 417–30). By the fifth century, Clytemnestra's character has been further blackened by the suggestions that this husband slayer would not even flinch from killing her

---

16. Davies and Finglass (2014), frg.180: 488–91, 503–7; Swift (2015), 127.

own son. In two vase paintings of the era she brandishes an ax in the direction of Orestes, who has just killed Aegisthus (see also Prag 1985).[17] Pindar (ca. 522–ca. 443), a Theban poet who wrote Choral lyric poetry, describes Clytemnestra as a ruthless and treacherous woman from whom Orestes had to be rescued after she killed his father (*Pythian* 11.17–21).

Although Orestes is consistently portrayed as a dutiful son in the case of his father, his role as a matricide is variously treated. In the *Odyssey*, he is cast as a heroic son avenging his father's murder, thus serving as a positive role model for Telemachus. Details of his mother's death are left vague, and moral questions that might undermine Orestes' heroic stature avoided. Alongside the gradually intensifying focus on Clytemnestra's guilt, the matricide motif becomes more prominent in later works. The fragmentary pseudo-Hesiodic *Catalogue of Women* (sixth century BCE) is the first known source to state clearly that Orestes killed not only his father's murderer (Aegisthus) but also his "man-slaying mother" (from 23 [a] M–W, 27–30). In a lost epic that recounts the heroes' return from Troy titled *Nostoi*, and Pindar (*Pythian* 11.36–37), he kills both Aegisthus and Clytemnestra.

The act of matricide was deemed such an abominable crime that it could not be justified even in the case of a depraved murderess with the potential to kill her own son. Therefore, a further exculpatory device was introduced: Apollo. As Jebb ([1894] 2004: xiii) explains, the god of light and all-seeing arbiter of purity had the power to measure homicidal guilt and to cleanse killers of the pollution caused by the shedding of kindred blood. All three tragedians present Apollo's oracle authorizing the vengeance and giving instructions for carrying it out. Apollo seems to have entered the story in the *Nostoi*, a lost epic that recounts the heroes' return from Troy in which Pylades of Phocis helps Orestes kill his father's murderers. In a poem by Stesichorus of Himera (*PMG* 217), Apollo gives Orestes a bow to fend off the Erinyes, or Furies, the primitive powers that punished the murderer of kin.[18]

Finally, Electra herself is a relative latecomer to the myth. In the *Iliad* (9.145, 287) Agamemnon is said to have three daughters, but Electra is not named among them. Proclus' fifth-century CE summary of the *Cypria* (of ca. late seventh century BCE) a post-Homeric epic, names four daughters: Chrysothemis, Laodice, Iphigenia, and Iphianassa. Aelian reports the first known reference to Electra in the now-lost *Oresteia* by Xanthus (seventh century BCE), who claimed she was the daughter Homer calls Laodice, nicknamed 'Electra' because she remained so long 'un-married,' *a-lektros* in Greek. The pseudo-Hesiodic *Catalogue of Women* identifies Electra as the daughter of Clytemnestra and Agamemnon, and Orestes as their son. It is also very likely that Stesichorus' *Oresteia*, P. Oxy. 2506 (*PMG* 217) mentioned Electra's recognition of Orestes by the lock of hair left on his father's grave, thereby placing Electra firmly in the story of the revenge and suggesting she played a role in it.

---

17. A red-figure *pelikē* by the Berlin Painter, Vienna, Kunsthistorisches Museum 3725, and a red-figure *stamnos* by the Copenhagen Painter, once Berlin F2184, now lost.

18. Davies and Finglass (2014), frg. 181a.14–24: 488–91, 509: Swift (2015), 127–32.

However, none of these sources indicate much about Electra's character, her role in avenging her father's murder, or her culpability.

DRAMATIC TREATMENTS OF THE MYTH

We have extant treatments by all three of the great Athenian tragedians of the revenge murders of Clytemnestra and Aegisthus. Aeschylus' *Libation Bearers,* the second part of his *Oresteia,* dated to 458 BCE, describes the revenge, as do the *Electra* plays of both Sophocles and Euripides. Scholars still debate the order of Sophocles' and Euripides' plays because of their many similarities and echoes. Sophocles' version is tentatively placed between 418 and 410, while that of Euripides might be between 422 and 417 or 415 and 413. In any case, the view maintained here is that both Sophocles and Euripides were reacting to Aeschylus' treatment, and that Sophocles' play preceded Euripides'.[19]

In Aeschylus, Orestes, the hero of both *Libation Bearers* and *Eumenides,* is alone responsible, while Electra plays a subordinate and limited role. Both Sophocles and Euripides shift the focus from Orestes to Electra, who is the protagonist, remaining on stage throughout most of the action. Sophocles' Electra enters at line 86 and, with the exception of one brief exit (lines 1383–98), stays on stage until the end of the play. The Sophoclean and Euripidean heroines are more complex characters than the younger, more innocent girl presented by Aeschylus. They both suffer from the loss of their father, hate his murderers, and eagerly await Orestes' return to wreak vengeance on them, then actively instigate the matricide after his arrival. Sophocles depicts an Electra absorbed by grief and emphasizes her deprivations and servitude in the home of the royal couple. Euripides' Electra resents her forced marriage to a poor peasant farmer and the loss of amenities due her royal status. Despite these differences, both playwrights show women whose bitterness, anger, and intransigence detract from the unadulterated sympathy the Aeschylean Electra could claim.

The playwrights also differ in their treatment of the central tension inherent in the myth: the collision of two strongly held moral injunctions: that sons must avenge wrongs to their fathers and that killing a parent is prohibited in all circumstances. A revenge beginning and ending with the killing of Aegisthus would have been unproblematic but also of little dramatic interest. In the moral code of the day, Orestes would have been entirely justified in killing the man who had stolen his father's wife, usurped his father's throne, murdered his father, and robbed him of his patrimony, while Electra's support would have been equally proper. They would have been remiss had they behaved differently. Matricide, however, is an instinctively heinous act, which violates the most basic of human obligations.

---

19. For discussion see Roisman and Luschnig (2011), 28–32 with bibliography; Finglass (2005); Finglass (2007), 1–3; Roisman (2017); see also Conacher (1967), 202n9.

Therefore, in doing right by their father, Orestes and Electra had to commit an act that no society sanctions.

Aeschylus deals with this dilemma by portraying Clytemnestra as ruthless and justifying Orestes' killing of her.[20] While revenge as a solution to a wrong was accepted in Athens in the first half of the fifth century when Aeschylus was writing, this view gradually lost its attractiveness in the wake of the protracted Peloponnesian War (431–404 BCE) and the ensuing political strife.[21] The rampant retaliations provoked fear and threatened civic order. Against this background, neither Euripides' nor Sophocles' play justifies the matricide. Euripides' *Electra* condemns the matricide; Sophocles' position is more ambiguous. While his Chorus repeatedly warn Electra of the disastrous consequences of her wallowing in grief and of opposing the royal couple, they also consistently remind the audience of the misdeeds of Clytemnestra and Aegisthus and endorse the vengeance. Neither Orestes nor Electra doubts the morality of their actions. Furthermore, both Orestes and Electra have qualities of character—Orestes' cold rationality and practicality, Electra's self-destructive hatred and grief—that raise questions about the rightness of their deeds.[22]

SETTING

In the following section I examine the significance of the setting of the play, that is, I ask what is the possible interrelationships between the fixed settings: the city (the macro level) and the palace (the micro level), and the texts, as the play progresses from scene to scene, with changes in content, theme, and mood. The settings would necessarily have had an affect on the audience both when the characters were addressing the audience and when they were engaged in dialogue with one another. Indeed, the visual presentation must have contributed to the audience's interpretation of the performance as a whole.

The City

Sophocles chose the city of Argos as the setting for his play, with the *skēnē* representing the palace of the rulers. By choosing the city, Sophocles avails himself of the conventional perception of the urban environment. The city was perceived to be positive in its offerings of education, culture, government, law, and civic engagement, but negative in its sophistry, immorality, political conniving, and betrayal. In setting his play in the city of Argos in front of the royal palace, Sophocles follows the *Libation Bearers* of Aeschylus, whose *Oresteia* is believed

---

20. For further discussion see Roisman (2008), 13.
21. Burnett (1998), xvi, 225–26.
22. For an overview of the play see Dugdale (2014b).

to have been revived a few years earlier.[23] This setting allows him to tap into both the political and the personal-familial dimensions of the myth of the House of Atreus.

The city location is particularly fitting for the political slant that Sophocles gives his rendition of the myth. Sophocles frames the revenge as much as an ideological and political act as a personal one.[24] Agamemnon's murder is presented as the source of a multitude of ills: the pollution that emanates from the murder of a king, cousin, and husband; the usurpation of the throne by his murderers; the sexual corruption of their adulterous affair; and the deprivations of the children: Orestes' exile and loss of his home and throne and Electra's pauperization, servitude, and exclusion. Each of these ills calls for rectification, which cannot be accomplished so long as Clytemnestra and Aegisthus are on the throne. All but the last, the deprivations of Agamemnon's children, are ills that damage the polity.

Because of the public ramifications of Agamemnon's murder, the revenge in this play is not only a private act to restore the avengers' personal honor and rights, but also a political act required to cleanse and restore order to the polity. Electra is characterized not only in personal terms as a lonely and frustrated woman, living under the thumb of her father's murderers and prevented by them from marrying (164–65, 187–88, 961–66). She is also, in political terms, a courageous idealist and revolutionary, determined to see justice done for her murdered father and to bring down a corrupt and illegitimate regime.[25] Sophocles endows his Electra with a

---

23. The assumption of the revival is based mainly on a reference from Aristophanes' *Acharnians*, produced in 425, in which Dicaeopolis describes how he had breathlessly anticipated a new performance of Aeschylus (Aristoph. *Ach.* 9–10), and a reference from the *Clouds*, first performed in 423 (though our version is a revision from 418/17), where Strepsiades, an Athenian man of the older generation, asks his son, Pheidippides, to recite for him something from the works of Aeschylus (Aristoph. *Cl.* 1365). Cf. *Vita Aeschyli* 12.

24. There is some debate as to the political dimensions of Sophocles' *Electra*. Knox (1982) contends that despite the fact that Sophocles' *Electra* opens with "the most precise location of the action in a city landscape to be found in extant Greek tragedy" (p. 7), and Euripides' play is set in a remote country farm, Sophocles' *Electra* is the least political of the three extant Electra plays and Euripides' *Electra* the most. According to Knox, Sophocles "concentrates our attention almost exclusively on the violent hatreds and internecine violence of a doomed and cursed family" (p. 8). The word *polis* is rarely mentioned, he points out, and the word freedom, he contends, usually refers to the characters' personal freedom rather than freedom from political tyranny. Griffin (1999a), 78–79 points out that Sophocles' Electra "mourns Agamemnon not as a political figure, a rightful king assassinated and replaced by a usurper, but as her father, pitifully dead." In contrast, Whitman (1951), 157, holds that "[o]f the three dramatists, Sophocles makes the most definite use of the political implications of the murder of Agamemnon." Blundell (1989), 154–55, points out that "[t]he language of rule and subjection suggest a political sphere extending beyond the household." Easterling (1987), 20, observes that "Aegisthus . . . is characterized as a cruel tyrant" and, more recently, MacLeod (2001), *passim* emphasizes the connection of the plot to the *polis*. Finglass (2005), attempting a middle road, suggests that ". . . occasional glimpses into the world of the polis cannot be ignored by interpreters of the play" and that "[s]uch hints of a broader reality behind the play's main action lend the events of the drama added significance" (p. 205). In my view, a play can be "political" without explicitly referring to the *polis*, and there is no reason to read the play in an either/or manner. Sophocles also combines the personal and political in *Philoctetes;* see Roisman (2005), *passim*, and *Antigone*.

25. The fact that her immediate focus is personal does not disqualify this view of her, as Aegisthus' wish to get rid of her if she does not stop her laments indicates.

high moral tone, as he has her emphasize the moral imperative of remembering the dead and giving them their due, rail against the affront to public decency in the royal couple's behavior, and excoriate her sister's accommodation to power in exchange for a comfortable life.

Two of the play's key themes are political in nature. One, explored in the scenes between Electra and Chrysothemis, is the question of how to behave in the face of immoral but superior political power. Chrysothemis counsels safe acquiescence, Electra reckless defiance. The play shows neither course to be entirely satisfactory. Chrysothemis is depicted as the kinder, more flexible, and more realistic sister, but Electra's heroic response is acknowledged as the morally right one. Electra's high-minded pursuit of vengeance is repeatedly described as just by the Chorus (473–77, 1386–88, 1422–23, 1440–1441), but she herself is depicted as rigid, fanatic, unrealistic, and life denying (e.g., 121–26, 137–79, 215–20, 231–32, 387–89, 399, 954–57, 1165–70).

The other related theme is the inevitable corruption of ideals as they are pursued in the real world. Sophocles suggests that to attain their idealistic goals, the avengers must act as political beings, with all the moral shortcomings of politicians. Orestes carries out the vengeance by using *dolos* (cunning, guile, stealth, trickery). The means he chooses, disseminating a false report of his death, is lying, which fifth-century Athenian audiences, no less than we, would have recognized as the staple of the politician (59–66).[26] He shows the politician's thick skin as he justifies the means with the morally compromising generalization that "no speech that brings profit is bad" (61) and the politician's opportunism as he instructs the Tutor to go into the palace to gather intelligence "when the opportunity arises" (39).[27]

Electra also acts like a politician. As she laments Agamemnon's death in public, her repeated, detailed descriptions of her father's murder and of the royal couple's mistreatment of her become public protests of the conduct of the ruling powers and reinforce the public perception of the illegitimacy of their rule. Her speech aimed at persuading Chrysothemis to join her in avenging their father's murder (954–89) demonstrates her own readiness to use misleading words to attain her ends. She pretends warmth and candor she does not really have, plays on the emotional bonds and mutual obligations that family members are supposed to feel for one another by referring to herself as Chrysothemis' sister (956, cf. 461), and keeps the horror of her intended matricide from Chrysothemis by implying that the sole target of their revenge will be their father's murderer (*ton autocheira*, 955)—that is, Aegisthus.[28]

26. Cf. Roisman (2005), 42–45, 57–71, 89–105 for Odysseus' rhetoric to convince Neoptolemus to use trickery in order to bring Philoctetes to Troy.

27. The translations of Sophocles' *Electra* are based on Roisman (2008) 2017.

28. Scholars have used three ways to explain Electra's not mentioning her mother as a target of her revenge: as an unconscious act, which serves to keep her true intentions not only from Chrysothemis but also from herself; as one of the many means Sophocles uses to suppress all mention of matricide in the play; and as an indication that Clytemnestra is not part of Electra's plan. For bibliography, see Macleod (2001), 141 n.7, who subscribes to the last view, as does March (2001) on 955–57. However, already in 582–83 and 604, Electra hints that her mother should be killed.

The vengeance is drawn as a horrific act, in which the avengers lose much of their humanity. In the choral ode preceding the vengeance (1384–97) the avengers are described as "inescapable hounds/hunting down evil" (1387–88) and are identified with the Furies.[29] When her mother cries that she has been stabbed, Electra brutally cheers Orestes on to "[s]trike her a second time, if you have the strength" (1415). The cool calculation with which she gets Orestes out of the way when Aegisthus approaches (1430, 1435), the deftness with which she sweet-talks Aegisthus into believing that she has turned over a new leaf, her gratuitous rejection of his request to be allowed to say some last words, and her urging to decline him proper burial (1487–88), all combine to appall and horrify. So does Orestes' conduct. His tricking Aegisthus into lifting the cover from Clytemnestra's corpse is positively grisly. His candid determination to make sure that Aegisthus' death will be bitter (1504) marks him as no less cruel and tyrannical than Aegisthus himself. Orestes' cavalier assertion that a painful death is the proper punishment for lawbreakers and the way to ensure there will be fewer criminals (1505–7) is the statement of a callow youth without clemency to match his power.

Sophocles' point is not that Orestes and Electra are to be condemned for their *real-politik* or that the revenge is wrong. Orestes acted as he had to under the circumstances. Young and robbed of his home and wealth, he is the weaker party in an uneven battle with powerful adversaries. Moving against them openly would be suicide. Failing to act quickly and to seize the opportunity would be risking detection. Electra, for her part, is a victim of her own heroic fantasies and desires. Sophocles' point is that however right the ideal, however just the cause, its realization is inevitably tainted. This is what makes the revenge so terrible even as it is both essential and just.

The Royal Palace

There are only two verbal indications that Sophocles' *Electra* is set in the city: at the beginning, directly, when the Tutor tells Orestes where they are (1–14) and later on indirectly, when Electra tells the Chorus that Aegisthus is not at home, but in the country (313). In contrast, the royal residence, variously designated,[30] is frequently referred to, thereby increasing the salience of its visual presence for the audience. The visual presence of the "house" functions, first and foremost, to support the point in the play that, as horrific as it is, the revenge, which will bring an end to the royal couple's unjust rule, is morally essential and cannot rightly be neglected.

It does so in two ways. The first is by keeping firmly in the audience's mind the crimes that must be punished. If, as is believed, Aeschylus' *Oresteia* had been revived some years earlier, many of the spectators had probably seen it. They would have seen Clytemnestra standing in

---

29. Winnington-Ingram (1980), 228; cf. Sale (1973), 6.
30. E.g., by δῶμα, στέγη, θύραι, θυράιος, θυρῶν, ἀντιθύρων, οἶκος.

front of the palace and luring her husband to his death. They would have seen Agamemnon walk into the palace on crimson tapestries, heard his cries as he was being murdered, seen his corpse (along with Cassandra's) brought outside, and seen and heard Clytemnestra and Aegisthus justifying and vaunting their deed as they stood nearby. Even if nothing were said about the house in Sophocles' play, its representation on the stage would have recalled the treachery of Agamemnon's murder and the murderers' lack of repentance.

The second way the palace setting underscores the morality of the revenge is through the jarring visual contrast, maintained throughout the play, between the royal palace and Electra's appearance as a distraught and mourning woman, emaciated and poorly dressed (189–92, 360–361, 448–52, 1181–99). This visual contrast underlines both Electra's own sense of isolation and the tremendous wrong of her marginalization and exclusion by the royal couple, who have reduced her to a servant in her father's home. The sight of the palace, with its connotations of luxury and status, constantly reminds the audience that Electra, the king's daughter, has been wrongly deprived of her rightful place in the house and her station in the polity as the price for her principled decision to remember her father's wrongful death.

By virtue of the associations it triggers and the contrasts it highlights, the representation of the palace on the stage supports the claims in the play that Agamemnon's murderers cannot be allowed to remain in power and that the deprivations of his children must not go unrectified. However, Sophocles does more than rely on the mere presence of the house on stage to provide subliminal support for the revenge. He foregrounds the house in the audience's consciousness by the Tutor's and Orestes' frequent mention of it as a house "plagued by disasters," or in need of restoration and purification. Such references make the house an important image, highlighting the violent history and pollution of the dynasty and endowing the physical stage house (which also represents the family) with the aura of violence and impurity.

The complexity of Sophocles' message in the play makes it vital that the audience constantly bear in mind the crimes that must be punished. Euripides' play explicitly condemns the matricide as morally wrong. Its message is quite clear. Sophocles' play, on the other hand, shows how revenge corrupts and dehumanizes its perpetrators, but no one in Sophocles' play ever says that it is morally wrong. The message of the play is that the revenge must be carried out despite the enormous damage it causes those who must commit it. This is a far more sophisticated message, and therefore more difficult to grasp. It is all too easy to see the perpetrators' corruption and dehumanization as a condemnation of the revenge, with this interpretation occasionally being presented.[31] Keeping Aegisthus' and Clytemnestra's crimes constantly in the eyes and minds of the spectators helps to avoid this oversimplification.

31. E.g., Sheppard (1927), 2–9; Kells (1973), 6–12.

The presence of the representation of the royal palace also serves to emphasize the contrast between inside and outside that is first made, then reimagined in the play. Early on the Tutor describes the house as "plagued by disasters" (10). Then, Orestes states that he will have to go into the house to purify it (69–70), and asks to be its restorer (72). These two statements are followed by Electra's highlighting that the murder was committed inside the house, where Aegisthus now sits on her father's chair, pours libations at his hearth, and sleeps with her mother in Agamemnon's bed (268–74). All of these references combine to identify the inside of the house as the place of evil. The outside, where the good Tutor delivers his prologue and Electra stands lamenting her father's death and telling of the ruling couple's crimes, is identified as the "good" or "moral" place from where their punishment will come.

This contrast between "inside" and "outside" the house is more or less maintained up until the end of the fourth episode; the sight of the house, laden with associations, reinforces it. In the reunion scene, the house is not mentioned during the recognition itself (1220–87), so as not to spoil the joy that bursts forth when brother and sister finally recognize each other. After the recognition, the house's presence in front of the audience's eyes lends validity to Orestes' and the Tutor's cautions, and helps to bring home the deadly consequences that Electra's ecstatic and overly loud expressions of joy could have. However, with Orestes' reminder that they will soon be going into the palace to carry out the revenge and with the Tutor's emergence from the palace, where Orestes had sent him to spy out the situation (39–43), the distance between inside and outside is reduced, as is the spatial and visual distinction between evil and good that had largely prevailed till this point in the play.

In the dramatization of the vengeance in the fifth episode, the distance between the evil of the inside and goodness of the outside is eliminated. Even though the stage-building-palace continues to stand as a visible reminder of the crimes that must be punished, it is now foregrounded in a way that blurs the distinction between inside and outside. The foregrounding occurs through the interplay of words that the audience hears and actions that they see. Orestes and Pylades go into the house to kill Clytemnestra. Then, for the first time in the play, Electra goes into the house (1383) with neither explanation nor evident reason. After she goes in, the Chorus inform the audience that "they've just gone into the house, / these inescapable hounds / hunting down evil" (1386–88). Fifteen lines later Electra rushes out again, telling the Chorus that she did so to make sure that Aegisthus does not surprise them with his return (1398–403). Those who entered the house are now tainted by its evil, and in turn taint the outside into which they emerge with the matricide committed within.

Thus in the depiction of the matricide, inside and outside intermingle. As Clytemnestra is being murdered in the palace, Electra stands outside, describing the action. Clytemnestra's cries are heard outside, where they are duly noted by Electra and the Chorus (1406–10). From outside the house, Electra shouts into it to reject her mother's plea for pity (1411–12) and to encourage Orestes to strike their mother a second time (1415). After killing his mother, Orestes emerges from the house with his bloodied sword (1422) and coldly declares that "all is well in the house, if Apollo prophesized well" (1424–25), before going back inside to wait for Aegisthus. By the end of the play, the evil inside/good outside dichotomy has been eradicated. The outside and those who enter the house from it can no longer be identified with the good. Likewise, the royal palace ceases to be identified solely with the evils that were committed within its walls. The purpose of this eradication of distinctions, however, is not to create a moral equivalence between Agamemnon's murderers and those who avenge his murder. The point is that the two worlds cannot be kept apart. When the justice and ideals of the world outside are brought into the world represented by the house, they inevitably partake of its corruption.

GUIDELINES FOR USING THE COMMENTARY

1. The commentary is based on *Sophoclis Fabulae*, edited by H. Lloyd-Jones and N.G. Wilson, Oxford Classical Texts (Oxford: Oxford University Press, 1990).

   The commentary also refers to the following commentaries in English:

Campbell, L. 1881	*Sophocles*. Vol. II. Oxford: Oxford University Press
Jebb, R.C. 1894	Sophocles.*Electra*. Part VI. Cambridge: Cambridge
(repr. 2004)	University Press; repr. London: Bristol Classical Press
Kells, J.H. 1973	*Sophocles: Electra*. Cambridge: Cambridge University Press
Kamerbeek, J.C. 1974	*The Plays of Sophocles, Part V: The Electra*. Leiden, The Netherlands: Brill
March, J. 2001	*Sophocles: Electra*. Warminster, UK: Aris and Phillips
Finglass, P.J. 2007	Sophocles.*Electra*. Cambridge and New York: Cambridge University Press

2. The commentary offers grammatical and syntactical explanations as well as translations. For enabling further study, references to relevant grammar and syntax books are included (see "Main Abbreviations").

3. The commentary offers a running vocabulary in the Notes and in the Glossary at the end of the Commentary, according to the following guidelines:

   Words are given as much as possible in their dictionary form to replicate the use of dictionaries. Usually next to the lemma of a verb in its lexical form, the text's form is also given in parenthesis to help the student. When a verb should be known, but the form in the text might be difficult to identify, I have put this form as a lemma, and in parentheses the verb in its lexical form.

   Words that appear only twice in the play are listed both times in the Commentary, unless the occurrences are fewer than fifty lines apart. These words are *not* listed in the *Glossary*.

   Words that appear more than twice are marked by a + sign. These are mentioned usually only once in the Notes, but are included in the Glossary. The student is expected to memorize these words.

   Words in the Glossary are given the range of meanings appearing in the play. Students are expected to learn these upon each word's first occurrence and subsequently to choose the meaning that best fits the context. The words in the glossary, especially their verbal forms, might be mentioned again in the commentary if they seem to need further comment, but their meanings are not usually repeated.

See the list in "Main Abbreviations" for further instructions.

4. All irregular verbs are marked by * sign. Their forms are to be found in the "Irregular (and Unpredictable) Principal Parts" list.

5. Translations are usually marked by single quotation marks, while double quotation marks represent the translation, or direct comment, of the preceded or following cited work. Grammatical and syntactical pointers appear alongside the translations, which use denotative and connotative meanings of the words. It *is important for students to notice that translations do not always match the lexical notes.* This distinction should help them understand the concept that literal translations are not always possible or should be preferred. Sometimes the preferable meaning of the Greek word is underlined.

6. Resolutions are noted in the spoken parts only (see "Meter and Prosody").

7. After line 100, *crasis* is not pointed out unless of special importance or difficulty. After about line 300, there are no longer page-references to the definitions of grammatical, rhetorical, literary figures, or metrical features. After about line 750, common syntactical features like genitive partitive or possessive are no longer noted. The last 400 lines have fewer references to syntactical sources and to literary devices if the phenomena have been frequently referenced before.

8. Line numbers for the notes are inserted for facilitating readability and do not necessarily relflect the syntax. Notes relate to the Greek text on top of the page. If any overflow is necessary, it will appear BENEATH the Greek text on the following page, e.g., p. 64.

METER AND PROSODY

Classical drama is written in verse. The dialogue parts are spoken, mostly in iambs. The choral odes and some other parts (e.g., *kommoi*) are sung (see Appendix A: "Metrical Analysis").

SCANNING GREEK IAMBS

Greek meters are described as the alterations of long and short syllables in regular patterns. The iambic metron is the closest to the rhythm of ordinary conversation (Aristotle, *Poetics* 1449a19; Demetrius, *On Style* 43). A syllable is long if it contains a long vowel or diphthong, or a short vowel followed by two or more consonants or a double consonant (ψ, ξ, ζ). The two consonants need not be in the same word. A mute (labial π, β, φ; guttural κ, γ, χ; dental τ, ζ, θ) followed by a liquid (λ or ρ), may not cause the preceding vowel to count as long. A syllable is *short* when its vowel is short (and is followed by only one consonant or be mute plus liquid). A vowel or diphthong at the end of a word, followed by a word beginning with a vowel, usually counts as short.

> **Iamb**   ⌣ – (short/long)

In dramatic verse iambs appear in groups of two, that is to say, in dipodic units. The most common line of dialogue consists of six iambs or three such groups:

⌣ – ⌣ – | ⌣ – ⌣ – | ⌣ – ⌣ –

The following substitutions are permitted:

> **Spondee**   – – (two longs) may substitute the first iamb of each unit, that is, the first, third, and fifth iamb

> **Tribrach**   ⌣ ⌣ ⌣ (three shorts) may be used for the first five iambs

> **Anapest**   ⌣ ⌣ – (short long short) may be used anywhere a spondee can occur, i.e., instead of the first iamb of each unit, that is, the first, third, and fifth iamb

Dactyl	– ◡ ◡ (long, short short) may be used anywhere a spondee can occur, i.e., in the first iamb of each unit, that is, the first, third, and fifth iamb

A final short in any line is counted as long (*syllaba anceps* X).

RESOLUTION

Resolution is the substitution of two shorts for either a long or a short in the iambic trimeter. The most common place for resolution is in position six, otherwise termed as third *longum* (Devine and Stephens [1980], 66–67).

The choral odes and lyric dialogues between a character and the Chorus (*kommoi*) are composed in lyric meters (for the analysis of which see Appendix A: "Metrical Analysis"). Electra's monody heard from the palace (86–120) is in chanted anapests.

Examples   (*Electra*, lines 1–3)

Ὦ τοῦ στρατηγήσαντος ἐν Τροίᾳ ποτὲ

– – ◡ – | – – ◡ – | – – ◡ X

Ἀγαμέμνονος παῖ, νῦν ἐκεῖν᾽ ἔξεστι σοι

◡ ◡ – ◡ ◡ | – – ◡ – | – – ◡ X   resolution in first position

παρόντι λεύσσειν, ὧν πρόθυμος ἦσθ᾽ ἀεί.

◡ – ◡ – | – – ◡ – | ◡ – ◡ X

CHORAL SONGS

In tragedy lyric meters, that is to say, meters that are sung rather than chanted or recited, are organized according to strophic structure.[1] This is a structure of pairs of stanzas, *strophē* and *antistrophē*, that have different words but the same metrical structure line by line (resolutions are often allowed). The metrical structure of each *strophē/antistrophē* unit is

---

1. For an excellent overview of meter in tragedy, see Battezatto (2014).

unique. Occasionally, after the last *antistrophē* in a song there follows a stanza with no metrical responsion; it is called an *epode*. An *epode* ends the song.

In its lyrics *Electra* uses a variety of meters, of which the more recurrent are the following:

1. Of Aeolic meters one finds the following: the glyconic ⏓ ⏓ – ⏑ ⏑ – ⏑ –; pherecratean ⏓ ⏓ – ⏑ ⏑ – –; tellesileus ⏓ – ⏑ ⏑ – ⏑ –; reizianum ⏓ – ⏑ ⏑ – –; aristophanean – ⏑ ⏑ – ⏑ – –; lecythion – ⏑ – ⏓ – ⏑ –; anacreontic ⏑ ⏑ – ⏑ – ⏑ – –; ithyphallic – ⏑ – ⏑ – ⏒. The Aeolic meters are analyzed not into feet but into *cola* of various kinds. A *colon* is a metrical sequence of not more than twelve syllables with a recognizable recurring pattern. A line of poetry can consist of one *colon,* or two or three cola may be strung together. In Aeolic meter there is no resolution (i.e., —into ⏑ ⏑) or contraction (i.e., ⏑ ⏑ into –, and the number of syllables in a given *colon* is always the same

2. One also finds dochmiacs in various configurations. Because of the various resolutions the dochmiac metron can be represented as ⏒ ⏖ ⏖ ⏒ ⏖

3. Of dactylic meters one finds dactylic tetrameter (– ⏑ ⏑ – ⏑ ⏑ – ⏑ ⏑ – ⏑ ⏑) and dimeter (– ⏑ ⏑ – ⏑ ⏑). Dactylic sequences in this play are often combined with Aeolic or other meter.

4. One also finds the chroriamb – ⏑ ⏑ – ; the iamb ⏑ –; the cretic – ⏑ – ; and the bacchiac ⏑ – – in various configurations with the previously mentioned meters.

DEFINITIONS OF GRAMMATICAL, RHETORICAL, AND LITERARY FIGURES USED IN THE COMMENTARY

alliteration   the repetition of consonant and vowel sounds in successive words or stressed syllables.

anaphora   the repetition of word, group of words, phrase, or cognate words at the beginning of successive verses, phrases, or lines (S #3010).

anastrophe   a shift back of an accent to the penult when preposition follows its noun or pronoun (S #175).

aphaeresis   the elision of ε at the beginning of a word after a word ending in a long vowel or diphthong (S #76).

apocope   in poetry a short vowel is sometimes cut off before a consonant.

apokoinu (ἀπὸ κοινοῦ)   ('in common') a word common to two clauses or two syntactical structures, carrying two syntactical functions.

asyndeton   absence of conjunction in a series of related and grammatically coordinated words or phrases (S #3016).

chiasmus   a rhetorical or literary figure in which words, grammatical constructions, or concepts are repeated in reverse order, in the same or a modified form (S #3020).

correption   the shortening of a long vowel before another vowel.

crasis   blending of syllables, contraction of vowels or diphthong at the end of a word with a vowel or diphthong at the beginning of the next word. It is marked with —'—, termed "coronis."

enallage   the substitution of one grammatical form in place of another; e.g., plural for singular (S #3023).

enjambment   the carrying over of a word or phrase to the next line; the breaking of a syntactical unit between two verses.

epanaphora, epanalepsis   see anaphora.

figura etymologica   the use of two or more words from the same root in close proximity; e.g., πρᾶγμα πράσσειν, πάθεα παθεῖν.

hendiadys   (one through two) one idea expressed by through two coordinate words, usually nouns connected by 'and': e.g., 'dangerous and divisive,' i.e., 'dangerously divisive' (S #3025).

hiatus   a break between two vowel sounds in adjoining syllables (S #46).

hypallage   an interchange in relationship among words in a phrase from a more fitting to a less appropriate one. When a word, instead of agreeing with a noun that it logically qualifies, grammatically agrees with another noun.

hyperbaton   the separation of words that naturally belong together; used for emphasis (S #3028).

metonymy   the substitution of one word for another that is closely associated with it (S #3033).

pluralis maiestatis   *majestic plural*, the royal 'we.' The use of plural to refer to a single person.

polyptoton   the repetition of words derived from the same root but with different endings in close proximity; a rhetorical device that can be used to reinforce the concept inherent in the repeated words.

pregnant construction   two actions condensed into one; the one stated implies more than it says. A form of brachyology.

prolepsis   the representation or assumption of a future act or situation as if existing in anticipation/before it actually happens.

resolution   the substitution of two shorts for a long or short element in the iambic trimeter (see "Meter and Prosody").

synecdoche   the use of part for whole, whole for part (S #3047).

synizesis   two vowels, or a vowel and a diphthong in successive syllables uniting to form a single syllable when pronounced but not in writing (S #60, 61).

tmesis   the separation of preposition from its verb (S #1650).

zeugma   a figure of speech in which a word, usually a verb or an adjective, applies to two or more words while appropriate to only one of them or making a different sense with each (S #3048).

MAIN ABBREVIATIONS

GMT	W.W. Goodwin, *Syntax of the Moods and Tenses of the Greek Verb*
GP	J.D. Denniston, *The Greek Particles* (2nd ed. rev. K.J. Dover)
LSJ	Liddell, Scott, Jones, *A Greek-English Lexicon*, 9th ed. with rev. supplement
S	H.W. Smyth, *Greek Grammar*, revised by G. M. Messing
SS	A.C. Moorhouse, *The Syntax of Sophocles*

SYMBOLS USED IN THE NOTES

⁺	words marked by a raised plus sign should be learned as they come up in the text. Their meaning won't be repeated, but each word appears in the Glossary at the end of the commentary
*	marks irregular and unpredictable verbs. Their forms are to be found in the "Irregular (Unpredictable) Principal Parts" list
·	hypothetical reconstruction, i.e., unattested form; or, see "Irregular (and Unpredictable) Principal Parts" list
+	and, i.e., compounded with, *or* with suffix
×	times (i.e., 8× = eight times)
<	comes from, is derived from
>	becomes, develops into
=	equals, equivalent to, identical with
/	varies between
(...)	usually the material within parentheses is grammatical explanation, cross-reference, occasionally translation
[...]	usually the material within square brackets contains words that do not occur in the text but need to be inserted in translation. Square brackets are also used to mark a single occurrence of a word in the play or in the extant plays of Sophocles, e.g., [1× Soph.] means that the word appears once in Sophocles

ABBREVIATIONS USED IN THE NOTES

acc.	accusative	obj.	object
act.	active (voice)	oft.	often
adj.	adjective, adjectively	opt.	optative (mood)
adv.	adverb(ial)	partit. genit.	partitive genitive
aor.	aorist (tense)	pass.	passive (voice)
artic.	articular	pcl.	particle
compd.	compound	pers.	person(s)/personal(ly)
conj.	conjunction	pf.	perfect (tense)
correl.	correlative	pl.	plural
dat.	dative	plupf.	pluperfect (tense)
demon.	demonstrative	possess.	possession/possessive
dep.	deponent (voice)	postpos.	postpositive
enclit.	enclitic	predicat.	predicative
etc.	Latin *et cetera*, 'and the rest,' 'and so on'	prep.	preposition
		pres.	present (tense)
fem.	feminine	privat.	privative
fut.	future	pron.	pronoun
genit.	genitive	ptc.	participle
impv.	imperative (mood)	relat.	relative, related
indecl.	indeclinable	seq.	sequence
indef.	indefinite	sg.	singular
indic.	indicative (mood)	subjv.	subjunctive (mood)
inf.	infinitive	substant.	substantive, substantival, substantivizing
intrans.	intransitive		
l.	line	supplem.	supplementary
lit.	literally	temp.	temporal
masc.	masculine	trans.	transitive
mid.	middle (voice)	usu.	usually
n.	note	vb.	verb
neut.	neuter	voc.	vocative

COMMENTARY ON SOPHOCLES' *ELECTRA*

ΗΛΕΚΤΡΑ

ΠΑΙΔΑΓΩΓΟΣ

Ὦ τοῦ στρατηγήϲαντοϲ ἐν Τροίᾳ ποτὲ
Ἀγαμέμνονοϲ παῖ, νῦν ἐκεῖν' ἔξεϲτί ϲοι
παρόντι λεύϲϲειν, ὧν πρόθυμοϲ ἦϲθ' ἀεί.

PROLOGUE 1–120

Scene: Dawn, before the royal palace of the Pelopidae at Mycenae, some eighteen years after the Trojan War and eight years after the murder of Agamemnon by Clytemnestra and Aegisthus.

Enter Tutor, leading Orestes and Pylades along a ramp (*eisodos*) on the spectators' right, indicating arrival from somewhere else in the territory of Mycenae. The Tutor (παιδαγωγός) is the faithful old servant who smuggled Orestes to Phocis and raised him.

The prologue consists of a dialogue between the Tutor and Orestes (lines 1–85) and Electra's anapestic lament delivered from the *skēnē* (86–120). Her lament is mostly 'recitative,' chanted with music but not sung.

LINE 1

ὦ . . . ποτὲ	The Oxford Classical Texts editors and many other editors consider line 1 authentic, but there are also major scholars (e.g., Haslam (1975), West (1984), Finglass) who consider it spurious, since, the argument goes, it's a feeble initial verse lacking the force of other Sophoclean openings and makes a "purposeless reference to Agamemnon's command at Troy" (Finglass 2007: on line). But ποτέ in line 1 is echoed in line 11 (both in final position) the first regarding Ag. as *victor of Troy*, the second as *victim of assassination* (so Pelliccia, *CR* 59.1, 2009, 35).
στρατ-ηγέω, -ήγησα	(στρατός + ἄγω) be a general (ptc. qualifies the noun as an *attributive* adj.: S #2049; SS 256–57; GMT #824); > 'Son of Ag., who once commanded.' Denominative vbs. in -έω are often intrans. (S#866.2). [1× *El*]
⁺ποτε (indef. adv.)	(enclitic) at some time; <u>once upon a time</u> (esp. in telling a story: LSJ III.1a)
⁺Ἀγαμέμνων, ονος, ὁ	murdered king of Mycenae. Resolution of 1st *anceps* in a trimeter is common with proper names (pp. 20–21, 24)
⁺παῖς, παιδός, ὁ/ἡ	child (voc.: S #248; ὦ for politeness: S #1284–85). The unit Ὦ . . . παῖ is separated by τοῦ . . . Ἀγαμέμνονος. Such transposition of words belonging together is called *hyperbaton* (S #3028); here it stresses the intervening clause.
⁺ἐκεῖνος (3)	(demon. pron.) *that* person/thing. ἐκεῖν' (acc. neut. pl.) = direct object of λεύσσειν and antecedent of ὧν (< ἐκεῖ *there* + suffix –ενος: S #333c)
⁺ἔξεστι (< ἔξ-ειμι)	it is possible for someone (*dat.*) + inf.; (⁺λεύσσειν = subject: S #1984–85)
⁺πάρ-ειμι	(ptc. παρ-ών, -όντος: S #305, 768) be present/near. σοι παρόντι = 'now *when you are here* (i.e., with present eyes) you can look upon those things'
⁺λεύσσω	see/<u>look upon</u> + acc. (poetic verb; pres. and impf. only)
πρό-θυμος, ον	willing, eager, <u>eager for</u> + objective genit., (LSJ I.2; S #1328; SS 52–53 §4); >'you can look upon those things which (ὧν) *you were eager to see*'; [1× *El*.]
⁺*εἰμί, ἦν	be (impf. ἦν, ἦσθα, ἦν, ἦμεν, ἦτε, ἦσαν: S #768)
⁺ἀεί (adv.)	[ἄ/ᾱ] ever, always (old locative < αἰών < αἰϝών, eternity: S #38)

τὸ γὰρ παλαιὸν Ἄργος οὑπόθεις τόδε,
τῆς οἰστροπλῆγος ἄλσος Ἰνάχου κόρης·
αὕτη δ᾽, Ὀρέστα, τοῦ λυκοκτόνου θεοῦ   5
ἀγορὰ Λύκειος· οὑξ ἀριστερᾶς δ᾽ ὅδε
Ἥρας ὁ κλεινὸς ναός· οἷ δ᾽ ἱκάνομεν,
φάσκειν Μυκήνας τὰς πολυχρύσους ὁρᾶν,

LINE 4

Ἄργος, εος, τό	a city in NE Peloponnese, 6 miles from Mycenae; here = <u>Argolid plain</u>; [1× *El.*]
⁺παλαιός (3)	(πάλαι, long ago) old in years, old in date, <u>ancient</u>
⁺*ποθέω	long for, yearn after (what is absent) + acc. (S #1349); <u>οὑπόθεις</u> = ὃ ἐ-πόθε-ε-ς (relative pron. contracts with vb. by *crasis*, i.e., mingling of a vowel at end of one word with initial vowel of following word: S #62)
⁺ὅ-δε, ἥ-δε, τό-δε	(demon. pron., S #333) this (ὅ -δε points out what is present or before one; hence it is called *deictic*: S #1241); > '<u>here</u> (τόδε) is the (τό) ancient Argos'

LINE 5

οἰστρο-πλήξ, πλῆγος ὁ/ἡ	(οἰστράω, sting + πλήσσω, strike) stung by a gadfly, driven wild; [1× Soph.]
ἄλσος, εος, τό	grove; esp. a sacred grove. Here in apposition to Argos.
Ἴναχος, ὁ	Inachus, the eponymous god of the river, which flows into the Argolid from the NW. He was the first king of Argos and father of Io; [1× Soph.]
⁺κόρη, ἡ	girl; <u>daughter</u> (refers to Io, priestess of Hera)
⁺οὗτος, αὕτη, τοῦτο	(demon. pron.: S #333) this, that one (sc. ἐστί); > '*this* is the Lycean agora'
⁺Ὀρέστης, ου, ὁ	(ὅρος, mountain) masculines in –της have vocative in short α (S #226); Soph. omits ὦ with names of persons that are without modification or complement; hence here plain Ὀρέστα (SS 27)
λῠκό-κτονος, ον	(λύκος, wolf + κτείνω) wolf-slaying; epithet of Apollo; [1× Soph.]

LINE 7

ἀγορά, ἡ	[ᾰ] (ἀγείρω, gather) marketplace; αὕτη ... ἀγορά = *hyperbaton*; [1× Soph.]
⁺Λύκειος, ον	[ῠ] belonging to a wolf (λύκος). As an epithet of Apollo, 'Lycean' sometimes refers to his role as wolf-slayer (protector of flocks), sometimes to his role as god of light (< *λύκη, light). >'Lycean market' alludes to Apollo's temple by the agora.
⁺ἐκ (+genit.)	out of (ἐξ before a vowel, movable σ :S #136); οὑξ = ὁ ἐξ (*crasis*: S #62)
ἀριστερός (3)	[ᾰ] <u>left</u>; ominous. οὑξ ἀριστερᾶς sc. χειρός (in common expressions a definite noun, e.g., χείρ, is often implied: S #1027 b); > 'and there [from the] on the left'
Ἥρα, ἡ	wife of Zeus, main goddess of the Argives. The *Heraion* was situated near Mt. Euboia, 5 miles NE of Argos and 2 miles SE of Mycenae; [1× Soph.]
⁺κλεινός (3)	(κλέος, rumor; good report; fame) renowned; ὁ κλεινὸς νᾱός: the article is used of the familiar/well known and often with κλεινός (SS 144 §13)
ναός, ὁ	temple (Doric form is metrically easier than Attic νεώς: S #238c); [1× *El.*]
⁺οἷ (relat. adv.)	to which place, whither (cf. correl. advs. ποῖ, ποι, ὅποι: S #346)
ἱκάνω, ἵκᾰνον	come; lengthened form of ἵκω, found in Epic and Lyric poetry, sometimes in Tragedy.
φά-σκω	say, think, <u>believe</u> (infinitive is often used as imperative in poetry: S #2013)
Μῠκῆναι, ῶν, αἱ	[ῠ] = ἡ Μῠκήνη (plural prevails in Attic, singular in Homer *metri causā*); [1× *El.*]
πόλυ-χρῡσος, ον	(χρῡσός, gold) rich in gold (fem. acc. pl.: only 2 endings, like most compd. adjectives: S #288). Homeric epithet of Mycenae. [1× *El.*]
⁺*ὁράω, εἶδον	(aor.² stem ἰδ-: S #529.2) see; > 'where we came now you may say you see'

πολύφθορόν τε δῶμα Πελοπιδῶν τόδε ,　　　　　　　　　　　　　　　　**10**
ὅθεν ϲε πατρὸϲ ἐκ φόνων ἐγώ ποτε
πρὸϲ ϲῆϲ ὁμαίμου καὶ καϲιγνήτηϲ λαβὼν
ἤνεγκα κἀξέϲωϲα κἀξεθρεψάμην
τοϲόνδ' ἐϲ ἥβηϲ, πατρὶ τιμωρὸν φόνου.

LINE 10

πολύ-φθοροϲ, ον — (φθόροϲ, ruin) of much destruction (strong antithesis in 9–10: 'rich in gold' vs. 'rich in murder'); cf. πολυφθόροϲ (act.) 'destroying many'; [1× *El.*]

⁺δῶμα, ατοϲ, τό — house (goes with τόδε; > 'and there [is] the house of the sons of Pelops')

Πελοπίδηϲ, ου, ὁ — (Πέλοψ, -οποϲ) son or descendant of Pelops (–ιδηϲ patronymic: S #845.4); Μυκήναϲ . . . πολυχρύϲουϲ/ πολύφθορόν . . . δῶμα (chiasmus); [1× Soph.]

LINE 11

ὅθεν (relat. adv.) — whence, from where (S #346); [1× *El.*]

⁺πᾰτήρ, πᾰτρόϲ, ὁ — father (syncopated noun: S #44, 262)

⁺φόνοϲ, ὁ — murder; homicide (generalizing plural refers to one deed: S #1000; SS 7 §4c); > '(whence I took/res-cued) you away *from/after the scene of your father's murder*' (SS 108 §9); cf. φόνουϲ πατρῴουϲ, 779. Some editors (e.g., Finglass) read not φόνων but φονῶν (< φονή, bloodshed, carnage ; always pl.); > '*from the moment of your father's bloody slaughter.*'

⁺πρόϲ (+ genit.) — from, at the hand of (with verbs of having, receiving, etc.: LSJ A.II.1)

⁺ὅμαιμοϲ, ὁ/ἡ — (ὁμόϲ, one and the same + αἷμα, blood) of the same blood, kinswoman (the motif of blood relations is highlighted from the outset)

⁺κᾰϲιγνήτη, ἡ — (κάϲιϲ, brother/sister; γίγνομαι, be born) sister; ὁμάιμου καὶ καϲιγνήτηϲ = *hen-dia-dys,* i.e., one idea expressed by two words (S #3025)

⁺*λαμβάνω, ἔλαβον — (aor.² ptc. act.) take, receive (circumstantial aor.² ptc. denoting time: S #1872c); 'taking/after taking'

⁺*φέρω, ἤνεγκα — bring, carry, bear; endure (on this irregular aor.¹ form see S #539.10)

ἐκ-⁺*ϲῴζω, -έϲωϲα — save, preserve from danger (κἀξέϲωϲα = καὶ ἐξέϲωϲα by *crasis*: S #67; in compd. vbs. ἐκ can signify 'ut-terly,' 'completely': S #1688.2; SS 111 §9)

ἐκ-τρέφω, -έθρεψα — rear from childhood, raise (the middle of the vb. does not differ semantically from the active. The *tricolon crescendo* of three successive actions rising to a climax [cf. 283, 1235] emphasizes the personal involve-ment of the Tutor in rescuing Orestes, as is the *three-word trimeter*, of which there are only 17 in Soph., see Marcovich 1984: 59–60, and see also 1002); > 'once after taking you from . . . I carried you, and saved you, and raised you.'

LINE 14

⁺τοϲόϲ-δε, τοϲή-δε, τοϲόν-δε — so great (demon. pron. τόϲοϲ with stronger demonstrative sense: S #340); > 'and raised you *to this stage of youthful vigor*'; cf. 961

⁺εἰϲ/ἐϲ (+ acc. only) — into; up to, until (in poetry many prepositions are postpositive: S # 1675a)

ἥβη, ἡ — manhood, youth, youthful prime

⁺τιμωρόϲ, ὁ — avenger (with objective genit.: S #1331; SS 53 §4); πατρί = dat. of advantage, oft. translated as dat. of possess. (SS 85 §9); > 'avenger of *your father's* murder'

πατρὶ τιμωρὸν φόνου — creates a ring composition with πατρὸϲ ἐκ φόνων at line 11 (Finglass)

νῦν οὖν, Ὀρέcτα καὶ cὺ φίλτατε ξένων

Πυλάδη, τί χρὴ δρᾶν ἐν τάχει βουλευτέον·

ὡc ἡμὶν ἤδη λαμπρὸν ἡλίου cέλαc

ἑῷα κινεῖ φθέγματ' ὀρνίθων cαφῆ

μέλαινά τ' ἄcτρων ἐκλέλοιπεν εὐφρόνη.

LINE 15

⁺οὖν (pcl.)   so now, therefore (marks transition to a new thought: S #2964; GP 426)

⁺ξένοc, ὁ   host, <u>guest-friend</u>; stranger (superlative with partit. genit.: #1306, 1315; SS 58 §10)

Πυλάδηc, ου, ὁ   (< πύλη, gate; patronymic in form: S #845.2) voc. coordinated with Ὀρέcτα (SS 31 §14); note the emphatic *enjambment*. He is son of Strophius and Ag.'s sister in Phocis; they gave Orestes refuge. He is a κωφόν πρόcωπον, mute character

⁺τίc, τί   [ῐ] (interrog. pron.; genit. τίνοc: S #334) who? what? L. *quis? quid?*

⁺χρή   (indecl. noun: 'necessity'; supply ἐcτί: S #793) it is necessary + infinitive

⁺τάχοc, εοc, τό   [ᾰ] swiftness, speed; ἐν τάχει 'quickly' (LSJ II)

βουλευτέοc, τέον   (verbal adj. ⁺βουλεύω) it must be decided (S #358.2.b; impersonal: S #2149.2); > 'so now ... what is necessary to do *must be decided* quickly [by you]'; [1× Soph.]

LINE 17

⁺ὡc (conj.)   inasmuch as, since, seeing that (causal, LSJ B.IV; S #3000)

ἡμὶν   (ῐ, *metri causā*; cf. ἡμῖν: S #325f) <u>for our sake</u> (ethical dat. or dat. of feeling to denote the speaker's interest: S #1486; SS 85§10)

⁺ἤδη (adv.)   (ἤ, really + δή, even) <u>already</u>, by this time, now, immediately

⁺λαμπρόc (3)   (λάμπω shine) bright, brilliant, radiant

⁺ἥλιοc, ὁ   sun

cέλαc, αοc, τό   bright light/ray, brightness, flame; lightning flash; [1× *El.*]

ἑῷοc (2/3)   (ἕωc, ἡ: cf. Ionic ἠώc) at daybreak, in/of the morning; [1× Soph.]

κῑνέω   set in motion, arouse, stir up; [1× *El.*)

φθέγμα, ατοc, τό   (φθέγγομαι, utter a sound) sound, voice; word

⁺ὄρνιc, ὄρνιθοc, ὁ/ἡ   bird; omen (declension S #285.20)

⁺caφήc, έc   clear, distinct (proleptic predicat. adj.; anticipates result of vb.'s action: S #3045; SS 167 §6: "arouses the birds' songs so that they are clearly heard.")

μέλᾱc, μέλαινα, μέλαν   black, dark (S #298; cf. τᾰλαc, τάλαινα, τάλαν); [1× *El.*]

⁺ἀcτήρ, έροc, ὁ   star; > 'starry night' (genit. of quality: S #1320; SS 54 §6)

⁺ἐκ-⁺⁺λείπω, -λέλοιπα   leave out, pass over; (intrans.) leave off, cease (LSJ II.4); > 'has departed'

εὐφρόνη, ηc, ἡ   (εὔφρων, cheerful) the kindly time; euphemism for νύξ, night, mainly poetic; μέλαινα ... εὐφρόνη, *hyperbaton* (p. 24) bracketing the line (S #3028); [1× *El.*]

πρὶν οὖν τιν' ἀνδρῶν ἐξοδοιπορεῖν cτέγηc,　　　　　　**20**
ξυνάπτετον λόγοιcιν· ὡc ἐνταῦθ' †ἐμὲν
ἵν' οὐκέτ' ὀκνεῖν καιρόc, ἀλλ' ἔργων ἀκμή.

OPECTHC

ὦ φίλτατ' ἀνδρῶν προcπόλων, ὥc μοι cαφῆ
cημεῖα φαίνειc ἐcθλὸc εἰc ἡμᾶc γεγώc.

LINE 20

⁺πρίν (conj.) — [ῐ] before (usually takes an inf. when subordinated to an affirmative clause: S #2454)

⁺τῐ́c, τι (indef. pron.) — <u>anyone</u>, anything; τιν' = acc. subject of inf. ἐξοδοιπορεῖν (S #1972)

⁺ἀνήρ, ἀνδρόc, ὁ — man (syncopated noun: S #44, 262; ἀνδρῶν, partit. genit.: SS 57–58 §10; S #1306, 1317); > 'before any of the men/any man exits'

ἐξ-οδοιπορέω — go out of, exit; [1× Soph.]

⁺cτέγη, ἡ — roof; roofed place; house

LINE 21

cυν-άπτω — (ξυνάπτετον = 2nd dual pres. impv.: S #462); tie together, unite; (intrans.) enter into conversation (LSJ B II); > 'you two take joint counsel'; [1× El.]

⁺λόγοc, ὁ — (⁺λέγω, tell) word (λόγοιcιν, dative of means: S #1507)

ἐνταῦθα (adv.) — there; ἐνταῦθα . . . ἵνα at the point . . . where (ἵνα for οὗ, S #2498); > 'since it is a point where it is no longer the time to hold back, but high time to act'

†ἐμέν — † 'dagger' or 'obelus' marks an insoluble textual problem. ἐμέν is not Attic, and ἐcμέν would not scan.

⁺ἵνα (relat. adv.) — where (S #2498; poetic)

⁺οὐκ-έτι (adv.) — no longer, no more, no further

⁺ὀκνέω — hesitate, hold back, shrink from doing (physically or morally)

⁺καιρόc, ὁ — right point of anything, right time for action, critical moment; supply ἐcτί; > 'since in this place it is no longer the right time to hesitate . . .'; the motif of 'the right time' recurs often: 75, 1259, 1368; cf. 1251

⁺ἔργον, τό — deed, action; (Doric: Ϝέργον: S #122)

⁺ἀλλά (conj.) — (neut. pl. of ἄλλος with changed accent) but, but rather (LSJ I; S #2775)

ἀκμή, ἡ — best or highest point of anything, most fitting time (LSJ III)

⁺πρόc-πολοc, ον — (προc-πολέω, attend, wait upon) servant, attendant; ὦ φίλτατ' προcπόλων 'dearest of my servants'; superlative with partitive genit.; cf. 15

⁺ὥc (relat adv.) — how! what! (exclamatory ὥc following the vocative: S #2682a, 2998)

LINE 24

cημεῖον, τό — (cῆμα, sign) mark, sign of token by which something is inferred; cαφῆ cημεῖα = object of φαίνειc, 'clear signs')

⁺*φαίνω — bring to light, <u>reveal</u>, <u>show</u>, disclose

⁺ἐcθλόc (3) — (poetic) good (= ἀγαθόc); (of persons) brave, <u>noble</u>; (morally) faithful

ἡμᾶc — us = me; pl. for sg. in pronouns can be used to enhance one's own importance, *pluralis maiestatis* (as probably here), or to de-emphasize one's uniqueness by avoiding specificity, *pluralis modestiae* (SS 6 §4a, 8–10 §5); ⁺εἰc with persons indicates attitude (SS 104–5 §7; S #1675a)

⁺*γίγνομαι — (γεγώc, perf.² ptc.: S #704b), become, <u>be</u>; (the perf. refers to the pres. state of the subject resulting from a completed action: S #1945; SS 197). Supplem. ptc. in indirect discourse depending on a verb of showing, φαίνειc (S #2106; GMT #904; SS 260 §12); > 'how you are showing me with clear signs that you *are* loyal to me'

ὥσπερ γὰρ ἵππος εὐγενής, κἂν ᾖ γέρων,   **25**
ἐν τοῖϲι δεινοῖϲ θυμὸν οὐκ ἀπώλεϲεν,
ἀλλ' ὀρθὸν οὖϲ ἵϲτηϲιν, ὡϲαύτωϲ δὲ ϲὺ
ἡμᾶϲ τ' ὀτρύνειϲ καὐτὸϲ ἐν πρώτοιϲ ἔπῃ.
τοιγὰρ τὰ μὲν δόξαντα δηλώϲω, ϲὺ δὲ

LINE 25

⁺ὥσπερ (conj.)	just as (introduces a comparative clause of quality: SS 305–6 §1)
⁺γάρ (postpos. conj.)	for (introducing a reason for the preceding statement: S #2803, 2810)
⁺ἵππος, ὁ	horse
εὐ-γενής, ές	(⁺·*γίγνομαι) high-bred, noble
κἂν	= καὶ ἐάν (*crasis*) although, even if; (concessive clause: S #2372; SS 282–83 §5)
⁺*εἰμί, ἤν	be (subjv. ὦ, ᾖς, ᾖ, . . .; opt. εἴην, εἴης, εἴη . . . S #768)
⁺γέρων, ον	(γέρων, οντος, old man) aged
⁺ἐν (+ dat)	in, at; (SS 106 §8: "denotes situation . . . in which the action takes place")
⁺δεινός (3)	(δέος, fear) fearful; τὰ δεινά, terrible moment, danger (attributive adjs. with the article are often used as nouns: S #1021, 1153a; SS 163 §1)
⁺θῡμός, ου, ὁ	breathe; soul; desire; temper; spirit, <u>courage</u> (LSJ II.3)
⁺ἀπ-όλλῡμι, -ώλεσα	kill, <u>lose</u> (gnomic aor. in pres. general condition: [S #2338; GMT #466] expresses a general truth: [S #1931; GMT #154; SS 196–97 §17] here with a punctual aspect); >'even though old, *does not lose* his courage in time of danger'

LINE 27

⁺ὀρθός (3)	straight, erect, upright
⁺οὖς, ὠτός, τό	(declension S #285.22) ear; handle
⁺*ἵ-στη-μι	cause to stand (transitive forms are in the pres., impf., fut., and aor.¹ act.); > 'but pricks up his ear'
ὡσαύτως (adv.)	just so, in the same manner (note the apodotic δέ, rare in Tragedy after the comparative protasis: S #2837, #2837; GP 179–80); > '*just like* a horse . . ., *in the same way* . . .'; [1× *El.*]
ὀτρύνω	[ῠ] stir up, rouse, urge; > '. . . you urge us forward'; [1× *El.*]
⁺αὐτός, αὐτή, αὐτό	(intensive pron.) -self; καὐτός = καὶ αὐτός (*crasis*); > 'and you yourself'; (in oblique cases personal pronoun of 3rd pers.: S #325d, 328)
⁺πρῶτος (3)	first (substant. adj. without article: SS 163 §1); > 'among the foremost [men]'
⁺*ἕπομαι	follow; > 'and you yourself follow among the foremost men'
τοί-γαρ (pcl.)	so then, thus, therefore (usually first word in an iambic line: GP 565–56)
⁺δοκέω, ἔδοξα	form an opinion, think (neut. acc. pl. aor¹. ptc.; articular substantive participle: S #2050–52; S 257–58 §9; GMT #825); 'thoughts'
⁺δηλόω, -ώσω	make known, disclose, reveal; > 'I will tell/disclose my thoughts'

ὀξεῖαν ἀκοὴν τοῖς ἐμοῖς λόγοις διδούς, 30
εἰ μή τι καιροῦ τυγχάνω, μεθάρμοσον.
ἐγὼ γὰρ ἡνίχ' ἱκόμην τὸ Πυθικὸν
μαντεῖον, ὡς μάθοιμ' ὅτῳ τρόπῳ πατρὶ
δίκας ἀροίμην τῶν φονευσάντων πάρα,

LINE 30

ὀξύς, ὀξεῖα, ὀξύ	sharp, keen
ἀκοή, ἡ	[ᾰ] (ἀκούω, hear, give ear) listening, the ear; [1× *El.*]
⁺*δίδωμι	give (the present ptc. emphasizes the continuous listening: SS 210 §33)
⁺τι	in some respect, somehow, by chance; either acc. of respect (S #1601c; SS 43 §14), or internal (adverbial) acc. (S #1607)
⁺*τυγχάνω, ἔτυχον	(τύχη, coincidence, chance) happen (+ ptc.); meet, <u>hit</u> (+ genit.: καιροῦ)
μεθ-αρμόζω	(aor.¹ act. impv.) correct; > 'if I fail to hit the mark, correct...'; (the direct obj. is probably implied με, but could be τὰ δόξαντα); [1× Soph.]

LINE 32

⁺γάρ (pcl.)	the fact is that (explanatory, often found "after an expression denoting the giving or receiving of information" GP 59.2)
⁺ἡνίκα (adv.)	at the time when (S #346, 2383A)
⁺*ἱκνέομαι, ἱκόμην	(aor.² with -ῑ-; lengthened form of ἵκω, come, reach) come, arrive
Πῡθικός (3)	(Πῡθώ, Pytho, region where Delphi was) Pythian (Delphic oracle was the most important oracle in Greece, belonging to the god Apollo)
μαντεῖον, τό	(μάντις, diviner) oracle, seat of an oracle (terminal acc. after a vb. of motion without preposition: S #1588); emphatic *enjambment*; [1× *El.*]
⁺ὡς (conj.)	in order to, so that (opens a final clause ὡς μάθοιμι: S #3000)
⁺*μανθάνω, ἔμαθον	(μάθοιμι, aor.² opt.) learn by inquiry (final clause in secondary sequence, following ἱκόμην: S #2197) > 'when I went to the Pythian oracle *in order to learn*'
ὅτῳ τρόπῳ	(ὅτῳ = ᾧτινι: S #339b) how, <u>in what way</u>
⁺δίκη, ἡ	custom; justice; consequence of action, <u>penalty, retribution</u> (LSJ IV.3)
ἄρνυμαι, ἠρόμην	(ἀροίμην, aor.² opt.) win, gain, <u>exact</u> (indirect question in secondary sequence, ἱκόμην: S #2663; SS 236; GMT #669.2); > 'to learn *how I might exact retribution* for my father from his murderers'; [1× Soph.]
φονεύω, ἐφόνευσα	murder, kill (τῶν φονευσάντων, articular substantive participle: S # 2050–52; SS 257–58 §9; GMT #825); > 'the murderers'; [1× *El.*]
⁺παρά (+ genit.)	from (πάρα: accent thrown back when disyllabic prep. follows its case; called *anastrophe*: S #175a)

χρῇ μοι τοιαῦθ' ὁ Φοῖβος ὧν πεύσῃ τάχα·   **35**
ἄσκευον αὐτὸν ἀσπίδων τε καὶ στρατοῦ
δόλοισι κλέψαι χειρὸς ἐνδίκου σφαγάς.

LINE 35

χράω	utter an oracle, proclaim (-άω contracted to η: S #394); (Tragedy prefers historical pres. for vivid portrayal of a past action. Usually translated by a past tense: S #1883; SS 184 §5; GMT #33); >'Phoebus *gave me this prophecy*'; [1× *El.*]
⁺τοιοῦτος, -αύτη, -οῦτο	such, of such kind, nature, quality, such as this (direct object of χρῇ: >'Phoebus proclaimed *these things to me/gave me this prophecy*'; antecedent of ὧν; *correption* -οι- shortened before the following diphthong; cf. 1001, 1024, 1338)
Φοῖβος, ὁ	epithet of Apollo; (as adj.) pure, bright, radiant, beaming
*πυνθάνομαι, πεύσομαι	(fut. indic. mid. 2sg.) inquire, <u>hear, learn of</u> + genit.· ὧν (S #1361); > 'which *you will hear* soon'

LINE 36

ἄ-σκευος, ον	(ἀ privat., σκεύη, equipment) unfurnished; [1× *El.*]
⁺αὐτόν	(intensive pron.) -self; > 'myself alone'
ἀσπίς, ίδος, ἡ	shield (ἄσκευον + genit.: SS 54–55 §7, 68–69 §31); [1× *El.*]
⁺στρατός, ὁ	<u>army</u>, people crowd; (ἀσπίδων τε καὶ στρατοῦ > 'unfurnished with [either shields or army=] armed force; *hendiadys*, one idea expressed by two words: S #3025)
⁺δόλος, ὁ	cunning, trickery (–οισι[ν] oft. in poetry: S #234; dat. of means: S #1507)
⁺κλέπτω, ἔκλεψα	(κλέψαι, aor.¹ act. inf.) steal; cheat; <u>do secretly or treacherously</u> (LSJ IV.1: "*execute* slaughter *by secret frauds*"; inf. in acc. and inf. construction after χρῇ; the subj. of the inf. is αὐτόν: S #1972)
⁺χείρ, χειρός, ἡ	hand (χειρὸς ἐνδίκου subjective genit.: S #1330; SS 53 §4); > 'that … by guile I should steal the slaughter *with my own righteous hand*'
ἐν-δῐκ-ος, ον	just, righteous (emendation to ἐνδίκου is an easy fix for the codd. ἐνδίκους, which leaves χειρός alone without an epithet: Finglass); [1× *El.*]
σφαγή, ἡ	(σφάζω, slay) slaughter, killing (generalizing plural: SS 7 §4b)

ὅτ' οὖν τοιόνδε χρησμὸν εἰσηκούσαμεν,
σὺ μὲν μολών, ὅταν σε καιρὸς εἰσάγῃ,
δόμων ἔσω τῶνδ', ἴσθι πᾶν τὸ δρώμενον, **40**
ὅπως ἂν εἰδὼς ἡμὶν ἀγγείλῃς σαφῆ.

LINE 38

⁺ὅτε (relat. adv.)	since (causal: S #2240; LSJ B)
⁺τοιόσδε, τοιάδε, τοιόνδε	such (in quality: S #333d, 340)
χρησμός, ὁ	(χράω, give an oracle) oracle; [1× *El.*]
⁺εἰσ-⁺*ἀκούω	<u>hear</u>, listen (either *pluralis maiestatis*, emphasizing his importance: S #1006; SS 6 §4a, or the plural includes Pylades)
σὺ μὲν ... ἡμεῖς δὲ	σὺ μὲν corresponds to ἡμεῖς δὲ in 51; > 'you must go inside this house and learn ..., we, on the other hand/meanwhile, ...'
⁺*βλώσκω, ἔμολον	(μολών, aor.² ptc.) come, <u>go</u> (poetic vb. occurring in Soph., only in aor.²)
ὅταν = ὅτε + ἄν	when (temporal clauses referring indefinitely to the future take subjv. with ἄν, or opt. without ἄν: S #2399, 1768; SS 294 §4)
εἰσ-⁺*ἄγω	lead in, into (subjv. in indef. temp. clause of single fut. act [SS 294 §4] with primary vb: ἴσθι; impv. moods count as primary because they point to the fut.: S #1858a); > 'when chance leads you in ...'; [1× *El.*]
⁺δόμος, ὁ	house, chamber (pl. because of the collection of rooms: SS 4 §3)
⁺ἔσω (=εἴσω + genit.)	to within, into (improper prep., i.e., an adv. used as a prep. but incapable of forming compounds: S #1647, 1700)
⁺*οἶδα	(ἴσθι, pf. impv.) know (pregnant construction: two actions condensed into one with the action stated implying more than it says: S #3044. ἴσθι = πυνθανόμενος ἴσθι 'know after having learned' > 'make sure to know.' The emphasis is on the 'learning,' although not mentioned explicitly)
⁺πᾶς, πᾶσα, πᾶν	all, every, everything (S #299)
⁺*δράω	do, accomplish (neut. articular substantive participle: S #2050–52; SS 257 §9; GMT #825); > 'all that is going on'; cf. 85, 1333

LINE 41

⁺ὅπως (conj.)	so that (opens final clause with subjv., ἀγγείλῃς, may or may not have ἄν without affecting meaning: SS 285–86 §3; S #2193, 2196; GMT #328)
⁺*ἀγγέλλω	bring tidings, announce, <u>report</u> (final clause in primary sequence, ἴσθι: S #2196, 1858a)
⁺σαφής, ές	clear, distinct (σαφῆ = neut. pl. acc. as adverb); > 'so that you can report to us with clear/accurate knowledge (εἰδώς= knowing clearly)'

οὐ γάρ σε μὴ γήρᾳ τε καὶ χρόνῳ μακρῷ
γνῶς᾽, οὐδ᾽ ὑποπτεύσουσιν, ὧδ᾽ ἠνθισμένον.
λόγῳ δὲ χρῶ τοιῷδ᾽, ὅτι ξένος μὲν εἶ
Φωκέως παρ᾽ ἀνδρὸς Φανοτέως ἥκων· ὁ γὰρ   45
μέγιστος αὐτοῖς τυγχάνει δορυξένων.

LINE 42

γῆρας, αος, τό	old age (γήρᾳ Attic, contraction of γήραϊ) dat. of cause (S #1517; SS 89 §17); [1× *El.*]
⁺χρόνος, ὁ	time
⁺μᾰκρός (3)	long, large
⁺*γιγνώσκω	(γνῶσι, aor.² subjv. S #687) know by observation, recognize (οὐ . . . μή + aor. subjv. indicates strong future denial [S #1804, 2754; GMT #295] linked here to an ordinary future denial: οὐδ᾽ ὑποτεύσουσιν: SS 337); > 'they *will never recognize* you or suspect'; emphatic *enjambment*
ὑπ-οπτεύω	suspect; [1× Soph.]
⁺ὧδε (adv.)	in this way, thus; so very, so exceedingly
ἀνθ-ίζω, ἤνθισμαι	(ἠνθίσμενον, pf. ptc. pass.) (ἄνθος, flower) strew/deck with flowers; dye, <u>color</u>, stain; > 'thus *disguised*' or 'with *silvered* hair' (LSJ 2); [1× Soph.]

LINE 44

χράομαι	(pres. impv. dep. 2nd sg., χρῶ < χράου: S #395) use, avail oneself of + dat., λόγῳ τοιῷδε (S #1509); > '*use such a story as this, that* . . .'
⁺ὅτι (conj.)	that (introduces indirect discourse with verb of saying/thinking, generally expresses objective fact whether true or not: S #2582; SS 313 §1)
⁺Φωκεύς, έως, ὁ	Phocian (Phocis, a region in northern Greece that includes Delphi; -εως in Φωκέως is pronounced as one syllable by *synizesis*: S #60–61)
ἀνδρός	⁺ἀνήρ indicates respect when attached to a character not mentioned beforehand; > 'the Phocian gentleman, Phanoteus'
Φανοτεύς, έως, ὁ	uncle and enemy of Strophius, Pylades' father, who was Ag.'s ally; Φανοτέως resolution in 6th position, pp. 20–21, 24
⁺ἥκω	have come/ arrived (like ⁺*οἴχομαι, a present with perfect sense: S #1886)
⁺αὐτοῖς	dat. of possession (S #1480; SS 83–84 '8); > 'their,' i.e., of Clyt. and Aeg.
⁺*τυγχάνω	(intrans.) happen to (often with supplementary participle which tells what the main action is, while the finite verb tells something about how the action is occurring: S #2096a; GMT #887; SS 261§12f; here ὤν is omitted: S #2119); > 'for he (*happens to be* =) *really is* their . . .'
δορύ-ξενος, ον	(δόρυ, spear; ξένος, friend) spear-friend, war-friend, <u>ally</u> (partitive genit. with superlative: S #1306, 1315; SS 58 §10); [1× *El.*]

ἄγγελλε δ' ὅρκον προστιθεὶς, ὁθούνεκα
τέθνηκ' Ὀρέστης ἐξ ἀναγκαίας τύχης,
ἄθλοισι Πυθικοῖσιν ἐκ τροχηλάτων
δίφρων κυλισθείς· ὥδ' ὁ μῦθος ἐστάτω.   **50**
ἡμεῖς δὲ πατρὸς τύμβον, ὡς ἐφίετο,
λοιβαῖσι πρῶτον καὶ καρατόμοις χλιδαῖς
στέψαντες, εἶτ' ἄψορρον ἥξομεν πάλιν,

LINE 47

ὅρκος, ὁ	oath; [1× *El.*]
προσ-⁺*τί-θη-μι	(προστιθείς, pres. ptc. act.: S #419) bestow, <u>add</u>
⁺ὀθούνεκα (conj.)	that (= ὅτι, introduces dependent sentence after verbs of 'saying'; restricted to Tragedy, especially Soph.: SS 313–14 §1; S #2578; GMT #710)
⁺*θνήσκω	(τέθνηκε, pf. act.) die; be dead (S #1946); > 'report that Or. is dead'
⁺ἐξ	SS 110 §9: "introduces the cause, the ground of action: *as the result of* an accident fate-ordained' "
ἀναγκαῖος (3)	(ἀνάγκη, constraint, necessity) constraining; [1× *El.*]
⁺τύχη, ἡ	fate, good/bad luck, chance, <u>accident</u>; > 'from a (constraining) *fatal* accident'
ἄθλος, ὁ	contest (-οισι: dat. of place: SS 87 §13; S #1530–31). The Pythian games were founded in 582 BCE. Tragedy is indifferent to anachronism; [1× *El.*]
τροχ-ήλατος, ον	(τροχός, wheel + ἐλαύνω, ride, drive) moved on wheels, <u>rapid</u>; [1× Soph.]
⁺δίφρός, ὁ	(δι-φόρος, bearing 2) chariot board (for both the driver and combatant)
*κυλίνδω, ἐκύλῑσα	(κυλισθείς aor.¹ ptc. pass.) roll; > 'rolled from his rapid chariot'; [1× *El.*]
⁺μῦθος, ὁ	word, speech; conversation; rumor, report; <u>story</u>
⁺*ἵ-στη-μι, ἕστηκα	(ἐστάτω, pf.² impv.: S #417) intransitive: stand (S #819; SS 218 §5); Kamerbeek: "let such be the basis of the story"

LINE 51

ἡμεῖς δὲ	answers σὺ μὲν of 39: 'we (Or. and Pyl.) on the other hand/meanwhile'
⁺τύμβος, ὁ	tomb, grave
⁺ὡς (relat. adv.)	as (S #2992)
⁺ἐφ-⁺*ίη-μι	(ἐφίετο, impf.) mid.: command (LSJ B) (the imperfect is often used in oracular responses and with verbs of command: SS 191 §11); ὡς ἐφίετο = 'as [the god, 38] commanded'
λοιβή, ἡ	(λείβω, pour) pouring, <u>libation</u> (in words denoting liquids, the plural indicates abundance, SS 6 §3)
καρά-τομος, ον	[ᾰ] (κάρα, head; τέμνω, cut) cut from the head; [1× Soph.]
χλιδή, ἡ	luxury; > 'with luxuriant hair cut from my head'
στέφω, ἔστεψα	(στέφος, poetic for στέφανος); crown, wreathe, honor; emphatic *enjambment*; > 'after having first honored...'; [1× *El.*]
⁺εἶτα (adv.)	then; πρῶτον ... εἶτα 'first ... then ...'
ἄψορρον (adv.)	(ἄψ, backward, back; ῥέω, flow) backward, back again
⁺πάλιν (adv.)	again, once more; > 'we will come back once more'

τύπωμα χαλκόπλευρον ἡρμένοι χεροῖν,
ὃ καὶ cὺ θάμνοιc οἶcθά που κεκρυμμένον,
ὅπωc λόγῳ κλέπτοντεc ἡδεῖαν φάτιν
φέρωμεν αὐτοῖc, τοὐμὸν ὡc ἔρρει δέμαc
φλογιcτὸν ἤδη καὶ κατηνθρακωμένον.

55

LINE 54

τυπώμα, ατος, τό	that which is formed or molded; [1× Soph.]
χαλκό-πλευρος, ον	with sides of bronze; > 'brazen urn,' 'urn of beaten bronze'; (1× Soph.)
*αἴρω, ἦρμαι	(ἑρμήνοι, pf. mid. ptc.) raise, <u>carry</u>; > *carrying* in our hands'; [1× *El.*]
⁺χεροῖν	dual is used for certain parts of the body (SS 2–3 §2; S #285–28)
⁺καί (adv.)	also, even (usually stresses the idea in the word that follows: S #2881)
θάμνος, ὁ	bush, shrub (dat. of place: SS 87 §13; S #1530–31); [1× Soph.]
⁺που (enclit. adv.)	Frequently qualifies an expression (οἶσθα):'I suppose,' 'surely,' 'no doubt'
⁺κρύπτω, κέκρυμμαι	(κεκρυμμένον, pf. pass. ptc.) hide; > 'which, as I believe you know, *is hidden* in the bushes'

LINE 56

⁺λόγος, ὁ	word, story, tale, fiction
⁺κλέπτω	cheat, steal, deceive; > 'deceiving them with our story'
⁺*φέρω	<u>bring</u>, carry, bear; endure (ὅπως . . . φέρωμεν final clause in 1st seq., ἥξομεν: S #2196; the subjv. is an emendation of the opt. φέροιμεν that appears in most mss. but is an anomaly after a primary tense: GMT #322); > 'so that . . . we may bring'
⁺ἡδύς, ἡδεῖα, ἡδύ	sweet, pleasant, welcome (S #296, 297); (667)
⁺φά-τις, εως, ἡ	[ᾰ] (⁺*φημί, speak) (oracular) speech, rumor, report, story (S #257)
⁺ὡς (conj.)	that (introduces indirect discourse in which what is said is false as it is here, or uncertain, or after negated verbs: S #3000; SS 314 §1); cf.1289
⁺ἔρρω	come to ruin, perish; go, vanish; > 'that my body is no more'
⁺δέμας, τό	(δέμω build) bodily frame, living/dead body; used in nom./acc.; τοὐμὸν = τὸ ἐμόν (*crasis*)
φλογιστός (3)	(φλόξ, flame, blaze) burnt up, set on fire; [1× Soph.]
κατ-ανθρακόω	(pf. ptc. pass.) (κατά, completely; ἄνθραξ, ὁ, charcoal) burnt to ashes; > 'that my body is no more and already *burnt to ashes*'; [1× Soph.]

τί γάρ με λυπεῖ τοῦθ᾽, ὅταν λόγῳ θανὼν
ἔργοιϲι ϲωθῶ κἀξενέγκωμαι κλέος;   **60**
δοκῶ μέν, οὐδὲν ῥῆμα ϲὺν κέρδει κακόν.
ἤδη γὰρ εἶδον πολλάκιϲ καὶ τοὺϲ ϲοφοὺϲ
λόγῳ μάτην θνήϲκονταϲ· εἶθ᾽, ὅταν δόμουϲ
ἔλθωϲιν αὖθιϲ, ἐκτετίμηνται πλέον·

LINE 59

⁺λῡπέω	(λύπη, pain, grief, distress) cause pain, grief, annoy
⁺ὅτε (adv.)	when (ὅταν = ὅτε + ἄν; temporal clauses referring indefinitely to the future take subjv. with ἄν, or opt. without ἄν: S #2399, 1768; SS 294 §4; the ὅταν-clause provides the subject); > 'For what harm does this do me, *when* in words I'm dead but in fact I am safe/alive and win renown?'
⁺ἔργον, τό	deed, action, work; ἔργοιϲι 'in fact'; (for the pl.: SS 4 §3); one of the most frequent antitheses in Greek literature is between 'word' and 'deed'; cf. 319, 357–58, 624–625
⁺*ϲώζω	(ϲωθῶ,¹ aor.¹ subjv. pass.) save, keep, <u>keep alive</u>
ἐκ-⁺*φέρω	(ἐξ-ενέγκωμαι, aor.² subjv. pass.) carry off; κἀξενέγκωμαι = καὶ ἐξενέγκωμαι (*crasis*)
κλέος, τό	fame, glory, renown (used only in nom. and acc., sg. and pl.; the very word used by Homer of Orestes' revenge at *Od.* 1.298; 3.204)
⁺δοκέω	<u>think</u>, imagine (personal construction of the vb. [S #1983] governs indir. statement in acc. & inf.: οὐδὲν … κακόν [εἶναι]); > 'I really (μέν) *think* that no word with gain [i.e., that brings gain] is bad'
⁺μέν	surely, indeed, really (μέν *solitarium*, i.e., with no corresponding δέ clause, is emphatic. Here stressing and affirming the idea of the verb: S #2896–98; GP 359–60).
ῥῆμα, ατος, τό	(ἐρῶ, will say) that which is said/spoken, word; [1× *El.*]
⁺κέρδος, εος, τό	(κερδοϲύνη, ἡ, cunning, shrewdness) gain, profit
⁺κακός (3)	bad (not in a moral sense), <u>ill-omened</u> (supply εἶναι)

LINE 62

⁺ἤδη (adv.)	already, by this time, now, immediately, <u>in the past</u>
πολλάκιϲ (adv.)	many times, <u>often</u>; > 'I have in the past often seen even …'
⁺ϲοφός (3)	<u>clever</u>, wise, prudent
⁺μάτην (adv.)	[ă] in vain, falsely
⁺*ἔρχομαι, ἦλθον	(ἔλθωϲιν, aor.² subjv.) come (see ὅταν with subjv. on 59; SS 295 §4: "I have observed many cases of men falsely reported dead; then, when they have come home again, they have been held in greater honour")
αὖθιϲ (adv.)	back, again, hereafter; [1× *El.*]
ἐκ-τῑμάω	(ἐκτετίμηνται, pf. indic. pass.) honor highly (gnomic/empiric pf. of general description: S #1948; SS 200 §21; GMT #154); [1× Soph.]
⁺πλέον (comparative adv.)	(⁺πολύς, πολλή, πολύ, much) more; = μᾶλλον (S #1068)

ὡς κἄμ' ἐπαυχῶ τῆσδε τῆς φήμης ἄπο   65
δεδορκότ' ἐχθροῖς ἄστρον ὡς λάμψειν ἔτι.
ἀλλ', ὦ πατρῷα γῆ θεοί τ' ἐγχώριοι,
δέξασθέ μ' εὐτυχοῦντα ταῖσδε ταῖς ὁδοῖς,
σύ τ', ὦ πατρῷον δῶμα· σοῦ γὰρ ἔρχομαι
δίκῃ καθαρτὴς πρὸς θεῶν ὡρμημένος·   70

LINE 65

+ὡς (adv. of manner)	just so, thus; = οὕτως (with an accent, LSJ Aa); some print ὡς = 'as'
κἄμ' = καί ἐμέ	*crasis;* acc. for expected nom. with inf. construction, since the subject of the inf. and the governing verb, ἐπαυχῶ, is the same (S #1973–74); κἄμ' parallels τοὺς σοφούς at 62, and emphasizes Or.'s position: (SS 317 §4)
ἐπ-αυχέω	lit.: boast of, exult in; with acc. and inf.: be confident that; [1× *El.*]
+φήμη, ἡ	(+*φημί, say) utterance, rumor
+ἀπό (+ genit.)	from, after, by, because of, as a result of; ἄπο *anastrophe,* see παρά 34n
+*δέρκομαι, δέδορκα	(δεδορκότα, pf. act. ptc.; pf. as pres) see (the Greeks equated seeing the light with being alive; praedicative function with ἐμέ: 'alive.')
+ἐχθρός (3)	hating, hostile, hateful (substant. adj. without article: SS 163 §1)
λάμπω	(λάμψειν, aor.¹ act. inf.) shine; metaphorically: 'blaze'; [1× *El.*]
+ἔτι (adv.)	yet, still; > 'I am confident (lit.: I boast) that as result of this report, I too (καί), alive, shall *yet* shine as a star upon my enemies'

LINE 67

πατρῷα/πατρῷον (l. 69)	Emphatic repetition that reflects Or.'s double goal: avenging his father and reclaiming his patrimony, repetition of words derived from the same root but with different ending. Play on different forms of the same word was greatly appreciated by the Greeks.
ἀλλά (pcl.)	but (with a prayer, making a transition to a desired future: GP 15)
+πατρῷος (3)	of one's father (Both Or.'s and El.'s prayers [110–18, 1376–83] will be fulfilled, but not Clyt.'s [634–59]. Clyt.'s belief in its immediate fulfillment will assure the success of Or.'s deceit.)
+γῆ, ἡ	earth, land
+θεός, ὁ	god
ἐγ-χώριος (2/3)	(χώρα, country) in/of the country; [1× *El.*]
+*δέχομαι, ἐδεξάμην	(δέξασθε, aor.¹ impv.) receive
+εὐ-τυχέω	(εὖ, τύχη, chance, fortune) be lucky, be well off, succeed; > 'receive' *me with good fortune*'
+ὁδός, ἡ	road, way, journey; (the plural according to SS 4 §3: "refers to the sum of the action, 'my journeying,' in the course of which many ὁδοί would be traversed")
καθαρθής, οῦ, ὁ	(κἄθαίρω, purify) purifier, cleanser (σοῦ objective genit.: SS 53 §4; S #1328; Kamerbeek notes that the word is "important for the understanding of Orestes' role as seen by himself."); > 'for I come in justice *as your purifier*'; [1× Soph.; not found in Aesch. or Eur.]
πρὸς θεῶν	= ὑπὸ θεῶν (πρός with genit. of agent is common in poetry: S#1678)
ὁρμάω	(ὡρμημένος, pf. mid. ptc.) speed, hasten, rush on; > 'sped by the gods'; Or. has no doubt that he has the gods on his side in seeking vengeance.

καὶ μή μ' ἄτιμον τῆςδ' ἀποστείλητε γῆς,
ἀλλ' ἀρχέπλουτον καὶ καταστάτην δόμων.
εἴρηκα μέν νυν ταῦτα· coì δ' ἤδη, γέρον,
τὸ còν μελέcθω βάντι φρουρῆcαι χρέοc.
νὼ δ' ἔξιμεν· καιρὸc γάρ, ὅcπερ ἀνδράcιν   75
μέγιcτοc ἔργου παντόc ἐcτ' ἐπιcτάτηc.

LINE 71

⁺ἄ-τῑμος, ον   (ἀ privat., τῑμή, honor, respect) without honor, dishonored

ἀπο-*cτέλλω, -έcτειλα   (ἀποcτείλητε, aor.¹ subjv.) send away from (μή + prohibitive aorist subjv.: S #1800a; SS 220 §6; GMT #259); > 'do not send me away'

ἀλλ' …   Supply a positive verb: > 'but [receive] me as'; cf. 650

ἀρχέ-πλουτος, ον   (ἀρχε-, πλοῦτος) master of one's wealth /riches; [1× Soph.]

κατα-cτάτης, ου, ὁ   (καθ-⁺*ίcτημι, set down) establisher; [1× Soph.]

LINE 73

εἴρηκα   (pf.) I said (S #529.3; ⁺*φημί, ⁺*λέγω, ἀγορεύω are used for the pres. tense); εἴρηκα μέν νυν … coì δ' ⁺ἤδη > 'this is what I had to say, but you now …'

⁺μέλω   (pres. impv. mid. 3sg.) be an object of care (+ dat., coί: S #1467)

⁺*βαίνω, ἔβην   (βάντι, aor.² ptc.) go (modifies coι); > 'make it your business to go'

φρουρέω   (προ + ⁺*ὁράω) keep watch, guard

χρέος, ους, τό   duty, <u>task</u> ; > ' … and keep watching over your task'; [1× El.]

νώ   we two, the two of us (nom. dual of ἐγώ: S #325 D1)

ἔξ-⁺ειμι   go out (εἶμι serves as the future of ἔρχομαι: S #773); > 'we two will be on our way'; [1× El.]

ἐπι-cτάτης, ὁ   (ἐφ-⁺*ίcταμαι, be set over) master, overseer (ὅcπερ … ἐπιcτάτης, emphatic *hyperbaton*); > 'for it is the right time, which is the greatest master/ruler of every action for men.' The emphasis on proper timing continues, cf. 22, 39.

Electra is heard from the doorway of the stage building that represents the palace.

ΗΛΕΚΤΡΑ

ἰώ μοί μοι δύϲτηνοϲ.

ΠΑ.   καὶ μὴν θυρῶν ἔδοξα προϲπόλων τινὸϲ
       ὑποϲτενούϲηϲ ἔνδον αἰϲθέϲθαι, τέκνον.

ΟΡ.   ἆρ' ἐϲτὶν ἡ δύϲτηνοϲ Ἠλέκτρα; θέλειϲ   **80**
       μείνωμεν αὐτοῦ κἀπακούϲωμεν γόων;

LINE 77

⁺ἰώ	(ἰ) Oh! (Exclamation frequently repeated twice; exclamations are inarticulate expressions represented in our texts by repeated letters, mainly vowels, sometimes separated by consonants. The line is in catalectic anapestic dimeter —— ˘ ˘ — —, and as such a prelude to her monody: Kamerbeek)
⁺δύϲτηνοϲ, ον	wretched, unhappy, unfortunate
καὶ μήν	Why! (calls attention to something just heard or seen: GP 356 §7)
θύρα, ἡ	door (genit. of place, largely poetic: 'from the doorway': SS 59 §11)
⁺προϲπόλων	partitive genit. (S #1306; SS 58). The Tutor cannot imagine El., the princess, at the gates, and at such an early hour.
ὑπο-⁺ϲτένω	sigh or groan softly/in a low tone (supplementary ptc. [not in indir. disc.] with vb. expressing feeling, αἰϲθέϲθαι: S #2088; GMT #877, 884; SS 260 §12); [1× *El.*]
⁺ἔνδον (+ genit.)	within
⁺*αἰϲθάνομαι, ἠϲθόμην	(αἰϲθέϲθαι, aor.² inf. dep.) perceive or apprehend by senses, <u>hear</u> (with acc. or genit., here τινὸϲ; when a subject of an inf. is the same as that of the governing vb., ⁺ἔδοξα, it is omitted: S #1973); > '*I thought I heard* from the doorway one of the servants moaning inside the house'
⁺τέκνον, τό	(⁺*τίκτω, bear, beget) child (often in addresses from elder to younger person, LSJ); > 'my son'
⁺ἄρα	interrog. pcl. indicating anxiety and impatience (LSJ 1; GP 46)
ἡ δύϲτηνοϲ Ἐλέκτρα	either Ἐλέκτρα is a predicate, i.e., 'Can the poor/wretched woman be El.?', or, the δύϲτηνοϲ serves as attribute to Ἐλέκτρα, i.e., 'Is this the poor/wretched El.?' If the latter, and Or. is aware of El.'s pitiful state, he would be remarkably callous.
⁺θέλω	= *ἐθέλω, poetic; will, desire, wish (θέλειϲ = 'do you wish' often precedes deliberative subjv: S #1806; GMT #287; SS 223–25 §11)
⁺*μένω, ἔμεινα	(μείνωμεν, aor.¹ subjv., deliberative) <u>stay</u>, wait
αὐτοῦ (adv.)	there, <u>here</u>, on the spot (properly genit. neut. of αὐτόϲ); [1× *El.*]
ἐπ-*ακούω, -ήκουϲα	(ἐπακούϲωμεν, aor.¹ subjv., deliberative) <u>listen</u>, overhear + genit; κἀπακούϲωμεν = καὶ ἐπακούϲωμεν (*crasis*); >'should we stay and listen . . . ?'; [1× *El.*]
⁺γόοϲ, ὁ	weeping, wailing, groaning (often in the plural· SS 4 §3)

43

ΠΑ. ἥκιστα. μηδὲν πρόσθεν ἢ τὰ Λοξίου
     πειρώμεθ' ἔρδειν κἀπὸ τῶνδ' ἀρχηγετεῖν,
     πατρὸς χέοντες λουτρά· ταῦτα γὰρ φέρειν
     νίκην τέ φημι καὶ κράτος τῶν δρωμένων.   85

LINE 82

⁺ἥκιστα (adv.)	least (in emphatic reply to a question: 'not at all, no')
⁺μηδείς, μία, ἕν	no one, nothing
⁺πρόσθεν ἤ	sooner than, <u>before</u> (S #2459)
Λοξίας, ου, ὁ	(Λοξιός, slanting, crosswise) epithet of Apollo (either because the sun traverses the ecliptic, or because of Apollo's 'crooked,' i.e., ambiguous, oracles, LSJ); τὰ Λοξίου = 'Apollo's commands'; [1× *El.*]
⁺πειράομαι	try, attempt (construe: μηδὲν πειρώμεθα ἔρδειν πρόσθεν ἢ τὰ Λοξίου; hortatory subjv.: S #1797; SS 222–23 §10; GMT #256)
ἔρδω	work, accomplish, <u>do</u> (inf. as complement of vbs. of wishing, striving, daring, trying; here: πειρώμεθα: SS 239 §4); Kells: "let us attempt to do nothing before [we do] the behest of Apollo"
ἀρχηγετέω	(ἀρχηγέτης, founder of a city) begin; solemn word; > 'and [let us attempt to] start with this, pouring libations to your father'; [1× Soph.]
χέω	pour (in its simple form used mostly by poets); [1× *El.*]
⁺λούτρον, τό	(λούω, wash) bath, washing (of the corpse); poetic: <u>libations</u>
⁺*φημί	(φα-, φη-) say, say yes (S #783); > 'I say that this brings victory and success ...'
⁺κράτος, εος, τό	strength, might, power, <u>mastery</u> (i.e., success)
τῶν ⁺δρωμένων	(objective genit.: SS 53 §4; S #1328; articular substant. ptc.: S#2050–2052; SS 257–58 §9; GMT #825); > 'in [of] what needs to be done'; cf. 40, 1333

ΗΛ.   ὦ φάοc ἁγνὸν
        καὶ γῆc ἰcόμοιρ' ἀήρ, ὥc μοι
        πολλὰc μὲν θρήνων ᾠδάc,
        πολλὰc δ' ἀντήρειc ᾔcθου
        cτέρνων πλαγὰc αἱμαccομένων,   **90**
        ὁπόταν δνοφερὰ νὺξ ὑπολειφθῇ·

The Tutor, Orestes, and Pylades exit on the left of the spectators, through the eisodos leading both to Agamemnon's tomb and the city. Electra comes out of the central door of the stage building.

Lines 86–120 are termed θρῆνος ἀπὸ σκηνῆς, a lyric lament from the stage building, delivered by the actor alone, not jointly with the Chorus (κομμός). Electra's lament is in mainly recitative anapests, not sung ones. Electra's garb befits a slave rather than a princess (cf. 190–191), and she probably wears a mask with short hair, a characteristic of women in mourning.

LINE 86

φάος, εος, τό	light, daylight; we know from lines 17–19 that dawn has already broken; [1× *El.*]
ἁγνός (3)	pure, holy, sacred; [1× *El.*]
⁺γῆς	'the air, whose portion is equal to that of the earth' (the genit. can be explained as genit. following compd. adj. that includes a noun as its base [ἰcόμοιρ']: SS 54 §7; and as following adjective of sharing, SS 60 §13: "Heaven, whose domain is equal to that of earth")
ἰcό-μοιρος, ον	[ῐ] ἴσος, equal; μοῖρα, part, portion) having an equal part; [1× Soph.]
ἀήρ, ἀέρος, ἡ	[ἄ] air; [1× Soph.]
μοι	(dat. of possession: S #1480; SS 83–84 §8); > 'my'
⁺πολύς, πολλή, πολύ	many; > 'how many of my doleful laments, how many blows aimed straight at my breast till it was bloodied have you heard … ?'
πολλὰς μὲν … πολλὰς δ'	*anaphora*; repetition with emphasis of the same word at the beginning of successive clauses (S #3010), here with antithesis
⁺θρῆνος, ὁ	(θρέομαι, lament) lamenting, funeral song, dirge
ᾠδή, ἡ	(ἀείδω, ᾄδω, sing) song, lay (contraction for ἀοιδή); [1× *El.*]

LINE 89

ἀντήρης, ες	(ἀντί, against) set over against, opposite; [1× Soph.]
cτέρνον, τό	breast, chest (objective genit.: S #1331–32; SS 52–53 §4); [1× *El.*]
πληγή, ἡ	(πλήσσω, strike) a blow, stroke, beating (πλαγάς: the only Doric alpha in 86–120; repeated Doricism is usually a mark of lyric, i.e., song with music; this is a recitative)
αἱμάσσω	(αἷμα, blood) to make bloody (attributive ptc.: S #2049; SS 256–57 §8; GMT #824; lit.: 'blows to my bloodied breast'; *prolepsis*, the participle denotes what the blows will cause); [1× *El.*]
⁺ὁπόταν	when, whenever (= ὁπότε + ἄν; temporal clauses referring indefinitely to the future take subjv. with ἄν, ὑπολειφθῇ, or opt. without ἄν: S #2399, 1768; SS 294 §4)
δνοφερός, ον	(δνόφος, darkness, gloom) dark, dusky, murky; [1× Soph.]
⁺νύξ, νυκτός, ἡ	night
ὑπο-⁺*λείπω	(ὑπολειφθῇ, aor.¹ pass., subjv.) fail; pass.: be left behind; >'*whenever* dusky night *has been left behind*'; [1× Soph.]

τὰ δὲ παννυχίδων κήδη ϲτυγεραὶ
ξυνίϲαϲ' εὐναὶ μογερῶν οἴκων,
ὅϲα τὸν δύϲτηνον ἐμὸν θρηνῶ
πατέρ', ὃν κατὰ μὲν βάρβαρον αἶαν   95
φοίνιοϲ Ἄρηϲ οὐκ ἐξένιϲεν,
μήτηρ δ' ἡμὴ χὠ κοινολεχὴϲ

LINE 92

παννὔχιϲ, ίδοϲ, ἡ	a vigil, keeping awake all night (genit. of explanation/apposition, explains the meaning of a more general word: S #1322); > 'sorrows of my sleepless nights'; [1× Soph.]
κῆδοϲ, εοϲ, τό	(κήδω, trouble) trouble, sorrow (conjecture for the not objectionable ἤδη [codd.] 'ere now,' "pointing to her prolonged grief" [Jebb]); [1× Soph.]
ϲτὔγεροϲ (3)	(ϲτὔγέω, hate) hated, hateful, abominated; [1× El.]
+ϲυν-είδω	(ξυνίϲαϲι, pf. indic. act. 3pl.) share in the knowledge (pf. with pres. sense)
+εὐνή, ἡ	bed (often in plural: SS 6 §3); > 'and my hateful bed in this afflicted house knows of…'
μογερόϲ (3)	toilsome, grievous, <u>afflicted</u>; [1× Soph.]
+οἶκοϲ, ὁ	house, abode, dwelling (pl. often stands for a single house)
+ὅϲοϲ (3)	as much as; (cf. correl. pron.: S #340); > 'how much I lament…'
θρενέω	(θρῆνοϲ, ὁ, dirge, lament) bewail, lament

LINE 95

+κατά (+ acc.)	over, throughout, among all along
βάρβᾰροϲ, ον	barbarian, foreign; [1× El.]
αἶα, ἡ	earth, <u>land</u> (poetic for γαῖα, γῆ); βάρβαρον αἶαν = Troy; [1× El.]
+φοίνιοϲ (2/3)	bloody (poetic for φόνιοϲ)
+"Ἄρηϲ, ὁ	god of war/warlike frenzy; (decln., S #285.1); son of Zeus and Hera
ξενίζω	(ξένοϲ, host) entertain hospitably; > 'whom the bloody War-god did not make his guest in a foreign land'; (irony—Ares' hospitality is wounds and death); [1× Soph.]
+μήτηρ, μητρόϲ, ἡ	mother (syncopated noun, S #44, 262)
ἡμή	= ἡ ἐμή (aphaeresis, initial ε elides with a long vowel or diphthong of the preceding word: S #76); χὠ = καὶ ὁ (crasis)
κοινολεχήϲ, ές	(κοινόϲ, shared, λέχοϲ, bed) sharing the same bed; [1× Soph.]

Αἴγισθος ὅπως δρῦν ὑλοτόμοι
cχίζουcι κάρα φονίῳ πελέκει.
κοὐδεὶc τούτων οἶκτος ἀπ᾽ ἄλληc
ἢ 'μοῦ φέρεται, cοῦ, πάτερ, οὕτωc
αἰκῶc οἰκτρῶc τε θανόντοc.
ἀλλ᾽ οὐ μὲν δὴ
λήξω θρήνων cτυγερῶν τε γόων,

100

LINE 98

⁺Αἴγισθος, ὁ	son of Pelops and his daughter (Pelopia), cousin of Agamemnon
⁺ὅπως (conj.)	as, like (opens a comparative clause of quality or manner: S #2463)
δρῦς, δρυός, ἡ	oak, any timber tree; [1× *El.*]
ὑλο-τόμος, ὁ	ὕλη, wood, forest; τεμεῖν < τέμνω, cut) woodcutter; [1× Soph.]
cχίζω	split, cleave (historical pres. for vividness: S #1883; SS 186 §5: "note the change to the present for the violent action . . ."; GMT #33); [1× Soph.]
⁺κάρᾱ, τό	[ᾰ] head; poetic for κεφαλή; > 'whom bloody Ares did not make his guest . . . but my mother and her bedfellow, Aegisthus, split his head . . .'
πέλεκῠς, εως, ὁ	double-edged ax; [1× Soph.]

LINE 100

οὐδείς, οὐδεμία, οὐδέν	and not one, not even one (S #349b); κοὐδεὶς = καὶ οὐδεὶς (*crasis*)
⁺τούτων	(objective genit.: SS 52–53 §4; S #1328); > '*and for this* no pity is offered by/comes from . . .'
οἶκτος, ὁ	(οἴζω, cry οἴ, lament) pity, compassion, lamentation; [1× *El.*]
ἀπ᾽ ἄλλης ἢ 'μοῦ	ἢ 'μοῦ = ἢ ἐμοῦ (*aphaeresis*, p. 23; emphatic genit. of ἐγώ; the fem. replaces the more general masc. ἄλλου, by attraction to the gender of Electra); > 'from/by anyone but me'
cοῦ . . . θανόντος	*hyperbaton* (p. 24); concessive or temporal genit. absolute (S #2070); > 'although/when you have died'
⁺οὕτως (adv.)	(⁺οὗτος, this) so, thus, in this manner
⁺αἰκῶς (adv.)	poetic = ἀεικῶς (ἀεικής, unseemly, shameful) shamefully; according to Kamerbeek, a keyword of this play; cf. 206, 216, 487, 511, 515
οἰκτρῶς (adv.)	(⁺οἰκτρός, pitiable, lamentable) pitiably; [1× *El.*]
ἀλλ᾽ . . . μὲν δή	'yet for all that . . .'; (adversative: GP 394)
⁺λήγω	cease from + genit.

ἔcτ᾽ ἂν παμφεγγεῖc ἄcτρων　　　　　　　　　　　　　　**105**

ῥιπάc, λεύccω δὲ τόδ᾽ ἦμαρ,

μὴ οὐ τεκνολέτειρ᾽ ὥc τιc ἀηδὼν

ἐπὶ κωκυτῷ τῶνδε πατρῴων

πρὸ θυρῶν ἠχὼ πᾶcι προφωνεῖν.

ὦ δῶμ᾽ Ἀίδου καὶ Περcεφόνηc,　　　　　　　　　　　**110**

ὦ χθόνι᾽ Ἑρμῆ καὶ πότνι᾽ Ἀρά,

cεμναί τε θεῶν παῖδεc Ἐρινύεc,

LINE 105

ἔc-τε (conj.) — as long as (ἔcτ᾽ ἄν … + subjv., λεύccω: SS 295 §7: "Subjunctive [pres. usually with ἄν] is used where the *duration* [of the act] is lying in the future …"); > 'I will not cease my pain-filled lamentations, *as long as I look* at the radiant sweep of the stars and this daylight'

παμ-φεγγήc, έc — (πᾶc, all; φάοc, light) all-shining, <u>radiant</u>; [1× Soph.]

ῥῑπή, ἡ — (ῥίπτω, throw) quivering, twinkling light (LSJ 3); [1× El.]

ἦμαρ, ἤμᾰτοc, τό — day (poetic for ἡμέρα)

μὴ οὐ … προφονεῖν — μὴ οὐ (*synizesis*, p. 24; with inf. after a vb. of denying that is itself negated; the inf. here can be an object, epexegetic, or consecutive; the sense would be the same if the infinitive had no negative attached: SS 328–29 §7i); > '[No,] I will not cease from lament … from raising/uttering a cry to all'

τεκν-ολέτειρα, ἡ — If we think of the myth in which Procne kills her son, Itys, for revenge on his father, it is 'having killed its young,' if not, 'having lost its young'; [1× Soph.]

ἀηδών, ἡ, Attic ὁ, — genit.: ἀηδόνοc/ἀηδοῦc; (ἀείδω, sing) songstress, i.e., the nightingale

LINE 108

κωκῡτόc, ὁ — (κωκύω [ῡ], shriek, wail, lament) shrieking, wailing; [1× El.]

⁺πρό (+ genit.) — before, in front of

ἠχώ, -όοc/-οῦc, ἡ — (acc. ἠχώ) ringing sound; loud cries (LSJ); [1× El.]

προ-⁺φωνέω — <u>utter</u> [1× El.]

LINE 110

⁺Ἀίδηc, Ἀίδᾱο, ὁ — (ἀ privat., + ἰδεῖν, unseen) Hades, the god of the world below

Περcεφόνη, ἡ — daughter of Zeus and Demeter, carried off by Hades; [1× El.]

χθόνιοc (2/3) — (χθών, earth) in/under the earth; χθόνιοc Ἑρμῆc, conductor of the dead

πότνιᾰ, ἡ — as substant.: mistress, lady; adj.: revered, august, awful (only in nom. and voc.); [1× El.]

Ἀρά, ἡ — Curse (personified; probably the curse uttered by the dying Ag.)

cεμνόc (3) — (cέβομαι, awe) august, solemn, holy; cult title of the Erinyes; [1× El.]

⁺Ἐρῑνύc, ύοc, ἡ — deity avenging wrongs done to kindred, both murder and adultery

αἳ τοὺς ἀδίκωϲ θνῄϲκονταϲ ὁρᾶθ',
αἳ τοὺς εὐνὰϲ ὑποκλεπτομένουϲ,
ἔλθετ', ἀρήξατε, τείϲαϲθε πατρὸϲ   115
φόνον ἡμετέρου,
καί μοι τὸν ἐμὸν πέμψατ' ἀδελφόν.
μούνη γὰρ ἄγειν οὐκέτι ϲωκῶ
λύπηϲ ἀντίρροπον ἄχθοϲ.   120

LINE 113

ἀ-δίκωϲ (adv.)	(ἄδικοϲ, unjust: ἀ privat., + δίκη) unjustly; [1× Soph.]
αἳ . . .αἳ	*anaphora* in *asyndeton* (p. 23; according to Kamerbeek, it stresses both the double function of the Erinyes and the double crime committed by Clyt. and Aeg. against Ag.); > 'you who see . . . [you who see, supplement ὁρᾶτε])'
ὑπο-⁺κλέπτω	steal surreptitiously (verbs of depriving take double acc., the person deprived of and the object taken; when the verb is used passively, as here, the 2nd acc. is often retained: SS 39 §8); > 'you who see *those who are robbed* of their marriage beds (εὐνάϲ)'; cf. κτῆϲιν at 960; [1× Soph.]

LINE 115

ἀρήγω	help, aid
*τίνω, <u>ἔτειϲα</u>/ἔτιϲα	mid.: (poetic) take payment, <u>avenge</u> (ἔλθετε, ἀρήξατε, τείϲαϲθε— vivid rising tricolon [cf. l. 13] with *asyndeton* [p. 23], which lends the imperative its great force: S #3016)
⁺*πέμπω	(πομπή, solemn procession) send
⁺ἀδελφόϲ, ὁ	[ἄ] (ἀ copulative, δελφύ, womb) son of the same mother, <u>brother</u>
⁺μοῦνοϲ (3)	<u>alone</u>, forsaken (Ion. for μόνοϲ)
⁺οὐκ-έτι (adv.)	no more, no longer, no further
ϲωκέω	(ϲῶκοϲ, the stout, strong one) to be strong or powerful; with inf.: to be in condition or state to do something; [1× *El.*]
⁺λῦπή, ἡ	pain of body or mind, <u>grief</u>
ἀντίρροποϲ, ον ἄχθοϲ, -εοϲ, τό	counterpoising, compensating for; weight, burden (the 'burden of grief' is 'counterpoised' to Electra herself); > 'For I am no longer strong enough to hold up alone against the burden of grief that weights me down'; [1× Soph.]

ΧΟΡΟΣ

    ὦ παῖ παῖ δυστανοτάτας   στρ. α’

    Ἠλέκτρα ματρός, τίν’ ἀεὶ

    λάσκεις ὧδ’ ἀκόρεστον οἰμωγὰν

    τὸν πάλαι ἐκ δολερᾶς ἀθεώτατα

    ματρὸς ἁλόντ’ ἀπάταις Ἀγαμέμνονα   125

    κακᾷ τε χειρὶ πρόδοτον; ὡς ὁ τάδε πορὼν

PARODOS (entrance song), LINES 121–250

Chorus of women of Mycenae have entered the orchestra from entry ramp during Electra's delivery of the last lines. Their song consists of three strophic pairs and an epode, each divided between themselves and Electra.

    Choral passages admit some Doric forms: ᾱ for η (S Introduction C, D #30, 32, 214.D1): e.g., δυστᾱνοτάτας = δυστηνοτάτης; μᾱτρός = μητρός; γενέθλᾱ = γενέθλη; Doric genit. pl. -άων > -ᾶν (S #214.D8).

FIRST STROPHE, Lines 121–136

LINE 121

λάσκω	scream, shout out (codd. have τάκεις [=τήκεις] 'melt away'; λάσκω governs two objects: an inner one: οἰμογάν: 'What lamentation do you shout out?' expanded by ὧδ’ ἀκόρεστον 'so insatiably'; and an external object τὸν Ἀγαμέμνονα, which is governed also by the verbal noun οἰμογάν); > 'Why do you shout out so insatiably *a lamentation for* Ag. trapped long ago most godlessly by the wiles of your deceitful mother . . . ?'; [1× *El.*]
ἀ-κόρεστος, ον	(ἀ privat., κορέννῡμι, satisfy) insatiate, unceasing; [1× *El.*]
οἰμωγή, ἡ	(οἰμώζω, cry οἴμοι) lamentation (verbal noun in acc. governing τὸν Ἀγαμέμνονα, 'lament for Agamemnon': SS 37 §5; τὸν . . . ἁλόντα . . . Ἀγαμέμνονα, *hyperbaton*); [1× *El.*]
⁺πάλαι (adv.)	long ago
δολερός (3)	(⁺δόλος) deceitful, treacherous; [1× *El.*]
ἀθέως (adv.)	in a godless fashion, in unholy fashion

LINE 125

*ἁλίσκομαι, ἑάλων/ἥλων	(ἁλόντα, aor.² ptc. defective pass., ⁺αἱρέω supplies active voice) be captured, seized (often used of enemies being overthrown and ruined); [1× *El.*]
ἀπάτη, ἡ	guile, deceit (dat. of means: S #1507; SS 88–89 §16); [1× *El.*]
⁺πρό-δοτος, ον	(προ-δίδωμι, betray) <u>betrayed</u>, abandoned
⁺ὡς	the unaccented exclamatory ὡς, which would equal εἰ γάρ, εἴθε (S #1815, 2999), seems to be preferred: 'if only' 'may,' 'would that'
⁺πόρω, ἔπορον	(aor.² ptc. act. masc. sg.) bring to pass, contrive (⁺πόρω, obsolete pres. of aor.²; articular substant. ptc.: S #2050–2052; SS 257–58 §9; GMT #825; the masc. serves as a generalizing masc. gender. The Chorus refer to anyone whom the description fits, whether Clyt. or Aeg., or both: S #1015; SS 12–13 §8); > may the doer perish/die'

ΗΛ.

ὄλοιτ', εἴ μοι θέμιϲ τάδ' αὐδᾶν.
ὦ γενέθλα γενναίων,
ἥκετ' ἐμῶν καμάτων παραμύθιον·
οἶδά τε καὶ ξυνίημι τάδ', οὔ τί με
φυγγάνει, οὐδ' ἐθέλω προλιπεῖν τόδε,
μὴ οὐ τὸν ἐμὸν ϲτενάχειν πατέρ' ἄθλιον.

130

LINE 127

⁺*ὄλ-λῡμι   (aor.² mid. opt.) destroy, ruin; mid.: perish, come to an end (optative of wish with an introductory word ὡς: SS 232 §15; GMT #726)

⁺θέμις, θέμιστος, ἡ   law, right (agreed-upon common consent or prescription); > 'if it is right for me to ...'

αὐδάω   (αὐδή, human voice) speak, talk, say

LINE 129

γενέθλη, ἡ   race, stock, family, <u>offspring</u> (LSJ I.2)

γενναῖος (2/3)   (γέννᾰ poetic for γένος, birth) true to one's descent, noble, high born, high minded

κάμᾰτος, ὁ   (κάμνω, be tired, distressed) weariness, distress, toil, trouble

παρα-μύθιον, τό   (παρα-μῡθέομαι, console) address; comfort, consolation (acc. in apposition to the sentence: the comforting is the purpose of their coming: SS 45 §17; Kamerbeek, Campbell, Jebb, Kells, Finglass: 'as a consolation'); > 'Oh offspring of noble parents, you have come to console (as a consolation to) my distress'; [1× Soph.]

⁺ξυν-*ίημι   = συν-ίημι, metaphorically: perceive, understand, know

LINE 132

φυγγάνω   (collateral form of φεύγω) flee, escape; > 'it does not escape me'; [1× Soph.]

προ-⁺*λείπω, -έλιπον   (προλιπεῖν, aor.² inf. act.) leave by going forth, forsake, i.e., give up (doing something); [1× *El.*]

μὴ οὐ   *synizesis*, adjacent vowels are pronounced together to give a single long syllable (S #60, 61)

⁺ϲτενάχω   [ᾰ](lengthened for ϲτένω) trans.: bemoan, bewail, lament (μὴ οὐ ... ϲτενάχειν, doubled negative as if a negated verb of preventing had preceded, see 107n; a sense construction, *constructio ad sensum*); > 'I do not wish to give this up, *not* to lament my poor father'

⁺ἄθλιος (2/3)   wretched, poor (the play abounds in words signifying misery, cf. δύστηνος, τάλας)

ἀλλ' ὦ παντοίας φιλότητος ἀμειβόμεναι χάριν,
ἐᾶτέ μ' ὧδ' ἀλύειν,   **135**
αἰαῖ, ἱκνοῦμαι.

XO.   ἀλλ' οὔτοι τόν γ' ἐξ Ἀίδα   ἀντ. α'
             παγκοίνου λίμνας πατέρ' ἀν-
             στάσεις οὔτε γόοισιν, οὐ λιταῖς·

LINE 134

παντοῖος (3)	(πᾶς, all every) of all sorts or kinds; [1× *El.*]
φῐλότης, ητος, ἡ	(φίλος, friend) friendship, love, affection; [1× *El.*]
ἀμείβω	[ᾰ] mid.: change with one another, exchange (with another) (ὦ ... ἀμειβόμεναι the voc. does not always necessitate the exclamatory ὦ, but it is needed when a participle takes the place of a substantive to indicate that the participle is not a predicative but attributive: SS 27, §9, 30 §10); > "You who repay kindness (χάριν) in every sort of friendship [with me]" (Lloyd-Jones); [1× *El.*]
⁺χάρις, -ιτος, ἡ	[ᾰ] (χάριν, acc. sg.) favor, pleasure, gratitude (declension: S #257)
⁺*ἐάω	[ᾰ] let, suffer, allow, permit
ἀλύω	[ᾰ, ῡ] be distraught, beside oneself
⁺αἰαῖ	alas (interjection of grief)

FIRST ANTISTROPHE, Lines 137–152

LINE 137

⁺οὔ-τοι (adv.)	indeed not
τόν ... πατέρα	*hyperbaton* (p. 24); > 'you will never bring your father back from the lake of Hades (Ἀίδα = Ἀίδου), where all of us will have to go'
⁺γε	at least (postpositive and enclitic particle in limitative function, i.e., "whether or not prayer is likely to be successful in other cases": GP 140–41)
παγ-κοίνος (3)	common to all; [1× *El.*]
λίμνη, ἡ	lake (SS 108 §9: "ἐκ is used with ablatival genitive . . . to denote *motion out of*, or *away from*"; λίμνᾶς = λίμνης); [1× *El.*]
ἀν-**ίστημι, -στάσεις	(fut. act.) raise up (ἀνστάσεις, apocope: cutting off a short vowel before a consonant, here ἀν for ἀνά); [1× *El.*]
λῐτή, ἡ	(λίσσομαι, pray) prayer (mostly in plural); [1× *El.*]

ἀλλ' ἀπὸ τῶν μετρίων ἐπ' ἀμήχανον   140
ἄλγος ἀεὶ cτενάχουcα διόλλυcαι,
ἐν οἷc ἀνάλυcίc ἐcτιν οὐδεμία κακῶν.
τί μοι τῶν δυcφόρων ἐφίῃ;

ΗΛ.   νήπιος ὅc τῶν οἰκτρῶc   145
οἰχομένων γονέων ἐπιλάθεται.

LINE 140

⁺ἀπό (+genit.)   from (with ablatival genit. indicates departure or absence from: SS 99 §5); > 'but (away from moderation =) leaving moderation behind you are destroying yourself [plunging] into incurable grief while lamenting forever'

μέτριος (2/3)   (μέτρον, measure) moderate; τὰ μέτρια, moderation; [1× *El.*]

⁺ἐπί (+ acc.)   to, toward, for (the acc. indicates here the goal attained or aimed at: S #1676 SS 113 §10); > 'into incurable grief'

ἀ-μήχᾰνος, ον   (ἀ privat., μηχανή) incurable, without remedy (LSJ 2b); [1× *El.*]

⁺ἄλγος, εος, τό   pain, sorrow, grief, distress

δι-⁺*ὄλλῡμι   mid.: destroy utterly, bring to naught

οἷς   The antecedent is in the general sense of what precedes (Kamerbeek); > 'in which there is no release whatsoever from your sorrows'

ἀνάλῠσις, εως, ἡ   (ἀναλύω, set free) loosing, releasing, dissolution (with objective genitive, κακῶν: SS 52–53 §4; S #1328); [1× Soph.]

LINE 144

τί (adv.)   why? how? wherefore? (LSJ B 8d); [1× Soph.]

μοι   ethical dat., indicates assurance of close concern or involvement (S #1486); SS 85 §10: "why, I ask you (why, pray), do you desire troubles?"

δύσ-φορος, ον   (δυσ-, φέρω) hard to bear, oppressive, insufferable, grievous; [1× *El.*]

⁺ἐφ-*ίη-μι   mid.: aim at, long, desire + genit. (LSJ B2; S #777)

νήπιος, ον   infant, child; childish, silly; generalizing masc. (SS 12–13 §8; see πάσχοντι 771n; νήπιος ὅς, epic expression, only here in Tragedy: Finglass); [1× *El.*]

⁺οἴχομαι   (dep.) come, go, be gone (of persons euphemistically for θνῄσκω, to have departed: LSJ II)

⁺γονεύς, έος, ὁ   (**γίγνομαι, be, become) begetter, father (mostly in pl.: parents; genitive with verbs of forgetting: SS 65 §23)

ἐπι-λήθομαι   forget, lose thought of + genit. (Doric: ἐπι-λάθομαι [ᾰ]); > 'only a simpleton forgets parents who died piteously'

ἀλλ' ἐμέ γ' ἁ στονόεςς' ἄραρεν φρένας,
ἁ Ἴτυν αἰὲν Ἴτυν ὀλοφύρεται,
ὄρνις ἀτυζομένα, Διὸς ἄγγελος.
ἰὼ παντλάμων Νιόβα, σὲ δ' ἔγωγε νέμω θεόν,   **150**
ἅτ' ἐν τάφῳ πετραίῳ,
αἰαῖ, δακρύεις.

LINE 147

στονόεις, -εσσα, -εν	(στόνος, στένω) mournful, wretched (= ἡ στονόεσσα); [1× *El.*]
ἀρᾰρίσκω, ἤρᾰρον	(ἄραρεν, aor.² indic. act. without temp. augment) intrans.: suit, fit (usually with dat. here with two accs.; Finglass views it as an intransitive pf.²: "is fixed in my mind"; in either case the accs. are of the whole and of the part: the first, ἐμέ, refers to the person, i.e., 'me,' and the second, φρένας, specifies the part, i.e., 'mind'; SS 41 §11); > 'but she who laments suits me, [that is, suits] my mind'; [1× Soph.]
⁺φρήν, φρενός, ἡ	midriff, mind (LSJ 3; often in plural)
Ἴτυς, υος, ὁ	son of Procne and Tereus; the length of -υ- changes: ἁ Ἴτῠν αἰέν Ἴτῦν; [1× Soph.]
ὀλοφύρομαι	lament (Procne, changed into a nightingale, mourns her son eternally); [1× Soph.]
⁺ὄρνις, ὄρνιθος, ὁ/ἡ	here: the nightingale
ἀτύζομαι	be distraught (from fear) (attributive participle: SS 256–57 §8); [1× Soph.]
⁺Ζεύς, Διός, ὁ	(Διϝός, declension: S #285.12)
ἄγγελος, ὁ/ἡ	messenger; the traditional messenger was the eagle. Jebb and Kells suggest that the nightingale was considered Zeus' messenger since his return to Attica heralds the Spring, which is sacred to Zeus, as are all the seasons, Ὧραι, who are his daughters; [1× *El.*]

LINE 150

παν-τλήμων, ον	all-wretched (genit. –ονος; = παντάλᾱς, αινα, αν; Doric: τλάμων [ᾱ]); (1× *El.*)
Νιόβη, ἡ	voc. (she had 6 sons and 6 daughters [or 7 and 7] and boasted that she was superior to Leto, who had only 1 each. In revenge, Apollo and Artemis killed Niobe's children. She turned into a rock on Mt. Sipylus in Lydia, with a spring of water forever flowing down her face like tears); Sophocles sees her as a goddess (Sale); (1× *El.*)
⁺ἔγωγε	emphatic for ἐγώ (S #325b)
⁺*νέμω	hold, <u>consider as</u>; apportion, assign, distribute; (Νέμεσις = Retribution)
ἅτ'	= ἅ τε (ἥ τε); here ὅς τε in its epic use indicates permanent/timeless action (SS 263 §2); > '*you who forever* shed tears in your rocky tomb'
⁺τάφος, ὁ	[ᾰ] (θάπτω, bury) grave, tomb
πετραῖος (3)	(πέτρα, rock) rock; (1× *El.*)
⁺δακρύω	weep, shed tears

XO.　　　　　　οὔτοι coì μούνα ,　　　　　　　　　　　　　　　　　　　　　στρ. β'
　　　　　　　　τέκνον, ἄχοc ἐφάνη βροτῶν,
　　　　　　　　πρὸc ὅ τι cὺ τῶν ἔνδον εἶ περιccά,　　　　　　　　　　　　　155
　　　　　　　　οἶc ὁμόθεν εἶ καὶ γονᾷ ξύναιμοc,
　　　　　　　　οἷα Χρυcόθεμιc ζώει καὶ Ἰφιάναccα,
　　　　　　　　κρυπτᾷ τ' ἀχέων ἐν ἥβᾳ
　　　　　　　　ὄλβιοc, ὃν ἁ κλεινὰ　　　　　　　　　　　　　　　　　　160

SECOND STROPHE, Lines 153–172

LINE 153

⁺βροτός, ὁ　　　　mortal person (poetic opposite to ἀθάνατος or θεός; as adj.: mortal); partitive genit. following adj. μούνᾳ (SS 58 §10)

ἄχος, εως, τό　　　pain, distress; [1× *El.*]

⁺*φαίνω　　　　(ἐφάνη [ă] = ἐφήνη, aor.²); bring to light, show, make known, reveal, disclose; intransitive: appear

⁺ὅστις, ἥτις, ὅ τι　　whoever, any one who, whatever, anything which (indefinite/general relative pron.: S #339); ὅ τι = acc. of respect; > 'Not to you alone among mortals, child, has grief appeared, in regard *to which* you are beyond (i.e., more afflicted than, Kamerbeek) those within/indoors'

⁺ἔνδον (adv.)　　τῶν ⁺ἔνδον supply ἀνθρώπων; an adv. with an article may be used to qualify a noun which is often omitted (S #1153e); genit. of comparison (S #1401–3); antecedent of οἷς, the masculine form can stand also for feminine, here referring to Chrysothemis and Iphianassa (S #105l SS 12–13 §8)

περιccός (3)　　(περί, exceedingly) more than sufficient, superfluous, beyond (LSJ 3)

LINE 156

ὁμόθεν (adv.)　　(ὁμός, same) from the same origin; [1× Soph.]

γονή, ἡ　　　　(⁺*γίγνομαι be, become), race, stock, family, lineage (LSJ 2); γονᾷ = γονῇ

ξύν-αιμος, ὁ/ἡ　　= cύν-αιμος (cύν, αἷμα) brother, <u>sister</u>, kinsman, kinswoman; > 'with whom by lineage you are sister; [1× *El.*]

⁺οἷος, οἵα, οἷον　　<u>such as</u>, of which sort (correl. pron., S #340) οἷα clarifies τῶν ἔνδον > 'such as Chr. who is living and Iph.'; some connect the words to περιccά and understand: 'considering the manner in which Chr. lives . . .'

Χρυcόθεμιc . . . Ἰφιάναccα　according to Homer, Ag. had three daughters: Chrysothemis, Laodicē, and Iphianassa, the last sometimes identified with Iphigenia (*Iliad* 9.145); Euripides (*Or.* 23) mentions Chrysothemis, Iphianassa, and Electra; (Ἰφιϝάναccα, 'ruling with power')

⁺*ζάω　　　　live (contracts to η when we expect ă: S #395); Ion.: ζώει = Attic: ζῇ

LINE 159

⁺κρυπτός (3)　　(κρύπτω, hide) hidden, secret, concealed, <u>secluded</u>

ἀχέων　　　　either genit. pl. following κρυπτᾷ, from τὸ ἄχος [ă] = sorrow, i.e., '[lives] in youth secluded from sorrows' (SS 68 §30, Finglass, Kells, Kamerbeek); or an uncontracted pres. ptc. from ἀχέω, grieve, i.e., 'who [lives] in sorrow/sorrowing . . .', i.e., he too is grieving (Jebb, Sale. *Synizesis*, adjacent vowels are pronounced together to give a single long syllable: S #60)

ἥβη, ἡ　　　　youth

ὄλβιος (2/3)　　(ὄλβος, happiness) happy, blest; [1× *El.*]

ὅν　　　　　　The subject of the supplied ζώει/ζῇ, Orestes, is the antecedent; > '[he lives] . . . whom . . .'

ἁ κλεινά　　　= ἡ κλεινή; see κλεινός 8n

55

ΗΛ.

γᾶ ποτε Μυκηναίων
δέξεται εὐπατρίδαν, Διὸς εὔφρονι
βήματι μολόντα τάνδε γᾶν Ὀρέσταν.
ὅν γ᾿ ἐγὼ ἀκάματα προσμένουσ᾿ ἄτεκνος,
τάλαιν᾿ ἀνύμφευτος αἰὲν οἰχνῶ,
δάκρυσι μυδαλέα, τὸν ἀνήνυτον
οἶτον ἔχουσα κακῶν· ὁ δὲ λάθεται
ὧν τ᾿ ἔπαθ᾿ ὧν τ᾿ ἐδάη. τί γὰρ οὐκ ἐμοὶ

165

LINE 161

⁺Μῠκηναῖος (3)	Mycenaean
εὐ-πᾰτρίδης, ου, ὁ	(εὔ, πᾰτήρ) of a noble sire, of a noble family
εὔ-φρων, ον	(εὔ, φρήν) cheerful; well minded, <u>well disposed</u>, kind; [1× El.]
βῆμα, ατος, τό	(⁺*βαίνω, go) pace, step, footstep, <u>guidance</u> (LSJ); [1× El.]
ὅν . . . Ὀρέσταν	hyperbaton (p. 24). The name is emphatically put last, and is attracted to the case of the relative pronoun; > 'whom the famous Mycenaean land will one day accept as heir of his noble father when he comes with the kindly guidance of Zeus to this land, Orestes.'

LINE 164

ὅν	the antecedent is Orestes
ἀ-κάμᾰτος (2/3)	(ἀ privat., κάμᾰτος) untiring, unresting (ἀκάμᾰτα = neut. acc. pl. as adv. = untiringly); [1× El.]
⁺προσ-⁺*μένω	abide, wait still or longer; await
ἄ-τεκνος, ον	(ἀ privat., τέκνον) childless; [1× Soph.]
⁺τάλᾱς, τάλαινᾰ, τάλᾰν	(᾿τλάω, suffer) suffering, wretched, enduring
ἀ-νύμφευτος, ον	(ἀ privat., νυμφεύω, wed) unwedded (ἄτεκνος, ἀνύμφευτος, *hysteron proteron:* arrangement reversing the natural order of events: S #3030. The more important reason for her unhappiness is stated first [her childlessness] although it depends on the latter, i.e., not being married); > 'Yes! And in waiting for whom without rest, I childless, *without a husband* live miserable forever'; [1× El.]
οἰχνέω	= ⁺*οἴχομαι go; generally: walk, <u>live</u>
δάκρυ, υος, τό	tear (= δάκρῠον, τό); [1× Soph]
μῠδᾰλέος (3)	wet, dripping, soaked; > 'drenched in tears'; [1× Soph.]
ἀν-ήνῠτος, ον	(ἀ privat., ἀνύω, accomplish) endless (= ἀν-ήνυστος); [1× Soph.]

LINE 167

οἶτος, ὁ	ill fate, lot, doom; > 'having an endless fate of sorrows'
⁺λήθω, λήθομαι	mid. and pass.: forget, lose the memory of + genit.
⁺*πάσχω, ἔπαθον	(ἔπαθε, aor.² act.) suffer, experience
᾿δάω	(ἐδάη, aor.² indic.) learn (an old root); > 'he forgets what (the things) he has suffered and what (the things) *he has learned*'; [1× El.]

ἔρχεται ἀγγελίας ἀπατώμενον;   170
ἀεὶ μὲν γὰρ ποθεῖ,
ποθῶν δ' οὐκ ἀξιοῖ φανῆναι.

XO.   θάρςει μοι, θάρςει,   ἀντ. β'
           τέκνον. ἔτι μέγας οὐρανῷ
           Ζεύς, ὃς ἐφορᾷ πάντα καὶ κρατύνει·   175
           ᾧ τὸν ὑπεραλγῆ χόλον νέμουσα
           μήθ' οἷς ἐχθαίρεις ὑπεράχθεο μήτ' ἐπιλάθου·
           χρόνος γὰρ εὐμαρὴς θεός.

LINE 170

ἀγγελία, ἡ   (ἀγγέλλω, bear a message) message (partitive genit.: SS 57 §10); [1× *El.*]

ἀπᾰτάω   (ἀπατή, cheating) cheat, trick, beguile; pass.: deceived, <u>belied</u> > 'what (τί) message (lit.: of his message) comes to me *that is not belied?*'; [1× *El.*]

⁺*ποθῶν   (ποθέω) concessive ptc. (SS 252 §3; S #2066); ποθεῖ . . . ποθῶν wordplay on different forms of the same word was greatly appreciated by the Greeks, here for emphasis.

ἀξιόω   think/deem worthy; think fit (with limiting/explanatory inf. φανῆναι: SS 238–39 §3a); Kells: "For he is always 'yearning' (to come); but although yearning, he does not think fit to appear."

SECOND ANTISTROPHE, Lines 173–192

LINE 173

⁺θαρσέω   (θάρσος, courage) be of good courage; θάρσει = impv.: take courage

μοι . . . τέκνον   'my child' (dat. of possession: S #1480; SS 83–84 §8)

οὐρᾰνός, ὁ   heaven (dat. of place: S #1531; SS 87 §13); > 'Zeus is still great in heaven'

ἐφ-⁺*οράω   look over/on, oversee, observe, survey

κρᾰτύνω   [ῠ] (κράτος, rule) rule, govern; [1× *El.*]

LINE 176

ὑπερ-αλγής, ές   (ὑπερ, ἄλγος) exceedingly grievous, painful; [1× Soph.]

χόλος, ὁ   gall, bile; bitter anger, wrath; [1× *El.*]

⁺οἷς   by attraction for οὕς, because ὑπερ-άχθομαι requires dat.; μήθ' ὑπεράχθεο (τούτοις) οὓς ἐχθαίρεις μήτε ἐπιλάθου = > 'commit (lit.: committing) to him (i.e., to Zeus) your grievous anger; do not be excessively vexed *with those whom you* hate, or forget them'

⁺ἐχθαίρω   (ἔχθος, hatred) hate

ὑπερ-άχθομαι   (ὑπεράχθεο = ὑπεράχθου, impv.) be exceedingly vexed + dative

εὐ-μᾰρής, ές   easy, convenient; <u>gentle</u> (LSJ 2); [1× Soph.]

θεός   *synizesis* (p. 24)

οὔτε γὰρ ὁ τὰν Κρῖσαν   **180**
βούνομον ἔχων ἀκτὰν
παῖς Ἀγαμεμνονίδας ἀπερίτροπος
οὔθ' ὁ παρὰ τὸν Ἀχέροντα θεὸς ἀνάσσων.

HΛ.   ἀλλ' ἐμὲ μὲν ὁ πολὺς ἀπολέλοιπεν ἤδη   **185**
βίοτος ἀνέλπιστον, οὐδ' ἔτ' ἀρκῶ·
ἅτις ἄνευ τεκέων κατατάκομαι,

LINE 180

Κρῖσα, ἡ — a city in Phocis, about two miles WSW of Delphi; includes the land stretching southward from the town to its harbor (see Jebb); [1× Soph.]

ἀκτή, ἡ — (ἄγνυμι, break) place where the waves break, i.e., beach, shore; [1× El.]

βού-νομος, ον — (βοῦς, νέμω, drive to pasture) cattle feeding; > 'for neither he who holds/occupies ('+ἔχων) the cattle-feeding coast at Crisa . . .' (the Crisean plain southward from Delphi to the Corinthian Gulf became untilled and sacred to Apollo ['cattle feeding'] only after ca. 585 BCE, when Delphi took over this region [Jebb]. Tragedy is indifferent to anachronism; cf. Πυθικοῖσιν 49n)

Ἀγαμεμνονίδης, ου, ὁ — son of Agamemnon (–ιδης patronymic: S #845.4); [1× Soph.]

ἀ-περί-τροπος, ον — (ἀ privat., περιτρέπω, turn round about) not returning, _heedless_ (predicate to both Orestes, and Hades/Agamemnon); > 'For neither is he who holds the cattle-feeding shore of Crisa _heedless_, the son of Ag., nor . . .'; [1× Soph.]

LINE 183

+παρά (+ acc.) — running along, beside

Ἀχέρων, ὁ — river in the Netherworld; [1× El.]

ἀνάσσω — [ᾰ] rule, hold sway (poetic verb mostly in present. Scholars who read ὁ θεός as subject: "nor is the god ruling" would assume him to be Hades [Jebb, Sale, March, Finglass], those who read θεός as predicate: "nor is he who rules as a god," would see reference to the spirit of Ag. [Kamerbeek, Kells]. El. has invoked the 'house of Hades and Persephone' at 110)

LINE 185

ἐμὲ +μὲν — μέν _solitarium_ emphasizes ἐμέ; see 61n

ἀπο-+*λείπω, -λέλοιπα — (ἀπολέλοπεν, pf. act.) leave behind one, abandon

βίοτος, ὁ — (βιόω, live) life

ἀν-έλπιστος, ον — (ἐλπίζω, hope) hopeless; > 'but best part/much of my life has already abandoned me without hope'; [1× El.]

+ἀρκέω — be strong, avail; aid, assist (+ dat.); > 'I have no strength anymore'

+ἄνευ (+ genit.) — without

τέκος, εος, τό — offspring, child (poetic for τέκνον); [1× Soph.]

κατα-τήκω — (Doric: τάκω); pass.: melt away; > 'I who melt away with no offspring'; (1× El.)

ἃς φίλος οὔτις ἀνὴρ ὑπερίςταται,
ἀλλ' ἀπερεί τις ἔποικος ἀναξία
οἰκονομῶ θαλάμους πατρός, ὧδε μὲν   190
ἀεικεῖ ςὺν ςτολᾷ,
κεναῖς δ' ἀμφίςταμαι τραπέζαις.

XO.   οἰκτρὰ μὲν νόςτοις αὐδά ,   στρ. γ'
οἰκτρὰ δ' ἐν κοίταις πατρῴαις,
ὅτε οἱ παγχάλκων ἀνταία   195
γενύων ὡρμάθη πλαγά.

LINE 188

⁺φίλος (2/3)	loved, near and dear (poetic with active sense: loving)
ὑπερ-ίςτᾰμαι	to stand over so as to protect one, shield, guard + genit.; > 'whom (ἃς = ἧς) no loving husband protects'; [1× Soph.]
ἀπερεῖ (adv.)	(ἅπερ, as, so as) just as if, even as (= ὡςπερεί); [1× Soph.]
ἔπ-οικος, ον	stranger, alien; [1× Soph.]
ἀν-άξιος (2/3)	(ἀ privat., ἄξιος) unworthy, worthless; [1× *El.*]

LINE 190

οἰκο-νομέω	(οἰκονόμος, οἶκος, νέμω) be a steward; > 'but as some worthless alien I serve/tend to the chambers of my father'; [1× Soph.]
θάλᾰμος ὁ	chamber; [1× *El.*]
ἀ-εικής, ές	(ἀ privat., εἶκος, fair, reasonable) unseemly, shameful; [1× Soph.]
ςτολή, ἡ	(ςτέλλω, furnish) fitting out, <u>clothes</u>; [1× *El.*]
⁺κενός (3)	empty, destitute, vain, mean
ἀμφ-⁺*ίςτημι	pass.: stand around; [1× *El.*]
τράπεζα, ἡ	[τρᾰ] table, dinner, meal; >'in such mean clothes I stand around bare tables'

THIRD STROPHE, Lines 193–212

LINE 193

⁺οἰκτρός (3)	pitiable, lamentable (οἰκτρά . . . οἰκτρά: anaphora, p. 23)
νόςτος, ὁ	(νέομαι, go, come) return home (SS 4 §3: "perhaps the abstract action causes the plural of νόςτος." Dat. of time (SS 88 §3; S #1528b); [1× *El.*].
μέν . . . δέ	complementary not adversative, common in *anaphora*. Here, emphasizing οἰκτρά; > 'pitiful was the cry at his homecoming, *and* pitiful was the cry when your father lay on the couch (lit.: on your father's couch)'
αὐδή, ἡ	human voice; metaphorically: any other sound
κοίτη, ἡ	(κεῖμαι, lie down) bed, couch; the plural probably imitates νόςτοις, in preceding line.
ὅτε (correl. adv.)	when (usually denotes same time as that of the main verb: S 2383a)
οἱ	dat. sg. 3rd pers. (*hiatus*, see p. 23) here between ὅτε and οἱ. Dat. of disadvantage or *incommodi*: S #1481); > 'when the stroke of the brazen blade of an axe came down straight (lit.: hastened) *at him*.'
παγχάλκος, ον	(πᾶς, χαλκός, bronze) all-brazen, all of brass; [1× *El.*]
ἀνταῖος (3)	(ἄντα, over against) set over, against, right opposite; [1× Soph.]
γένῠς, υος, ἡ	lit.: jaw; edge of an axe, axe, <u>blade of an axe</u> (LSJ II)

δόλος ἦν ὁ φράσας, ἔρος ὁ κτείνας,
δεινὰν δεινῶς προφυτεύσαντες
μορφάν, εἴτ᾽ οὖν θεὸς εἴτε βροτῶν
ἦν ὁ ταῦτα πράσσων.

200

ΗΛ.   ὦ πασᾶν κεῖνα πλέον ἁμέρα
ἐλθοῦσ᾽ ἐχθίστα δή μοι·
ὦ νύξ, ὦ δείπνων ἀρρήτων
ἔκπαγλ᾽ ἄχθη.

ὁρμάω, ὡρμήθην	(Doric: ὡρμάθη, aor.¹ pass.) pass.: speed, hasten, rush on, make a start
πληγή, ἡ	(Doric: πλαγά) blow, stroke

LINE 197

⁺δόλος, ὁ	cunning, deceit
⁺φράζω, ἔφρασα	devise, plan (artic. substant. ptc.: S #2050, 2052; SS 257–58 §9; GMT #825)
ἔρος, ὁ	love, desire (Homeric form of ἔρως; occurs only here in Sophocles, does not appear in Aeschylus and only once in Euripides)
⁺*κτείνω, ἔκτεινα	kill (see ὁ φράσας previously; > 'guile was the plotter, passion was the killer'
⁺δεινὰν δεινῶς	extension of *polyptoton* (p. 24); play on different forms of the same word was greatly appreciated by the Greeks; δεινῶς (adv.)
προ-φῠτεύω	(προφυτεύσαντες, aor.¹ act. ptc.) plant before; metaphorically: <u>engender</u>; [1× Soph.]
μορφή, ἡ	shape, form, figure; > '[the two] terribly bred a terrible shape'
⁺εἴ-τε οὖν … εἴ-τε	either … or, whether … or; often for εἴτε … εἴτε
⁺*πράσσω	do, achieve, effect, <u>bring to pass</u> (Kamerbeek = εἴτ᾽ οὖν ὁ ταῦτα πράσσων ἦν θεός [τις], εἴτε [τις] βροτῶν) > 'whether [some] god or [someone] of mortals brought this to pass'

LINE 201

⁺πασᾶν	= πασῶν; comparative genit. (S #1069; SS 69–70 §32)
κεῖνος (3)	poetic for ⁺ἐκεῖνος (3)
⁺πλέον (adv.)	neut. of πλέων used here instead of μᾶλλον (S #1068) to create comparative of the omitted ἐχθρά; > 'Oh, that day by far most hateful, *more [hateful]* than all days that have come to me'
⁺ἡμέρα, ἡ	(Doric: ἁμέρα) day

LINE 203

ἔχθιστος (3)	irregular superlative of ⁺ἐχθρός (3); = ἐχθίστη
δή (postpos. pcl.)	emphasizes the superlative ἐχθίστα (GP 206); > 'by far most hateful'
δεῖπνον, τό	meal, feast (poetic plural: SS 7§4); [1× *El.*]
ἄρρ-ητος (2/3)	(ἀ privat., ῥηθῆναι > ἐρῶ, say) that cannot be told, unspeakable
ἔκ-παγλος, ον	metathesis: ἐκπλάγος (ἐκπλαγῆναι, ἐκπλήσσω, scare) frightful; > 'Oh, fearful anguish (lit.: 'burdens') of the unspeakable feast'

τοῖς ἐμὸς ἴδε πατὴρ   205
θανάτους αἰκεῖς διδύμαιν χειροῖν,
αἳ τὸν ἐμὸν εἷλον βίον
πρόδοτον, αἵ μ' ἀπώλεσαν·
οἷς θεὸς ὁ μέγας Ὀλύμπιος
ποίνιμα πάθεα παθεῖν πόροι,   210
μηδέ ποτ' ἀγλαΐας ἀποναίατο
τοιάδ' ἀνύσαντες ἔργα.

LINE 205

τοῖς	= οἷς (antecedent: δείπνων ἀρρήτων)
ἴδε	(aor.[2] act. 3sg., [+*]ὁράω); temporal augment omitted = εἷδε
αἰκής, ές	= [+]ἀεικής, ές
θάνᾰτος, ὁ	[ᾰ] death (probably poetic plural for emphasis: SS 6–7 4a); [1× El.]
δίδῠμος (3/2)	(δίς, twice) double (δυδύμαιν χειροῖν, dat. dual. The hand of Clyt. and the hand of Aegisthus;); > 'at which my father saw his shameful death by *their twin hands*'; [1× El.].
[+*]αἱρέω	take away, seize, overpower; see ἁλίσκομαι 125n
πρόδοτον	predicative and proleptic (see p. 24; Kamerbeek; SS 167–68 §6); > 'hands] that took away (εἷλον) my *betrayed* life' i.e., '[hands] that betrayed me and took away my life'
[+*]ἀπ-[+*]όλλῡμι, -ώλεσα	(ἀπώλεσαν, aor.[1] act.) destroy utterly, kill, slay; > '[hands] that *utterly destroyed* me'; αἵ … αἵ = *anaphora* in *asyndeton* (p. 23) between the two relative clauses, cf. 113–14

LINE 209

[+]οἷς	the antecedent is Clyt. and Aeg.
Ὀλύμπιος (3)	dwelling on Olympus; i.e., Zeus; [1× El.]
ποίνῐμος, ον	(ποινή vengeance) avenging, punishing; [1× El.]
πάθος, εος, τό	(παθεῖν, πάσχω suffer) suffering, misfortune; [1× El.]
[+*]πάσχω, ἔπαθον	(παθεῖν, aor.[2] inf. act.) suffer, be affected by anything good or bad (πάθεα παθεῖν—*figura etymologica*, see p. 23. παθεῖν, final/ consecutive inf. following vb. of giving, πόροι: SS 237§2: "May the god give them in return [i.e., as revenge] *sufferings to endure*")
[+*]πόροι	(aor.[2] opt.) bring to pass (opt. of wish: S #1814; GMT #721, 722); π alliteration, here repetition of word-initial consonant sounds.
ἀγλᾰΐα, ἡ	ἀγλαός, splendid) splendor, beauty, festive joy; (1× Soph.)
ἀπ-ονίνημαι, -ωνήμην	(Attic: ἀπόναιτο, aor.[2] opt. mid.) mid.: have enjoyment (opt. of wish negated by μή: S #1814; GMT #721, 722); [1× Soph.]
ἀνύω	accomplish; > 'may they who accomplished such things never have joy of their splendor'; (1× El.)

XO.   φράζου μὴ πόρcω φωνεῖν.   ἀντ. γ΄
        οὐ γνώμαν ἴcχεις ἐξ οἵων
        τὰ παρόντ᾽; οἰκείαc εἰc ἄταc   215
        ἐμπίπτειc οὕτωc αἰκῶc;
        πολὺ γάρ τι κακῶν ὑπερεκτήcω,
        cᾷ δυcθύμῳ τίκτουc᾽ αἰεὶ
        ψυχᾷ πολέμουc· τάδε—τοῖc δυνατοῖc
        οὐκ ἐριcτά—τλᾶθι.   220

THIRD ANTISTROPHE, Lines 213–232

LINE 213

πόρcω (adv.)	hereafter, forward; (1× *El.*)
⁺φωνέω	(φωνή, sound) speak loud or clearly (Jebb: "Be advised to say no more")
⁺γνώμη, ἡ	(γνῶναι, γιγνώcκω, perceive) mind, judgment
ἴcχω	<u>hold</u>, restrain (γνώμαν ἴcχεις periphrasis for γιγνώcκεις: Finglass)
⁺πάρ-⁺⁺ειμι	be present (τὰ παρόντα = present situation); > 'don't you understand from what kind of things [words/ deeds] the present situation [emerged]?'
οἰκεῖος (2/3)	(οἶκος, house) belonging to the house; <u>one's own</u> (LSJ III.2); >'disasters *of your own making*'; [1× *El.*]
⁺ἄτη, ἡ	(ἀάω, infatuate) state of infatuation or the ruin arising from it, <u>disaster</u>
ἐμ-⁺⁺πίπτω	fall upon, plunge; [1× *El.*]

LINE 217

ὑπερ-κτάομαι	(ὑπερεκτήcω, aor.¹ mid.) acquire over and above; [1× Soph.]
δύς-θῡμος, ον	(δυς-, θῡμος) dispirited, despondent, anxious, <u>disaffected</u>
⁺⁺τίκτω	give birth, beget
⁺ψῡχή, ἡ	spirit, soul
πόλεμος, ὁ	war, battle; >'you have acquired a large portion of your suffering over and above by constantly breeding *battles* for your disaffected soul'; [1× *El.*]
τάδε ... τλᾶθι	(= τλῆθι, aor.² impv., < *τλάω, <u>ἔτλην</u>, endure) 'endure this' (τάδε ... τλᾶθι is conjecture of Jackson's for τά δὲ, and of Wakefield's for codd. πλάθειν: 'to approach [in hostile sense].' Jebb accepts the codd. and sees πλάθειν as epexegetic inf. that further explains the meaning of ἐριcτά: "but those things [i.e., such wars] cannot be waged against the powerful, *so that one should come in conflict with them.*" The Jackson-Wakefield conjecture is recommended due to its simplicity and is in line with the core advice of the Chorus: 'Endure this [i.e., the situation]! You cannot struggle against those in power.')
δῠνατός (3)	(δύναμαι, be able) strong, mighty, powerful; [1× *El.*]
ἐριcτός (3)	(ἐρίζω, rival with) be disputed; [1× Soph.]

ΗΛ.   ἐν δεινοῖς δείν' ἠναγκάσθην·
              ἔξοιδ', οὐ λάθει μ' ὀργά.
              ἀλλ' ἐν γὰρ δεινοῖς οὐ σχήσω
              ταύτας ἄτας,
              ὄφρα με βίος ἔχῃ.   225
              τίνι γάρ ποτ' ἄν, ὦ φιλία γενέθλα,
              πρόσφορον ἀκούσαιμ' ἔπος,
              τίνι φρονοῦντι καίρια;
              ἄνετέ μ' ἄνετε παράγοροι.
              τάδε γὰρ ἄλυτα κεκλήσεται·   230
              οὐδέ ποτ' ἐκ καμάτων ἀποπαύσομαι
              ἀνάριθμος ὧδε θρήνων.

LINE 221

⁺δεινοῖς δείνά   *polyptoton,* see δεινὰν δεινῶς 198n

⁺ἀναγκάζω   (ἠναγκάσθην, aor.¹ pass.) force a person to do something; > 'I've been forced [to do] dreadful things in dreadful circumstances'

⁺ἐξ-⁺*οιδα   I know full well (for ⁺οἶδ, see 40, 41, 55; for ἐκ, see 7, 13)

⁺*λήθω   (Doric: λάθει) act.: escape or elude notice (+ acc. of person: μέ); > 'I know it well; my passion *does not escape me.*'

ἀλλ' ... γὰρ   assumes an ellipse (GP 101: "what precedes is irrelevant unimportant, or subsidiary, and is consequently to be ruled out of discussion"); >'But no! For I shall not curb these disastrous ways'

⁺*ἔχω, <u>σχήσω</u>/ἔξω   have, hold (for 2 futures, see S #1911. In verse ἔχω is often used as κατέχω, <u>hold back, curb</u>)

LINE 225

ὄφρα (conj.)   so long as (ἄν omitted; ἔχῃ, subjv. pres. act. in primary sequence, σχήσω (S #2193 a); > 'as long as life keeps hold of me'; [1× Soph.]

⁺βίος, ὁ   life

⁺τίνι   Moorhouse sees it as dat. with verbs of obeying or addressing, 82 §5: "from whom could I hear a suitable word (of comfort) from whom that thinks aright?"

πρόσ-φορος, ον   (προσφέρω, bring to) useful, profitable, suitable; [1× *El.*]

⁺*ἀκούω   (ἀκούσαιμι, aor.¹ act. opt.) hear, listen (potential opt. in independent clause with ἄν for timeless reference to the future: S #1824; SS 230 §14); > '*could I hear* (possibly in the future)'

⁺ἔπος, εος, τό   word

⁺φρονέω   think, have an understanding

καίριος (3/2)   (⁺καιρός) seasonable, happening at the right/critical time; [1× *El.*]

LINE 229

⁺ἀν-*ίημι   (ἄν-ετε, aor.² impv. act) let go (S #777)

παρήγορος, ον   (παρα, ἀγορεύω) consoling, soothing; > 'leave me, leave me, you who console me'; [1× Soph.]

ἄλυτος, ον   (ἀ privat., λύω loosen) not to be loosed, insoluble; [1× Soph.]

⁺*κἄλέω   call, call by name (fut. pf. pass. indic., κεκλήσεται, indicates a completed action in the future with permanent result: S #1852 b3) > 'for these things/this *will be called* insoluble'

XO.	ἀλλ' οὖν εὐνοίᾳ γ' αὐδῶ,	ἐπ.
	μάτηρ ὡϲεί τιϲ πιϲτά,	
	μὴ τίκτειν ϲ' ἄταν ἄταιϲ.	235
ΗΛ.	καὶ τί μέτρον κακότατοϲ ἔφυ; φέρε,	
	πῶϲ ἐπὶ τοῖϲ φθιμένοιϲ ἀμελεῖν καλόν;	

κάμᾰτοϲ, ὁ	(κάμνω, be tired) toil, trouble, weariness, distress
ἀπο-παύω	mid.: cease from; [1× El.]
ἀν-άριθμοϲ, ον	(ἀ privat., ἀριθμόϲ, number) without number; > 'for I will never cease from my labors and am in this way *infinite* in my lamentations'; [1× El.]

LINE 233

ἀλλ' οὖν ... γε	well, at least (GP 442–43: "following upon the rejection of a suggestion … usually … introduces a more moderate suggestion")
εὔνοιᾰ, ἡ	goodwill, loyalty (dat. of cause or reason: SS 89 §17); > because of/ out of goodwill'; [1× El.]
αὐδάω	(αὐδή, human voice) speak, talk, say
ὡϲ-εί (adv.)	as if, just as (GMT #873); > 'as some faithful mother'; (in a ring composition the Chorus conclude with the theme of the mother image, they started at 112, casting themselves as the opposite of Clytemnestra); [1× El.]
⁺πιϲτόϲ (3)	reliable, faithful, loyal
ἄταν ἄταιϲ	*polyptoton* (see δεινὰν δεινῶϲ, 198n) for effect and emphasis. Dat. of what is added to; SS 85 §9: "I tell you not to breed misery upon misery."

LINE 236

⁺καί (adv.)	and (for stress, the query is an indignant comment on the preceding statement); > '*and* what has nature produced as a measure of evil?'
μέτρον, τό	measure, standard, rule; [1× El.]
κᾰκότηϲ, ητοϲ, ἡ	(κακόϲ, bad) badness, wickedness; [1× El.]
⁺*φύω, ἔφυν	[ῠ] (aor.² act) bring forth, produce
⁺*φέρε	'come,' 'now,' 'well' (used like ἄγε: S #2010)
⁺πῶϲ	how?
⁺ἐπί (+ dat.)	on, by, upon, on the surface of, in addition to; for, over
⁺φθίω/φθίνω	decline, decay, wane (φθίμενοι = the dead; τοῖϲ φθινομένοιϲ artic. substant. ptc.: S #2050; SS 257–58 §9; GMT #825)
ἀ-μελέω	(ἀμελήϲ, uncared for) be careless, negligent, not to care; > 'Come, how can it be honorable *not to care* for the dead?' [1× El.]
⁺κᾰλόϲ (3)	beautiful, good, noble

ἐν τίνι τοῦτ' ἔβλαστ' ἀνθρώπων;
μήτ' εἴην ἔντιμος τούτοις
μήτ', εἴ τῳ πρόσκειμαι χρηστῷ,   240
ξυνναίοιμ' εὔκηλος, γονέων
ἐκτίμους ἴσχουσα πτέρυγας
ὀξυτόνων γόων.
εἰ γὰρ ὁ μὲν θανὼν γᾶ τε καὶ οὐδὲν ὢν   245
κείσεται τάλας,
οἱ δὲ μὴ πάλιν
δώσουσ' ἀντιφόνους δίκας,

LINE 238

τοῦτ'	= τοῦτο, 'this' (i.e., the idea that such a behavior would be καλόν)
+*βλαστάνω, ἔβλαστον	(ἔβλαστε, aor.² act.) bud, sprout; > 'in whom among men has this shot forth?' = "Who among men has such an instinct?" (Lloyd-Jones) (Verbs denoting creation and breeding are recurrent in El.'s language.)
μήτ' . . . μήτ'	*anaphora* (p. 23)
ἔν-τῑμος, ον	(ἐν, τιμή) in honor, honored; [1× *El.*]
μήτ' εἴην ἔν-τῑμος	'may I never be honored among those' (optative of wish in independent sentence: S #1814; GMT #721–22)
+πρὸς-+κεῖμαι	lie with, lie near, be attached, placed near
χρηστός (3)	(χράομαι, use) useful, good; > 'if I am attached to any good thing'

LINE 241

συν-ναίω	dwell along with (μήτ'. . . ξυναίοιμι opt. of wish in independent sentence: S #1814; GMT #721–22); > 'may I never dwell in tranquility . . .'; [1× *El.*]
εὔκηλος, ον	(lengthened form of ἕκηλος) tranquil, free from care, fear; [1× *El.*]
+γονέων	Electra puts 'parents' in the plural even though she must be referring only to her father, cf. 146, 187. Objective genit.: 'dishonor _my father_' (SS 53; §4; S #1328)
ἔκ-τῑμος, ον	(ἐκ, τῑμή) without honor, dishonoring; [1×Soph.]
πτέρυξ, ῠγος, ἡ	wing; [1× *El.*]
ὀξύ-τονος, ον	(ὀξύς, τόνος; τείνω, stretch) stretched to a point, piercing, sharp; > 'if I hold back (ἴσχουσα) the wings of piercing lamentation so as to dishonor my father'; [1× *El.*]

LINE 245

οὐδὲν ὢν	οὐδέν negates ὢν
+κεῖμαι	lie down, be situated, be placed/laid; ὁ μέν is opposed by οἱ δέ; > 'for if he . . . while they . . .'
+*δίδωμι	(δώσουσι, fut. act.) + δίκας: give satisfaction/suffer punishment
ἀντί-φονος, ον	in return for slaughter; [1× *El.*]

ἔρροι τ' ἂν αἰδὼс

ἁπάντων τ' εὐcέβεια θνατῶν.   250

XO.   ἐγὼ μέν, ὦ παῖ, καὶ τὸ còν cπεύδουc' ἅμα

καὶ τοὐμὸν αὐτῆc ἦλθον· εἰ δὲ μὴ καλῶc

λέγω, cὺ νίκα· coὶ γὰρ ἑψόμεcθ' ἅμα.

HΛ.   αἰcχύνομαι μέν, ὦ γυναῖκεc, εἰ δοκῶ

πολλοῖcι θρήνοιc δυcφορεῖν ὑμῖν ἄγαν.   255

LINE 249

εἰ κείcεται ... μὴ	This is a mixed condition constructed with fut. indic. in protasis and potential opt. in apodosis. The po-
δώcουcι ... ἔρροι τ' ἂν	tential opt. either can have its distinctive force or can express a softened expression of fut. indic. (GMT #505c). Fut. indic. in protasis (instead of ἐάν with subjv.) contains a strong appeal to the feelings, or a threat, or warning, and therefore a favorite construction in Tragedy (GMT #447; SS 277–78 §1a); > 'if the dead man (ὁ μὲν θανών) *is to lie* as earth and nothingness (οὐδὲν ὤν), a wretched being, and they (οἱ δ') *are not to pay back* a penalty in return for slaughter ...'; †πάλιν, 'in return' points to retributory justice.
αἰδώc, όοc/οῦc, ἡ	sense of shame; [1× *El.*]
†ἄ-παc, ἅπᾱcα, ἅπαν	(ἅμα, πᾶc, strengthened for πᾶc) quite all, all together
†εὐcέβεια, ἡ	reverence toward the gods, piety
†θνητόc (2/3)	mortal (θνητοί = 'mortals'); > 'shame and reverence of all mortals would vanish'

FIRST EPISODE, LINES 251–471

In lines 251–327, Electra continues to justify her behavior. The Coryphaeus (Chorus leader) comforts her with the hope of Orestes' return. The dialogue is conducted in ordinary iambic trimeters. Lines 328–471 present a new character. Chrysothemis enters from the palace, sent by Clytemnestra to take offerings to Agamemnon's tomb. A dialogue between the two sisters ensues from which we learn about the different temperaments and attitudes of the two sisters.

LINE 251

†μέν	surely, indeed; μέν *solitarium*; see μέν 61n
τὸ còν, τοὐμὸν αὐτῆc	'your interest,' 'my very own interest'; τοὐμόν = τὸ ἐμόν; αὐτῆc stresses ἐμόν, which is the equivalent of ἐμοῦ; > 'promoting your cause and at the same time my very own' (possessive genit.: SS 51 §3, 140–141 §9)
cπεύδω	promote/further zealously (exceptionally the pres. ptc. serves in final capacity; usually it is the function of fut. ptc.: SS 252 §3); 'I came in order to further your cause and my own at the same time'
†ἅμα (adv.)	at the same time

LINE 254

νῑκάω	win, win over, overcome (εἰ ... νίκα simple condition (implies nothing as to actual fulfillment)
*αἰcχύνω	(αἰcχύνη, dishonor) shame, dishonor; mid.: feel shame
†δοκέω	seem, appear (πολλοῖcι θρήνοιc, dat. of cause or reason: SS 89 §17)
δυc-φορέω	be impatient, vexed, angry; [1× Soph.]
†ἄγᾱν (adv.)	very, much, very much; too much; > 'if I seem *too* impatient with my numerous laments'

ἀλλ' ἡ βία γὰρ ταῦτ' ἀναγκάζει με δρᾶν,
cύγγνωτε. πῶc γάρ, ἥτιc εὐγενὴc γυνή,
πατρῷ' ὁρῶcα πήματ', οὐ δρῴη τάδ' ἄν,
ἁγὼ κατ' ἦμαρ καὶ κατ' εὐφρόνην ἀεὶ
θάλλοντα μᾶλλον ἢ καταφθίνονθ' ὁρῶ;   260
ἢ πρῶτα μὲν τὰ μητρόc, ἥ μ' ἐγείνατο,
ἔχθιcτα cυμβέβηκεν· εἶτα δώμαcιν
ἐν τοῖc ἐμαυτῆc τοῖc φονεῦcι τοῦ πατρὸc

LINE 256

ἀλλ' … γὰρ	unlike in 223, both particles are independent: while ἀλλά goes with the main clause, γάρ with the dependent one (GP 98); > 'but forgive me, *since* a violent force compels me to do this'
+βίᾱ, ἡ	violent force, might
cυγ-+*γιγνώcκω	(cύγνωτε, aor.² impv. act) excuse, pardon (LSJ IV); emphatic *enjambment*; [1× *El.*]
ὅcτιc, ἥτιc, ὅ τι	any-who, any-which, any one who, whatever, etc. (S #339)
εὐ-γενήc, έc	high bred, noble
+γῠνή, γυναικόc, ἡ	woman
+πῆμα, ατοc, τό	misery, calamity, suffering (antecedent of ἃ in ἁγὼ, i.e., ἃ ἐγὼ)
δρῴη	(+δράω, pres. act. opt.) potential optative; > 'looking at the sufferings of her father, how (πῶc) *could* any noble woman *not do* this. . . ?'

LINE 258

ἦμαρ, ἥμᾰτοc, τό	day (poetic for ἡμέρα) (κατ' ἦμαρ = 'day by day')
εὐφρόνη, ηc, ἡ	the kindly time; euphemistically: night
θάλλω	bloom, flourish, swell, shoot out
+μᾶλλον ἤ	(comparative of μάλα) more than, rather than (S #1065)
κατα-+φθίνω	waste away, decay; > 'sufferings that I see . . . always grow and flourish rather than wither'; [1× *El.*]

Line 261

ἤ	relat. pron. with causal force = ἐμοὶ γάρ (dat. required by cυμβέβηκεν); '*for*, first, *my* relationship with my mother (τὰ μητρόc) turned (fell upon me as) hostile'
πρῶτα μέν … εἶτα …	first . . . next . . .
γείνομαι	trans.: bear, bring forth; beget; [1× *El.*]
ἐχθιcτόc (3)	irregular superlative of +ἐχθρόc; most hateful, hostile, rancorous
cυμ-+*βαίνω, -βέβηκα	(cυμβέβηκε, perf. act.) fall in with, fall to one's lot (+ dat.; usually with either infinitive or participle, but is found often just as τυγχάνω without the expected participle; [1× *El.*]
δώμαcιν τοῖc ἐμαυτῆc	'next, I am living <u>in my own home</u>' (El. as the rightful heiress of Ag. should own the palace.)
+φονεύc, έωc, ὁ	murderer, slayer

ξύνειμι, κἀκ τῶνδ' ἄρχομαι κἀκ τῶνδέ μοι
λαβεῖν θ' ὁμοίως καὶ τὸ τητᾶσθαι πέλει.
ἔπειτα ποίας ἡμέρας δοκεῖς μ' ἄγειν,
ὅταν θρόνοις Αἴγισθον ἐνθακοῦντ' ἴδω
τοῖσιν πατρῴοις, εἰσίδω δ' ἐσθήματα

265

LINE 264

⁺σύν-⁺⁺ειμι	associate, live with (emphatic *enjambment*)
κἀκ	καὶ ⁺ἐκ (*crasis*) = καὶ ὑπό (+ τῶνδε, genit. of agent: S #1678, SS 109 §9); > 'I am ruled *by them*'
κἀκ τῶνδε . . . κἀκ τῶνδε	a variation on *epanaphora, epanalepsis,* or *anaphora* (p. 23), rhetorical figure in which successive phrases or clauses begin with the same word, phrase, or cognate words; see below ἴδω 267, εἰσίδω 268, ἴδω 271.
⁺⁺ἄρχω	begin; <u>govern</u>, <u>rule</u>
ὁμοίως (adv.)	(ὅμοιος, like, resembling) in like manner, like, alike
τητάομαι	pass.: be in want, bereft, deprived (while the aorist aspect of λαβεῖν points to a punctual act of receiving, the present infinitive τετᾶσθαι indicates a continuous state of deprivation); [1× *El.*]
πέλω	be (the articular infs. [τό] λαβεῖν and τό τετᾶσθαι are subjects of πέλει: SS 241–42 §5, 153 §21. The article makes the infinitive more prominent as a noun in the sentence: GMT #789. The articular inf. was especially developed in Tragedy and favored by Soph., who used it more frequently in dialogue than in lyric: SS 245–46 §10); > '[and my *receiving* or *being left* deprived *is* up to them' =] 'and it is up to them whether I receive or am left deprived'; [1× *El.*].

LINE 266

⁺ἔπειτα (adv.)	(ἐπί, εἶτα) then, thereafter, thereupon (El. loses sight of her own question as she continues to enumerate her unhappy experiences)
⁺ποῖος (3)	of what sort, what kind
μ' ἄγειν	*hiatus*: μὲ ἄγειν (p. 23; acc. and inf. required by δοκεῖς); > 'And then what kind of days do you think *I pass/spend*'
θρόνος, ὁ	chair of state, <u>throne</u>; [1× *El.*]
ἐν-θᾱκέω	sit in/on; [1× *El.*]
ὅταν . . . ⁺⁺ἴδω . . .	'when I see Aegisthus sitting on my father's throne . . .' (temporal clauses referring indefinitely to the future take subjunctive with ἄν [ὅτε + ἄν], or optative without ἄν: S #2399; SS 294 §4)
ἴδω (267), εἰσίδω (268), ἴδω (271)	a variation on *epanaphora, epanalepsis,* or *anaphora;* see κἀκ τῶνδ'. . . κἀκ τῶνδε 264n, indicating El.'s growing indignation
⁺εἰσ-⁺⁺οράω, -εῖδον	(εἰσίδω, aor.² subjv.) look at/upon
ἔσθημα, ατος, τό	(ἐσθής, clothe) garment, dress; [1× Soph.]

φοροῦντ' ἐκείνῳ ταὐτά, καὶ παρεστίους
cπένδοντα λοιβὰc ἔνθ' ἐκεῖνον ὤλεcεν,
ἴδω δὲ τούτων τὴν τελευταίαν ὕβριν,
τὸν αὐτοέντην ἡμὶν ἐν κοίτῃ πατρὸc
ξὺν τῇ ταλαίνῃ μητρί, μητέρ' εἰ χρεὼν
ταύτην προcαυδᾶν τῷδε cυγκοιμωμένην·

270

LINE 269

⁺φορέω — carry constantly, wear (frequentative of φέρω, implying repeated or habitual action: LSJ III; S #867)

⁺ἐκεῖνος (3) — the person there, that person/thing (usually with reference to what has gone before; ἐκείνῳ = πατρός; dat. of possession: S #1476, SS 83–84 §8)

ταὐτά — = τὰ αὐτά (*crasis*); > 'wearing the same clothes that he did'

παρ-έστιος, ον — (παρά, ἑστία) by/at the hearth (at a sacrifice or feast the first libation was made to Hestia by the master of the house); [1× *El.*]

σπένδω — pour drink offering; [1× *El.*]

λοιβή, ἡ — libation; see 52n

⁺ἔνθα (relat. adv.) — where; > 'and pouring libations at the very hearth at which he murdered him'

LINE 271

τελευταῖος (3) — (τελευτή, end) final, last; [1× *El.*]

τούτων — can be neut. pl; > 'and when I see the final outrage *of all this*'; or fem., i.e., ὕβρεων > 'outrage of outrages'; or, masc., i.e., Αἰγίσθου καὶ Κλυταιμνήστρας

⁺ὕβρις, εος, ἡ — [ῠ] outrage

αὐτο-έντης, ου, ὁ — murderer; [1× *El.*]

κοίτη, ἡ — bed, couch;

ἡμίν — for accent see ἡμίν 17n; dat. of possession: SS 84 §8: "when I see the murderer in our father's bed"

⁺χρεών (indecl.) — that which must be (ἐστί omitted after expression of necessity: S #944b);> '[if there is a need to =] if one should address her as/call her a mother …'

προσ-αυδάω — speak to, address, accost

συγ-κοιμάομαι — sleep with, lie with; > 'who sleeps with him'; [1× Soph.]

ἡ δ' ὧδε τλήμων ὥστε τῷ μιάστορι   275
ξύνεστ', Ἐρινὺν οὔτιν' ἐκφοβουμένη·
ἀλλ' ὥσπερ ἐγγελῶσα τοῖς ποιουμένοις,
εὑροῦς' ἐκείνην ἡμέραν, ἐν ᾗ τότε
πατέρα τὸν ἀμὸν ἐκ δόλου κατέκτανεν,
ταύτῃ χοροὺς ἵστησι καὶ μηλοσφαγεῖ   280
θεοῖσιν ἔμμην' ἱερὰ τοῖς cωτηρίοιc.

LINE 275

ὧδε . . . ⁺ὥστε . . . ⁺ξύνεστι   'she is *so* reckless *that she lives* with the polluter' (ὥστε with indic. implies an actual result: S #2251, 2257; SS 311 §3; GMT #601. ξύνεστι, emphatic *enjambment*)

⁺τλήμων, ονος, ὁ/ἡ   (⁺τλάω) suffering, endwretched, abandoned (with moral connotation)

μιάστωρ, ορος, ὁ   (μιαίνω, defile, pollute) polluter (Aeg. is the polluter not only because of adultery, but because as Ag.'s cousin, he also spilled kindred blood)

ἐκ-φοβέω   pass.: fear greatly (with acc.; Kells: "the compound verb used [as frequently in Sophocles] not intensively, but in the same sense as the simple verb φοβουμένη")

ἐγ-γελάω   [ă] laugh at, mock (Sophoclean heroes are oversensitive to mockery); [1× *El.*]

⁺ποιέω   make, do (articular substant. ptc.: S #2050; SS 257–58 §9; GMT #825); > 'gloating over what she has done'

⁺*εὑρίσκω, ηὗρον/εὗρον   (εὑροῦσα, aor.² ptc. act.) find (since the verb indicates Clyt. has not remembered the exact day, scholars suspect the soundness of the verb, but time has elapsed between the murder and the institution of this custom. The calendar was by no means as easy to manage as nowadays); > '*having* [*found*]= *ascertained* that day on which . . .'

⁺τότε (adv.)   at that time, then, next.

LINE 279

ἀμός (3)   [ă] in Attic, poetic for ἐμός (S #330D, 1)

κατα-⁺*κτείνω,   (κατέκτανε, poetic aor.² act.) kill, slay, put to death

χόρος, ὁ   dance; chorus; [1× *El.*]

μηλο-σφαγέω   (μῆλον, σφᾰγέω) slay sheep, offer sheep (in sacrifice) (compound verbs made of a noun and a verb may take an acc. object, here ἱερά: SS 38 §6: "[she]sacrifices sheep as monthly offerings"); [1× Soph.]

ἔμ-μηνος, ον   (ἐν, μήν) in a month, monthly; [1× *El.*]

ἱερός (2/3)   sacred (as substantive: ἱερά ='offerings', LSJ III.1); [1× *El.*]

σωτήριος, ον   (σωτήρ, savior) saving, delivering (Zeus and Apollo were the main θεοὶ σωτήριοι associated with the house. Clyt. has a celebratory thanksgiving every month on the day of Ag.'s murder. Soph. may be offering an etiology for an existing ritual); > 'on that day she holds dances and offers monthly sheep sacrifice to the gods *who saved her.*'

ἐγὼ δ' ὁρῶσα δύσμορος κατὰ στέγας
κλαίω, τέτηκα, κἀπικωκύω πατρὸς
τὴν δυστάλαιναν δαῖτ' ἐπωνομασμένην
αὐτὴ πρὸς αὑτήν· οὐδὲ γὰρ κλαῦσαι πάρα   285
τοσόνδ' ὅσον μοι θυμὸς ἡδονὴν φέρει.

LINE 282

δυσ-μόρος, ον	ill fated, ill starred
κατὰ στέγας	'in the house' (El. cries in her room, staying away from the celebration)
⁺*κλαίω	weep, lament, wail (*enjambment*. The *tricolon* crescendo of three successive actions rising to a climax. Cf. ἐκτρέφω 13n; τίνω 115n; ἐμόλετ' . . . εἴδεσθ' 1235n)
⁺*τήκω	pine, melt away (pf. act. is used as intransitive and denotes a state achieved in the pres. The *asyndeton*, i.e., absence of conjunction, between κλαίω and τέτηκα functions as a *hendiadys* [p. 23] = 'I melt in tears')
ἐπι-κωκύω	[ῡ] lament over (κἀπικωκύω = καὶ ἐπικωκύω, *crasis*; ὁ Κωκῡτός, Cocytus, the River of Wailing in the Netherworld)
δυσ-⁺ταλάς, ᾰν	very wicked, most miserable; [1× *El.*]
δαίς, δαιτός, ἡ	meal, feast (usually a meal following a sacrifice. It is unclear whether El. refers to the 'original' banquet in which Ag. was killed and of which the current ones remind her, or to the feast inaugurated by Clyt.); [1× *El.*]
ἐπ-ονομάζω, -ωνόμασμαι	(ἐπωνομασμένη, pass. ptc.) name after (+ genit.); > 'I lament over the abominable feast named after my father'; [1× Soph.]

LINE 285

αὐτὴ πρός αὑτήν	'all by myself and to myself alone' (since lamentation is usually a communal experience, El. points again to her isolation, emphasized even further by the *enjambment*)
οὐδέ (μηδέ) (adv.)	not even (S #2931)
⁺*κλαῦσαι	the aor.[1] inf. rather than the present ⁺κλαίειν points out that she not only is not allowed to indulge continuously in weeping, but not even on one occasion
πάρα	impersonal use: it is allowed, it may be done (= πάρεστι; S #175b)
⁺τοσόνδ' ⁺ὅσον	as much as
⁺θῡμος, ὁ	soul, spirit, heart (any vehement passion: anger, wrath, courage)
⁺ἡδονή, ἡ	delight, enjoyment, pleasure; > 'as much as my heart takes pleasure in'

αὕτη γὰρ ἡ λόγοισι γενναία γυνὴ
φωνοῦσα τοιάδ' ἐξονειδίζει κακά,
"ὦ δύσθεον μίσημα, σοὶ μόνῃ πατὴρ
τέθνηκεν; ἄλλος δ' οὔτις ἐν πένθει βροτῶν;   **290**
κακῶς ὄλοιο, μηδέ σ' ἐκ γόων ποτὲ
τῶν νῦν ἀπαλλάξειαν οἱ κάτω θεοί."
τάδ' ἐξυβρίζει· πλὴν ὅταν κλύῃ τινὸς
ἥξοντ' Ὀρέστην· τηνικαῦτα δ' ἐμμανὴς

LINE 287

γενναῖος (2/3)	noble
⁺λόγοισι	'this high-born woman, as shown by her words' (modal dat.: SS 90–92 §19. αὕτη = ἡ αὐτή, crasis. Sarcasm: Clyt.'s following words show what her 'nobility' consists of [Kamerbeek])
ἐξ-ονειδίζω	(strengthened for ὀνειδίζω) cast in one's teeth; reproach; > '[shouting =] cries out and casts insults such as these'; [1× El.]
δύσ-θεος, ον	godless (= hated by the gods [Finglass]. Since Clyt. thinks the gods are on her side, El., in Clyt.'s mind, must be hated by the gods); [1× Soph.]
μίσημα, ατος, τό	(μισέω, hate) an object of hate; > 'godless, hateful creature'; [1× Soph.]
⁺ἄλλος, η, ο	other (of several: S #335, 1271)
⁺οὔ-τις, οὔ-τινος	no one, nobody (for accent: S #164a)
σοὶ μόνῃ	'Are you the only one whose father has died? No one else of men is in mourning? (El. recasts the Chorus' words to her [153], but without the consolatory tone. ⁺*τέθνηκεν, emphatic *enjambment*)
πένθος, εος, τό	grief, sorrow; misfortune

LINE 291

⁺ἀπ-αλλάσσω	set free, release (⁺*ὄλοιο . . . μηδέ . . . ἀπαλλάξειαν = opt. of wish without an introductory word: SS 232 §15, GMT #721.I, 722; S #1814); > 'may you perish miserably . . . and may the gods below never release you . . .'
⁺κάτω (adv.)	below (οἱ κάτω θεοί = 'the gods below.' Substant. use of article with an adverb: S #1153e. El. invoked these deities as avengers in 110–18)
τάδ'	one would expect therefore ταῦτ' and not τάδ', but for El. everything Clyt. says is hybristic
ἐξ-υβρίζω	break into insolence; [1× Soph.]
⁺πλήν (adv.)	besides, unless, save, except
⁺κλύω	hear, listen (with genit.: S #1361, 1365. ὅταν κλύῃ, relative pres. condition, with subjv. in protasis, and pres. indic. in apodosis, βοᾷ: S #2295.1, 2561); > 'she upbraids me, except *whenever she hears* from someone that . . . then maddened with rage she stands by me *and shouts*'

LINE 294

⁺ἥξοντ' ⁺Ὀρέστην	(⁺ἥκω) supplem. ptc. in indir. disc after vb. of perception, κλύῃ (S #2110, 2112.b; SS 318 §6; GMT #904, 914); > '*that Orestes will come*'
τηνικαῦτα (adv.)	at this particular time, then; [1× El.]
ἐμ-μανής, ές	mad, frantic, raving; [1× Soph.]

βοᾷ παραστᾶς', "οὐ σύ μοι τῶνδ' αἰτία;   295
οὐ σὸν τόδ' ἐστὶ τοὔργον, ἥτις ἐκ χερῶν
κλέψασ' Ὀρέστην τῶν ἐμῶν ὑπεξέθου;
ἀλλ' ἴσθι τοι τείσουσά γ' ἀξίαν δίκην."
τοιαῦθ' ὑλακτεῖ, σὺν δ' ἐποτρύνει πέλας
ὁ κλεινὸς αὐτῇ ταὐτὰ νυμφίος παρών,   300
ὁ πάντ' ἄναλκις οὗτος, ἡ πᾶσα βλάβη,
ὁ σὺν γυναιξὶ τὰς μάχας ποιούμενος.
ἐγὼ δ' Ὀρέστην τῶνδε προσμένουσ' ἀεὶ
παυστῆρ' ἐφήξειν ἡ τάλαιν' ἀπόλλυμαι.

LINE 295

⁺*βοάω	shout
παρ-⁺*ίστημι	(παραστᾶσα, aor.² ptc. fem. sg.) make stand beside; aor.² = stand beside
μοι	dat. of disadvantage (SS 84–85 §9)
αἴτιος (3)	blamable, guilty; [1× *El.*]
ὑπ-εκ-⁺*τίθημαι	(ἔθου, aor.² indic. mid. 2sg.) carry safely away; [1× Soph.]
⁺τοι	therefore, accordingly; in truth, verily
*τίνω, τείσω/τίσω	pay a price, pay a penalty, repay, atone, expiate
⁺ἄξιος (3)	worthy, befitting, deserving
ἀλλ' ἴσθι . . . τείσουσα	'well, know that you really will pay' (τείσουσα, supplem. ptc. in indirect discourse after vb. of knowing, ἴσθι. The fut. tense corresponds to the tense of indic. as if it were a finite vb.: S # 2106, 2112.b; SS 318 §6; GMT #904, 914)

LINE 299

ὑλακτέω	[ῠ] (= ὑλάω) bark, bay, howl (used in pres. and impf.); [1× Soph.]
⁺σύν	adv. (Jebb): together, at once, jointly, besides, moreover; or (less likely in *tmesis* [p. 23] with ἐποτρύνω; LSJ offers the latter under σύν (B) and under συν-επ-οτρύνω = join in urging on)
ἐπ-οτρύνω	excite, stir up, urge on
⁺πέλᾰς	near, hard by, close (improper prep. with genit. and also with dat.: S #1699)
ταὐτά	= τὰ αὐτά 'the same things' preferable to the codd. ταῦτα = 'these things'
⁺κλεινός (3)	renowned (ὁ κλεινὸς νύμφιος: see κλεινός 8n, SS 145 §13: "ironical of Aeg.: followed by three further uses of the article, spoken in contempt.")
νυμφίος, ὁ	(νύμφη, young wife, bride) bridegroom, husband; > 'and her illustrious bridegroom, always at her side (⁺πάρ-⁺*ειμι + dat.) eggs her on [in her abuse]'; [1× *El.*]

LINE 301

πάντ'	'completely,' 'utterly' (adv. acc., or acc. of respect: S #1600; SS 42–43 §13,14)
ἄν-αλκις, ιδος, ὁ/ἡ	(ἀ privat., ἀλκή, bodily strength) without strength, impotent, unwarlike; [1× Soph.]
ὁ . . . ὁ . . . ὁ	*anaphora* in three consecutive lines (300–302)
⁺βλάβη, ἡ	[ᾰ] (βλάπτω, hinder, harm) harm, damage; > 'a complete bane'
μάχη, ἡ	[ᾰ] battle, fight; > 'one who fights his battles with women's help'; [1× *El.*]
παυστήρ, ῆρος, ὁ	(παύω, stop) one who stays/calms, an allayer, assuager (Ὀρέστην . . . παυστῆρ' *hyperbaton*. With objective genit., ⁺τῶνδε : S #1328); [1× *El.*]
ἐφ-⁺ήκω	to have arrived at (a rare verb); > 'But I'm forever waiting for Orestes to come (as one who stops =) and stop these things'; [1× *El.*]

μέλλων γὰρ ἀεὶ δρᾶν τι τὰc οὔcαc τέ μου   **305**
καὶ τὰc ἀπούcαc ἐλπίδαc διέφθορεν.
ἐν οὖν τοιούτοιc οὔτε cωφρονεῖν, φίλαι,
οὔτ' εὐcεβεῖν πάρεcτιν· ἀλλ' ἐν τοῖc κακοῖc
πολλή 'cτ' ἀνάγκη κἀπιτηδεύειν κακά.

ΧΟ.   φέρ' εἰπέ, πότερον ὄντοc Αἰγίcθου πέλαc   **310**
      λέγειc τάδ' ἡμῖν, ἢ βεβῶτοc ἐκ δόμων;

ΗΛ.   ἦ κάρτα. μὴ δόκει μ' ἄν, εἴπερ ἦν πέλαc,
      θυραῖον οἰχνεῖν· νῦν δ' ἀγροῖcι τυγχάνει.

LINE 305

⁺μέλλω   be on the point of doing (with pres./fut. inf. forms the periphrastic fut. pres. inf. usually expresses will: S #1959); > 'for by always *intending* to do something (τι, Finglass: "something of value, cf. 336")'

⁺ἄπ-⁺ειμι   be away, be absent (ἀπούcαc, attributive ptc.: SS 25 7§8. The polar expression οὔcαc/ἀπούcαc covers all of El.'s hopes. Cf. similar polar expression in Clyt.'s words in 780–781, pointing further to the resemblance between mother and daughter.); > ' he has utterly destroyed *the hopes I had and the hopes I didn't have.*

⁺ἐλπίc, ίδοc, ἡ   hope

δια-⁺φθείρω, -έφθορα   (2nd pf.) destroy utterly; [1× *El.*]

cωφρονέω   (cώφρων, of sound mind) be temperate, moderate, of sound mind

⁺φίλη, ἡ   near and dear, <u>friend</u>

LINE 307

εὐcεβέω   (εὐcεβήc, pious) be pious; [1× *El.*]

⁺πάρεcτι   (⁺πάρειμι) impersonal: it is in one's power (+ dat.)

ἐν τοῖc κακοῖc   'in [the existing] bad circumstances' (⁺πολλή 'cτ' = πολλή ἐcτί *aphaeresis* and *elision*, p. 23)

ἐπιτηδεύω   (ἐπιτηδέc adv. formed from ἐπὶ τάδε, for a special purpose) pursue (The vb. formed as if it were a compd. of ἐπί and τηδεύω that does not exist. El. ends her speech in a ring composition, returning to both the idea of a bad situation and the need to behave in the same manner, as well as her direct address to the Chorus, 256–57); [1× Soph.]

LINE 310

φέρ'   φέρε, ἄγε, ἴθι may emphasize the imperative and its subject (S #1010; GMT #251); > '*come*, tell me . . .'

⁺εἶπον   (ἐπ- for ϝεπ-, defective, other tenses supplied by +*λέγω) said (εἰπέ, aor.² impv., for accent: S #424.b)

⁺πότερον/πότερα . . . ἤ   whether . . . or (S #2656. Introduces direct alternative questions with πότερον/ πότερα frequently left untranslated in English)

⁺*ὄντοc Αἰγίcτου . . .   genits. absolute; > 'is Aegisthus nearby when you are saying these things, or staying away from home?'
⁺*βεβῶτοc

⁺ἦ (adv.)   in truth, truly, verily (confirms with κάρτᾰ [adv.], very, very much); > 'Of course he is away'

XO.   ἢ δή ἂν ἐγὼ θαρcοῦcα μᾶλλον ἐc λόγουc
        τοὺc coὺc ἱκοίμην, εἴπερ ὧδε ταῦτ᾽ ἔχει.   315

ΗΛ.   ὡc νῦν ἀπόντοc ἱcτόρει· τί coι φίλον;

XO.   καὶ δή c᾽ ἐρωτῶ, τοῦ καcιγνήτου τί φῄc,
        ἥξοντοc, ἢ μέλλοντοc; εἰδέναι θέλω.

ΗΛ.   φηcίν γε· φάcκων δ᾽ οὐδὲν ὧν λέγει ποεῖ.

οἰχνέω	= ⁺*οἴχομαι go (contrary-to-fact statement in acc. and inf., ἄν ... οἰχνεῖν, following δόκει [impv.] μ᾽ ἄν); > 'do not think that I would be going outdoors, if he were close by'
θυραῖοc (2/3)	(θύρα, door) outside the door
ἀγρόc, ὁ	land, field; country (dat. of place: SS 87; S #1528); [1× *El.*]
⁺*τυγχάνει	'but now (*he happens to be* =) he is in the country' (ὤν omitted, see 46n)

LINE 314

⁺δή (pcl.)	of course, indeed, quite (postpositive; adds explicitness [*voilà*], i.e., marks something as immediately present and clear to the mind: S #2840; S #2865: "ἦ δή expresses lively surprise." δή ἂν synizesis, see p. 24)
⁺εἴπερ	if indeed, if at all events (introduces sort of concessive meaning, especially when the truth of the statement is implicitly denied or doubted: S #2379)
ἂν ἐγὼ ... ἔχει	'I would (come into words =) talk to you with more confidence, if this is indeed so' (a combination of a mixed condition: protasis in pres. indic., ἔχει, and apodosis with potential opt. + ἄν, ἱκοίμην, each clause maintaining its proper force: GMT #503a)

LINE 316

ἱcτορέω	(pres. impv.) learn by inquiry, question, inquire (punctuation after ἱcτόρει makes τί coι φίλον, a direct question: = 'He is away now [ἀπόντοc genit. absolute], so ask your question; what do you want to know?': SS 266–67 §5)
καὶ δή	'very well then' (GP 251: "in response to a definite command, often with word of command echoed")
ἐρωτάω	ask; [1× *El.*]
⁺καcίγνητοc, ὁ	(κάcιc, brother/sister, γενέcθαι, be, become) brother
τοῦ καcιγνήτου ... ἥξοντοc	'what do you say of your brother, will he come, or is he delaying? (The simple genit. without περί is frequent in Soph. [Kells])
⁺*φηcίν γε	'Well (γε), he says [he is coming] (γε = 'yes, well ...'; confirmative, as often in replies: S #2825; GP 130, II, i)
φά-cκω	say (concessive ptc.: SS 252 §3, S #2066. φηcίν, φάcκων, λέγει: Soph. favors variation, i.e., instead of repeating a word, an exact synonym is being used [Kells]; cf. 350); > 'but although he says so'
οὐδὲν ὧν λέγει ποεῖ	= οὐδὲν τούτων ἃ λέγει ποεῖ (relative attraction with omitted antecedent, S #2522); > 'he does none of the things that he says [he will do]'

ΧΟ.	φιλεῖ γὰρ ὀκνεῖν πρᾶγμ' ἀνὴρ πράccων μέγα.	**320**
ΗΛ.	καὶ μὴν ἔγωγ' ἔcωc' ἐκεῖνον οὐκ ὄκνῳ.	
ΧΟ.	θάρcει· πέφυκεν ἐcθλόc, ὥcτ' ἀρκεῖν φίλοιc.	
ΗΛ.	πέποιθ', ἐπεί τἂν οὐ μακρὰν ἔζων ἐγώ.	
ΧΟ.	μὴ νῦν ἔτ' εἴπῃc μηδέν· ὡc δόμων ὁρῶ	
	τὴν cὴν ὅμαιμον, ἐκ πατρὸc ταὐτοῦ φύcιν,	**325**
	Χρυcόθεμιν, ἔκ τε μητρόc, ἐντάφια χεροῖν	
	φέρουcαν, οἷα τοῖc κάτω νομίζεται.	

LINE 320

⁺φιλέω	love, welcome = be wont to, use to, tend to (+ inf.)
⁺ὀκνέω	hesitate, hold back, shrink from doing (physically or morally)
⁺πρᾶγμα, ατοc, τό	(⁺πράccω, do) deed (πρᾶγμα πράccειν = *figura etymologica*, p. 23); > 'When a man is engaged in a great undertaking he tends to hesitate'
καὶ μήν	and yet (a strong adversative: GP 357–58)
ὄκνοc, ὁ	hesitation, shrinking (from doing); [1× *El.*]
⁺ἐcθλόc (3)	(poetic adj.) good; (of persons) brave, <u>noble</u> (morally); faithful
⁺ὥcτε (conj.)	so as to (with inf. [outside indirect discourse] opens a result clause, it implies a possible or intended result or a tendency rather than actual fact: S #2251, 2254; GMT #582, 587); > 'so as to help those dear to him'

LINE 323

⁺*πείθω	persuade; pf.² πέποιθα = trust, <u>believe</u>, rely, have confidence in (S #1946: "When the perfect marks the enduring result rather than the completed act, it may often be translated by the present")
μακράν (adv.)	(acc. f. of μακρόc, used as adv.) long (μακρὰν ζῆν = 'livelong')
πέποιθ'... ἔζων	'I believe it . . .otherwise I would not have lived this long' (contrary-to-fact statement for the present time)
μή	'say no more now' (prohibitive subjv.; μή with aor. subjv. in 2nd pers.: S #1800a; SS 220 §6; GMT #259)
⁺δόμων	'carrying from home' (genit. with verbs of motion: SS 66 §26)

LINE 325

τὴν cὴν ὅμαιμον... Χρυcόθεμιν... φέρουcαν	two instances of *hyperbaton* (p. 24) expressing the Chorus' sense of urgency
ταὐτοῦ	= τοῦ αὐτοῦ
⁺φύcιc, εωc, ἡ	[ῠ] (φύω, bring forth) nature, inborn quality; natural origin (acc. of respect: S #1601b, 1516a, SS 43 §14); > 'by birth'
Χρυcόθεμιc, εωc, ἡ	resolutions in positions 2 and 10 (Χρῡcόθεμιν), 10 (ἐντάφια), (see pp. 20–21, 24)
ἐν-τάφιοc, ον	(ἐν, τάφοc) of or used for burial (τὰ ἐντάφια = obsequies, burial offerings; [1× Soph.]
⁺*νομίζω	believe, think, <u>hold as custom or usage, practice as custom</u>; > 'such as *are customary* for those below'

ΧΡΥϹΟΘΕΜΙϹ

τίν᾽ αὖ ϲὺ τήνδε πρὸϲ θυρῶνοϲ ἐξόδοιϲ
ἐλθοῦϲα φωνεῖϲ, ὦ καϲιγνήτη, φάτιν,
κοὐδ᾽ ἐν χρόνῳ μακρῷ διδαχθῆναι θέλειϲ   330
θυμῷ ματαίῳ μὴ χαρίζεϲθαι κενά;
καίτοι τοϲοῦτόν γ᾽ οἶδα κἀμαυτήν, ὅτι
ἀλγῶ ᾽πὶ τοῖϲ παροῦϲιν· ὥϲτ᾽ ἄν, εἰ ϲθένοϲ
λάβοιμι, δηλώϲαιμ᾽ ἂν οἷ᾽ αὐτοῖϲ φρονῶ.

LINE 328

τίν᾽ ... τήνδε ... φάτιν   through the *hyperbaton* emphasizing ⁺φάτιν and the *figura etymologica* (p. 23) ⁺φωνεῖϲ ... ⁺φάτιν, Chr. underscores her concern that El. is talking too much.

⁺αὖ (adv.)   again, anew, once more (cf. Clyt.'s words in 516–17)

⁺πρός (+ dat.)   hard by, near, at (LSJ B)

θυρών, ῶνος, ὁ   [ῠ] hall, antechamber, vestibule, space immediately inside the main door; [1× *El.*]

ἔξ-οδος, ἡ   way out, exit (LSJ II, 1); > 'What sort of remarks are you making again, Oh sister having come near the exit from the vestibule ... ?'

⁺*διδάϲκω   (διδαχθῆναι, aor.¹ pass. inf.) teach, explain

LINE 331

μάταιος (3/2)   [ᾰ] (μάτη, folly, fault) foolish, vain, idle, trifling, thoughtless (θῡμῷ ματαίῳ: dat. after a verb indicating attitude or feeling toward it: SS 82–83 §6: "not to give vain indulgence [χαρίζεϲθαι κενά] to pointless anger")

χᾰρίζομαι   to gratify or indulge (a passion) + dat.; [1× Soph.]

⁺κενός (3)   empty, destitute, vain, futile

⁺καί-τοι (pcl.)   and yet, although (GP 556, S #2893); κἀμαυτήν = καὶ ἐμαυτήν

⁺ἀλγέω   suffer pain, grieve, be troubled, distressed (ἀλγῶ ᾽πί = ἀλγῶ ἐπί, *aphaeresis*, p. 23. ὅτι ἀλγῶ, indirect statement after vb. signifying knowledge, οἶδα: GMT #912); > 'and yet this much I know about myself, *that I too am distressed* because of/by the present circumstances'

τοῖς παροῦσιν   τὰ παρόντα = 'circumstances' (dat. of means/cause: SS 88–89 §§16,17, S #1507)

σθένος, εος, τό   strength, might, power

ὥϲτ᾽ ἄν, εἰ ...⁺δηλώϲαιμ᾽ ἄν   'so that if I had the strength, I would show them the thoughts I have about them' (fut. less vivid condition: S #2297, 2329; GMT #392.2 with repeated ἄν to emphasize the result: S #1765; GMT #223). The protasis pointing to what is unlikely or impossible. SS 279 §1d,i: "Chr. would like to have the strength to oppose, but rules it out as not practicable"; for doubling of ἄν, cf. ἄν ... ⁺*γένοιτ᾽ ἄν 558–59n)

νῦν δ' ἐν κακοῖς μοι πλεῖν ὑφειμένη δοκεῖ,　335
καὶ μὴ δοκεῖν μὲν δρᾶν τι, πημαίνειν δὲ μή.
τοιαῦτα δ' ἄλλα καὶ cὲ βούλομαι ποεῖν.
καίτοι τὸ μὲν δίκαιον οὐχ ἧ 'γὼ λέγω,
ἀλλ' ἧ cὺ κρίνεις. εἰ δ' ἐλευθέραν με δεῖ
ζῆν, τῶν κρατούντων ἐcτὶ πάντ' ἀκουcτέα.　340

ΗΛ.　δεινόν γέ c' οὖcαν πατρὸc οὖ cὺ παῖc ἔφυc
κείνου λελῆcθαι, τῆc δὲ τικτούcηc μέλειν.
ἄπαντα γάρ coι τἀμὰ νουθετήματα

LINE 335

πλέω　sail (a nautical metaphor, cf. 730)

ὑφ-ίημι　(ὑφειμένη, pf. ptc. mid., agrees with μοι) mid.: lower one's sails (LSJ III; descriptive ptc. of attending circumstances: S #2068; GMT #843); > 'But now, in these bad circumstances, it seems best to me to sail *with slackened sail*'; [1× *El.*]

+*δοκεῖ　it seems (quasi-impersonal when the indefinite 'it' anticipates an infinitive as the subject, δρᾶν: S #933b; SS 241 §5. δρᾶν τι 'to do something of value', cf. μέλλω 305n)

μὴ δοκεῖν　The inf. depends on +*δοκεῖ in 335. Fifth-century poets were not subjected to the modern convention of refraining from using the same word twice if it was the right word to employ (Kamerbeek, Finglass)

πημαίνω　make suffer, harm, distress; > 'and not on the one hand, to appear to be doing something, while on the other, not to do [them] harm'; [1× *El.*]

τοιαῦτα δ' ἄλλα　'And I wish you would do the same [lit.: such and other things]'

LINE 338

+ἧ (adv.)　(dat. sg. fem. relat. pron.) in the way in which; i.e., 'as'; ' γώ' = ἐγώ *aphaeresis* (p. 23)

+*κρίνω　[ῑ] put apart, pick out, choose; judge; > 'And yet (καίτοι) the right course is not as/in what I say, but as/in what you have chosen' (Chr. objects to her own course of action)

+ἐλεύθεροc (3)　free

+δεῖ　it is necessary (quasi-impers. vb.: S #933b); > lit.: 'but if it is necessary that I live as a free woman', i.e., 'but if I am to (should) live a free woman'

+κρᾰτέω　(κράτος, rule, power) rule, be master, lord (τῶν κρατούντων articular substant. ptc.: S #2052; SS 257–58 §9; GMT #825); > 'those in power'

ἀκουcτέον/ἀκουcτέα　(verbal adj., ἀκούω, hear) one must hear, one must hearken to (+ genit., τῶν κρατούντων); > 'I [supply μοι] *must listen* to those in power in everything'

LINE 341

δεινόν　supply ἐcτί; the subjects are λελῆcθαι and μέλειν

τῆc +τικτούcηc　(+τίκτω pres. act ptc.) articular substant. ptc. (S #2052; SS 257–58 §9; GMT #825). Note the present aspect of the participle, which emphasizes Chr.'s relation with her mother.

+*λελῆcθαι　(λανθάνω, pf. inf. mid.) 'to be *in a state* of forgetfulness' (i.e., to have forgotten completely [Kells]. cέ οὖcαν subject of the inf. The two infs. λελῆcθαι and μέλειν: and genits. κείνου and τικτούcηc, parallel the antithesis between Ag. and Clyt.); > 'it is terrible that you (lit.: being, οὖcαν, of your father) daughter of your father, whose child you are, *forget* him, but think [only] of your mother'

κείνης διδακτά, κοὐδὲν ἐκ cαυτῆc λέγεις.
ἐπεί γ᾽ ἑλοῦ cὺ θἄτερ᾽, ἢ φρονεῖν κακῶς,   345
ἢ τῶν φίλων φρονοῦcα μὴ μνήμην ἔχειν·
ἥτις λέγεις μὲν ἀρτίως, ὡς εἰ λάβοις
cθένος, τὸ τούτων μῖcος ἐκδείξειας ἄν·
ἐμοῦ δὲ πατρὶ πάντα τιμωρουμένης
οὔτε ξυνέρδεις τήν τε δρῶσαν ἐκτρέπεις.   350

νουθέτημα, ατος, τό	(⁺νοῦς, ⁺⁺τίθημι) admonition, warning (τἀμὰ = τὰ ἐμά, poss. adj. for the expected objective genit.: τὰ νουθτήματα μου: SS 53 §4, S #1328); > 'all your warnings/scolding of me'; [1× Soph.]

LINE 344

⁺κείνης	possibly genit. of agent (SS 75–76 §41). Finglass suggests that the genit. might be formed by analogy with μανθάνω + genit: 'I learn from'; > 'you have learned from her'
δῐδακτός (3)	(verbal adj. ⁺⁺δῐδάσκω) taught, learnt (with the force of pf. pass. ptc., S #358.2b); [1× *El.*]
σαυτοῦ, σαυτῆς	thyself (= σεαυτοῦ, σεαυτῆς reflexive pron. referring back to the subject of the sentence: S #329); > 'nothing of what you say comes *from* yourself'
θἄτερα	other of two (= τὰ ἕτερα: S #69, 1271); > 'Then choose (ἑλοῦ < ⁺⁺αἱρέω, aor.² mid. impv.) one or the other'
μνήμη, ἡ	(μνάομαι, remember) remembrance, memory; [1× *El.*]
ἢ ... ἔχειν	'either to think wrongly, or, to think rightly (φρονοῦσα [εὖ]) but forgetful of your nearest and dearest' (El. gives Chr. a choice between being 'imprudent,' i.e., if she is to follow El.'s example, or being 'prudent' i.e., compliant, as Chr. is now, which necessitates forgetting her loved ones [Jebb])

LINE 347

⁺ἥτις	'you who' (marking the character and quality of a person: S #2496)
⁺ἀρτίως (adv.)	(ἄρτιος, complete) just now, exactly
⁺μῖσος, εος, τό	hatred, grudge (with τούτων as objective genit. [S #1328, SS 53 §4])
ἐκ-⁺⁺δείκνῡμι,	show off, display (εἰ λάβοις ... ἐκδείξειας ἄν, future less vivid condition, protasis: εἰ + opt., apodosis: optative + ἄν :GMT #392.2; S #2561); > 'if you had the strength, *you would show* your hatred of them.' El. recites Chr.'s words at 333–34, and uses them against Chr.); [1× *El.*]
τῑμωρέω	(τῑμωρός, ον, avenging) avenge one, exact vengeance for (middle voice, τιμωρουμένης, equals active voice = τιμωρεῖν [τινί]. ἐμοῦ ... τιμωρουμένης temporal genit. absolute: S #2058, 2070a; SS 76–77 §42, in a *hyperbaton*.); '*but while I do* all I can to avenge my/our father ...'
συν-έρδω	join in a work, cooperate; [1× *El.*]
ἐκ-τρέπω	divert, deter, dissuade (τήν ... δρῶσαν articular substant. ptc. Moorhouse points out that the pres. ptc. δρῶσαν, is timeless, or of conative function, and the pres. indic. ἐκτρέπεις may also be conative: SS 257–58 §9, 183 §2, S #1878a); 'you do not cooperate [with me] and even (*try to*) deter [me] the one (*who attempts* to take)/takes action'; [1× *El.*]

οὐ ταῦτα πρὸς κακοῖςι δειλίαν ἔχει;
ἐπεὶ δίδαξον, ἢ μάθ᾽ ἐξ ἐμοῦ, τί μοι
κέρδος γένοιτ᾽ ἂν τῶνδε ληξάςῃ γόων.
οὐ ζῶ; κακῶς μέν, οἶδ᾽, ἐπαρκούντως δ᾽ ἐμοί.
λυπῶ δὲ τούτους, ὥςτε τῷ τεθνηκότι   355
τιμὰς προςάπτειν, εἴ τις ἔςτ᾽ ἐκεῖ χάρις.
ςὺ δ᾽ ἡμὶν ἡ μιςοῦςα μιςεῖς μὲν λόγῳ,
ἔργῳ δὲ τοῖς φονεῦςι τοῦ πατρὸς ξύνει.
ἐγὼ μὲν οὖν οὐκ ἄν ποτ᾽, οὐδ᾽ εἴ μοι τὰ ςὰ

LINE 351

δειλία, ἡ   cowardice, timidity (Kamerbeek: "does not this [have] involve cowardice in addition to our misery?"; οὐ can introduce a question expecting the answer 'yes,' or imply that it should be so: SS 320 §3)

⁺ἐπεί (conj.)   since, seeing that (causal ἐπεί with imperative is used paratactically according to SS 303–4, §3 it "introduces a fact which proves the correctness of what has been said [and which was not previously known to, or adequately recognized by the person addressed]"; GMT #718); > '*For* explain to me, or learn from me'

⁺* διδάςκω, ἐδίδαξα   (δίδαξον, aor.¹ impv.) teach, explain (the aorist aspect pointing to a single act, is more suitable than the present: SS 217–18 §5)

τί ... γένοιτ᾽ ἂν ... ᾽ληξάςῃ   ληξάςῃ = εἰ λήξαιμι, ptc. for the protasis of future less vivid condition (GMT #392.2, S #2297, 2329); > 'what gain would I have, if I should cease from these lamentations'

ἐπ-αρκούντως (adv.)   (ἐπαρκέω, be sufficient) sufficiently; [1× Soph.]

LINE 354

τῑμή, ἡ   honor

προς-άπτω   attach to, apply to, confer upon

⁺ὥςτε ... προςάπτειν   'so *as to confer* on the dead' (τῷ τεθνηκότι, articular substant. ptc. ὥςτε with inf. [outside indirect discourse] opens an alleged result clause; it implies a possible or intended result or a tendency rather than actual fact: S #2251, 2254; GMT #582, 587)

⁺*ἔςτι   'if any pleasure *exists* there (where the dead are)' (accented on the penult ἔςτι expresses existence: S #187b)

ἐκεῖ   there

LINE 357

μῑςέω   (⁺μῖςος, hatred) hate (ἡ μιςοῦςα = articular substant. ptc. see τῆς τικτούςης, line 342n. μιςοῦςα μιςεῖς = the brachylogy served by the *figura etymologica*; p. 23; emphasizes the vehemence of El.'s accusation. According to Finglass ἡ μιςοῦςα = ἡ μιςεῖν φάςκουςα, i.e., 'you who claim to hate'); [1× *El.*]

μὲν λόγῳ, ἔργῳ δὲ   'but you who would like us/me (ἡμίν, ethical dat., for accent, see ἡμίν 17n), to believe that you hate, you hate [only] in word, but in deed/in fact you are on the side of your father's murderers.' The antithesis between 'word' and 'deed' runs as a leitmotif through the play' see at lines 59–60

μέλλοι τις οἴσειν δῶρ', ἐφ' οἷςι νῦν χλιδᾷς, 360
τούτοις ὑπεικάθοιμι· coὶ δὲ πλουсία
τράπεζα κείсθω καὶ περιρρείτω βίος.
ἐμοὶ γὰρ ἔсτω τοὐμὲ μὴ λυπεῖν μόνον
βόσκημα· τῆς сῆς δ' οὐκ ἐρῶ τιμῆс λαχεῖν.
οὐδ' ἂν cύ, сώφρων γ' οὖсα. νῦν δ' ἐξὸν πατρὸς 365

LINE 360

δῶρον, τό
(δίδωμι, give) gift; here: 'privileges' (the word implies reward for Chr.'s compliance [Kamerbeek]); [1× *El.*]

χλιδάω
(χλιδή, luxury) live luxuriously; + ἐπί τινι = pride oneself upon a thing, <u>revel in</u>; [1× Soph.]

ὑπ-είκω, -είκαθον
(ὑπεικάθοιμι, aor.² opt., poetic) yield (with dat. LSJ 2; οὐκ ἄν ποτ' . . . ὑπεικάθοιμι = *hyperbaton*, p. 24. Fut. less vivid condition, see 353n: εἰ μέλλοι . . . ἂν ὑπεικάθοιμι); > 'I would never yield to them, not even if someone were to bestow (μέλλοι οἴσειν) on me *your* (τὰ σά; contemptuous) privileges in which you now revel'; [1× *El.*]

πλούσιος (3)
rich, wealthy; abundant, ample; [1× *El.*]

τράπεζα, ἡ
[ᾰ] table, dinner, meal

περι-ρρέω
(περιρρείτω, impv. pres. 3sg.) overflow on all sides (LSJ II,4) (*chiasmus*: τράπεζα κείσθω/περιρρείτω βίος); > 'let your life *overflow with abundance*'; [1× Soph.]

LINE 363

⁺λῡπέω
(λύπη, pain, distress) cause pain, distress, annoy (τοὐ μέ μὴ λυπεῖν = τὸ ἐμέ μὴ λυπεῖν, articular inf. as nom. taking an object, ἐμέ: Kamerbeek; SS 246 §11. The article makes the inf. more prominent as a noun: GMT #789); > 'may not *causing pain* to myself be my only sustenance'

βόσκημα, ατος, τό
(βόσκω, feed) food, sustenance (emphatic *enjambment*)

ἐράω
desire passionately (only in pres., impf., and aor.¹); [1× *El.*]

⁺*λαγχάνω, ἔλαχον
[ᾰν] (λαχεῖν, aor.² act. inf.) obtain by lot (+ partit. genit. = become possessed of a thing, LSJ II. Infinitive as complement of ἐρῶ: SS 239 §4); > 'I have no desire *to obtain* any of your honors'

σώφρων, ον, ονος
(σῶς, φρήν) of sound mind, temperate; [1× *El.*]

οὐδ' σύ ἄν . . . οὖσα
'neither would you [desire them], if you were of sound mind' (ellipsis of vb.: ἐρῴης [opt.]/ἤρας [indic.] 'desire' in apodosis after ἄν; protasis: οὖσα = εἰ εἴης [opt.]/ἦσθα [indic.]. Either less vivid fut. condition, or contrary to fact for pres. time: GMT #410; S #2564; SS 280–281 §3a)

ἐξ-όν
(⁺ἔξ-εστι, it is allowed, possible) it being possible (impers. ptc. in acc. absolute with inf. ⁺*κεκλῆσθαι: S #2076; GMT #851); > lit.: 'it is possible [for you] to be called'

πάντων ἀρίστου παῖδα κεκλῆcθαι, καλοῦ
τῆc μητρόc. οὕτω γὰρ φανῇ πλείcτοιc κακή,
θανόντα πατέρα καὶ φίλουc προδοῦcα coύc.

XO. μηδὲν πρὸc ὀργὴν πρὸc θεῶν· ὡc τοῖc λόγοιc
ἔνεcτιν ἀμφοῖν κέρδοc, εἰ cὺ μὲν μάθοιc   370
τοῖc τῆcδε χρῆcθαι, τοῖc δὲ coῖc αὕτη πάλιν.

XP. ἐγὼ μέν, ὦ γυναῖκεc, ἠθάc εἰμί πωc
τῶν τῆcδε μύθων· οὐδ' ἂν ἐμνήcθην ποτέ,
εἰ μὴ κακὸν μέγιcτον εἰc αὐτὴν ἰὸν
ἤκουc', ὃ ταύτην τῶν μακρῶν cχήcει γόων.   375

LINE 366

⁺*κεκλῆcθαι (καλέω, pf. pass. inf.) pass.: be called by name; > 'But now, though you could be called the daughter of the noblest father of all men, be called (καλοῦ, impv.) the daughter [supply παῖδα with μητρόc] of your mother' (for the use of the same vb. see μὴ δοκεῖν 335–36n.)

πλειcτοῖc (superlative of ⁺πολύc) (substantival use of adj. without the article: SS 163 §1); > 'indeed (γάρ) you'll appear *to most people* . . .'

προ-⁺*δίδωμι (προδοῦcα, aor.² ptc. act.) betray; > 'as one who betrayed your dead father and your own'; [1× *El.*]

μηδὲν πρὸc ⁺ὀργήν 'nothing in [the manner of] anger' (for πρὸc with acc. of manner, see 464, 921, 1462, S #1608. Understand εἴπηc. For prohibition with omission of vb., see Diggle 1996: 8. πρὸc ⁺θεῶν 'in gods' name!')

⁺ἔν-⁺*ειμι be within, be in *or* among (ἔνεcτι . . . εἰ μάθοιc = mixed conditional construction: pres. indic. in the apodosis and opt. in the protasis "is sometimes merely emphatic future expression": GMT #500.b); > 'there is profit to be had in both your words, if you [El.] would learn to make use of hers, and she in turn, of yours'

ἄμφω both; ἀμφοῖν dual genit. and dat. (S #349e; SS 2–3); [1× *El.*]

LINE 371

⁺χράομαι mid.: use (+ dat. LSJ CII2; S #1509, 1734.20)

ἠθάc, άδοc, ὁ, ἡ (ἦθος, custom) used, accustomed, habituated (to a thing) + genit.; [1× Soph.]

⁺πωc (adv.) somehow, in any way

*μιμνήcκω, ἐμνήcθην (aor.² pass.) mid. and pass.: remember, call to mind, remind oneself; (apodosis: ἂν ἐμνήcθην; protasis: εἰ μὴ . . . ἤκουc'; contrary-to-fact condition for the past: S #2564; GMT #410; SS 281 §3b); > 'I would never have mentioned [this, what she said in 328–29], had I not heard . . .'

LINE 373

⁺*εἶμι (ἰόν, neut. sg. acc. ptc.) (will) go (for its future meaning see S #1880, for conjugation S #773. Ptc. ἰών, ἰοῦcα, ἰόν. Supplem. ptc. in indir. disc. following vb. of perception, ἤκουcα: S #2145; GMT #904); > '*had I not heard* that great evil *coming upon* her.'

⁺μᾱκρόc (3) long, large (τῶν μακρῶν . . . ⁺γόων anaphoric article, i.e., refers to what has been mentioned already beforehand: SS 143–44 §13: "which will restrain her [*cχήcει, ἔχω] from *these* long laments of hers.")

⁺γόων repeated at the end of l. 379 as well; an emphatic repetition: neither Clyt. nor Aeg. can stop El.'s lamentations that are her sole weapon.

ΗΛ.　φέρ' εἰπὲ δὴ τὸ δεινόν. εἰ γὰρ τῶνδέ μοι
　　　μεῖζόν τι λέξεις, οὐκ ἂν ἀντείποιμ' ἔτι.
ΧΡ.　ἀλλ' ἐξερῶ coι πᾶν ὅcον κάτοιδ' ἐγώ.
　　　μέλλουcι γάρ c', εἰ τῶνδε μὴ λήξεις γόων,
　　　ἐνταῦθα πέμψειν ἔνθα μή ποθ' ἡλίου　　　　　　　　380
　　　φέγγοc προcόψῃ, ζῶcα δ' ἐν κατηρεφεῖ

LINE 376

⁺φέρ' ⁺εἰπέ　　　　　　see 310n

⁺μείζων, μεῖζον　　　　bigger (comparative of ⁺μέγας; with genit.: τῶνδε: S #1066, 1431)

ἀντ-εῖπον　　　　　　(ἀντείποιμι, aor.² without pres.) speak in answer, gainsay (εἰ λέξεις . . . ἂν ἀντείποιμ', fut. indic. in protasis instead of ἐάν with subjv., contains a strong appeal to the feelings, or a threat, or warning, and therefore a favorite construction in Tragedy: GMT #447; SS 277–78 §1a. When a fut. indic. in protasis is followed by a potential opt. in the apodosis, "there is sometimes a distinct potential force in the apodosis, and sometimes the optative with ἄν is merely a softened expression for the fut. indic.": GMT #505c); > *'for if you are going to tell me* something bigger (i.e., worse) than these things (i.e., my present circumstances), I *will not argue with you anymore';* [1× *El.*]

LINE 378

ἀλλ'　　　　　　　　well (with fut. [ἐξερῶ] expresses "practical consent . . . willingness to act in a certain way" after the first speaker speaks in imperative: φέρ' εἰπέ: GP 17)

⁺ἐξ-ερῶ　　　　　　speak out, proclaim (fut. without any present in use)

⁺κατ-⁺*οῖδα　　　　　know well, be assured of

⁺γάρ　　　　　　　　'the fact is that' (explanatory; see 32n)

⁺*μέλλουσι . . . εἰ μὴ ⁺*λήξεις　condition with fut. indic. in protasis may express present intention, threat, or necessity for the future with no commitment for realization (SS 277–78 §1a; GMT #447); > 'they plan/intend to . . . if you do not [intend to] stop'

LINE 380

ἐνταῦθα . . . ⁺ἔνθᾰ　　there . . . where

φέγγος, εος, τό　　　　light; [1× *El.*]

προσ-⁺*οράω, -όψομαι　(indic. fut. dep. 2sg.) look at (μή . . . προσόψῃ, Soph. is fond of μή with indic. rather than οὐ); > 'there where you will never see the light of the sun'

κατ-ηρεφής, ές　　　　(κατά, ἐρέφω) covered over, roofed over, vaulted; [1× *El.*]

⁺χθών, χθονός, ἡ　　　the earth, ground, <u>land</u>, <u>country</u>

στέγη χθονὸς τῆςδ' ἐκτὸς ὑμνήςεις κακά.
πρὸς ταῦτα φράζου, καί με μή ποθ' ὕςτερον
παθοῦςα μέμψῃ. νῦν γὰρ ἐν καλῷ φρονεῖν.

ΗΛ.   ἢ ταῦτα δή με καὶ βεβούλευνται ποεῖν;   385
ΧΡ.   μάλιςθ'· ὅταν περ οἴκαδ' Αἴγιςθος μόλῃ.
ΗΛ.   ἀλλ' ἐξίκοιτο τοῦδέ γ' οὕνεκ' ἐν τάχει.

LINE 382

⁺ἐκτός	without, outside, out of, beyond (+ genit.)
ὑμνέω	tell over and over again, sing; > 'you will tell your troubles over and over again'; [1× *El.*]
πρὸς ταῦτα	in regard to this, therefore (the phrase often comes with an impv. [φράζου] in warning or menace [Jebb]); > 'in view of these things, think'
ὕστερον (adv.)	(ὕςτερος, the latter) after, afterward, hereafter, <u>in the future</u>
μέμφομαι	blame, reproach, find fault with (+ acc.); > "and do not blame me later, after you have suffered (παθοῦσα)" (Lloyd-Jones); [1× *El.*]
ἐν καλῷ φρονεῖν	'it is high time to think/be prudent (i.e., use your head)' (supply ἐστι)

Lines 385–404 are structured in *stichomythia*, a rapid exchange of one- or two-liners, a common rhetorical device in Greek tragedy to convey emotional agitation. It is concise in expression, and grammatical constructions are at times extended from line to line for the sake of speed and brevity.

LINE 385

ἢ . . . δή	really? (formula that points to El.'s great surprise and astonishment)
⁺καί (conj.)	GP 316, iv: "καί without an interrogative, and not opening a question, sometimes means 'actually,' and conveys surprise or indignation . . . and coheres closely with the following word and emphasizes it."
⁺βουλεύω	(βεβούλευνται, pf. mid.) to take counsel, consider, determine (the perfect emphasizes the decisiveness of their resolve; cf. at 947; με secondary acc. to an already complete verbal phrase: SS 37 §5); > 'Really?! *Are they actually determined* to do this to me?'
⁺μάλιστα (adv.)	(superlative of μάλα, exceedingly) yes (emphatic), of course, especially
⁺πέρ	(postpos. and enclit.) much, very, just, even (adds force to the word to which it is annexed: S #2965. ὅταν περ = 'just as soon as')
ὅταν . . . ⁺*μόλῃ	(⁺*βλώσκω. subjv. aor.² act.) Subjv. with ἄν in a temporal clause referring indefinitely to the future (S #2399, 1768; SS 294 §4); > 'just as soon as Aeg. comes home'
οἴκάδε (adv.)	[ᾰ] to one's house, home, homeward; [1× *El.*]
ἐξ-⁺*ικνέομαι, -ικόμην	(ἐξίκοιτο, aor.² opt) arrive, reach (optative of wish without an introductory word εἴθ'· SS 232 §15; GMT #721,723); [1× *El.*]

LINE 387

⁺οὕνεκα	on account of, for the sake of (+ genit., τοῦδε; usually postpositive); > 'as far as this is concerned'
⁺τάχος, εος, τό	[ᾰ] swiftness, speed; ἐν τάχει <u>'quickly'</u> (LSJ II)

ΧΡ.	τίν’, ὦ τάλαινα, τόνδ’ ἐπηράσω λόγον;
ΗΛ.	ἐλθεῖν ἐκεῖνον, εἴ τι τῶνδε δρᾶν νοεῖ.
ΧΡ.	ὅπως πάθῃς τί χρῆμα; ποῦ ποτ’ εἶ φρενῶν; 390
ΗΛ.	ὅπως ἀφ’ ὑμῶν ὡς προσώτατ’ ἐκφύγω.
ΧΡ.	βίου δὲ τοῦ παρόντος οὐ μνείαν ἔχεις;
ΗΛ.	καλὸς γὰρ οὑμὸς βίοτος ὥστε θαυμάσαι.
ΧΡ.	ἀλλ’ ἦν ἄν, εἰ σύ γ’ εὖ φρονεῖν ἠπίστασο.
ΗΛ.	μή μ’ ἐκδίδασκε τοῖς φίλοις εἶναι κακήν. 395

LINE 388

ὦ τάλαινα — the voc. does not always necessitates the exclamat. ὦ, but in Soph. it is needed when the adj. is not accompanied by a noun (SS 27 §8ii)

ἐπ-αράομαι, -ηρᾱσάμην — (ἐπηράσω, aor.[1] indic. mid. 2sg) imprecate curses upon (the instantaneous, immediate, or contemporary aorist indicates an action that has occurred just a moment before. English uses a present tense: Kells; SS 196 §16. ἐπαρᾶσθαι λόγον = 'utter an imprecation'; τόνδε λόγον = internal acc. of ἐπηράσω: SS 34–35 §2, S #1554a, 1555); > 'what curse is this you utter . . . ?'; [1× Soph.]

ἐλθεῖν ἐκεῖνον — 'that he should come' (acc. and inf. required by supplied ἐπηρασάμην understood from the preceding ἐπηράσσω; syntax in *stichomythia* extends from line to line)

νοέω — think, mind, deem

LINE 390

⁺ὅπως . . . ὅπως — *anaphora* (p. 23); final clause with subjv. (⁺*πάθῃς, ἐκ-⁺*φύγω) in Soph. usually follows a primary tense in the main clause, but here subjv. follows a secondary tense: ἐπηράσσω (SS 284–85 §2); according to GMT #321, the subjv. "makes the language more vivid by introducing more nearly the original form of thought of the person whose purpose is stated"

χρῆμα, ατος, τό — (χράομαι, experience) matter, business; τὶ χρῆμα = τί 'what'; [1× El.]

⁺ποῦ (adv.) — where? > 'So that you may suffer what? Where are you in your mind (i.e., What are you thinking?)?'

προσώτατα (adv.) — (προσώτατος, superlative of πρόσω) furthest, as far as possible; [1× El.]

ἐκ-⁺*φεύγω, -έφυγον — (ἐκφύγω, aor.[2] subjv.) flee out/away, escape; > "So that I can escape as far as possible from you people" (March); [1× El.]

βίου . . . τοῦ ⁺παρόντος — 'you have no concern for the life you still have?' (objective genit.: SS 53 §4; S #1328)

μνεία, ἡ — remembrance, memory; <u>care, thought, concern</u>; [1× Soph.]

LINE 393

⁺γάρ — indeed, forsooth (according to Jebb, ironic)

βίοτος, ὁ — (βιόω, live) life

θαυμάζω — (θαυμάσαι, aor.[1] inf. act.) wonder (ὥστε with inf. [outside indirect discourse] opens a result clause implying a possible or intended result rather than actual fact: S #2254; GMT #582, 587); lit.: 'because (γάρ, laden with irony if intonated rightly) my life is wonderful so as to wonder [at it]' [1× El.]

⁺ἐπίστᾰμαι — know how (to do) (contrary-to-fact condition for pres. time. The aor. in the apodosis refers to the present time—as the protasis does, but without the duration of time a vb. in the impf. would express, GMT #414); > 'it would be, if you knew how to be sensible'

*ἐκ-διδάσκω — teach thoroughly; (621)

ΧΡ.	ἀλλ' οὐ διδάσκω· τοῖς κρατοῦσι δ' εἰκαθεῖν.
ΗΛ.	σὺ ταῦτα θώπευ'· οὐκ ἐμοὺς τρόπους λέγεις.
ΧΡ.	καλόν γε μέντοι μὴ 'ξ ἀβουλίας πεσεῖν.
ΗΛ.	πεσούμεθ', εἰ χρή, πατρὶ τιμωρούμενοι.
ΧΡ.	πατὴρ δὲ τούτων, οἶδα, συγγνώμην ἔχει.
ΗΛ.	ταῦτ' ἐστὶ τἄπη πρὸς κακῶν ἐπαινέσαι.
ΧΡ.	σὺ δ' οὐχὶ πείςῃ καὶ συναινέσεις ἐμοί;

400 (margin, opposite line ΧΡ. πατὴρ)

LINE 396

οὐ διδάσκω	supplement: τοῖς φίλοις εἶναι κακήν
τοῖς ⁺κρατοῦσι	'the rulers, those in power' (articular substant. ptc.: S #2052; SS 257–58 §9; GMT #825. Dat. with vbs. of withdrawing or giving up, εἰκαθεῖν: SS 82 §4)
εἴκω, εἴκᾰθον	(aor.² inf., poetic) yield, give way, draw back, retire; > 'I am not teaching you [that], but to yield to those in power'
θωπεύω	flatter on (ταῦτα as adv. or internal acc.: SS 34–35 §2, 41–42 §12; S #1554. Supply external object: αὐτούς); > 'you flatter them like that!'; [1× *El.*]
ἐμούς	SS 168 §6 : "the ways of which you are speaking are not mine"; predicative adjective that emphatically affirms the noun
⁺γε μέντοι (pcl.)	(μέν+τοί) all the same, and yet, however (combination found in drama. Adversative and here introduces an objection in dialogue: GP 412,1)
ἀ-βουλία, ἡ	(ἀ privat.) ill council, thoughtlessness; [1× *El.*]
⁺*πίπτω, ἔπεσον	(πεσεῖν, aor.² inf. act.) fall, fail; > 'and yet, it is as well not to fall (i.e., come to grief) through folly'

LINE 399

τῑμωρούμενοι	see 349n (masc. pl. is used of and by a single woman in self-reference: SS 10 §5, 14–15 §8. Morwood attributes this usage of masc. gender to "boldness and resolution" on El.'s part. The use of participial masc. for women is most frequent in the speeches of El.: SS 9 §5); > 'I'll come to grief, if need be, avenging my father'
συγ-γνώμη, ἡ	(συγ-γιγνώσκω) forgiveness (with objective genit., τούτων: SS 53 §4; S #1328); > Kells: "But our father makes allowances (συγγνώμην ἔχει), I know, for this situation", i.e., yielding to their enemies; [1× *El.*]
τἄπη	= τὰ ⁺ἔπη
⁺ἐπ-*αινέω, -ήνεσα	(ἐπαινέσαι, inf. aor.¹ act.) approve, sanction, commend (αἰνέω keeps a short vowel in the aor. and fut.: S #488b. ταῦτα here amounts to τοιαῦτα [Kamerbeek] followed by epexegetic inf.: SS 238–39b; GMT #759); > 'Such words are (lit.: on the side of, πρός) for the base persons to commend'
συν-*αινέω	agree or come to terms with a person (notice the wordplay on El.'s ἐπαινέσαι, which may indicate that Chr. is annoyed as well as calm)

ΗΛ.	οὐ δῆτα. μή πω νοῦ τοσόνδ' εἴην κενή.
ΧΡ.	χωρήϲομαί τἄρ' οἷπερ ἐϲτάλην ὁδοῦ.
ΗΛ.	ποῖ δ' ἐμπορεύῃ; τῷ φέρεις τάδ' ἔμπυρα ;	405
ΧΡ.	μήτηρ με πέμπει πατρὶ τυμβεῦϲαι χοάς.
ΗΛ.	πῶς εἶπας; ἦ τῷ δυϲμενεϲτάτῳ βροτῶν;
ΧΡ.	ὃν ἔκταν' αὐτή· τοῦτο γὰρ λέξαι θέλεις.
ΗΛ.	ἐκ τοῦ φίλων πειϲθεῖϲα; τῷ τοῦτ' ἤρεϲεν;
ΧΡ.	ἐκ δείματός του νυκτέρου, δοκεῖν ἐμοί.	410

LINE 403

+οὐ δῆτα — indeed/certainly not! (emphatic negative answer. Here the denial is expected: GP 274, II.ii)

πω (enclit. pcl.) — up to this time, ever yet (μή πω = never. εἴην, opt. of wish); > 'Certainly not! May I never be so (τοσόνδε) devoid of thought'

+νοῦς, ὁ — mind, thought

+χωρέω — go forward, advance, go, come

τἄρ = +τοι ἄρα — +ἄρα then, therefore (postpostive confirmatory pcl. marking the immediate succession of events and thoughts while adding a lively feeling of interest: S #2787; GP 32–35);'Well! Then . . .'

οἷπερ — whither (S #346)

*στέλλω, ἐστάλην — (aor.² pass.) send

+ὁδός, ἡ — partit. genit. with adv. (S #1306; SS 58 §10) separated from οἷπερ by *hyperbaton* (p. 24) and semantically superfluous: > 'where I was sent to on my journey'

LINE 405

+ποῖ — where? (S #346)

ἐμ-πορεύομαι — be on a journey; [1× *El.*]

τῷ — 'for whom?' (= τινι, interrog. pron.: S #343)

ἔμ-πῠρος, ον — (ἐν, πῦρ) in/on the fire, burnt; ἔμπυρα (ἱερά) = burnt offerings; [1× *El.*]

χοή, ἡ — (χέω, pour) drink-offering for the dead mixed of honey, wine and water

τυμβεύω — (τύμβος, mound of earth heaped over ashes) bury, burn, entomb a corpse (χοὰς τυμβεῦσαι τινι = pour libations as an offering on one's grave. Final infinitive 'to pour libations' after a verb of motion, πέμπει: GMT #770; SS 237 §2); [1× *El.*]

+δυσ-μενής, ές — bearing ill will, hostile

LINE 408

ἐκ τοῦ φίλων — = ὑπὸ τινὸς φίλων; > 'convinced by whom of her friends?'; τινος = genit. of agent (S #1491; SS 109 §9); φίλων, partit. genit. (S #1306, 1317)

*ἀρέσκω, ἤρεσα — (aor.¹ act.) be pleasing to, gratify, please, be agreeable + dat.; > 'to whom was this pleasing?'; [1× *El.*]

δεῖμα, ατος, τό — (δείδω, be afraid) fear, terror (του = τινός, indefinite. pron., S #334)

νύκτερος (3) — (νύξ) nighttime (note the *anaphora* of ἐκ in 409–10); > 'from/by some night terror'; [1× *El.*]

+δοκεῖν — limiting inf. closely allied with epexegetic and consecutive uses of the inf, and thus should be preceded by ὡς or ὥστε, often omitted in familiar speech (Kells; GMT #778); > 'as it seems to me'

ΗΛ.	ὦ θεοὶ πατρῷοι, cυγγένεcθέ γ' ἀλλὰ νῦν.
ΧΡ.	ἔχεις τι θάρcος τοῦδε τοῦ τάρβους πέρι;
ΗΛ.	εἴ μοι λέγοις τὴν ὄψιν, εἴποιμ' ἂν τότε.
ΧΡ.	ἀλλ' οὐ κάτοιδα πλὴν ἐπὶ cμικρὸν φράcαι.
ΗΛ.	λέγ' ἀλλὰ τοῦτο. πολλά τοι cμικροὶ λόγοι
	ἔcφηλαν ἤδη καὶ κατώρθωcαν βροτούς.
ΧΡ.	λόγος τις αὐτήν ἐcτιν εἰcιδεῖν πατρὸς
	τοῦ cοῦ τε κἀμοῦ δευτέραν ὁμιλίαν
	ἐλθόντος ἐc φῶc· εἶτα τόνδ' ἐφέcτιον

415

LINE 411

cυν-⁺*γίγνομαι	[ῐ] be with, come to assist [1× Soph.]
⁺ἀλλὰ νῦν	now at least, <u>now at long last</u> (GP 13.3)
⁺θάρcος, εος, τό	[ᾰ] courage, boldness, confidence
τάρβος, εος, τό	fright, alarm, terror; [1× El.]
⁺πέρι	= ⁺περί, of, about, concerning (+ genit.; *anastrophe*, p. 23; S #175)
ὄψις, εως, ἡ	(ὄψομαι) sight, vision, apparition; [1× El.]

LINE 414

cμῑκρός (3)	= μῑκρός; small, little, trivial, insignificant; [1× El.]
⁺φράcαι	epexegetic inf. almost redundant; can depend either on κάτοιδα, or on ἐπὶ cμκρόν; 'I do not know and can tell only a little' or 'I do not know except for a very little to tell.' The essential meaning is the same.
⁺πολλά	often (adverbial acc.: SS 42 §12)
εἰ ⁺λέγοις ... ⁺εἴποιμ' ἂν	future less vivid condition (S #2297, 2329; GMT #392.2)
*cφάλλω, ἔcφηλα	trip up, deceive
κατ-ορθόω	set up straight, erect (both verbs stand in a gnomic aorist expressing general truth: S #1931); [1× El.]

LINE 417

αὐτήν ... ⁺εἰcιδεῖν	(εἰc-⁺*οράω, aor.² inf act.) (acc. and inf. construction following λόγος τις ... ἐcτιν: S #1972, 2016)
πατρὸς ... ⁺*ἐλθόντος	temporal genit. absolute in a *hyperbaton* (p. 24); (S #2058, 2070a; SS 76–77 §42)
δεύτερος (3)	second, once more; [1× El.]
ὁμῑλία, ἡ	being/living together, intercourse, companionship (some assume companionship [Jebb, Finglass]. Others assume sexual intercourse [Kamerbeek, Kells]); > 'there is a word that she saw a second companionship with your father and mine after he had come to the daylight/life [again]'; [1× El.]
⁺φῶc, φωτός, τό	light, daylight (usually signifies life versus the darkness of the Netherworld.)
ἐφ-έcτιος, ον	(ἐπὶ ἐcτία) by the hearth (predicative and proleptic, see p. 24; SS 167–68 §6. I.e., he planted it in a way it would be by the hearth); > 'having taken the scepter, he planted it by the hearth'; [1× El.]

πῆξαι λαβόντα cκῆπτρον οὐφόρει ποτὲ   420
αὐτόc, τανῦν δ' Αἴγιcθοc· ἔκ τε τοῦδ' ἄνω
βλαcτεῖν βρύοντα θαλλόν, ᾧ κατάcκιον
πᾶcαν γενέcθαι τὴν Μυκηναίων χθόνα.
τοιαῦτά του παρόντοc, ἡνίχ' Ἡλίῳ
δείκνυcι τοὔναρ, ἔκλυον ἐξηγουμένου.   425
πλείω δὲ τούτων οὐ κάτοιδα, πλὴν ὅτι
πέμπει μ' ἐκείνη τοῦδε τοῦ φόβου χάριν.

LINE 420

*πήγνῡμι, ἔπηξα	fix in, make fast, plant
cκῆπτρον, τό	(cκήπτω, prop, support) a staff, scepter; (ὑφόρει = ὃ +ἐφόρει)
+τανῦν (adv.)	now at present (= τὰ νῦν)
τοῦδε	ὅδε in anaphoric (referring back) use; > 'and from *it* (i.e., the staff) grew up a fruitful young shoot'
+ἄνω (adv.)	(ἀνά) upward, up
βρύω	[ῡ] full of, swell, teem with; [1× *El.*]
θαλλόc, ὁ	(θάλλω) a young shoot (ᾧ = dat. of means: SS 88–89 §16); [1× *El.*]
κατά-cκῐοc, ον	(κατά, cκία) overshadowed (acc. and inf. following λόγοc τιc ἐcτιν: κατάcκιον τὴν χθόνα γενεcθαι, into the relative clause starting with ᾧ: SS 262–63 §1: "[it is said that] a fruitful bough grew up from it, and with it (ᾧ) *all the land was overshadowed*"); [1× Soph.]

LINE 424

+του +παρόντοc	'someone (= τινόc) present'; indef. pron. and pres. ptc. of +πάρειμι in genit. after +ἔκλυον
+*δείκνῠμι	show, declare, reveal (historical present for vividness, standing mostly for narrative aorist or descriptive imperfect: S #1883; SS 186 §5; GMT #33)
ὄναρ, τό	dream (used in nom. and acc. only τοὔναρ = τὸ ὄναρ. Occurs only here in Soph. and in a fragment); [1× Soph.]
ἐξ-ηγέομαι	narrate, describe, tell at length (LSJ III); > 'This is what I heard told in detail by someone (present) who was there when . . .'; [1× *El.*]
πλείω	= πλείονα (acc. pl. neut. comparative of +πολύc: S #319.8, with genit. of comparison τούτων: SS 69–70); > 'more than this I do not know'
+φόβοc, ὁ	fear, terror, fright, dismay
+χάριν + genit.	for the sake of, on account of (χάριc, acc. sg. as a postpositive improper prep., i.e., an adv. used as a prep. but unable to form compounds: S #1665a, 1700; LSJ A VI,1)

[πρός νυν θεῶν cε λίccομαι τῶν ἐγγενῶν
ἐμοὶ πιθέcθαι μηδ' ἀβουλίᾳ πεcεῖν·
εἰ γὰρ μ' ἀπώcῃ, cὺν κακῷ μέτει πάλιν.]   **430**

ΗΛ.   ἀλλ', ὦ φίλη, τούτων μὲν ὧν ἔχεις χεροῖν
τύμβῳ προcάψῃc μηδέν· οὐ γάρ cοι θέμιc
οὐδ' ὅcιον ἐχθρᾶc ἀπὸ γυναικὸc ἱcτάναι
κτερίcματ' οὐδὲ λουτρὰ προcφέρειν πατρί·
ἀλλ' ἢ πνοαῖcιν ἢ βαθυcκαφεῖ κόνει   **435**
κρύψον νιν, ἔνθα μή ποτ' εἰc εὐνὴν πατρὸc
τούτων πρόcειcι μηδέν· ἀλλ' ὅταν θάνῃ,

LINE 428

Most mss. assign lines 428–30 to Chr., others to El. Jebb, Kamerbeek, Kells attribute them to Chr.; Finglass assumes that they are a reworking and amplification of l. 398 and square-brackets them.

λίccομαι	beg, pray, entreat
ἐγ-γενής, ές	(ἐν, γένος) <u>native</u>, inborn (ἐγγενεῖς . . . θεοί = gods of the family or country. *Hyperbaton*, p. 24)
⁺ἀπ-ωθέω, -ωcα	(ἀπώcῃ, ind. fut. mid. 2sg.) mid.: reject, disdain, repulse; > 'for if you reject me'
μέτ-ειμι	(μετά, εἶμι) <u>go to, approach</u>, go after, visit with vengeance (the indic. pres. of εἶμι has a future meaning: S #774, 1880); > 'you will come to me when things are bad (lit.: with /) for you'

LINE 431

προc-άπτω	(προcάψῃc, subjv. aor.¹ act.) attach to, apply to, confer upon (prohibitive subjunctive: 'do not . . .': S #1800a; SS 220 §6; GMT #259)
τούτων . . . μηδέν	partitive genit., (SS 57–58 §10; S #1306, 1317); ὧν = ἅ, relative attraction in which the relat. pron. is attracted from its proper case into the case of its antecedent—τούτων; i.e., instead of acc. ἅ, there is genit. ὧν (S #2522a); > 'do not (attach to) place on the tomb any of the things in your hands'
ὅcιος (3)	pious, scrupulous; > 'it is not lawful nor *pious* for you to . . .'; [1× *El.*]
κτερίcματα, τά	(κτερίζω, bury with due honors) funeral honors, obsequies (= κτέρεα, in 931 the term includes libations; here it doesn't)
προc-⁺*φέρω	bring to
⁺πατρί	*apokoinu*, ἀπὸ κοινοῦ, a word common to two clauses or two syntactical structures, carrying two syntactical functions; here with both infinitives, ἱcτάναι and προcφέρειν; > 'to place funeral honors (*to our father*) or bring libations *to our father*'

LINE 435

⁺ἀλλ'	but (with commands and exhortations: GP 13–14; repeated twice more in this speech, 435, 437)
πνοή, ἡ	wind, blast, air, breath
βαθυ-cκᾰφής, ές	(βαθύς, cκάπτω) deep dug; [1× Soph.]
⁺κόνις, εως, ἡ	dust; > 'hide them deep in the dust'
⁺κρύψον	*zeugma* (p. 24). The verb goes only with βαθυcκαφεῖ κόνει. δός or μεθές, to be supplied with πνοαῖcιν. The aorist imperative indicates a specific action to be begun and whose termination is also envisaged (SS 217 §5): it will be hidden until Clyt. dies.
νιν	= αὐτά (S #325e)
⁺ἔνθα μὴ ποτ'	⁺ἔνθᾰ: where (μή reflects the subjective wish and thought of El.)
πρόc-⁺*εἶμι	approach, come to (⁺*εἶμι and its compounds serve as future); [1× Soph.]
τούτων . . . μηδέν	partit. genit. (S #1306; SS 58); > 'where nothing of them will ever come to our father's resting place'

κειμήλι' αὐτῇ ταῦτα cῳζέcθω κάτω.
ἀρχὴν δ' ἄν, εἰ μὴ τλημονεcτάτη γυνὴ
παcῶν ἔβλαcτε, τάcδε δυcμενεῖc χοὰc   440
οὐκ ἄν ποθ' ὅν γ' ἔκτεινε τῷδ' ἐπέcτεφε.
cκέψαι γὰρ εἴ cοι προcφιλῶc αὐτῇ δοκεῖ
γέρα τάδ' οὖν τάφοιcι δέξεcθαι νέκυc

LINE 438

κειμήλιον, τό (⁺κεῖμαι, lie down) anything stored up as valuable, treasure (predicative: 'as a treasure'); [1× Soph.]

⁺αὐτῇ dat. of advantage (*commodi*) often translated as dat. of possession (SS 84 §9); > 'as a treasure *for her/ for her sake*'

⁺cῳζέcθω the aspect of the pres. impv. points to action to be begun and be continued (SS 217 §5); > '*let these be kept safely* for her as a treasure below for whenever she dies.' (a sarcastic comment suggesting that no one else will offer libations for Clyt, when she dies, whenever it that may be: ὅταν ⁺*θάνῃ)

ἀρχή, ἡ a beginning, first cause, origin (ἀρχήν, adverbial acc., = 'to begin with,' 'at all.' Mostly preceding negative sentences. SS 42 §13: "'would not have poured libations *for a start*', i.e., '*not at all*'"); [1× *El.*]

⁺τλήμων, ονος, ὁ/ἡ suffering, enduring, wretched, miserable; <u>bold, daring, reckless, rash</u> (superlative with partit. genit. παcῶν: S #1306, 1315; SS 58 §10)

⁺*ἔβλαcτε (βλαcτάνω, aor.² act.); ἔβλ(αcτε) counted as a short syllable, but long in 238. Soph. tends to use this verb as variation of φύομαι, γίγνομαι, and even εἰμί more often than Aesch. or Eur. (in *El.*: 238, 590, 966, 1060, 1081, 1095, Kamerbeek)

LINE 441

⁺τῷδε 'to the man whom she killed'; antecedent of ὅν in an inverted order

ἐπι-cτέφω surround with (χοὰc ἐπιcτέφειν τινι = offer libations as an honor to the dead; ἀρχήν ἄν, εἰ . . . ἔβλαcτε . . . ἄν . . . ἐπέcτεφε: contrary-to-fact condition: protasis for past time, apodosis for pres. time; repeated ἄν emphasizes the impropriety of the libations: S #1765, 2297, GMT #223); > '*had she not been the most shameless* of all women, *she would certainly never have offered* these hateful libations to begin with'; [1× Soph.]

cκέπτομαι (cκέψαι, aor.¹ impv. mid.) look to, view, examine, consider; [1× *El.*]

προcφιλῶc (adv.) kindly (here with αὐτῇ); [1× Soph.]

γέρας, αος, τό gift of honor (Epic contraction: γέρα = γέρατα, nom. pl.)

οὖν = ὁ ἐν with νέκυc

⁺δέξεcθαι δέξαcθαι in codd., but the sense demands future (SS 209 §31), thus the emendation δέξεcθαι is a preferable reading.

νεκύς, ύος, ὁ a dead body, corpse; <u>dead man</u>; > 'for consider if you believe (cοι δοκεῖ) that the dead man in the tomb would receive these honors *with kindly feelings toward the woman*'; [1× *El.*]

ὑφ᾽ ἧς θανὼν ἄτιμος ὥστε δυσμενὴς
ἐμασχαλίσθη κἀπὶ λουτροῖσιν κάρα   445
κηλῖδας ἐξέμαξεν. ἆρα μὴ δοκεῖς
λυτήρι᾽ αὐτῇ ταῦτα τοῦ φόνου φέρειν;
οὐκ ἔστιν. ἀλλὰ ταῦτα μὲν μέθες· σὺ δὲ
τεμοῦσα κρατὸς βοστρύχων ἄκρας φόβας
κἀμοῦ ταλαίνης, σμικρὰ μὲν τάδ᾽, ἀλλ᾽ ὅμως   450
ἄχω, δὸς αὐτῷ, τήνδε λιπαρῆ τρίχα
καὶ ζῶμα τοὐμὸν οὐ χλιδαῖς ἠσκημένον.
αἰτοῦ δὲ προσπίτνουσα γῆθεν εὐμενῆ

LINE 444

ὑφ᾽ ἧς 'by whose hand he died' (⁺ὑπό with genit. of personal agent: S #1493; the antecedent is αὐτῇ, 442)

μασχᾱλίζω put under the armpits, mutilate; > either 'he died without honor as an enemy and his corpse *was mutilated*,' or 'he died without honor and *was mutilated* as an enemy'; [1× Soph.]

κηλίς, ῖδος, ἡ stain, spot, defilement; [1× *El.*]

ἐκ-μάσσω wipe off; > 'and by way of cleaning, *she wiped off* the [blood]stains on his head'; [1× Soph.]

⁺ἆρα μή 'You don't think that . . . do you?' (= μῶν); interrogative pcl. expecting the answer 'no': SS 320)

⁺λῠτήριος (3) (⁺λύω, loosen) losing, delivering; λουτήρια <u>atonement</u> (LSJ II) (substantival use of adj. without article: SS 163 §1. Predicative with τοῦ φόνου as objective genit.: SS 53 §4, S #1328); > '*as atonement / absolution* for her [αὐτῇ] of the murder'

LINE 448

οὐκ ἔστιν it is impossible (the supposition is rejected; a quasi-impersonal use of ⁺*εἰμί = ⁺ἔξεστι. The subject, ταῦτα, is omitted: S #1985)

⁺μεθ-⁺ίημι, (μέθες, aor.² impv.: S #777) set loose, let go; + acc. throw

⁺τέμνω, ἔτεμον (τεμοῦσα, aor.² ptc. act.) cut

βόστρῠχος, ὁ curl, lock of hair

⁺ἄκρος (3) (ἀκή, edge) at the end

φόβη, ἡ lock, curl, hair; foliage; > 'having cut the tips of your locks'; [1× *El.*]`

⁺ὅμως (adv.) nevertheless, still (ἀλλ᾽ ὅμως = but still: S #2786)

LINE 451

ἄχω = ἃ ἔχω; > 'and from poor me, these [are] small things, but [all] I have'

λῐπᾰρής, ές persisting, persevering, earnest (Scholia: λιπαρῇ, the codd. have ἀλῐπαρῇ = 'not sleek'; however, the quantity of the iota disagrees, and the word is found nowhere else. The text calls for 'unkempt', which λιπαρῇ does not fit semantically, unless iironic. The epithet of τρίχα remains a crux: Kamerbeek)

θρίξ, τριχός hair; [1× *El.*]

ζῶμα, ατος, τό (ζώννυμι, gird) girdle, belt; [1× Soph.]

χλιδή, ἡ luxury, adorments

⁺ἀσκέω (ἠσκημένον, pf. pass. ptc.) adorn, fashion, dress up, decorate; > 'and give them to him, this earnst (?) hair and my girdle not decorated with adornments'

αἰτέω (pres. impv. mid.) ask, beg, request (followed by two acc. and inf. structures: εὐμενῆ . . . ἀρωγὸν αὐτὸν and . . . μολεῖν and παῖδ᾽ Ὀρέστην . . . ἐπεμβῆναι)

ἡμῖν ἀρωγὸν αὐτὸν εἰс ἐχθροὺс μολεῖν,
καὶ παῖδ' Ὀρέсτην ἐξ ὑπερτέραс χερὸс   455
ἐχθροῖсιν αὐτοῦ ζῶντ' ἐπεμβῆναι ποδί,
ὅπωс τὸ λοιπὸν αὐτὸν ἀφνεωτέραιс
χερсὶ сτέφωμεν ἢ τανῦν δωρούμεθα.
οἶμαι μὲν οὖν, οἶμαί τι κἀκείνῳ μέλειν

προс-πίτνω | fall upon, embrace; prostrate, supplicate (poetic for προс-+*πίπτω)
εὐμενής, ές | well disposed, kind, propitious, beneficent; [1× El.]

LINE 454

ἡμῖν | 'request that he come to us as a beneficent helper'; (dat. of advantage: SS 845 §9)
+ἀρωγός, ὁ | helper
ὑπέρτεροс (3) | (comparative adj. of ὑπέρ) upper, higher; stronger, mightier (ἐκ ὑπερτέραс χερός = 'with upper hand.' For ἐκ see ἐξ at 48)
+*ζῶντ' | = ζῶντα (pres. ptc. acc. sg. masc., not dat. sg., because dat. sg. of 3rd declension does not elide in Tragedy: Finglass)
ἐπ-εμ-+*βαίνω | (ἐπεμβῆναι, aor.² inf. act.) step upon, tread upon; trample upon (with dat., ἐχθροῖсιν)
+πούс, ποδός, ὁ | foot (dat. of means: SS 88–89 §16); > 'that his (αὐτοῦ) son Orestes, with upper hand, alive, trample his enemies under/with his foot'

LINE 457

+λοιπός (3) | (+*λείπω, leave) remaining (τὸ λοιπόν = the remainder, the future)
ἀφνεός (3) | rich, wealthy (= ἀφνειός, 3/2); [1×Soph.]
ὅπωс . . . +сτέφωμεν | 'so that in the future we may honor him with richer hands than [with which] we now bring him gifts.' Final clause in subjv. in primary sequence, αἰτοῦ. Imperative moods count as primary because they point to the future (S #1858a; SS 284–85 §2)
δωρέομαι | give, present one with, bring a gift
+*οἶμαι | (= οἴομαι) think, suppose (emphatic repetition. οὖν emphasizes prospective μέν: GP 473. οἶμαι μέν is answered by ὅμωс δ' in 461); > 'Yes, (although) I think, I think that he . . . but nonetheless'
+μέλειν + dat. | A necessary emendation (Blaydes) to codd. μέλον. οἶμαι requires usually an inf., not a participial construction; >'Yes, I think that it *was of some (τι) interest (care)* to him (ἐκείνῳ) to send these horrible dreams to her'

πέμψαι τάδ' αὐτῇ δυσπρόσοπτ' ὀνείρατα·   **460**
ὅμως δ', ἀδελφή, σοί θ' ὑπούργηςον τάδε
ἐμοί τ' ἀρωγά, τῷ τε φιλτάτῳ βροτῶν
πάντων, ἐν Ἅιδου κειμένῳ κοινῷ πατρί.

XO.   πρὸς εὐσέβειαν ἡ κόρη λέγει· cὺ δέ,
ει cωφρονήcειc, ὦ φίλη, δράcειc τάδε.   **465**

XP.   δράcω· τὸ γὰρ δίκαιον οὐκ ἔχει λόγον
δυοῖν ἐρίζειν, ἀλλ' ἐπιcπεύδει τὸ δρᾶν.
πειρωμένη δὲ τῶνδε τῶν ἔργων ἐμοὶ
cιγὴ παρ' ὑμῶν πρὸς θεῶν ἔcτω, φίλαι.

LINE 460

δυσ-πρόσωπτος, ον	(δυσ-, πρόσωπον) of ill aspect, sour looks; [1× *El.*]
⁺ὄνειρον, τό	dream (pl. ὀνείρατα)
⁺ἀδελφή, ἡ (ᾰ)	(ἀ copulative, δελφύς, womb) daughter of the same mother, sister (it is the first time, El. addresses Chr. as her sister.)
σοί	= σεαυτῇ; together with μοι depends on ἀρωγά
ὑπουργέω	(ὑπουργός, rendering service) assist, serve, render; [1× *El.*]
ἀρωγός, ον	helping, aiding
⁺κοινός (3/2)	shared in common, kindred; > 'but nevertheless/all the same, do these things as a service both to yourself and to me, and to the dearest of all mortals, the father *of us both* who lies in Hades'
τῷ ... πατρί	an emphatic *hyperbaton*, see p. 24
πρὸς εὐσέβειαν	'the girl speaks out of reverence' (πρὸς with acc. of manner: S #1608, = εὐσεβῶς, cf. 369, 921, 1462)
σωφρονέω	be of sound mind (the future indic. is especially emphatic when the condition contains a strong appeal to the feelings of the addressee, as such is a favorite construction with the tragedians: GMT #447); > 'and you, if you are *of sound mind*, my dear, you will do as she says'

LINE 466

δύο	two (declension S #349; dual; *enjambment*)
ἐρίζω	(ἔρις, strife) strive, wrangle, quarrel; [1× Soph.]
ἐπι-σπεύδω	urge on; hasten (codd. have the inf. ἐπιcπεύδειν. In either case, it takes the articular inf. τὸ ⁺*δρᾶν either as a complementary inf. to mean 'urges to do.' Or if it is transitive, τὸ ⁺*δρᾶν is a direct object in acc. 'urges/hastens doing/accomplishing [it]': SS 239 §4; GMT #791); [1× Soph.]
τὸ ... δίκαιον ... δρᾶν	τὸ δίκαιον: either (a) anticipatory acc. of respect, with οὐκ ἔχει λόγον as impersonal with the epexegetic infs. ἐρίζειν and ἐπιcπεύδειν: 'for *in regard to what is right*, it makes no sense for two people to argue about it, but to urge accomplishing/doing it.' Or, (b) subject of οὐκ ἔχει: 'for *what is right (to do) does not permit* (οὐκ ἔχει λόγον) two persons to argue about it, but urges accomplishing/doing it.'
⁺*πειράομαι	(pres. ptc. dep.) try, attempt; the participle agrees with μοι.
τῶνδε τῶν ἔργων	objective genit. (SS 52–53 §4; S #1331–32); > 'while I attempt these things'
σιγή, ἡ	silence
παρ' ὑμῶν	'on your part'
ἔστω	(εἰμί, impv. pres. 3g.) 'let there be'

ὡς εἰ τάδ' ἡ τεκοῦσα πεύσεται, πικρὰν   470
δοκῶ με πεῖραν τήνδε τολμήσειν ἔτι.

XO.   εἰ μὴ 'γὼ παράφρων μάντις ἔφυν καὶ   στρ.
γνώμας λειπομένα σοφᾶς,
εἶσιν ἁ πρόμαντις   475
Δίκα, δίκαια φερομένα χεροῖν κράτη·

LINE 470

ἡ τεκοῦσα	(⁺*τίκτω, aor.² act.) mother, the one who give birth (articular substantive participle: S #2050–2052; SS 257–58 §9; GMT #825)
πυνθάνομαι, πεύσομαι	(fut.) hear, earn, inquire (fut. condition with fut. indic. in protasis; see μέλλουσι . . . λήξεις 379n); > 'for if my mother will hear of this . . .'
⁺πικρός (2/3)	bitter, harsh, cruel (predicative adj.: 'as a bitter one')
πεῖρα, ἡ	experience (internal acc.: S #1554, recalling πειρωμένη in 468); [1× *El.*]
τολμάω	undergo, endure, venture, risk (με τολμήσειν = acc. with inf. for expected nominative with infinitive because of the personal construction in which the leading verb δοκῶ and the infinitive share the same subject: S #1973–74, cf. at 65–66; με is thus emphasized.)
⁺ἔτι	menacing as in 66: 'I think I will *yet* venture this endeavor as a bitter one'

Chrysothemis exits via the eisodos on the spectators' left, indicating she is going to Agamemnon's tomb outside the city.

FIRST STASIMON, LINES 472–515

The first Choral song that the Chorus sing and dance after they position themselves in the *orchestra*. Electra, who remains onstage, is silent. Encouraged by the account of Clytemnestra's dream, they envision a personified Justice, the axe that had been used to murder Agamemnon, and the Furies all coming together to punish the murderers. The song divides into strophe, 472–487, antistrophe, 488–503, and epode, 504–515.

STROPHE, Lines 472–487

LINE 472

μὴ 'γὼ	= μὴ ἐγὼ; aphaeresis (p. 23)
παρά-φρων, ον	(παρά, φρήν) out of one's right mind, out of one's wits; false; [1× Soph.]
⁺μάντῖς, εως, ὁ	(μαίνομαι) a diviner, soothsayer, seer, prophet; (as fem.) a prophetess; > 'If I was not born (⁺*ἔφυν) a deranged prophetess'
γνώμας λειπομένα σοφᾶς	= ⁺γνώμης ⁺*λειπομένη ⁺σοφῆς; > 'bereft of sound judgment'
πρό-μαντις, εως	prophetic (ἁ πρόμαντις Δίκα, Justice gave forewarning on the issue via Clyt.'s dream); > 'Justice, *who has already sent a sign*, will come carrying just victory in her hands'; [1× Soph.]

μέτεισιν, ὦ τέκνον, οὐ μακροῦ χρόνου.
ὕπεστί μοι θάρσος
ἀδυπνόων κλύουσαν   480
ἀρτίως ὀνειράτων.
οὐ γάρ ποτ' ἀμναστεῖ γ' ὁ φύ-
cac c' Ἑλλάνων ἄναξ,
οὐδ' ἀ παλαιὰ χαλκόπλη-   485
κτος ἀμφήκης γένυς,
ἅ νιν κατέπεφνεν αἰσχίσταις ἐν αἰκείαις.

LINE 477

μέτ-⁺*ειμι | (μετα, εἶμι; μέτεισι, pres. with future indication) <u>go after, visit with</u> <u>vengeance</u>, go to, approach; > 'she will visit in vengeance, soon, my child'

⁺μακροῦ ⁺χρόνου | genit. of time is used of the period of time within which something happens (SS 58–59 §11.i; S #1444); > 'in no short space of time'

ὕπ-*ειμι | be under; support; > 'confidence *supports* me'; [1× Soph.]

ἡδύ-πνοος (2) | (ἡδύς, πνοή) sweet-breathing; [1× Soph.]

κλύουσαν | (⁺κλύω); acc. qualifies the dat. μοι, because of construction according to the sense, as if ὑπέρχεται με θάρσος preceded κλύουσαν; > 'confidence supports me, now that I have heard the sweet-breathing dream'

LINE 482

ἀμνηστέω | be unmindful, forget; [1× Soph.]

⁺*φύσας | (φύω, aor.¹ act. ptc.) 'your begetter,' 'who begot you.' Articular substantive participle; see ἡ τεκοῦσα, line 470

Ἕλλην, ηνος, ὁ | Greek

⁺ἄναξ, ακτος, ὁ | lord, king; > 'For he who sired you, the lord of the Greeks, is never unmindful'

LINE 485

χαλκό-πληκτος (2) | (χαλκός, πλήσσω) forged or welded of brass; [1× Soph.]

ἀμφ-ήκης, ες | (ἀμφί, ἀκή) two edged; [1× El.]

γένῠς, υος, ἡ | (blade of an) axe; > 'nor is the ancient two-edged bronze axe'

κατα-φένω | (reduplicated aor.² with no pres. in use) kill, slay; [1× Soph.]

αἴσχιστος (3) | Superlative of ⁺αἰσχρός (2/3) (αἶσχος, τό, shame) shameful, disgraceful

⁺αἰκία, ἡ | [ῐ] injurious treatment, outrage (codd.: αἰκίας; αἰκείαις: Porson); > 'that killed him in a most despicable assault'

ἥξει καὶ πολύπους καὶ πολύχειρ ἁ   ἄντ.
δεινοῖς κρυπτομένα λόχοις   490
χαλκόπους Ἐρινύς.
ἄλεκτρ᾽ ἄνυμφα γὰρ ἐπέβα μιαιφόνων
γάμων ἁμιλλήμαθ᾽ οἷσιν οὐ θέμις.
πρὸ τῶνδέ τοι θάρσος   495
μήποτε μήποθ᾽ ἡμῖν
ἀψεγὲς πελᾶν τέρας

ANTISTROPHE, Lines 489–503

LINE 489

πολύ-πους, ποδος, ὁ/ἡ	(πολύς, πούς) many footed; [1× Soph.]
πολύ-χειρ, χειρος, ὁ/ἡ	(πολύς, χείρ) many handed; [1× Soph.]
λόχος, ὁ	(λέγω, lay to sleep; λέγομαι, lie down) ambush, place of lying in wait; [1× El.]
χαλκό-πους, ποδος, ὁ/ἡ	(χαλκός, πούς) brazen footed; [1× El.]

LINE 492

ἄ-λεκτρος, ον	(ἀ privat., λέκτρον, marriage bed) without a marriage bed, unwedded, <u>unhallowed marriage</u> (LSJ)
ἄ-νυμφος, ον	(ἀ privat., νύμφη, bride) not bridal, unwedded
ἐπι-⁺*βαίνω + dat	(ἐπέβα = ἐπέβη, aor.²) attack, set upon, assault; [1× El.]
μῖαι-φόνος (2)	(μιαίνω, defile; φόνος) blood stained, defiled with blood; [1× Soph.]
γάμος, ὁ	[ᾰ] marriage, wedding (some think the plural comes from repeated intercourse; others note the use of plural for festivals and festivities: SS 6 §3)
ἁμίλλημα, ατος, τό	(ἁμιλλάομαι, compete) contest, conflict, <u>striving, craving</u> (logically the epithets ἄλεκτρα and ἄνυμφα describe the γάμοι, but are transferred here to the passionate craving for the marriage); > 'for an unwedded, brideless *craving* for a blood-defiled marriage came upon those who had no right [to marry]'; [1× Soph.]

LINE 495

πρὸ τῶνδε	'for (= on account of) these things' (Jebb)
μήποτε	μή is usually the negation of the infinitive, here with πελᾶν (SS 327 §6)
ἡμῖν	the Chorus refer to itself in both singular and plural, combined at times in the same passage (SS 10 §6); > 'because of this, *I am sure* beyond doubt (⁺τοι)'
ἀ-ψεγής, ές	(ἀ privat., ψέγω, blame) unblamed, blameless, harmless (predicative adj.: 'as harmless'; [1× Soph.]
πελάω	Attic fut. of πελάζω; approach, draw near; [1× El.]
τέρας, ατος, τό	portent, sign

τοῖς δρῶϲι καὶ ϲυνδρῶϲιν. ἤ-
τοι μαντεῖαι βροτῶν
οὐκ εἰϲὶν ἐν δεινοῖς ὀνεί-
ροις οὐδ' ἐν θεϲφάτοις,   **500**
εἰ μὴ τόδε φάϲμα νυκτὸς εὖ καταϲχήϲει.

ὦ Πέλοποϲ ἀ πρόϲθεν   *ἐπ.*
πολύπονοϲ ἱππεία ,   **505**
ὡϲ ἔμολεϲ αἰανὴϲ
τᾷδε γᾷ.
εὖτε γὰρ ὁ ποντιϲθεὶϲ
Μυρτίλοϲ ἐκοιμάθη,

LINE 498

ϲυν-⁺*δράω	[ᾰ] do together; τοῖς δρῶϲι καὶ ϲυνδρῶϲιν = articular substantive participles (S #2050–52; SS 257–58 §9; GMT #825) and a wordplay on Clyt. and Aeg.; > 'that never ever will the nightmare come harmless upon the killers and their accomplices'
⁺ἤτοι (conj.)	probably disjunctive: 'or else' (GP 554)
μαντεία, ἡ	prophesying; prophesy (with objective genit. βροτῶν: SS 52–53 §4; S #1328); > 'divination for men'
θέϲφᾰτος (2)	(θεός, φημί) spoken by god, decreed (τὰ θέϲφατα = oracles); [1× El.]
⁺φάϲμα, ατος, τό	(φαίνω) apparition, phantom
⁺κατ-⁺*έχω	hold, withhold; reach destination safely (ἤ-τοι … εἰϲὶν … κατασχήϲει; future condition with fut. indic. in protasis commitment of realization: SS 277–78 §1a; GMT #447; cf. μέλλουϲι … εἰ μὴ λήξεις 379); > 'or else there is no prophecy for humankind in dreadful dreams and oracles, if this nighttime portent *is not to reach its due fulfillment*'

EPODE, Lines 504–515

LINE 504

ἱππεία, ἡ	driving, racing, horsemanship (Pelops' race to win Oenomaus' daughter, Hippodemeia, was the origin of the woes of the house of Atreus); [1× Soph.]
⁺πολύ-πονος, ον	(πολύς, πόνος) much-suffering; causing much pain, painful (repeated in 515 in the same metrical spot.)
αἰᾱνής, ές	(probably < αἰεί) everlasting; dismal, horrible; > 'Oh, Pelops' ancient horsemanship, cause of so much suffering, how you came *without end* upon this land'; [1× El.]
εὖτε (adv.)	when, at the time when, since, seeing that (poetic for of ὅτε)
ποντίζω	(ποντιϲθείς, aor.¹ pass. ptc.) (πόντος, sea) plunge in the sea, pass.: be drowned; [1× Soph.]
Μύρτιλος, ὁ	the charioteer of Oenomaus, bribed and thrown into the sea by Pelops; [1× Soph.]
κοιμάω	(ἐκοιμάθη = ἐκοιμήθη, aor.¹ pass. ptc.) lull to sleep; > 'sunk to sleep'; [1× Soph.]

παγχρύϲων δίφρων   510
δυϲτάνοιϲ αἰκείαιϲ
πρόρριζοϲ ἐκριφθείϲ,
οὔ τί πω
ἔλιπεν ἐκ τοῦδ᾽ οἴκου
πολύπονοϲ αἰκεία.   515

ΚΛΥΤΑΙΜΗϹΤΡΑ

ἀνειμένη μέν, ὡϲ ἔοικαϲ, αὖ ϲτρέφῃ.
οὐ γὰρ πάρεϲτ᾽ Αἴγιϲθοϲ, ὅϲ ϲ᾽ ἐπεῖχ᾽ ἀεὶ
μή τοι θυραίαν γ᾽ οὖϲαν αἰϲχύνειν φίλουϲ·

LINE 510

πάγ-χρῡϲοϲ, ον	(πᾶϲ, χρύϲοϲ) all gold, of solid gold; [1× *El.*]
πρό-ρριζοϲ, ον	(πρό, ῥίζα, root) by the roots
ἐκ-ρίπτω	(ἐκριφθείϲ, aor.¹ pass. ptc.) throw out, cast off; [1× *El.*]
πω (pcl.)	up to this time, yet, ever (mostly with negative); > 'For since Myrtilus was plunged into the sea, sunk to sleep, hurled in an execrable outrage headlong from a golden chariot, since then never has affliction, full of trouble, left this house'; [1× *El.*]

SECOND EPISODE, LINES 516–822

The Episode divides into two parts: lines 516–659 and 660–822.

LINES 516–659: Clytemnestra enters from the palace, accompanied by a maidservant carrying fruit offerings for Apollo. She engages in a formal debate (*agōn*) with Electra about the justice of Agamemnon's murder.

LINE 516

⁺ἀν-⁺ειμένη	(ἀνίημι, pf. pct. pass.: S #777) let go; > 'on the loose,' 'at large'
⁺μέν	μέν *solitarium* often begins speeches in drama (Finglass); emphasizes ἀνειμένη; see 61n
⁺*ἔοικα	(pf. with pres. sense) seem (personal use of impersonal ἔοικε.) English idiom is impersonal: 'it seems'
⁺αὖ (adv.)	cf. Chr.'s words in 328–29; > 'So you are out and about *again*, it seems'
ϲτρέφω	turn; mid. > 'you are turning', 'you are out and about'; [1× *El.*]
ἐπ-⁺*ἔχω	keep in, hold back (the impf. expresses frequent repetitive/customary act: S #1893, emphasized by ἀεί); > 'who always kept you in/restrained you'
θυραῖοϲ (2/3)	(θύρα, door) outside the door
μή τοι . . . γε	in indirect discourse with inf. 'at any rate not' (GP 546–47). The limiting γε stresses the adj. θυραίαν (GP 141). μή with inf., αἰϲχύνειν, in forbidding function (SS 328 §6 iv); > '(restrained you) *from shaming your kin, at least* (γε) outside the house'
*αἰϲχύνω	(αἰϲχύνη, shame, dishonor) shame, dishonor

νῦν δ' ὡς ἄπεστ' ἐκεῖνος, οὐδὲν ἐντρέπῃ

ἐμοῦ γε· καίτοι πολλὰ πρὸς πολλούς με δὴ   **520**

ἐξεῖπας ὡς θρασεῖα καὶ πέρα δίκης

ἄρχω, καθυβρίζουσα καὶ σὲ καὶ τὰ σά.

ἐγὼ δ' ὕβριν μὲν οὐκ ἔχω, κακῶς δέ σε

λέγω κακῶς κλύουσα πρὸς σέθεν θαμά.

πατὴρ γάρ, οὐδὲν ἄλλο, σοὶ πρόσχημ' ἀεί,   **525**

ὡς ἐξ ἐμοῦ τέθνηκεν. ἐξ ἐμοῦ· καλῶς

ἔξοιδα· τῶνδ' ἄρνησις οὐκ ἔνεστί μοι.

ἡ γὰρ Δίκη νιν εἷλεν, οὐκ ἐγὼ μόνη,

ᾗ χρῆν σ' ἀρήγειν, εἰ φρονοῦσ' ἐτύγχανες.

LINE 519

ἐν-τρέπω	mid.: give heed or regard; respect, pay deference + genit. of person; [1× *El.*]
ἐμοῦ γε (520), ἄρχω (522), ἔξοιδα (527), λύπης (533), δύσθυμος (550)	*enjambment*s; Clyt. emphasizes her stance and role
⁺καίτοι (pcl.)	adversative: 'you don't heed me at all, *and yet . . .*,' '. . . *and further . . .*'
⁺πολλά adv. acc.	= πολλάκις; often, <u>many times</u>; πολλὰ πρὸς πολλούς *polyptoton*, see δεινὰν δεινῶς 198n.
⁺ἐξ-⁺*εἶπον	(aor.² act. indic.) tell of (in use for ἐξ-αγορεύω, ⁺ἐξ-ερῶ); > '*you have reported* often many things about me to many people that . . .'
θρασύς, εῖα, ύ	bold
⁺πέρα + genit.	beyond, exceeding; πέρα δίκης = 'above justice,' 'unjustly'; > that I am (bold) insolent and that I rule *unjustly*'
καθ-⁺υβρίζω	(pres. act. ptc.) treat despitefully, insult + acc.; > 'insulting you and what's yours'; [1× *El.*]

LINE 523

⁺σέθεν	old poetic form of σοῦ, genit. of σύ
θαμά (adv.)	often, ofttimes, frequently; [1 × *El.*]
πρόσχημα, ατος, τό	(προ-⁺*ἔχω, hold before) what is held forth, <u>pretext</u>; ornament, showpiece

LINE 526

ἐξ ἐμοῦ	genit. of agent, comes with ἐκ, πρός and ὑπό (SS 75 §41; S #1678; note the emphatic repetition); > 'for your father, nothing else, is always your pretext, how he died *by my hand*. [Yes] *by my hand*'
ἄρνησις, εως, ἡ	(ἀρνέομαι, deny) denial; > 'I can't deny it'; [1× *El.*]
νίν	acc. of 3rd pers. pron. sg.
χρῆν	= ⁺χρή +ἦν (S #793) 'it was necessary' (with inf. it takes the acc.: σ': S #1562); > 'whom (ᾗ, 'Justice' is the antecedent) you should have helped'
ἀρήγω	help, aid
⁺*ἐτύγχανες	with φρονοῦσα, as supplem. ptc., which tells what the main action is, while the main verb tells something about how the action is occurring (S #2096a; GMT #887; SS 261 §12f); > 'if (*you happened to have any sense =*) *if you had any sense*'

ἐπεὶ πατὴρ οὗτος cóc, ὃν θρηνεῖς ἀεί, 530
τὴν cὴν ὅμαιμον μοῦνος Ἑλλήνων ἔτλη
θῦcαι θεοῖcιν, οὐκ ἴcον καμὼν ἐμοὶ
λύπης, ὅτ' ἔcπειρ', ὥcπερ ἡ τίκτουc' ἐγώ.
εἶέν· δίδαξον δή με ⟨τοῦτο⟩· τοῦ χάριν
ἔθυcεν αὐτήν; πότερον Ἀργείων ἐρεῖc; 535
ἀλλ' οὐ μετῆν αὐτοῖcι τήν γ' ἐμὴν κτανεῖν.

LINE 530

πατὴρ οὗτος cóc	Finglass: "The combination of οὗτος and cóc is probably contemptuous ('that father of yours,' Lloyd-Jones, similarly Jebb)"
⁺ἐπεί (conj.)	since, seeing that (LSJ; S #2240, cf. 352n); > '*for* that father of yours . . . alone of all the Greeks, had the heart to sacrifice your sister. . .'
θρηνέω	(θρῆνος, ὁ, dirge, lament) bewail, lament
Ἑλλήνων	partitive genit. with ⁺μοῦνος: SS 58 §10; > 'alone of the Greeks'
*τλάω, ἔτλην	(aor.², never found in pres.) endure, dare
⁺θύω	sacrifice
⁺ἴσος (3)	equal in size, strength, or number + dat.; here an adv.
*κάμνω, ἔκαμον	(καμών, aor.² ptc.) <u>labor</u>, be weary or sick; [1× *El.*]
*σπείρω, ἔσπειρα	(aor.¹) sow; engender, beget
⁺ὥσπερ (conj.)	as (introducing a comparison: SS 305–6 §1)
⁺*τίκτουσα	(pres. act. ptc.) articular substant. ptc. (cf. 342, 470); note the present aspect: the pain of labor is still with her; > 'although he did not suffer the same amount of pain when he sired her, *as did I who bore her*'

LINE 534

εἶεν (pcl.)	<u>well</u>, good, quite so; used in oratory in passing to the next point
⁺*δίδαξον	(διδάσκω, aor.¹ impv.) the aorist aspect is more suitable than the present (SS 217–18 §5)
⁺χάριν + genit.	τοῦ χάριν = τινὸς χάριν; > 'Fine. Just (δή) explain this to me, for whose sake did he sacrifice her'
⁺Ἀργεῖος (3)	of or from Argos, Argive
πότερον . . ., ἀλλὰ . . . δῆτα	πότερον is here continued not by ἤ, but by ἀλλὰ . . . ἀλλὰ . . . δῆτα used in questions that follow a rejected suggestion (GP 273), usually left untranslated in English; > '*Will* you say it was for the Argives? *But* they had no right to kill who was mine. *But then* having killed/if he killed my child because of his brother Menelaus, was he not to/ought he not (οὐκ ⁺*ἔμελλε) pay the penalty to me?' πότερον: resolution in 6th position; in line 539 the resolution in 1st position.
⁺ἐρῶ	I will say; ⁺*φημί, ⁺*λέγω, and ἀγορεύω used as pres. and εἶπον as aor.²
μέτ-⁺*ειμι	(μετῆν, impf. 3sg.) impers.; have share in, claim to + dat., αὐτοῖσι; > 'but they (αὐτοῖσι) had no claim/no right to kill <u>my</u> daughter'; [1× in *El.*]

ἀλλ' ἀντ' ἀδελφοῦ δῆτα Μενέλεω κτανὼν
τἄμ' οὐκ ἔμελλε τῶνδέ μοι δώσειν δίκην;
πότερον ἐκείνῳ παῖδες οὐκ ἦσαν διπλοῖ,
οὓς τῆσδε μᾶλλον εἰκὸς ἦν θνῄσκειν, πατρὸς
καὶ μητρὸς ὄντας, ἧς ὁ πλοῦς ὅδ' ἦν χάριν;
ἢ τῶν ἐμῶν Ἅιδης τιν' ἵμερον τέκνων

540

LINE 537

⁺ἀντί (+ genit.)	instead of; because of (SS 99 §4)
⁺Μενέλαος, ὁ	(genit.) resolution in 8th position, Μενέλεω; cf. 545, 576.
τἄμ'	= τὰ ἐμά neuter used for persons, cf. 972, 1208 (SS 14–15 §10)
⁺*δώσειν δίκας	give satisfaction/suffer punishment
ἐκείνῳ	dat. of possession (S #1476; SS 83 §8)
⁺διπλοῦς, ῆ, οῦν	two, twofold

LINE 540

⁺οὕς	acc., subject of the infinitive θνῄσκειν.
⁺ὅδε, ἥδε, τόδε	τῆσδε, genit. of comparison with μᾶλλον. According to Morwood, the pron. τῆσδε refers "to what is especially prominent in the speaker's mind" (SS 155 §23); > 'who (antecedent: παῖδες) should have properly (εἰκὸς ἦν) died *rather than* she (i.e., my daughter, Iphigenia)'
⁺εἰκός	(neut. pct. of ⁺ἔοικα) probable, <u>reasonable</u>, <u>proper</u>
πατρός καὶ μητρὸς ὄντας	possessive genits. in adverbial use; > 'since they were children *of the father and the mother*'
ἧς	the antecedent is Helen, the cause of the voyage is in Clyt.'s mind. Menelaus is irrelevant to her; > (mother) <u>for whose</u> sake the voyage took place'
πλοῦς, ὁ	sailing voyage; [1× in *El.*]
⁺ἤ (conj.)	or (continues πότερον in 539. Notice the *anaphora* in lines 542, 543, 544. Clyt. must have considered the reasons repeatedly)
ἵμερος, ὁ	[-ῐ-] longing, desire; [1× in *El.*]

ἢ τῶν ἐκείνης ἔϲχε δαίϲαϲθαι πλέον;
ἢ τῷ πανώλει πατρὶ τῶν μὲν ἐξ ἐμοῦ
παίδων πόθος παρεῖτο, Μενέλεω δ᾽ ἐνῆν;
οὐ ταῦτ᾽ ἀβούλου καὶ κακοῦ γνώμην πατρός;
δοκῶ μέν, εἰ καὶ ϲῆϲ δίχα γνώμης λέγω.
φαίη δ᾽ ἂν ἡ θανοῦϲά γ᾽, εἰ φωνὴν λάβοι.
ἐγὼ μὲν οὖν οὐκ εἰμὶ τοῖϲ πεπραγμένοιϲ

545

LINE 543

δαίνῠμαι — (δαίϲαϲθαι, aor.[1] inf. mid.) feast (epexegetic inf. with τἀμὰ τέκνα to be understood as the object: Kamerbeek. ἢ … πλέον frame the line in reverse order); > 'or (ἢ, l. 542) did Hades have some desire to feast on my children more (πλέον) than (ἢ, line 543) on hers?; [1× in *El.*]

παν-ώλης, ες — (+πᾶς, ++ὄλλῡμι, destroy) all-destructive, <u>murderous</u> (alliteration, 5× π, in the most important words might indicate Clyt.'s passionate indignation: Kamerbeek); [1× *El.*]

πόθος, ὁ — (ποθέω, love, yearn for) love, desire

+παρ-+ίημι, -εῖμαι — (παρεῖτο, aor.[2] indic. pass.) give up, slacken; > 'Or (ἢ, l. 544) had your murderous father's love for my children *abated*, while [his love] for Menelaus' [children] stayed the same (+ἐν ++ἦν)?'

ἄ-βουλος, ον — (ἀ privat., βουλή) inconsiderate, ill-advised, <u>thoughtless</u>

+γνώμην — acc. of respect (S #1601c; SS 43); > 'wasn't this [the conduct] of a thoughtless father, one *with poor judgment*?' Note the triple use of γνώμη in lines 546, 547, 551, in which Clyt. tries to set a contrast between her 'standards' and El.'s. For the repetition see 67n on πατρῷα/πατρῷον.

LINE 547

+δοκέω — <u>think</u>, imagine (personal constr.: S #1983 with μέν *solitarium*, see 61n); > 'I certainly think so'

εἰ καί — even if (concessive clause. Pres. indic. in protasis admits the condition, but denies the difficulty: S #2372; SS 282–83 §5)

δίχᾰ + genit. — (-ῐ-) apart from; > 'even if I differ from your judgment'

+*φαίη … ἄν …, εἰ … — (+*φημί, pres. opt.: S #783–86) say (less vivid condition, opt. in protasis and in apodosis, λάβοι [λαμβάνω,
+*λάβοι — aor.[2] opt.], with ἄν for what is impossible: SS 279 §1d, ii); > 'she who had died (ἡ +*θανοῦϲα) *would surely* (γ᾽) *say so, if she could acquire* a voice'

φώνη, ἡ — voice; [1× in *El.*]

+οὖν (conj.) — so now, therefore, then, in fact, at all events (inferential: marks transition to a new thought: S #2964; GP 426)

τοῖϲ +*πεπραγμένοιϲ — (πράϲϲω, pf. pass. ptc.) do (articular substant. ptc.: S #2052; SS 257–58 §9; GMT #825. Dat. of cause/ reason: S #1517; SS 89 §17); > 'by what was done'

δύcθυμοc· εἰ δὲ coì δοκῶ φρονεῖν κακῶc,   **550**
γνώμην δικαίαν cχοῦcα τοὺc πέλαc ψέγε.

ΗΛ.   ἐρεῖc μὲν οὐχὶ νῦν γέ μ' ὡc ἄρξαcά τι
λυπηρὸν εἶτα coῦ τάδ' ἐξήκουc' ὕπο·
ἀλλ' ἥν ἐφῇc μοι, τοῦ τεθνηκότοc θ' ὕπερ
λέξαιμ' ἄν ὀρθῶc τῆc καcιγνήτηc θ' ὁμοῦ.   **555**

ΚΛ.   καὶ μὴν ἐφίημ'· εἰ δέ μ' ὧδ' ἀεὶ λόγουc
ἐξῆρχεc, οὐκ ἂν ἦcθα λυπηρὰ κλύειν.

ΗΛ.   καὶ δὴ λέγω coι. πατέρα φῄc κτεῖναι. τίc ἄν

LINE 550

δύc-θυμος, ον
(δυσ-, ⁺*θῦμος) dispirited, anxious, disaffected (emphatic *enjambment*); > So, for my part *I am not upset* because of/by what was done'

⁺*cχοῦσα
(ἔχω, aor.² pass. ptc.) temporal ptc. (SS 252–53 §4; GMT §833)

τοὺς ⁺πέλας
'those near by'; substantival use of article with an adverb (S #1153e)

ψέγω
blame, <u>find fault with</u>; > 'acquire (after having acquired) a just perception [then] find fault with those around you')

LINE 552

⁺ἐρεῖς ... μ'
'This time you shall not say about me'

⁺ὡς (conj.)
that ('subjective' use introducing indirect discourse after negated vb.: SS 314 §1)

⁺*ἄρξασα
(ἄρχω, aor.¹ act. ptc.) Kells: "legalistic, since Greek law laid guilt on anyone who *began* a dispute"

λῡπηρός (3)
(⁺λύπη [ῡ]) painful, distressing; [1× *El.*]

ἐξ-⁺*ακούω
(aor.¹ act.) give an ear to + acc.; > 'that I have started something hurtful, before (εἶτα) I heard such things (the same kind of things, i.e., hurtful) from you'; [1× *El.*]

⁺ἐφ-*ίη-μι
(ἐφῇς, aor.² subjv. act.) metaphorically: permit, allow (mixed condition: ἥν [ἐάν] with subjv. in protasis and potential opt., λέξαιμ ἄν, in apodosis. The latter implies a softened expression of the fut. indic.: GMT #505); > 'but *if you permit, I should like to speak* truthfully on behalf of the dead man and my sister as well (ὁμοῦ)'

⁺ὀρθῶς (adv.)
⁺(ὀρθός, straight) rightly, <u>truthfully</u>, justly

⁺ὁμοῦ (adv.)
(neut. genit. of ὁμός, joint) together, at once

LINE 556

ἐξ-⁺*άρχω
begin (the verb has an internal object, λόγους, and an external object μέ: S #1619–20; SS 37 §5. In a contrary-to-fact condition, it is sometimes difficult to decide if the impf. denotes present or past time: SS 280 §3a; GMT #410, 412); > 'If *you had always begun* your speeches to me in such a manner you would have not be hurtful to listen to'; [1× Soph.]

⁺κλύειν
limiting (explanatory) infinitive with adjective (SS 239 §3b)

πατέρα
resolution in 6th position: πᾰτέρᾰ.

⁺*φῄς ⁺*κτεῖναι
indirect discourse, same subject for main verb and inf. (S #1982): '*you* say that *you* killed'

ἄν ... ⁺*γένοιτ' ἄν
(γίγνομαι, aor.² opt.) potential optative. The doubling of ἄν has no syntactical significance, but semantically it can emphasize the words with which the ἄν is joined (GMT #223), here possibly the disgrace of Clyt's utterance. Cf. ὥcτ' ἄν, εἰ ... δηλώσαιμ' ἄν 333n

τούτου λόγος γένοιτ' ἂν αἰςχίων ἔτι,
εἴτ' οὖν δικαίως εἴτε μή; λέξω δέ coι,   560
ὡς οὐ δίκῃ γ' ἔκτεινας, ἀλλά c' ἔcπαcεν
πειθὼ κακοῦ πρὸς ἀνδρός, ᾧ τανῦν ξύνει.
ἐροῦ δὲ τὴν κυναγὸν Ἄρτεμιν τίνος
ποινὰς τὰ πολλὰ πνεύματ' ἔcχ' ἐν Αὐλίδι·
ἢ 'γὼ φράcω· κείνης γὰρ οὐ θέμις μαθεῖν.   565
πατήρ ποθ' οὑμός, ὡς ἐγὼ κλύω, θεᾶς
παίζων κατ' ἄλcος ἐξεκίνηςεν ποδοῖν
cτικτὸν κεράcτην ἔλαφον, οὗ κατὰ cφαγὰς

LINE 559

⁺εἴ-τε οὖν … εἴ-τε	whether … or ; > 'whether you [did it] justly or not'
cπάω, ἔcπᾰcα	draw, drag aside, pervert; [1× in *El.*]
πειθώ, οῦς, ἡ	persuasion, <u>influence</u>; > 'but the influence of the wicked man with whom you are living now, lured you on'; [1× in *El.*]

LINE 563

ἔρομαι, ἠρόμην	(ἐροῦ, aor.² impv. dep. 2sg.) ask, inquire; [1× *El.*]
κῠν-ᾱγός (2)	dog-leading; <u>hunter</u>; [1× Soph.]
⁺Ἄρτεμις, ιδος, ἡ	Artemis (hunting is among her functions)
ποινή, ἡ	price paid, satisfaction, <u>penalty</u> (τινός objective genit.: SS 53, S #1328); > 'as a penalty for what'; [1× Soph.]
πνεῦμα, ατος, τό	wind; [1× in *El.*]
Αὔλις, ιδος, ἡ	port town in Boeotia, where the Greek fleet gathered to set off for Troy; [1× Soph.]
'γώ	= ἐγώ; aphaeresis.
κείνης	= ⁺ἐκείνης; genit. of source after verbs of learning (S #1361, SS 66–67 §28); > 'for from her it is forbidden to learn'
⁺θέμις [ἐστί]	'it is right'

LINE 566

οὑμός	= ὁ ἐμός
παίζω	make sport (contemporary pres. ptc. sets the context: SS 210 §33); [1× Soph.]
ἄλcος, εος, τό	grove; especially a sacred grove; > 'when he was having sport in a sacred grove of the goddess'
ἐκ-κῑνέω, -ηκίνησα	move out: out up, <u>rouse</u>; [1× *El.*]
⁺πούς, ποδός, ὁ	foot (Soph. usually uses dual when metrically convenient, but here ποcί would have been also been metrically suitable: S #999; SS 2 §2)
cτικτός (3)	(cτίζω, make a mark, brand) marked, spotted, dappled; [1 × in *El.*]
κεραcτής, οῦ, ὁ	(κέρας, τό, horn) horned; [1× *El.*]
ἔλᾰφος, ὁ/ἡ	deer, stag/hind (resolution in 6th position; [1× *El.*]
cφαγή, ἡ	(cφάζω, slay, kill) slaughter, killing (generalizing plural (SS 7 §4b)

ἐκκομπάσας ἔπος τι τυγχάνει βαλών.
κἀκ τοῦδε μηνίσασα Λητῷα κόρη   570
κατεῖχ' Ἀχαιούς, ἕως πατὴρ ἀντίσταθμον
τοῦ θηρὸς ἐκθύσειε τὴν αὑτοῦ κόρην.
ὧδ' ἦν τὰ κείνης θύματ'· οὐ γὰρ ἦν λύσις
ἄλλη στρατῷ πρὸς οἶκον οὐδ' εἰς Ἴλιον.
ἀνθ' ὧν βιασθεὶς πολλά τ' ἀντιβὰς μόλις   575
ἔθυσεν αὐτήν, οὐχὶ Μενέλεω χάριν.

LINE 569

ἐκ-κομπάζω | +κατά τι (aor.[1] ptc. act.) boast loudly; [1× Soph.]

+*τυγχάνει | historical present for vividness, standing mostly for narrative aorist (with supplem. ptc. ἐκκομπάσας: S #1883; SS 186 §5; GMT #33. When an aorist ptc. is used with τυγχάνω, λαγχάνω or φθάνω in present or imperfect indicative, it is *not* coincidental with the finite verb but retains its own reference to past time: S #2096b, GMT #146; SS 261 §12f); > 'about whose killing (οὗ κατὰ σφαγάς) he (*happened to have slipped*) *slipped* some boastful word after hitting (βαλών) it'

*βάλλω, ἔβαλον | (βαλών, aor.[2] ptc. act.) throw, cast, hurl in, <u>strike, hit</u>; [1× El.]

μηνίω | (μηνίσασα, aor.[1] ptc. act.) (μῆνις, wrath) be wroth against; [1× El.]

Λητῷος (3) | born of Leto (Λητώ), the mother of Artemis and Apollo; [1× in Soph.]

Ἀχαιός (3) | Achaean

ἕως (conj.) | as long as, until (referring to coextensive actions: S #2383 C)

ἀντί-σταθμος, ον | (ἀντί, στάθμή carpenter's line) counterposing, balancing; metaphorically: in compensation for; [1× in extant Tragedy]

LINE 572

θήρ, θηρός, ὁ | wild beast (genit. after compound adjs., ἀντίσταθμον: SS 54 §7); [1× El.]

ἐκ-*θύω | [ῡ] (ἐκθύσειε, aor.[1] opt. act.) <u>sacrifice</u> (the compd. vb. is used in the same sense as the simple vb; see ἐκφοβουμένη 276n, ἐξαπώλεσας 588n. After a secondary tense, κατεῖχε, ἕως with aor. opt. in temporal clause may imply a purpose, the attainment of which is aimed or expected by the subject of the main vb.: S #2418, 2420; GMT #614.1); > 'She detained the Achaeans, *until the time when* in requital for the beast my father *sacrificed* his own (αὑτοῦ = ἑαυτοῦ) daughter.'

θῦμα, ατος, τό | (+*θύω, sacrifice) sacrifice (the plural might indicate the occurrences behind the act: SS 4–6 §3); > 'This is how she came to be sacrificed'

λύσις, εως, ἡ | [ῠ] (λύω, loosen) release; [1× El.]

Ἴλιος, ου, ἡ | [ῑλ] the city of Ilus (mythic founder of Troy), Troy; [1× El.]

LINE 575

+ἀντί (+ genit.) | in return for, in retribution for; ἀνθ' ὧν 'in exchange for these things' = 'wherefore,' 'because of' (SS 99 §4, 303 §1)

βιάζω | (βιασθείς, aor.[1] pass. ptc.) constrain; pass.: be hard pressed; [1× El.]

+πολλά | adverbial acc.: greatly, much (Kells sees it as *apokoinou*, here with both participles βιασθείς and ἀντιβάς: 'after being *hard* pressed and resisting *mightily*'

εἰ δ' οὖν, ἐρῶ γὰρ καὶ τὸ cόν, κεῖνον θέλων
ἐπωφελῆcαι ταῦτ' ἔδρα, τούτου θανεῖν
χρῆν αὐτὸν οὕνεκ' ἐκ cέθεν; ποίῳ νόμῳ;
ὅρα τιθεῖcα τόνδε τὸν νόμον βροτοῖc   580
μὴ πῆμα cαυτῇ καὶ μετάγνοιαν τίθηc.
εἰ γὰρ κτενοῦμεν ἄλλον ἀντ' ἄλλου, cύ τοι
πρώτη θάνοιc ἄν, εἰ δίκηc γε τυγχάνοιc.
ἀλλ' εἰcόρα μὴ cκῆψιν οὐκ οὖcαν τίθηc.

ἀντι-⁺*βαίνω	(ἀντιβάς, aor.² act. pct.) go against, withstand, <u>resist</u>; [1× Soph.]
⁺μόλἲς (adv.)	<u>with difficulty</u>, hardly, scarcely
⁺χάριν	+ genit.; > 'For which reason he sacrificed her after being hard pressed and resisting mightily, not *for sake of* Menelaus'
⁺εἰ δ' οὖν	GP 465: "particularly used when a speaker hypothetically grants a supposition which he denies, doubts, or reprobates"; > 'but if so-and-so *did* happen'
τὸ cόν	'for I will state *your claim*,' referring to 537–45

LINE 578

ἐπ-ωφελέω	(aor.¹ act. inf.) help, succor; > 'he did (ἔδρα) this wishing to *help* him
τούτου . . . ⁺οὕνεκα	emphatic *hyperbaton* for Clyt.'s reason; χρῆν = χρὴ ἦν
⁺ἐκ ⁺cέθεν	= ὑπὸ cοῦ (see κἀκ 264n); > 'was that a reason he had to die *by your hand?*'
⁺νόμος, ὁ	(νέμω, assign) custom, convention, law; > 'according to what law?'
⁺*τίθημι	(pres. act. ptc.) put, <u>establish</u>; τιθεῖcα . . . τίθηc enforcing rhetorical repetition.
μὴ . . . ⁺*τίθηc	emphatic *hyperbaton*; μή with pres. indic. after a verb of caution (ὅρα) expresses a danger that is very actual in the present (GMT #369); > 'see that in making this rule, *you are not establishing* suffering and remorse for yourself'
μετά-γνοιᾰ, ἡ	repentance, remorse; [1× Soph.]

LINE 582

εἰ . . . *θάνοῖς ἄν	mixed condition: fut. indic. in protasis and potential opt., in apodosis not as a softened future (GMT #505), but in a potential sense (Jebb) > 'if we kill . . . then you would be the first to die'
εἰ . . . *τυγχάνοις	second protasis in opt. with preceding apodosis with potential opt. to describe "an ideal or imaginary case which is proposed for the sake of argument, and the interest of drawing conclusion from it in the [preceding] apodosis" (SS 279d, §1), as such it creates a future less vivid condition (S #2297, 2329; GMT #392.2); > 'if you should meet with justice'
cκῆψις, εως, ἡ	(cκήπτω, defend oneself) pretext, excuse; legally: plea; [1× Soph.]
οὐκ οὖcαν	'unreal,' 'false'; > 'Be very careful not to put forth a false excuse'

εἰ γὰρ θέλεις, δίδαξον ἀνθ' ὅτου τανῦν   **585**
αἴσχιστα πάντων ἔργα δρῶσα τυγχάνεις,
ἥτις ξυνεύδεις τῷ παλαμναίῳ, μεθ' οὗ
πατέρα τὸν ἁμὸν πρόσθεν ἐξαπώλεσας,
καὶ παιδοποιεῖς, τοὺς δὲ πρόσθεν εὐσεβεῖς
κἀξ εὐσεβῶν βλαστόντας ἐκβαλοῦσ' ἔχεις.   **590**

LINE 585

ἀνθ' ὅτου	wherefore, for what reason (S #1683.2)
αἴσχιστος (3)	(superlative of ⁺αἰσχρός) most shameful, disgraceful
⁺*δρῶσα τυγχάνεις	τυγχάνω with supplem. ptc., δρῶσα, which tells what the main action is, while the main vb. tells something about how the action is occurring (S #2096a; GMT #887; SS 261 §12f); > 'Explain to me, if you will, for what reason you are right now (τανῦν) committing the most disgraceful acts of all (πάντων, partit. genit.)'
⁺ἥτις	indefinite/general relative pron., here marking the character and quality of a person (S #2496); > 'you who'
ξυν-εύδω	sleep with; [1× in *El.*]
παλαμναῖος, ὁ	(πᾰλάμη, palm of the hand, hand) murderer; [1× *El.*]
ἁμός (3)	[ᾱ] in Attic poetic for ἐμός (S #330D, 1)
ἐξ-απ-⁺*όλλυμι	(ἐξαπώλεσας, aor.¹ indic. act.) destroy utterly (Kells: "the compound verb used . . . not intensively, but in the same sense as the simple verb"; see ἐκφοβουμένη 276n, ἐκθύσειε 572n); [1× *El.*]

LINE 589

παιδο-ποιέω	(παῖς, ποιέω) bear children; [1× *El.*]
τοὺς . . . ⁺πρόσθεν	(sc. παῖδας) substantival use of article (S #1153e); > 'but your earlier lawful [children] born of lawful marriage you cast out'
εὐσεβής, ές	pious, hallowed, <u>legitimate</u> (εὐσεβεῖς . . . εὐσεβῶν *polyptoton.* Such wordplay was highly appreciated); [1× *El.*]
⁺ἐκ-*βάλλω	(ἐκβαλοῦσα, aor.² ptc.) throw out, cast out (ἐκ-βαλοῦσ' ἔχεις—⁺*ἔχω as an auxiliary verb with aorist participle yields a "transitive, resultative perfect": SS 206 §29d, which emphasizes the present existence of the result. Characteristic usage of Soph.)

πῶς ταῦτ' ἐπαινέσαιμ' ἄν; ἢ καὶ ταῦτ' ἐρεῖς
ὡς τῆς θυγατρὸς ἀντίποινα λαμβάνεις;
αἰσχρῶς δ', ἐάν περ καὶ λέγῃς. οὐ γὰρ καλὸν
ἐχθροῖς γαμεῖσθαι τῆς θυγατρὸς οὕνεκα.
ἀλλ' οὐ γὰρ οὐδὲ νουθετεῖν ἔξεστί σε,   595
ἢ πᾶσαν ἵῃς γλῶσσαν ὡς τὴν μητέρα
κακοστομοῦμεν. καί σ' ἔγωγε δεσπότιν
ἢ μητέρ' οὐκ ἔλασσον εἰς ἡμᾶς νέμω,

LINE 591

⁺ἐπ-*αινέω	(ἐπαινέσαιμι, aor.¹ act. opt.) αἰνέω keeps a short vowel in the aorist and future (S #488b). Potential optative with ἄν (GMT #236, S #1824); > 'How can I praise these things?'
θυγάτηρ, θυγατρός, ἡ	daughter; [1× *El.*]
ἀντί-ποινα, τά	(ἀντί- ποινος, ον, in requital) requital, retribution; > 'Or will you say that in this too you are taking as retaliation for your daughter?'; [1× *El.*]
ἐάν . . . λέγῃς	the protasis ἐάν + subjv. expresses a general present supposition (GMT #394–95, a); ⁺περ see 386n; > 'if you *do* (καί) in fact (περ) say it'
⁺ἐχθροῖς	substantival use of adj. without the article (SS 163 §1) and generalizing plural (SS 7 §2b) > 'it is not honorable to mate *with enemies*.' El. scrutinizes Clyt.'s conduct in terms of a general maxim.
γᾰμέω	in mid. = give oneself in marriage; [1× *El.*]

LINE 595

νουθετέω	(⁺νοῦς, ⁺*τίθημι) bring to mind, warn, admonish, advise
⁺ἔξεστι	(ἐξ-⁺*ειμι) it is possible, in one's power (with inf. νουθετεῖν as subject: S #1984–1985); > 'for it is not possible to admonish you'
*ἵημι	(ἵῃς, pres. act. 2sg) send away, dismiss, let go; [1× *El.*]
γλῶσσα, ἡ	tongue
κακο-στομέω	(κακός, στόμα) speak evil of; > '(lit.: you send your whole tongue) i.e., you raise every manner of outcry *that I speak evil* of my mother'; [1× Soph.]
καί	'and indeed'
δεσπότις, ιδος, ἡ	= δέσποινα, mistress; [1× in *El.*]
ἐλάσσον	(< ἐλάσσων, ον, comparative of ⁺μικρός); in a lesser degree (neuter as adv.)
ἡμᾶς	'indeed I consider you (lit.: a tyrant no less than a mother =) more a tyrant than a mother toward *us*' (unclear whether referring to Electra alone or to both Electra and Orestes)

ἢ ζῶ βίον μοχθηρόν, ἔκ τε coῦ κακοῖc
πολλοῖc ἀεὶ ξυνοῦca τοῦ τε cυννόμου.   600
ὁ δ' ἄλλος ἔξω, χεῖρα cὴν μόλιc φυγών,
τλήμων Ὀρέcτηc δυcτυχῆ τρίβει βίον·
ὃν πολλὰ δή μέ coι τρέφειν μιάcτορα
ἐπῃτιάcω· καὶ τόδ', εἴπερ ἔcθενον,
ἔδρων ἄν, εὖ τοῦτ' ἴcθι. τοῦδέ γ' οὕνεκα   605
κήρυccέ μ' εἰc ἅπανταc, εἴτε χρῇc κακὴν

LINE 599

+*ζάω	meaning enables only internal object: βίον μοχθηρόν (SS 34–35 §2)
μοχθηρός (3/2)	suffering hardship, in sore distress, wretched; [1× Soph.]
cύν-νομος, ἡ/ὁ	(+cυν, **νέμω) partnermate, <u>paramour</u> (ἐκ τε cοῦ . . . [ἐκ] τοῦ τε cυννόμου); > 'with many miseries that come from you and your paramour'; [1× El.]
ὁ δ 'ἄλλος	'and that other one' (i.e., of your children, a male one, i.e., Orestes)
ἔξω (adv.)	(ἐξ) outside
+*φεύγω	(φυγών, aor.² act. ptc.) flee, run away; > 'having barely escaped'
+δυc-τυχής, ές	(δυc-, τύχη) unlucky, unfortunate
τρίβω	rub away; τρίβειν βίον wear away life; [1× Soph.]

LINE 603

μῐάcτωρ, οροc, ὁ	(μῐαίνω, defile, pollute) polluter, avenger (cοι dat. of disadvantage: SS 84–85 §9); > ; 'as an avenger *to you* (= your avenger)'
ἐπ-αιτιάομαι	(ἐπῃτιάcω, aor.¹ indic. dep. 2nd sg;) bring a charge against one, <u>accuse</u> (requires με . . . τρέφειν as acc. and inf.; emphatic *enjambment*); > 'many times *you have accused* me that *that I brought* him *up* (ὅν) as your (cοι) avenger'
καί	'and indeed')
+cθένω	<u>have power</u>, be strong (εἴπερ ἔcθενον ἔδρων ἄν 'if I had had the power I would have done this'; contrary-to-fact condition, the impf. sometimes can refer to past time: SS 280 §3a; S #2304; GMT #410)
κηρύccω	proclaim, announce
χράω	eager for (LSJ AIII) (χρῇc 2 sg. pres. indic. = χρήζειc 'you wish.' Contracts to -η- instead of -α-: S #395. The rare use of the verb in this meaning must have caused the mss corruption to χρή); [1× El.]

εἴτε cτόμαργον εἴτ' ἀναιδείας πλέαν.
εἰ γὰρ πέφυκα τῶνδε τῶν ἔργων ἴδρις,
cχεδόν τι τὴν cὴν οὐ καταιcχύνω φύcιν.

XO.   * * * * *

ὁρῶ μένοc πνέουcαν· εἰ δὲ cὺν δίκῃ   610
ξύνεcτι, τοῦδε φροντίδ' οὐκέτ' εἰcορῶ.

ΚΛ.   ποίαc δ' ἐμοὶ δεῖ πρόc γε τήνδε φροντίδοc,
ἥτιc τοιαῦτα τὴν τεκοῦcαν ὕβριcεν,
καὶ ταῦτα τηλικοῦτοc; ἆρά cοι δοκεῖ
χωρεῖν ἂν ἐc πᾶν ἔργον αἰcχύνηc ἄτερ;   615

ΚΛ.   εὖ νυν ἐπίcτω τῶνδέ μ' αἰcχύνην ἔχειν,   .

LINE 607

cτομαργόc, ον — noisily prating, loud mouthed; [1× Soph.]

πλέοc, α, ον — + genit., ἀναιδείαc: full, filled

ἀναίδεια, ἡ — shamelessness; > 'proclaim to all, if you wish, that I am bad, or strident, or *full of shamelessness*'; [1× Soph.]

⁺*πέφυκα — (φύω, pf. act.) πέφυκα ... φύcιν wordplay, a pun (Kells), *figura etymologica*. > 'For *if by nature* I am accomplished in any of these deeds (τῶνδε τῶν ἔργων)'

ἴδριc, εωc, ὁ/ἡ — (οἶδα); + genit.; experienced in, knowing, skillful, <u>accomplished</u>; [1× *El.*]

cχέδον (adv.) — (ἔχω, cχεῖν) perhaps (cχέδον τι 'perhaps in some way'; 'almost'); [1× *El.*]

κατ-⁺*αιcχύνω — shame, disgrace, dishonor; [1× *El.*]

LINE 610

μένοc, εοc, τό — force, strength; ardor, <u>fury</u>; [1× *El.*]

πνέω — breathe; [1× *El.*]

φροντίc, ίδοc — (φρονέω, think) thought, care, consideration (⁺ποίαc ... φροντίδοc, *hyperbaton* framing the line); > 'but whether she has justice on her side, I no longer see her giving any thought to this'

⁺*δεῖ — it is necessary (quasi-impersonal verb, i.e., its subject may be derived from the context: S #933b. δεῖ μοι τινοc "I have need of something": S #1400); > 'what sort of consideration must I have for her ... ?'

τοιαῦτα — (⁺τοιοῦτοc, τοιαύτη, τοιοῦτο) such (usually refers to what precedes: S #333e, 1245. Adverbial accusative 'in such a way' 'so')

⁺ὑβρίζω — outrage, insult, maltreat

LINE 614

καὶ ταῦτα — 'and that'; SS 157 §24: "she who has so abused her mother, *and that too* at such an age as she is"

τηλικοῦτοc, -αύτη or -οῦτοc, -οῦτο — of such an age (SS 13 §8); [1× *El.*)

⁺ἆρα — according to context here it stands for ἆρ' οὐ = '*don't* you think?' (Kells)

⁺χωρεῖν ⁺πρὸc ⁺ἔργον — come to action (χωρεῖν ἂν = ὅτι χωροίη ἄν); > 'don't you think that she would proceed to any deed without shame?' Clyt. talks 'at' El., not to her, although El. addresses her mother directly.

αἰcχύνη, ἡ — (ῡ) shame, disgrace, dishonor

ἄτερ (+ genit.) — without, except, besides (usually postpositive improper prep.: S #1647, 1700)

κεἰ μὴ δοκῶ cοι· μανθάνω δ' ὁθούνεκα
ἔξωρα πράccω κοὐκ ἐμοὶ προcεικότα.
ἀλλ' ἡ γὰρ ἐκ cοῦ δυcμένεια καὶ τὰ cὰ
ἔργ' ἐξαναγκάζει με ταῦτα δρᾶν βίᾳ·   **620**
αἰcχροῖc γὰρ αἰcχρὰ πράγματ' ἐκδιδάcκεται.

ΚΛ.   ὦ θρέμμ' ἀναιδέc, ἦ c' ἐγὼ καὶ τἄμ' ἔπη
καὶ τἄργα τἀμὰ πόλλ' ἄγαν λέγειν ποεῖ.

LINE 617

⁺ἐπίστω   = ἐπίστασο, pres. impv. dep. 2sg.

μ' ... ἔχειν   acc. and inf. after a verb of *knowing*, ἐπίστω (SS 317 §4; GMT 915.2b); > 'Do know that I (have) feel shame for this (τῶνδε objective genit.: S #1328; SS 53 §4)'

κεἰ   = καὶ εἰ 'even if' opens concessive condition (S #2369–72, SS 282–83 §5)

ἔξ-ωροc, ον   (ὥρα, season) untimely, out of season, <u>unfitting</u>; [1× Soph.]

προc-⁺έοικα   (προcεικότα, pf. act. ptc. acc. pl. neut.) be like, seem fit (pf. with pres. sense); > 'And I know that (ὁθούνεκα = ὅτι) my behavior is unfitting (ἔξωρα πράccω) and (*unlike me =) contrary to my nature*'; [1× El.]

ἀλλ' ... γάρ   GP 101: "'but, as a matter of fact,' is the meaning in the great majority of cases ... The sense conveyed is that what precedes is irrelevant, unimportant, or subsidiary, and is consequently to be ruled out of discussion...." Kells: "But (I cannot help myself) for ..."

δυc-μένεια, ἡ   (δυc-, μένος) ill will, enmity (ἐκ cοῦ points to actual activity on Clyt.'s part and hence more emphatic than ἡ cὴ δυc-μένεια); > 'the enmity that comes *from you*'

LINE 620

ἐξ-ἀναγκάζω   force, compel utterly; [1× El.]

αἰcχροῖc ... αἰcχρά   *polyptotpon*, although here αἰcχρά accompanies πράγματα.

ἐκ-⁺*διδάcκω   teach thoroughly

θρέμμα, ατος, τό   (τρέφω, nourish) nursling, <u>creature</u> (here as a term of reproach); [1× El.]

ἀν-αίδηc, εc   (ἀ privat., αἰδώc, shame) shameless; [1× El.]

⁺ἦ   in truth, in sooth, verily (asseverative prepositive pcl.: S #2866); > 'Truly, I and my words and my deeds make you say (cέ ... λέγειν) too much'

τἄμ', τἄργα, τἀμά   = τὰ ἐμά, τά ἔργα, τὰ ἐμά

HΛ.   σὺ τοι λέγεις νιν, οὐκ ἐγώ. σὺ γὰρ ποεῖς
      τοὔργον· τὰ δ' ἔργα τοὺς λόγους εὑρίσκεται.   625

KΛ.   ἀλλ' οὐ μὰ τὴν δέσποιναν Ἄρτεμιν θράσους
      τοῦδ' οὐκ ἀλύξεις, εὖτ' ἂν Αἴγισθος μόλη.

HΛ.   ὁρᾷς; πρὸς ὀργὴν ἐκφέρῃ, μεθεῖσά με
      λέγειν ἃ χρῄζοιμ', οὐδ' ἐπίστασαι κλύειν.

KΛ.   οὔκουν ἐάσεις οὐδ' ὑπ' εὐφήμου βοῆς   630
      θῦσαί μ', ἐπειδὴ σοί γ' ἐφῆκα πᾶν λέγειν;

HΛ.   ἐῶ, κελεύω, θῦε, μηδ' ἐπαιτιῶ
      τοὐμὸν στόμ'· ὡς οὐκ ἂν πέρα λέξαιμ' ἔτι.

LINE 624

νιν
: (= αὐτά; enclitic 3rd pers. pron.) the plural is rare; here refers to everything Clyt. has said.

μά
: [ă] asseverative adv. + acc. of the deity or thing appealed to. Neither affirmative nor negative by itself (LSJ; S #2894); > 'Now, by the mistress Artemis.' Elsewhere in Tragedy only unmarried girls invoke Artemis.

⁺θράσος, εος, τό
: = ⁺θάρσος; courage, confidence, <u>overboldness, rashness, insolence</u>

ἀλύσκω
: [ă] shun, avoid, escape (with genit. of cause, τοῦδε. SS 68 §30: "you will not go scot-free because of this [yours] boldness"; cf. Jebb, Campbell); [1× *El.*]

εὖτε (adv.)
: when, at the time when, since, seeing that (poetic for ὅτε. εὖτ' ἄν = ὅταν, opens temporal clause referring indefinitely to the future: S #2399, 1768; SS 294 §4. Here with aorist subjv., ⁺*μόλη, for a single occurrence); > 'when Aeg. comes'

LINE 628

ἐκ-⁺*φέρω
: (ἐκφέρῃ, pres. pass.) pass.: being carried away beyond bounds (LSJ 3); > 'You see? You are carried away onto anger'

⁺χρῄζω
: (χρῄζοιμι, opt. pres. act.) desire, like, wish (opt. depending on μεθεῖσα < μεθίημι, aor.² act. ptc.; the opt. reflects ἄν + subjv. of the direct speech in which Clyt. is imagined to have said, 'I grant you permission to say ἃ ἂν χρῄζῃς: 'whatever you like'); > 'after having set me free to say, *whatever I liked*'

⁺οὔκουν (adv.)
: (= οὐκ οὖν) and so not? not therefore? not then? (often with 2nd pers. fut. indic., or opt. with ἄν, at an opening of a speech: GP 431); > 'won't you let me [⁺*ἐάσεις] then . . . ?'

οὐδέ . . . ⁺*θῦσαι
: οὐδέ reinforces οὔκουν

εὔ-φημος, ον
: (⁺εὔ, ⁺φήμη) abstaining from inauspicious words (i.e., religiously silent)

⁺βοή, ἡ
: cry, shout, outcry; > 'in silent clamor,' i.e., 'in silence'

LINE 632

κελεύω
: bid, command (ἐῶ, κελεύω, θῦε in *asyndeton*: S #2165, 3016)

θῦε
: pres. impv. indicates an action that is to be begun and continued, or just continued. SS 217 §5: "you can proceed with the offering."

ἐπ-αιτιάομαι
: (ἐπαιτιῶ= ἐπαιτιάου; impv. pres. dep. 2sg).; blame; > 'do not blame'

στόμα, τος, τό
: mouth, speech, words, language

πέρα (adv.)
: beyond measure, excessively

ἄν . . . λέξαιμι
: potential opt. in 1st pers. pointing to the fut. indicating intention with some reserve or reluctance (SS 230–31 §14); > 'for I will say no more'

ΚΛ.	ἔπαιρε δὴ σὺ θύμαθ᾽ ἡ παροῦσά μοι

	πάγκαρπ᾽, ἄνακτι τῷδ᾽ ὅπως λυτηρίους	635

	εὐχὰς ἀνάσχω δειμάτων, ἃ νῦν ἔχω.

	κλύοις ἂν ἤδη, Φοῖβε προστατήριε,

	κεκρυμμένην μου βάξιν. οὐ γὰρ ἐν φίλοις

	ὁ μῦθος, οὐδὲ πᾶν ἀναπτύξαι πρέπει

	πρὸς φῶς παρούσης τῆσδε πλησίας ἐμοί,	640

LINE 634

ἐπ-αίρω
    lift, raise (Clyt. walks away from El. toward the statue of Apollo, turns here to the maidservant, who holds the fruit offerings, and turns back to Apollo); [1× *El.*]

θῦμα, ατος, τό
    (⁺*θύω, sacrifice) offering, sacrifice

ἡ ⁺παρ-⁎⁎οῦσα
    (πάρειμι, pres. ptc. act. fem. sg.) SS 25 §5: "The articular use of the nominative of a noun [here substantive participle, in apposition to σύ] in address generally occurs in speech to inferiors."; > 'you who are with me'

πάν-καρπος, ον
    of all kinds of fruit (θύματα . . . πάγκαρπα), *hyperbaton* and *enjambment* for emphasis; [1× *El.*]

⁺ἄναξ, ακτος, ὁ
    lord, king; here Apollo

ἀν-⁎⁎έχω
    (ἀνάσχω, aor.² subjv.) offer prayers (perhaps with uplifted hands. Subjv. in final clause may or may not have ἄν without affecting meaning, in primary sequence, ἔπαιρε: SS 284–86 §1–3; S #2193). Impv. moods count as primary because they point to the future: S #2196, 1858a)

εὐχή, ἡ
    (εὔχομαι, pray) <u>prayer</u>, vow; [1× *El.*]

δεῖμα, ατος, τό
    (δείδω, be afraid) fear, terror; > 'so that (⁺ὅπως) I offer up prayers for release from the fears I now (have) suffer'

LINE 637

⁺κλύω
    κλύοις ἄν, 2nd pers. potential opt. + ἄν can have a force of exhortation or a respectful form of a wish (GMT §237; SS 231§14); > 'please hear me now'

Φοῖβος, ὁ
    epithet of Apollo; (as adj.) pure, bright, radiant, beaming

προστᾰτήριος, ον
    (προ-ἵσταμαι, stand before) protecting, guarding

βάξις, εως, ἡ
    (βάζω, speak) saying, report, announcement; > 'my secret words'

ἀνα-πτύσσω
    (ἀναπτύξαι, aor.¹ act. inf.) unfold, disclose; [1× *El.*]

πρέπω
    fit, be proper (mostly impersonal. '<u>It is proper</u>' both of outward circumstances and moral fitness)

πλήσιος (3)
    (πέλας, near, close) near, hard by, close to

⁺παρ-⁎⁎ούσης ⁺τῆσδε πλησίας
    genit. absolute expressing attending circumstances (S #2058, 2070e; SS 76–77 §42); > 'with her present/standing beside me'

μὴ cὺν φθόνῳ τε καὶ πολυγλώccῳ βοῇ
cπείρῃ ματαίαν βάξιν εἰc πᾶcαν πόλιν.
ἀλλ' ὧδ' ἄκουε· τῇδε γὰρ κἀγὼ φράcω.
ἃ γὰρ προcεῖδον νυκτὶ τῇδε φάcματα
διccῶν ὀνείρων, ταῦτά μοι, Λύκει' ἄναξ,   645
εἰ μὲν πέφηνεν ἐcθλά, δὸc τελεcφόρα,
εἰ δ' ἐχθρά, τοῖc ἐχθροῖciν ἔμπαλιν μέθεc·

LINE 641

φθόνος, ὁ — ill will, envy, jealousy, <u>grudge, malice</u>

πολύ-γλωσσος, ον — (πολύς, γλῶσσα) many tongued, loud voiced, often repeated

*σπείρω, ἔσπειρα — (σπείρῃ, aor.¹ subjv.) sow; engender, beget (μὴ . . . σπείρῃ—μή introduces a fear clause with subjv. after primary tense, πρέπει: S # 2221; SS 227 §12.iv; GMT #365); > 'lest with her malice and garrulous tongue *she spread* vain rumor all over the city'

μάταιος (3/2) — [ᾰ] (μάτη, folly, fault) foolish, <u>vain</u>, idle, trifling, thoughtless

ὧδε . . . τῇδε — 'But listen to me <u>like this</u>, for <u>in this way</u> I too (for my part) will speak,' i.e., cryptically

⁺*ἄκουε — (pres. impv.) In Soph. aorist imperative is much more common in prayers than the present imperative. The latter is used when there is a close link between the request and the situation at hand, and when the action is required to begin at once and not left to the discretion of the addressee. The opposite is true of the aorist, i.e., the action is not expected to be performed at once. In an address of a human to a god, the present imperative is thus rare. It occurs in only four passages: two in *Ajax* (74, 844), and two in *El.* here and 792 (SS 218–19 §5).

LINE 644

ἃ — relative pronoun precedes the antecedent φάσματα, which is kept for the main clause (S #2541). The two frame the line. ⁺γάρ is explanatory: 'the fact is that'; see 32n

προσ-⁺*οράω — (προσεῖδον, aor.²) look at

⁺νυκτί — dat. of time. SS 88 §15: "I saw last night"; (S #1447, 1539–40)

δίσσος (3) — (δίς) twofold, double, of two kinds, <u>ambiguous</u>; [1× *El.*]

⁺*πέφηνεν — (φαίνω, pf. act.) > 'on the one hand, if they reveal good [tidings]'

⁺*δός — (δίδωμι, aor.² impv.); see ἄκουε 643n

τελεσ-φόρος, ον — able to fulfill, or accomplish; > 'grant their realization'; [1× *El.*]

⁺ἐχθρά . . . ἐχθροῖσιν — *polyptoton*, see 198n on δεινὰν δεινῶς.

ἔμπαλιν (adv.) — back, backward; .> 'make them rebound on my enemies'; [1× *El.*]

⁺μέθ-*ες — (μεθίημι, aor.² impv.), see ἄκουε 643n

καὶ μή με πλούτου τοῦ παρόντος εἴ τινες
δόλοισι βουλεύουσιν ἐκβαλεῖν, ἐφῇς,
ἀλλ' ὧδέ μ' αἰεὶ ζῶσαν ἀβλαβεῖ βίῳ
δόμους Ἀτρειδῶν σκῆπτρά τ' ἀμφέπειν τάδε,
φίλοισί τε ξυνοῦσαν οἷς ξύνειμι νῦν,
εὐημεροῦσαν καὶ τέκνων ὅσων ἐμοὶ
δύσνοια μὴ πρόσεστιν ἢ λύπη πικρά.

650

LINE 648

+πλοῦτος, ὁ	wealth, riches (genit. required by ἐκ-*βαλεῖν)
ἐκ-*βάλλω	(ἐκβαλεῖν, aor.² inf.) + genit.: throw out, cast out; > 'cast me out / rob me of the wealth')
μή . . . ἐφῇς; με . . . ἐκβαλεῖν	two long instances of *hyperbaton* in one sentence emphasizing her request
ἀλλ' ὧδέ μ'	*zeugma* (S #3048) in which the positive concept needs to be supplied out of the negative one, supply: ἐφῇς or δός; > 'do not allow . . ., but grant that. . . . Accusative and infinitive structure follows the imperative: μέ . . . +ζῶσαν . . . ἀμφέπειν; cf. ἀλλ' . . . 72n
ἀ-βλᾰβής, ές	(ἀ privat., βλάβη, harm) without harm (ἀβλαβεῖ +βίῳ dat. of accompanying circumstances that here parallels internal accusative, i.e., ἀβλαβῆ βίον: SS 91 §19); > 'that I forever live life unharmed' [1× *El.*]
+δόμος, ὁ	house (plural probably because of the notion of collection of rooms: SS 4§3)
Ἀτρείδης, ὁ	son of Atreus (–ιδης patronymic: S #845.4)
σκῆπτρον, τό	(σκήπτω, prop, support) a staff, scepter (τ' connects it to δόμους, whose plural it might be imitating, i.e., a 'sympathetic' plural: SS 7 §4)
ἀμφι-έπω	be busy about, look after; > 'but grant that I, living (+ζῶσαν) always as I am now in an unharmed way of life *looking after* the house of the Atreidae and this scepter (i.e., kingdom) . . .'; [1× *El.*]

LINE 652

+ξυν-+*οῦσαν	(σύνειμι, pres. act. ptc.) circumstantial ptc. ξυνοῦσα . . . ξύνειμι, *figura etymologica*. Here the use of a verb together with a cognate participle. > 'living with friends with whom I now live'
εὐ-ημερέω	spend one's days cheerfully; > 'enjoying my days with cheer'
+τέκνων	probably partit. genit., in which case an antecedent needs to be supplied: [τοσούτοις] τέκνων ὅσων. SS 57 §9: "in company with friends and [*those*] of my children who have [= from who there is] no enmity for me." It could also be the case of the inverse relative attraction in which τέκνοις assumes the case of ὅσων (S #2533).
δύσ-νοια, ἡ	ill will, malevolence; [1× Soph.]
πρός-+*ειμι	be there, be present; [1× *El.*]

ταῦτ᾽, ὦ Λύκει᾽ Ἄπολλον, ἵλεως κλυὼν   655
δὸς πᾶcιν ἡμῖν ὥcπερ ἐξαιτούμεθα.
τὰ δ᾽ ἄλλα πάντα καὶ cιωπώcηc ἐμοῦ
ἐπαξιῶ cε δαίμον᾽ ὄντ᾽ ἐξειδέναι·
τοὺc ἐκ Διὸc γὰρ εἰκόc ἐcτι πάνθ᾽ ὁρᾶν.

ΠΑ. ξέναι γυναῖκεc, πῶc ἂν εἰδείην cαφῶc   660
εἰ τοῦ τυράννου δώματ᾽ Αἰγίcθου τάδε;
ΧΟ. τάδ᾽ ἐcτίν, ὦ ξέν᾽· αὐτὸc ἤκαcαc καλῶc.
ΠΑ. ἦ καὶ δάμαρτα τήνδ᾽ ἐπεικάζων κυρῶ
κείνου; πρέπει γὰρ ὡc τύραννοc εἰcορᾶν.

LINE 655

ἵλεωc — propitious, gracious, kindly (declension S #289); resolution in 8th position: ἵλεωc.

+κλυών — According to West (1984:174–75), it is aor.² act. ptc. giving the sense that the god "hears" the prayer, accepts it and decides to respond.

ἐξ-αιτέω — mid.: ask for oneself; > 'mercifully hearing these [prayers] grant them to us all as we ask'; [1× *El.*]

τὰ δ᾽ ἄλλα πάντα — 'as for all the rest'

cῐωπάω — (cιωπώcηc, pres. act. ptc.) keep silent, say nothing (concessive genit. absolute: SS 76 §42; S #2070); > 'even if I say nothing'; [1× *El.*]

LINE 658

ἐπ-αξιόω — (ἄξιοc, worthy) deem it right; <u>expect, believe</u> (with acc. and inf.)

+δαίμων, ονοc, ὁ — <u>god</u>, fate; > 'I believe that you, being a god, know [it] full well'

τοὺc ἐκ +Διόc — noun-forming use of article with genit. (S #1153d); > 'the sons of Zeus'

LINES 660–822: The Tutor enters from the wing (*eisodos*) on the spectators' right, indicating arrival from somewhere else in the territory of Mycenae. He poses as a stranger from Phocis (44–45), who comes to report Orestes' death. Dramatically he functions as a conventional tragic messenger. However, unlike a conventional messenger, his report is false. To Clytemnestra the news will seem like the answer to her prayer.

πῶc ἂν +*εἰδείην — (*οἶδα, pf. opt. act.) potential opt. used to indicate a polite request (S #1824; SS 231 §14); > 'how can I know'

cαφῶc (adv.) — (+cαφήc, distinct) distinct; clearly, for certain; [1× *El.*]

τύραννοc, ὁ/ἡ — [ῠ] ruler, sovereign; [1× *El.*]

+δῶμα, ατοc, τό — house (usually plural form in Tragedy, probably because it is a collection of rooms: SS 7 §3; with τάδε 'this house'. τοῦ τυράννου δώματ᾽ Αἰγίcθου τάδε *chiasmus*: S #3020)

LINE 662

εἰκάζω; ἐπ-εικάζω — (ἤκαcαc, aor.¹ act.) make a guess; surmise, guess; >'you yourself have guessed right'; [1× *El.*]

+ἦ (pcl.) — asseverative; with καί in animated questions (S #2864–65); > 'Am I also right . . . ?'

δάμαρ, αρτοc, ἡ — [ᾰ] (δαμάζω, make subject to) wife

+κῠρέω — (poetic for τυγχάνω) hit the mark (with supplem. ptc. containing the main idea, ἐπεικάζων: S #2096 a, b. κείνου emphatic *enjambment*); > 'in guessing that this is his wife?'

+εἰc-+*ορᾶν — limiting (explanatory) infinitive. SS 238 §3a: "she is like a royal person *to look at*"; with partitive genit. πάντων of supreme reality (LSJ iii); > 'most assuredly'

117

ΧΟ.	μάλιστα πάντων· ἥδε coι κείνη πάρα.	665
ΠΑ.	ὦ χαῖρ᾽, ἄναccα. coὶ φέρων ἥκω λόγουc	
	ἡδεῖc φίλου παρ᾽ ἀνδρὸc Αἰγίcθῳ θ᾽ ὁμοῦ.	
ΚΛ.	ἐδεξάμην τὸ ῥηθέν· εἰδέναι δέ cου	
	πρώτιcτα χρῄζω τίc c᾽ ἀπέcτειλεν βροτῶν.	
ΠΑ.	Φανοτεὺc ὁ Φωκεύc, πρᾶγμα πορcύνων μέγα.	670
ΚΛ.	τὸ ποῖον, ὦ ξέν᾽; εἰπέ. παρὰ φίλου γὰρ ὢν	

LINE 665

ἥδε ... κείνη
⁺ὅδε "refers primarily to what is present or near in place (deictic)." Often translated by 'here.' ⁺κείνη "refers to the mention by the previous speaker of one being sought" (SS 154 §23); > 'here is the one you asked about.' Cf. τόνδε 1228n, ἐκεῖνο 1178n

πάρα
in poetry = πάρεcτι (< πάρ-⁺*ειμι) (S #175b)

LINE 666

⁺ὦ
exclamatory ὦ linked with impv. rather than with the voc. (SS 28 §9)

⁺*χαίρω
rejoice (impv. a common form of greeting either at meeting or parting)

ἄναccα, ἡ
queen, lady; [1× El.]

⁺λόγουc/⁺ἡδεῖc
ἡδεῖc stands in enjambment; > 'welcome news'

ἐδεξάμην
(*δέχομαι, aor.¹ act.) receive (dramatic/instantaneous aorist, used often in dialogues in 1st pers. implying that the expressed judgment was already formed while the other person was speaking. Translated usually in the present. Here it expresses politeness: Lloyd 1999: 36; S #1937); > 'I accept what has been said/the message'

τὸ ῥηθέν
(aor.¹ ptc. pass. in acc. neut. sg., ⁺ἐρῶ) say, proclaim, announce

πρώτιcτα (adv.)
(⁺πρῶτοc) first of all; [1× El.]

ἀπο-*cτέλλω, -έcτειλα
(aor.¹) send away; > 'who among mortals sent you?'

LINE 670

Φανοτεύc, έωc, ὁ
uncle and enemy of Strophius, Pylades' father, who was Ag.'s ally (and brother-in-law)

⁺Φωκεύc, έωc, ὁ
Phocian; Phocis = a region in northern Greece that includes Delphi

πορcύνω
(ῡ) forward; > 'conveying a great/important matter'; [1× El.]

⁺μέγαc, μεγάλη, μέγα
big, large, great

τὸ ⁺ποῖον
anaphoric article, i.e., refers to what has been mentioned already. SS 143- 4 §13: "What was that?"; (S #1120b)

εἰπέ
(⁺*λέγω) (aor.²); the imperative of εἶπον is oxytone (S #424b)

ἀνδρός, cάφ' οἶδα, προσφιλεῖc λέξεις λόγουc.

ΠΑ. τέθνηκ' Ὀρέcτηc· ἐν βραχεῖ ξυνθεὶc λέγω.

ΗΛ. οἲ 'γὼ τάλαιν', ὄλωλα τῇδ' ἐν ἡμέρᾳ.

ΚΛ. τί φήc, τί φήc, ὦ ξεῖνε; μὴ ταύτηc κλύε. 675

ΠΑ. θανόντ' Ὀρέcτην νῦν τε καὶ πάλαι λέγω.

ΗΛ. ἀπωλόμην δύcτηνοc, οὐδέν εἰμ' ἔτι.

ΚΛ. cὺ μὲν τὰ cαυτῆc πρᾶcc', ἐμοὶ δὲ cύ, ξένε,
τἀληθὲc εἰπέ, τῷ τρόπῳ διόλλυται;

LINE 672

σάφᾰ — adv. (⁺σαφής) clearly, plainly, assuredly; [1× *El.*]

προσ-φιλής, ές — friendly, well disposed; [1× *El.*]

⁺*τέθνηκε — the perfect denotes a completed action, the effects of which continue in the present (S#1852b, 1945); > 'Orestes is dead'

⁺βραχύς, εῖα, ύ — short, brief; ἐν βραχεῖ in short, briefly

συν-⁺*τίθημι — [ῐ] (ξυνθείς, aor.² ptc. act.) put together; > 'I say, having put it succinctly'; [1× *El.*]

LINE 674

οἲ — Exclamation of pain. Here with nom. οἲ 'γώ—*aphaeresis*.

⁺τάλαινᾰ — nom. used in exclamation; here in reference to self (SS 23 §4)

⁺*ὄλωλα — (ὄλλυμι, pf.² indic. act.) pf.²: "I am undone/ruined" (S #819, LSJ Biii)

ταύτης — genit. demanded by ⁺κλύω; > 'Don't listen to *her*!'

⁺*θανόντα — ptc. in indirect discourse extended from verbs of knowing and perceiving. Since λέγω takes regulary the inf. or ὡς and ὅτι in indir. disc., the use of a ptc. might suggest emphasis on the Tutor's part, effected further by νῦν τε καὶ πάλαι (SS 318 §6; GMT #910; Finglass); > '*Orestes is dead,* I say now and [as I said] before.' Cf. ἐκεῖνον ὡς παρόντα 882n

ἀπ-⁺*ωλόμην — (⁺ἀπ-όλλυμι, aor.² indic.) mid.: perish, die (S #819) (the immediate or contemporary aor. indicates here an action that has just taken place or is contemporary: SS 317–18 §16). Translate in pres. tense: > 'I am no more'

τὰ cαυτῆς ⁺*πρᾶσσε — 'you mind your own affairs!'

ἀληθής, ές — (ἀ privat., λήθω, escape notice) truthful, sincere; τἀληθές = τὸ ἀληθές; substantival use of article with an adjective (S #1021, 1153a; SS 163 §1); > 'the truth'; (1046)

τῷ — = ⁺τίνι interrog. pron. (S #340, 1263)

δι-⁺*όλλυμι — mid.: destroy utterly, bring to naught (historical pres.: S #1883); > 'In what way/how did he die?'

ΠΑ.   κἀπεμπόμην πρὸς ταῦτα καὶ τὸ πᾶν φράcω.   **680**
κεῖνοc γὰρ ἐλθὼν ἐc τὸ κλεινὸν Ἑλλάδοc
πρόcχημ' ἀγῶνοc Δελφικῶν ἄθλων χάριν,
ὅτ' ᾔcθετ' ἀνδρὸc ὀρθίων γηρυμάτων
δρόμον προκηρύξαντοc, οὗ πρώτη κρίcιc,
εἰcῆλθε λαμπρόc, πᾶcι τοῖc ἐκεῖ cέβαc·   **685**
δρόμου δ' ἰcώcαc τῇ φύcει τὰ τέρματα
νίκηc ἔχων ἐξῆλθε πάντιμον γέραc.
χὥπωc μὲν ἐν παύροιcι πολλά cοι λέγω,
οὐκ οἶδα τοιοῦδ' ἀνδρὸc ἔργα καὶ κράτη·

LINE 680

καί ... καί   "as I was sent for that purpose, so ..." (Jebb)

κἀπεμπόμην   = καὶ +*ἐπεμπόμην. imperfect rather than the aorist because the mission has not been full executed yet. The aorist would have pointed out to its completion (SS 191 §11)

+γάρ   'the fact is that'; explanatory, see 32n

Ἑλλάς, άδος, ἡ   Greece (possessive genit.: S #1297)

προόσχημα, ατος, τό   (+προ-+*ἔχω, hold before) what is held forth, <u>showpiece</u>

+ἀγών, ῶνος, ὁ   [ă] gathering, <u>place of contest</u>, games (epexegetic/appositional genit.: #1322); > 'having gone to the renowned showpiece of Greece, *the contest*'

Δελφικός (3)   (Δέλφοι) Dephic, Delphian; [1 × *El.*]

ἄθλον, τό   prize of contest; > 'for the sake of Delphic prizes'; [1× *El.*]

LINE 683

ὄρθιος (3)   (ὀρθός, straight, excited) high pitched, shrill, <u>loud</u>; [1× *El.*]

γήρῡμα, ατος, τό   (γηρύω speak) sound (genit. following ᾔσθετο: S#1361); [1× Soph.]

+δρόμος, ὁ   (δραμεῖν, run) course, race; lap

προ-κηρύσσω   (προκηρύξαντος, aor.¹ ptc. act.) proclaim publically, proclaim by herald; > 'when he heard the ringing proclamation *of the man who proclaimed* the race'; [× Soph.]

κρίσις, εως, ἡ   [ῐ] (κρίνω decide) decision, judgment; > '(the race) of which deciding was first,' i.e., which was held first; [1× *El.*]

+εἰσ-+*ἔρχομαι   (εἰσῆλθε, aor.²) come into, enter (technical term of entering a race)

ἐκεῖ   there (τοῖς ἐκεῖ [ἀνθρώποις]. Substantival use of article with an adv. to qualify a noun that is often omitted: S #1153e); > 'those there'

σέβας, τό   (σέβομαι feel awe or fear) reverential awe (only in nom. acc. and voc.); [1× *El.*]

LINE 686

ἰσόω   [ῐ] make equal (τίνι τι); (1× *El.*)

τέρμα, ατος, τό   end, goal; > 'having matched the result of the race to his looks'

νίκη, ἡ   victory

πάν-τῑμος, ον   (πᾶς, τίμη) all-honorable; [1× *El.*]

γέρᾰς, αος, τό   gift of honor, prize

+ἐξ-+*ἔρχομαι   (ἐξῆλθε, aor.²) come out of/away; > 'he came away with a (all-honorable =) celebrated prize of victory'

ἓν δ᾿ ἴσθ᾿· ὅσων γὰρ εἰσεκήρυξαν βραβῆς,　　　　　　690
[†δρόμων διαύλων πένταθλ᾿ ἃ νομίζεται , †]
τούτων ἐνεγκὼν πάντα τἀπινίκια
ὠλβίζετ᾿, Ἀργεῖος μὲν ἀνακαλούμενος,
ὄνομα δ᾿ Ὀρέστης, τοῦ τὸ κλεινὸν Ἑλλάδος
Ἀγαμέμνονος στράτευμ᾿ ἀγείραντός ποτε.　　　　　　695
καὶ ταῦτα μὲν τοιαῦθ᾿· ὅταν δέ τις θεῶν
βλάπτῃ, δύναιτ᾿ ἂν οὐδ᾿ ἂν ἰσχύων φυγεῖν.

χὤπως	= καὶ ὅπως with final subjv. λέγω in *hyperbaton*
⁺παῦρος (3)	little, small, <u>short</u>; > 'and in order to tell much *in few words*'
⁺κράτη	'I do not know the achievements and victories/strengths of any other such man'

LINE 690

⁺εἷς, μία, ἕν	one (declension: S #349)
εἰς-κηρύσσω	(εἰσεκήρυξαν, aor.¹ act.) proclaim by herald; [1× Soph.]
βρᾰβεύς, εως, ὁ	judge at the games; [1× Soph.]
δίαλος, ὁ	[ῐ] double track; [1× Soph.]
πέντ-αθλον, τό	(πέντε, ἄθλον prize for contest) contest of five exercises (jumping, discus throwing, racing, wrestling, boxing. Line 691 is assumed to be corrupt due to unsatisfactory scanning and meaning); > Lloyd-Jones: ["the races on the double track that are the custom"]; [1× Soph.]
ἐνεγκών	<⁺*φέρω, aor.² ptc. act.
ἐπι-νίκιον, τό	(ἐπι, νίκη) victory song; τἀπινίκια = τὰ ἐπινίκια > 'prizes'; [1× *El.*]

LINE 693

ὀλβίζω	deem or pronounce happy (*enjambment*); >'for of every contest the judges announced, having carried off all the prizes *he was deemed happy/fortunate*'; [1× *El.*]
ἀνα-κᾰλέω	call again and again; [1× *El.*]
ὄνομα, ατος, τό	name (acc. of respect: S #1601c; SS 43); > 'he was announced as an Argive, *by name Orestes*, son of…'; [1× *El.*]
τὸ κλεινὸν … στράτευμα	The article is used of the familiar/well known, often with κλεινός (SS 144 §13); *hyperbaton* with στράτευμα, army; [1× *El.*]
ἀγείρω, ἤγειρα	(ἀγείραντος, aor.¹ act.) collect, gather; [1× *El.*]

LINE 696

καὶ … τοιαῦθ᾿	'this is how things were'
ὅταν	= ὅτε + ἄν; just as soon as, when
βλάπτω	(βλάπτῃ, subjv.) damage, hurt; [1× *El.*]
δύνᾰμαι	[ῠ] be able, strong enough; [1× *El.*]
ὅταν … βλάπτῃ … δύναιτ᾿	mixed condition. When subjv. with ἄν (ὅταν) in protasis has potential opt. in apodosis, there is sometimes a "distinct potential force in the apodosis, and sometimes the opt. with ἄν is merely a softened expression for the future indicative" (GMT #505). The implication here, however, is a rather clear statement of impossibility, emphasized perhaps further by the repetition of ἄν (Kells); > 'but when one of the gods sends harm, not even a strong man *can possibly* (following such a deed) *get away*'
ἄν … ἄν	

κεῖνος γὰρ ἄλλης ἡμέρας, ὅθ' ἱππικῶν
ἦν ἡλίου τέλλοντος ὠκύπους ἀγών,
εἰσῆλθε πολλῶν ἁρματηλατῶν μέτα.   700
εἷς ἦν Ἀχαιός, εἷς ἀπὸ Cπάρτης, δύο
Λίβυες ζυγωτῶν ἁρμάτων ἐπιστάται·
κἀκεῖνος ἐν τούτοισι Θεσσαλὰς ἔχων
ἵππους, ὁ πέμπτος· ἕκτος ἐξ Αἰτωλίας
ξανθαῖσι πώλοις· ἕβδομος Μάγνης ἀνήρ·   705

ἰσχύω	be strong in one's body (non-articular substant. ptc. for indefinite or general reference: SS 258–59 §10; GMT #827. Should have been τὶς ἰσχύων 'someone strong.' 'a strong man'); [1× *El.*]

LINE 698

†ἄλλης †ἡμέρας	genit. of time is used of the period of time within which something happens (SS 58–59 §11.i; S #1444); > 'on another day'
τέλλω	= ἀνα-τέλλω rise (temporal genit. absolute: S #2058); > 'at sun rise'; [1× Soph.]
ὠκύ-πους, ὁ, ἡ, -πουν, τό	swift footed; > 'swift contest of horse chariots'; [1× *El.*]`
ἁρμα-τηλάτης, ου, ὁ	[λᾰ] charioteer (nine altogether); [1× Soph.]
μέτα (+ genit.)	= †μετά; together with (*anastrophe*: S #175a)

LINE 701

Ἀχαιός (3)	Achaean; probably from the area on the south side of the Gulf of Corinth
Cπάρτη, ἡ	Sparta; [1× *El.*]
δύο	two (declension: S #349. With plural rather than with dual form: SS 3 §2)
Λίβῠς, ῠος, ὁ	[ῐ] form Libyan; [1× Soph.]
ζῠγωτός (3)	(ζῠγόω yoke) yoked; [1× Soph.]
ἅρμα, ατος, τό	chariot
ἐπιστάτης, ὁ	(ἐφ-ίσταμαι, be set over) master, overseer; > 'masters of yoked chariots'
ἐν τούτοισι	'then he (Orestes) *among them* with his Thessalian mares was the fifth.' Kamerbeek: "Orestes and the four mentioned before evidently form a group, among which he is the fifth"
Θεσσαλός (3)	Thessalian, from the region of northern Greece; [1× Soph.]

LINE 704

πέμπτος (3)	(πέντε five) fifth; κἀκεῖνος . . . ὁ πέμπτος emphatic *hyperbaton*; [1× *El.*]
ἕκτος (3)	(ἕξ six) sixth
Αἰτωλία, ἡ	Aetolia, region on the north coast of the Gulf of Corinth; [1× Soph.]
ξανθός (3)	yellow, <u>chestnut</u>; [1× Soph.]
†πῶλος, ὁ	young horse, whether colt or filly (dat. of accompaniment: SS 90 §19; S #1526); > 'with chestnut fillies'
ἕβδομος (3)	(ἑπτά, seven) seventh
Μάγνης, ητος, ὁ	Magnesian (i.e., dweller of Magnesia in Thessaly); [1× Soph.]

ὁ δ' ὄγδοος λεύκιππος, Αἰνιὰν γένος·
ἔνατος Ἀθηνῶν τῶν θεοδμήτων ἄπο·
Βοιωτὸς ἄλλος, δέκατον ἐκπληρῶν ὄχον.
στάντες δ' ὅθ' αὐτοὺς οἱ τεταγμένοι βραβῆς
κλήροις ἔπηλαν καὶ κατέστησαν δίφρους,   710
χαλκῆς ὑπαὶ σάλπιγγος ἦξαν· οἱ δ' ἅμα

LINE 706

ὄγδοος (3)	eighth; [1× Soph.]
λεύκ-ιππος, ον	riding or <u>driving</u> white horses (usually owned by gods or heroes); [1× Soph.]
Αἰνίαν	the Aenianes tribe dwelt in the south of Thessaly
⁺γένος	accusative of respect (S #1601c; SS 43 §14)
ἔνατος (3)	(ἐννέα nine) ninth; [1× Soph.]
Ἀθῆναι, αἱ	Athens
θεό-δμητος (3/2)	(θεός, δέμω) god-built; [1× Soph.]
ἄπο + genit.	(=⁺ἀπό) from; *anastrophe*
Βοιωτός, ὁ	Boeotian; [1× Soph.]
ἐκ-πληρόω	fill up, make up (to a certain number); [1× Soph.]
ὄχος, ὁ	carriage, chariot; > ' another, a Boeotian, filling the tenth chariot'; [1× *El.*]

LINE 709

⁺*στάντες	(⁺*ἵστημι, aor.² ptc. act.) 'having taken their spots,' 'standing'
ὅθι	poetic for οὗ 'where' (S #346 D2,); [1× *El.*]
⁺*τάττω	(τεταγμένοι, pf. pass. ptc.) form, arrange; pass.: be posted, stationed; > *the appointed* judges'
κλῆρος, ὁ	that which is assigned by lot; [1× *El.*]
πάλλω, ἔπηλα	(aor.¹, act.) sort by lot; > 'where the appointed judges had sorted them by lot'; [1× Soph.]
καθ-⁺*ίστημι	(κατέστησαν, aor.¹ act.) station, set; > 'and stationed their chariots'; [1× *El.*]
χάλκεος, έα, εον	brazen; [1× *El.*]
σάλπιγξ, ιγγος, ἡ	trumpet (ὑπαί poetic for ὑπό) >'at the sound of the brazen trumpet'
ἀίσσω	[ῑ] (ἦξαν, aor.¹ act.) shoot, dart
οἱ δ' ἅμα	'and they at the same moment'; i.e., all together at the same moment

ἵπποις ὁμοκλήσαντες ἡνίας χεροῖν
ἔσεισαν· ἐν δὲ πᾶς ἐμεστώθη δρόμος
κτύπου κροτητῶν ἁρμάτων· κόνις δ' ἄνω
φορεῖθ'· ὁμοῦ δὲ πάντες ἀναμεμειγμένοι   715
φείδοντο κέντρων οὐδέν, ὡς ὑπερβάλοι
χνόας τις αὐτῶν καὶ φρυάγμαθ' ἱππικά.
ὁμοῦ γὰρ ἀμφὶ νῶτα καὶ τροχῶν βάσεις
ἤφριζον, εἰσέβαλλον ἱππικαὶ πνοαί.
κεῖνος δ' ὑπ' αὐτὴν ἐσχάτην στήλην ἔχων   720

LINE 712

ὁμοκλάω	+ dat.; call or shout to, encourage; [1× Soph.]
ἡνία, ἡ	bridle, reins
σείω	shake (οἱ δ' ἅμα . . . ἔσεισαν emphatic *hyperbaton*); [1× *El.*]
ἐμ-μεστόομαι	(ἐμεστώθη, aor.¹ pass.) be filled (ἐν . . . ἐμεστώθη either adv. ἐν, or in *tmesis*: S #1650; SS 94 §1b); [1× *El.*]
κτύπος, ὁ	[ῠ] crash, bang, din; [1× *El.*]
κροτητός (3)	rattling, bumping (onomatopoeia with κ, τ, ρ, (S #3034); > 'and the entire racetrack filled with the din of rattling chariots'; [1× Soph.]
⁺φορεῖτο	like φείδοντο in the following line, the syllabic augment is omitted. A phenomenon common in choral odes, rare in dialogue parts. Outside lyrics, there are 17 unaugmented past tense verbs in Tragedy; all occur in messenger speeches (Finglass; S #438); > 'and dust rose up'
ἀνα-μείγνῡμι	(pf. pass. ptc.) often in pass.: be mixed with; [1× Soph.]

LINE 716

φείδομαι	(ind. impf.); spare; augment omitted. See φορεῖτο in previous line. [1 × *El.*]
κέντρον, τό	(κεντέω prick, goad) horse goad, spur; partit. genit. (S #1306; SS 58 §10); [1 × *El.*]
ὑπερ-*βάλλω, -έβαλον	(ὑπερβάλοι, aor.² opt.) overtake, outstrip, pass (final clause in secondary sequence, (ἐ)φείδοντο: S #2197); [1× Soph.]
χνόη, ἡ	the iron box of a wheel in which the axle turns, nave, axle; [1× *El.*]
τις αὐτῶν	= ἕκαστος τις αὐτῶν (Kamerbeek)
φρύαγμα, ατος, τό	[ῠ] neighing; > 'so that each would overtake the axle-naves and neighing horses of the others'; [1× Soph.]

LINE 718

⁺ἀμφί (+ acc.)	about
νῶτον, τό	back; [1× *El.*]
τρόχος, ὁ	(τρέχω run) wheel (genit. of definition: SS 53 §5); [1× *El.*]
βάσις, εως, ἡ	[ᾰ] (βαίνω step) stepping, step (Jebb: τροχῶν βάσεις = τρχοὺς βαινόντας); > 'whirling wheels'; [1× *El.*]
ἀφρίζω	(ἀφρέω, foam) foam; [1× Soph.]
εἰσ-*βάλλω	intransitive: throw oneself into (LSJ ii) (*asyndeton*, with ἤφριζον for emphasis); [1× *El.*]
πνοή, ἡ	wind, blast, breathing hard, panting; > 'at once for the horses' breaths foamed and flung (about) against their backs and the whirling wheels'
⁺ὑπό (+ acc.)	indicates motion to (SS 129 §19)

ἔχριμπτ' ἀεὶ cύριγγα, δεξιὸν δ' ἀνεὶς
cειραῖον ἵππον εἶργε τὸν προσκείμενον.
καὶ πρὶν μὲν ὀρθοὶ πάντες ἔστασαν δίφροις·
ἔπειτα δ' Αἰνιᾶνος ἀνδρὸς ἄστομοι
πῶλοι βίᾳ φέρουσιν, ἐκ δ' ὑποστροφῆς   725
τελοῦντες ἕκτον ἕβδομόν τ' ἤδη δρόμον
μέτωπα cυμπαίουcι Βαρκαίοιc ὄχοιc.

ἔσχᾰτος (3/2)	farthest (probably predicative usage: 'the edge of the turning post' rather than attributive: 'the farthest turning post at the end of the course')
στήλη, ἡ	stone, monument, pillar, turning post
⁺*ἔχων	supply: τοὺς ἵππους

LINE 721

χρίμπτω	bring near; [1× Soph.]
σύριγξ, ιγγος, ἡ	pipe (anything like a pipe, including a hole in the nave of a wheel: LSJ ii.2, and by metonymy the nave, the wheel itself); > 'Orestes having/driving [his horses] close to the edge of the turning post, grazed it each time with his wheel'
δέξιος (3)	on the right hand or side; [1× El.]
σειραῖος (3)	(σεῖρα cord) joined by a cord (of a horse: 'fastened by a rope outside'); [1× El.]
εἴργω	= ἔργω confine in, check; [1× El.]
⁺προς-⁺κείμενον	'placed near'; > 'having loosened (ἀνείς, < ἀνίημι) the reins of his right- hand trace-horse he held back the horse *on the inner side* (placed near)'.

The most dangerous places in a chariot race were the two turning points, each marked by a stone post or pillar. The skilled charioteer would try to make the most economical turn possible by getting as close as possible to the post without touching it, lest he brake his wheel. Orestes was driving a four-horse chariot. The two middle horses were fastened by harness to the chariot-pole, whereas the outer two horses were secured by a trace—a strap connecting the horse's harness to the chariot—and controlled by the reins. This helped the charioteer manage the chariot on the turn. Orestes was turning the post from right to left. He thus retained the inner horse, which was on his left and closest to the post, while giving room to the right trace-horse to make a larger turn. In other words, he did what had to be done to round the post as close to it as possible. There were twelve rounds of the course, which is thought to be almost five and a half miles (Jebb on 726f). Until the accident, Orestes managed to bring his nave as close as possible to the post in each of the rounds. Scholars assume that the disaster happened in the twelfth round.

LINE 723

⁺*ἔστασαν	(ἵστημι, aor.¹ act.) stood; > 'at first they all stood upright/safely in their chariots'
ἄ-στομος, ον	(ἀ privat., στόμα) hard-mouthed (i.e., insensitive to the bit); [1× Soph.]
⁺φέρουσιν	Historical present most often replaces a narrative aorist, but at times a descriptive imperfect (S #1883). According to Morwood (SS 185 §5), the historical present of φέρουσιν 725, ἀνοκωχεύει 732, διώκει 738, ἑλίσσεται 746, stands for the descriptive imperfect.
⁺βίᾳ	'the hard-mouthed colts carrying him *with violent force*/bolted'
ὑπο-στροφή, ἡ	turning about, wheeling round; > 'in wheeling around [the turning post]'; [1× Soph.]
⁺τελέω	accomplish; > 'having finished the sixth lap [and starting on the seventh]'

κἀντεῦθεν ἄλλος ἄλλον ἐξ ἑνὸς κακοῦ
ἔθραυε κἀνέπιπτε, πᾶν δ' ἐπίμπλατο
ναυαγίων Κρισαῖον ἱππικῶν πέδον.   730
γνοὺς δ' οὐξ Ἀθηνῶν δεινὸς ἡνιοστρόφος
ἔξω παρασπᾷ κἀνοκωχεύει παρεὶς
κλύδων' ἔφιππον ἐν μέσῳ κυκώμενον.

μέτωπον, τό	(μετά, ὄψ) space between the eyes, forehead, front; (1× Soph.)
συμ-παίω	dash together/against (historical present: S #1883. According to Morwood [SS 185 §5], the historical present of συμπαίουσι 727, παρασπᾷ 732, λανθάνει [παίσας] 744–45, stands for the narrative aorist, see φέρουσιν 725n); [1× Soph.]
Βαρκαῖος (3)	Barcan, Libyan; Barca was a city in Cyrenaica; > 'and they dashed their heads against/ran head-first into the chariot from Barca'; [1× Soph.]

LINE 728

ἐντεῦθεν (adv.)	hence, henceforth
θραύω	break in pieces, shatter; [1 × *El.*]
ἀνα-+*πίπτω	fall back, recline; > 'from this one mishap one chariot shattered another and *smashed up*'; [1× Soph.]
πίμπλημι	fill
ναυᾱγία, ἡ	shipwreck (nautical metaphor, cf. 335)
Κρισαῖος (3)	of Crisa, a city in Phocis near Delphi; chiastic structure of the line; [1× Soph.]

LINE 731

+*γνοῦς	(γιγνώσκω aor.[2] act. ptc.) 'having realized [this]'
ἡνιοστρόφος, ὁ	(ἡνία, στρέφω) guiding by reins, charioteer; > 'the cunning charioteer from Athens'; [1× Soph.]
ἔξω (adv.)	(ἐξ) on the outside
παρα-σπάω	pull forcibly aside (historical present, see συμπαίουσι 727n); [1× *El.*]
ἀνοκωχεύω	hold back, stay (historical present, see φέρουσιν); [1× Soph.]
+παρ-*είς	(παρίημι, aor.[2] act. ptc.) 'bypassing'
κλύδων, ωνος, ὁ	[ῠ] wave, billow, surge; [1× *El.*]
ἔφ-ιππος, ον	(ἐπί, ἵππος) on horseback (κλύδων ἔφιππος 'wave of horses': LSJ 2. I.e., 'surge of chariots'); [1× Soph.]
+μέσος (3)	middle
κυκάω	pass.: be thrown into confusion; > 'pulls [his horses] forcibly away and holds them back, bypassing the *tumultuous* surge of chariots in the middle'; [1× Soph.]

ἤλαυνε δ' ἔϲχατος μέν, ὑϲτέρας ἔχων
πώλους, Ὀρέϲτης, τῷ τέλει πίϲτιν φέρων·   735
ὅπως δ' ὁρᾷ μόνον νιν ἐλλελειμμένον,
ὀξὺν δι' ὤτων κέλαδον ἐνϲείϲας θοαῖϲ
πώλοις διώκει, κἀξιϲώϲαντε ζυγὰ
ἠλαυνέτην, τότ' ἄλλος, ἄλλοθ' ἅτερος
κάρα προβάλλων ἱππικῶν ὀχημάτων.   740

LINE 734

ἐλαύνω	drive
ἔϲχᾰτος (3)	the farthest, uttermost, extreme
ὕϲτερος (3)	latter; [1 × *El.*]
τέλος, εος, τό	an end; [1× *El.*]
πίϲτις, εως, ἡ	<u>trust</u>, that which gives trust, assurance, proof of reliability; > 'Orestes was driving last, having/keeping his horses in the rear, trusting the end [result]'
⁺ὅπως (conj.)	when (S #2383)
ἐλ-⁺*λείπω	(ἐλλελειμένον, pf. pass. ptc.) leave in; > 'but when he saw that he [the Athenian] was the only one *remaining/ left*'; [1× *El.*]
ὀξύς, ὀξεῖα, ὀξύ	sharp, keen;
⁺διά (prep.)	through (in Soph. mostly with genit. ὤτων: SS #102–4 §6)
κέλᾰδος, ὁ	clamor, din, cry; [1× Soph.]
ἐν-ϲείω	shake in or into, hurl; [1× *El.*]
θόος, (3)	swift, fast; [1× *El.*]

LINE 738

διώκω	pursue, go after (historical present, see φέρουϲιν 725n); > 'having sent a sharp cry through the ears of his swift fillies, *he gives chase*'
⁺ἐξ-ῐϲόω	(aor.¹ ptc. dual) <u>make equal, level</u>; pass.: be equal, be match for (κἀξιϲώϲαντε = καὶ ἀξιϲώϲαντε, dual)
ζῠγόν, τό	yoke (ἀξιϲώϲαντε ζυγά: 'bring the teams abreast'; ἠλαυνέτην, dual): > 'and the two of them after they brought their teams abreast, they drove on'; [1× *El.*]
ἄλλοτε (adv.)	(ἄλλος, ὅτε) at another time
ἅτερος	= ἕτερος other of the two
προ-*βάλλω	throw before, put forward, hold before; [1× *El.*]
ὄχημα, τό	(ὀχέω hold) carriage, chariot; > 'now one driver, then the other, thrusts (thrusting) his horse chariot ahead of [his rival's]'; [1× Soph.]

καὶ τοὺς μὲν ἄλλους πάντας ἀσφαλὴς δρόμους
ὠρθοῦθ' ὁ τλήμων ὀρθὸς ἐξ ὀρθῶν δίφρων·
ἔπειτα λύων ἡνίαν ἀριστερὰν
κάμπτοντος ἵππου λανθάνει στήλην ἄκραν
παίσας· ἔθραυσε δ' ἄξονος μέσας χνόας,   745
κἀξ ἀντύγων ὤλισθε· σὺν δ' ἑλίσσεται
τμητοῖς ἱμᾶσι· τοῦ δὲ πίπτοντος πέδῳ
πῶλοι διεσπάρησαν ἐς μέσον δρόμον.

LINE 741

ἀσφάλης, ες	[ᾰ] steadfast; [1× *El.*]
ὀρθόω	pass.: stand straight; [1× *El.*]
+ὀρθός ... ὀρθῶν	*polyptoton* for emphasis (SS 169–70 §10)
ὁ +τλήμων	proleptic, refers to Or. > 'Unfortunate Orestes stood safely upright throughout all the other laps, upright in his upright chariot'
+λύω	[ῠ] loosen
ἀριστερός (3)	[ᾰ] (lit.: better, ἄριστος, best) <u>left</u>; ominous
κάμπτω	guide a horse around the turning post; [1× *El.*]
+*λανθάνω	escape notice of (historical present with supplementary participle παίσας (see next line); see συμπαίουσι 727n
+ἄκραν	predicative: 'edge of the turning post'

LINE 745

παίω	strike, strike against (supplem. ptc. with λανθάνει in emphatic *enjambment*, carries the main idea. When an aorist participle is used with λανθάνω, τυγχάνω or φθάνω in the present or imperfect, it does not coincide with the verb but retains its own reference to past time: S #1873, 2096b; GMT #146); > 'and unawares (it was unknown to him that he had struck) he struck the edge of the turning post ...'
ἄξων, ονος, ὁ	axle; > 'he broke the axle-box right in the center'; [1× Soph.]
ὀλισθάνω, ὤλισθον	(ὤλισθε, aor.² act.) slip, slide, fall; [1× Soph.]
ἄντυξ, ῠγος, ἡ	rail round the front of the chariot rail; > 'and slid over the rail'; [1× *El.*]
ἑλίσσω	turn round, roll (σὺν ... ἑλίσσεται tmesis. SS 94 §1b: "he was entangled in the reins." Historical present, see φέρουσιν 725n); [1× *El.*]
τμητός (3)	(τέμνω cut) cut, shaped by cutting
ἱμάς, αντος, ὁ	[ῐ] leathern strap, thong, <u>reins</u>; > 'sharp-cut reins'; [1× Soph.]
τοῦ ... +*πίπτοντος	temporal genitive absolute (S #2070)
πέδον, τό	(πούς foot) earth, ground (dat. of place: SS 87 §13; S #1530–1)
δια-σπείρω	(διεσπάρησαν, aor.¹ pass) scatter, spread about; pass.: be scattered; > 'and when he fell to the ground, his mares *bolted wildly* into the center of the course'

στρατὸς δ' ὅπως ὁρᾷ νιν ἐκπεπτωκότα
δίφρων, ἀνωτότυξε τὸν νεανίαν,   750
οἷ' ἔργα δράσας οἷα λαγχάνει κακά,
φορούμενος πρὸς οὖδας, ἄλλοτ' οὐρανῷ
σκέλη προφαίνων, ἔστε νιν διφρηλάται,
μόλις κατασχεθόντες ἱππικὸν δρόμον,
ἔλυσαν αἱματηρόν, ὥστε μηδένα   755
γνῶναι φίλων ἰδόντ' ἂν ἄθλιον δέμας.
καί νιν πυρᾷ κέαντες εὐθὺς ἐν βραχεῖ
χαλκῷ μέγιστον σῶμα δειλαίας σποδοῦ
φέρουσιν ἄνδρες Φωκέων τεταγμένοι,
ὅπως πατρῴας τύμβον ἐκλάχῃ χθονός.   760

LINE 749

ἐκ-⁺**πίπτω	(pf. act. pct.) fall out of/down from (⁺**ὁρᾷ historical present: S #1883); [1× El.]
ἀνοτοτύζω	break out into wailing; > 'and when the crowd saw him falling out of the chariot *they broke out into wailing* for the young man'; [1× Soph.]
νεᾱνίας, ου, ὁ	young man; [1× El.]
*λαγχάνω	[χᾰ] obtain by lot; > 'the kind of deeds he accomplished, and the kind of misfortune that *befell him*'
οὖδας, εος, τό	surface of the earth, ground; [1× Soph.]
οὐρᾰνός, ὁ	sky, heaven
σκέλος, εος, τό	leg; [1× Soph.]
προ-⁺**φαίνω	show forth; > 'at one moment borne earthward, at another flinging his legs to the sky'
ἔσ-τε (conj.)	(ἐς, τε) till, until
διφρηλάτης, ου, ὁ	[ᾰ] charioteer; [1× Soph.]

LINE 752

αἱμᾰτηρός (3)	(αἷμα blood) bloody; > 'having with difficulty stopped (κατασχεθόντες <⁺κατ-⁺**ἔχω aor.² act. ptc.) the horses, they untangled *him all covered with blood*'
⁺**γνῶναι	(γιγνώσκω, aor.² act. inf.) ὥστε with inf. implies a possible result or a tendency, here underscored by ἂν as representing potential opt. (S #2250– 54, 2270), the subject of which is μηδένα accompanied by ἰδόντα; > 'so that none of his friends who saw him *could possibly have recognized* his wretched body'
⁺ἄθλιον	the play abounds in words signifying misery, cf. ⁺δύστηνος, ⁺τάλας, ⁺δείλαιος

LINE 757

πῠρά, ἡ	funeral pyre
καίω	(κέαντες, aor.¹ act. ptc. nom. pl., epic and poetic) burn (the subject is a vague. Kamerbeek, Jebb: 'they'); [1× El.]
⁺εὐθύς (adv.)	straightaway, at once; > 'and straightaway they burned him on a pyre'
χαλκός, ὁ	(poetic) anything made of brass or metal, a brazen vessel, urn; [1× Soph.]
⁺σῶμα, ατος, τό	body, dead body; > 'in a little urn his mighty body'
⁺δείλαιος (3)	(lengthened form of δειλός, miserable, wretched) wretched, sorry, paltry
⁺σποδός, ἡ	ashes (genit. of definition SS 53 §5: "the body which is [reduced to] sad dust")

τοιαῦτά coι ταῦτ' ἐcτὶν, ὡc μὲν ἐν λόγοιc
ἀλγεινά, τοῖc δ' ἰδοῦcιν, οἵπερ εἴδομεν,
μέγιcτα πάντων ὧν ὄπωπ' ἐγὼ κακῶν.

XO.   φεῦ φεῦ·τὸ πᾶν δὴ δεcπόταιcι τοῖc πάλαι

        πρόρριζον, ὡc ἔοικεν, ἔφθαρται γένοc.   765

KΛ.   ὦ Ζεῦ, τί ταῦτα, πότερον εὐτυχῆ λέγω,

        ἢ δεινὰ μέν, κέρδη δέ; λυπηρῶc δ' ἔχει,

        εἰ τοῖc ἐμαυτῆc τὸν βίον cῴζω κακοῖc.

⁺ἄνδρες ... ⁺*τεταγμένοι	(⁺*τάττω, pf. pass. ptc.); > 'men appointed from the Phocians'
ἐκ-*λαγχάνω	[χἄ] obtain by lot or fate (final clause in primary sequence, φέρουσιν: S #2196; GMT #317); > 'so that he draws a lot for a grave in his father's land'

LINE 761

coι	ethical dat. with pers. pronouns; SS 85 §10: "a form of dat. of interest used in intimate address"; > 'such is the story *for you*'
ὡς (conj.)	limitative: so far as (introducing comparative clause. SS 305 §1: "'painful if only [as far as] in report' [contrasted with the effect on those who saw it])"
ἀλγεινός (3)	(ἄλγος pain) painful; [1× *El.*]
τοῖς ἰδοῦσιν	(ὁράω, εἴδομαι aor.² ptc. act. dat. pl.) articular substant. ptc. (S #2050–52; SS 257–58 §9; GMT #825. ἰδοῦσιν ... εἴδομεν, wordplay for emphasis); > 'to those who saw'
ὧν	relative attraction for ἅ (S #2522a)
ὄπωπα	(Ion. pf. mid. of ⁺*ὁράω) see; > 'as much as painful in words, to those who saw it, (we who did) as we did, the greatest disaster of all that I have ever seen'

LINE 764

δεσπότης, ου, ὁ	master (dat. of possession: S #1476); [1× *El.*]
τοῖς ⁺πάλαι	an article and adverb following in attributive function a noun with no article, δεσπόταισι. In this arrangement the adverb is added by way of explanation (S #1159); > 'of our masters, those of old'
πρό-ρριζος, ον	(πρό, ῥίζα root) by the roots, root and branch (neut. πρόρριζον, adv.)
*φθείρω	(ἔφθαρται, pf. pass) ruin, destroy
τὸ πᾶν ... ⁺γένος	*hyperbaton*; > 'Alas, alas! The whole family of our ancient masters, it seems, is all destroyed root and branch'

LINE 766

πότερον ... ἤ	whether ... or (S #2656; introduces direct alternative questions with πότερον, frequently left untranslated in English)
εὐ-τῠχής, ές	successful, lucky, fortunate
⁺*λέγω	deliberative subjv. (S #2639; SS 223–25 §11); > 'what am I to say of these things; are they fortunate, or terrible yet profitable?'
λῠπηρῶς	painfully (ἔχω with adv. is often used as a periphrasis for an adj. with εἶναι: S #1438; apodosis to the following protasis); > 'it is painful'; [1× *El.*]
⁺*cῴζω	present condition whose protasis can be seen as causal clause (SS 279–80 §2); > 'if/since I save my life through my own misfortunes'

ΠΑ.	τί δ' ὧδ' ἀθυμεῖς, ὦ γύναι, τῷ νῦν λόγῳ;	
ΚΛ.	δεινὸν τὸ τίκτειν ἐςτίν· οὐδὲ γὰρ κακῶς	770
	πάςχοντι μῖςος ὧν τέκῃ προςγίγνεται.	
ΠΑ.	μάτην ἄρ' ἡμεῖς, ὡς ἔοικεν, ἥκομεν.	
ΚΛ.	οὔτοι μάτην γε. πῶς γὰρ ἂν μάτην λέγοις;	
	εἴ μοι θανόντος πίςτ' ἔχων τεκμήρια	
	προςῆλθες, ὅςτις τῆς ἐμῆς ψυχῆς γεγώς,	775
	μαςτῶν ἀποςτὰς καὶ τροφῆς ἐμῆς, φυγὰς	
	ἀπεξενοῦτο· καί μ', ἐπεὶ τῆςδε χθονὸς	
	ἐξῆλθεν, οὐκέτ' εἶδεν· ἐγκαλῶν δέ μοι	
	φόνους πατρῴους δείν' ἐπηπείλει τελεῖν·	

LINE 769

ἀ-θυμέω (ἀ privat., ⁺θυμος spiritless) be disheartened, despair at; [1× El.]

⁺*πάσχω the masculine participle, πάσχοντι, indicates the proverbially generalizing nature of Clyt.'s comment, even though the person can be only a woman here (S #1015; SS 12 §8); see νήπιος 145n

⁺*τέκῃ (τίκτω, aor.² subjv.) generalizing subjv. in relative clause without ἄν (SS 225–26 §12); see ⁺*βλάστωσιν . . . ⁺*εὕρωσι 1060–62n

⁺μῖσος, εος, τό hatred, grudge (ὧν: relative attraction = [τινὶ] τούτων οὕς: S #2522)

προσ-⁺*γίγνομαι [ῐ] + dat.: τινὶ; accrue, come to, happen to; > 'It is a wondrous thing to give birth. For even when one is wronged (κακῶς πάσχοντι), (there is no hatred for =) one does not hate those one has borne'; [1× El.]

⁺μάτην (adv.) in vain, pointlessly

ἡμεῖς (ἐγώ) *majestic plural* (poetic) to lend dignity (SS 6 §4; S #1006) > 'so I've come, it seems, pointlessly'

LINE 773

⁺πῶς . . . ⁺λέγοις potential optative with ἄν > 'how can you say "pointlessly"?'; apodosis to the following protasis.

⁺*θανόντος (θνῄσκω, aor.² act. ptc.) non-articular substant. ptc. for indefinite or general reference (SS 258–59 §10). Clyt. continues to generalize and not mention her son's name (cf. lines 770–1) in spite of a clearly understood reference to Orestes. Does she try to distance herself emotionally?

⁺τεκμήριον, τό proof, sign

προσ-⁺*έρχομαι (προσῆλθες, aor.² act.) come forth; [1× El.]

⁺ὅστις (indefnite/general relative pron.) whoever (antecedent: θανόντος; the generalization continues)

εἴ . . . προσῆλθες the εἰ has again a causal tilt; see 768; Clyt. must be using it as causal while the spectators know better (Finglass); >' if/since you came bringing me a reliable proof of the death of one who . . .'

⁺*γεγώς (γίγνομαι, pf. act. ptc.); > 'who sprang from my life' (metaphoric)

LINE 776

μαστός, ὁ breast; [1× El.]

⁺τροφή, ἡ (τρέφω, make firm) nourishment, rearing (note the repeating possessives that are not necessary)

ἀφ-⁺*ίστημι (ἀποστάς, aor.² inf. act.) stand away, withdraw, keep off

φῠγάς, -άδος, ὁ (⁺*φεύγω) fugitive, banished person;

ἀπο-ξενόω (⁺ξένος) pass.: live away from home; > 'having left my breast and my nurture, he lived away from his home as a fugitive'; [1× Soph.]

ὥcτ’ οὔτε νυκτὸc ὕπνον οὔτ’ ἐξ ἡμέραc   **780**

ἐμὲ cτεγάζειν ἡδύν, ἀλλ’ ὁ προcτατῶν

χρόνοc διῆγέ μ’ αἰὲν ὡc θανουμένην.

νῦν δ’ —ἡμέρᾳ γὰρ τῇδ’ ἀπηλλάγην φόβου

πρὸc τῆcδ’ ἐκείνου θ’· ἥδε γὰρ μείζων βλάβη

ξύνοικοc ἦν μοι, τοὐμὸν ἐκπίνουc’ ἀεὶ   **785**

ψυχῆc ἄκρατον αἷμα—νῦν δ’ ἔκηλά που

τῶν τῆcδ’ ἀπειλῶν οὕνεχ’ ἡμερεύcομεν.

καὶ μ’ ... οὐκετ’ ⁺*εἶδεν	*hyperbaton;* > 'and after he left this land he never saw me again'
ἐγ-⁺*κᾰλέω	blame, censure; [1× *El.*]
ἐπ-ἀπειλέω	hold out a threat to one, threaten besides; > 'but charging me with his father's murder he threatened to do horrible things'; [1× *El.*]

LINE 780

cτεγάζω	cover, protect (ὥcτε with inf., outside indirect discourse, implies a possible result or a tendency: S #2251, 2254; GMT #582, 587. The negation by οὐ is an exception it should have been μή with the inf.: SS 322 §4.c.i; GMT #598); > 'so that neither by night nor by day would sweet sleep cover me'; [1× Soph.]
νυκτόc ... ἡμέραc	(⁺νύξ, ⁺ἡμέρα) genit. of time (S #1444; SS 58–59 §11.i)
προ-cτᾰτέω	(προcτάτηc chief, ruler) stand before, rule; [1× Soph.]
δι-⁺*ἄγω	carry over; [1× *El.*]
ὡc ⁺*θανουμένην	(θνήcκω, fut. dep. ptc.) > 'but time standing over me kept me always as one about to die'

LINE 783

⁺πρόc (+ genit.)	from the side of (SS 153, 157 §23: "⁺ὅδε refers primarily to what is present or near in place [deictic]"; ⁺ἐκεῖνοc refers to what is more distant"); > 'for on this day I've been released (⁺ἀπ-αλάccω, aor.² pass.) from the dread (*from the side of*) of this girl here and of him'
ξύν-⁺οικοc, ον	= cύνοικοc (cύν, οἰκέω inhabit) living with
ἐκ-πίνω	[ῐ] drink out, drain; [1× *El.*]
ἄ-κρᾱτοc, ον	(κεράννυμι, mix) unmixed, pure (ἄκρατον πιεῖν: 'to drink umixed wine.' It was a sign of hard drinking.); > 'For she was the greater harm, living at my side and constantly drinking up *my true life's blood*'; [1× *El.*]
ἔκηλοc (3)	at rest, at one's ease (neut. pl. used adverbially)
που (pcl.)	GP 491.i: "ironically expressing quiet assurance" to the effect of "Now, if I mistake not, I shall have peace."
ἀπειλή, ἡ	usually in plural; threats (LSJ ii); [1× *El.*]
ἡμερεύω	pass the day; > 'now we shall spend our days, I think, in peace from any threats of hers'; [1× Soph.]

ΗΛ.	οἴμοι τάλαινα· νῦν γὰρ οἰμῶξαι πάρα,	
	Ὀρέστα, τὴν cὴν ξυμφοράν, ὅθ' ὧδ' ἔχων	
	πρὸς τῆcδ' ὑβρίζῃ μητρόc. ἆρ' ἔχω καλῶc;	790
ΚΛ.	οὔτοι cύ· κεῖνοc δ' ὡc ἔχει καλῶc ἔχει.	
ΗΛ.	ἄκουε, Νέμεci τοῦ θανόντος ἀρτίωc.	
ΚΛ.	ἤκουcεν ὧν δεῖ κἀπεκύρωcεν καλῶc.	
ΗΛ.	ὕβριζε· νῦν γὰρ εὐτυχοῦcα τυγχάνειc.	
ΚΛ.	οὔκουν Ὀρέcτηc καὶ cὺ παύcετον τάδε;	795
ΗΛ.	πεπαύμεθ' ἡμεῖc, οὐχ ὅπωc cὲ παύcομεν.	
ΚΛ.	πολλῶν ἂν ἥκοιc, ὦ ξέν', ἄξιοc φίλοc,	
	εἰ τήνδ' ἔπαυcαc τῆc πολυγλώccου βοῆc.	

LINE 788

οἰμώζω   cry οἴμοι, wail, lament; [1× *El.*]

πάρα   (⁺πάρειμι) = πάρεcτι + dat. (missing here) (impersonal: it is in one's power: S #175b); > 'for now it is allowed [to me] =) now I can lament your misfortune, Orestes'

⁺Ὀρέcτα   masculines in –τηc have voc. in short α (S #226). (Soph. omits ὦ with persons' names without modification or complement: SS 27 §9)

⁺ξύμφορα, ἡ   = cύμφορα (cύν, φέρω) bringing together, event, mishap, misfortune

⁺πρόc   'by' with genit. of agent is common in poetry (S #1755); > 'when this is your situation and you are insulted *by* this mother of yours'

⁺ἆρα   interrog. pcl. indicating anxiety and impatience (LSJ 1; GP 46); > 'Am I not well off?'

LINE 791

⁺οὔ-τοι (adv.)   'You are *certainly not* [well off], but he, as he is, is well off'

⁺*ἄκουε   (pres. impv.) see 643n on ἄκουε

Νέμεcιc, εωc, ἡ   impersonation of divine retribution. (resolution in 4th position Νέμεcι); > 'Hear [this] Nemesis, of the one who just (⁺ἀρτίωc) died'

ὧν   probably masculine for Clyt. and Aeg.; > 'She heard those who should (δεῖ) be heard'

ἐπι-κῡρόω   = καὶ ἐπεκύρωcεν; confirm, sanction, ratify; > 'and ratified these matters well'; (1× Soph.)

LINE 794

⁺εὐ-τῠχέω   (εὖ, τύχη, chance, fortune) be lucky, be well off, succeed (supplem. ptc. with ⁺*τυγχάνω, which contains the main idea: S #2096a, GMT #887, SS 261 §12f); > 'go on with your insults; for now *is your moment of luck*'

⁺οὔκουν   often with 2nd pers. fut. indic. or opt. with ἄν (GP 431)

⁺παύcετον   (⁺παύω, 2nd pers. dual. fut. indic.) stop (notice the repetition of the verb framing the following line); > 'Then will you two not stop this?'

οὐχ ⁺ὅπωc   Kells: "elliptical for οὐ (λέγω) ὅπωc"; > 'we ourselves have been stopped; I can't say *how* we shall stop you'; GMT #708: "we have been stopped ourselves; *there is no talk* of our stopping you"

⁺πολλῶν   genit. following ⁺ἄξιοc (LSJ ii.2); > 'worthy of great reward'

ἂν ⁺ἥκοιc   opt. with ἄν might indicate here a cautious variant of the present = "urbane ἥκειc" (Kamerbeek); > 'you are coming, stranger, as a friend worthy of . . .'

ΠΑ.	οὔκουν ἀποστείχοιμ' ἄν, εἰ τάδ' εὖ κυρεῖ;	
ΚΛ.	ἥκιστ'· ἐπείπερ οὔτ' ἐμοῦ κατάξι' ἂν	800
	πράξειας οὔτε τοῦ πορεύσαντος ξένου.	
	ἀλλ' εἴσιθ' εἴσω· τήνδε δ' ἔκτοθεν βοᾶν	
	ἔα τά θ' αὑτῆς καὶ τὰ τῶν φίλων κακά.	
ΗΛ.	ἆρ' ὑμὶν ὡς ἀλγοῦσα κὠδυνωμένη	
	δεινῶς δακρῦσαι κἀπικωκῦσαι δοκεῖ	805
	τὸν υἱὸν ἡ δύστηνος ὧδ' ὀλωλότα;	

+ἔπαυσας	εἰ with the aorist indicative "introduces a supposition that is regarded as certain: 'if *really* you did . . .'" (Kamerbeek)
πολύ-γλωσσος, ον	(πολύς, γλῶσσα) many-tongued, loud-voiced, oft repeated (LSJ)
+βοή, ἡ	cry, shout, outcry (genit. with verbs of separating. SS 67 §30: "stopped her from [making] her noise")

LINE 799

ἀπο-στείχω	go away, go back; [1× *El.*]
+εὖ κῠρεῖ	(poetic for εὖ τυγχάνει); > 'Then may I be on my way, if all is well?'
ἥκιστα (adv.)	least; in reply to a question: not at all, <u>no</u> (emphatic)
κατάξιος, ον	quite worthy of (κατάξια acc. neut. plural, adverbial)
+*πράξειας	(πράττω, aor. opt. act); potential optative with ἄν, expressing an opinion (S #1826)
πορεύω	bring, carry, convey; > 'since you would not fare worthily of me and of the friend who sent you.' Clyt. refers to Phanoteus, cf. 670–72; [1× *El.*]
+εἴσ-*ειμι	(εἴσιτε, impv.) go in, go into
+εἴσω	to, within, into; + genit.; to within, into
ἔκτοθεν	(adv. ἐκτός, ἐκ) outside, from without; [1× Soph.]
+*ἐάω	[ᾰ] (impv.) > 'let her to scream outside about her own sorrows and those of her near and dear.' This is the last time we see Clyt. and hear her before her death cry.

Clytemnestra, the maidservant, and the Tutor go into the palace. Electra and the Chorus remain outside.

LINE 804

ἆρα	interrog. pcl. indicating anxiety and impatience; here expecting the answer 'no' (GP 46 II.2)
ἀλγέω	suffer pain, grieve, be troubled, distressed
ὀδῠνάω	κὠδυνωμένη = καὶ ὀδυνωμένη; cause pain; pass: feel pain, suffer; [1× *El.*]
ἐπι-κωκύω	[ῠ] κἀπικωκῦσαι = καὶ ἐπικωκῦσαι; (κωκῡτός, ὁ, Cocytus, the river of Wailing in the Netherworld); lament over
δοκεῖ	personal use sharing a subject with infs. δακρῦσαι and ἐπικωκῦσαι: 'she,' accompanied by two circumstancial ptcs. in nom.: ἀλγοῦσα and ὀδυνωμένη (S #1973); > '*Does she seem* to you to cry in pain and suffering, the poor woman, and lament her son who died in this way?'
υἱός, ὁ	son; [1× *El.*]
+*ὀλωλότα	(ὄλλυμι, pf. act. ptc.) τὸν . . . ὀλωλότα *hyperbaton* sandwiching the subject ἡ δύστηνος, 'the poor woman,' in between.

ἀλλ' ἐγγελῶcα φροῦδοc. ὦ τάλαιν' ἐγώ·
Ὀρέcτα φίλταθ', ὥc μ' ἀπώλεcαc θανών.
ἀποcπάcαc γὰρ τῆc ἐμῆc οἴχη φρενὸc
αἵ μοι μόναι παρῆcαν ἐλπίδων ἔτι,   810
cὲ πατρὸc ἥξειν ζῶντα τιμωρόν ποτε
κἀμοῦ ταλαίνηc. νῦν δὲ ποῖ με χρὴ μολεῖν;
μόνη γάρ εἰμι, cοῦ τ' ἀπεcτερημένη
καὶ πατρόc. ἤδη δεῖ με δουλεύειν πάλιν
ἐν τοῖcιν ἐχθίcτοιcιν ἀνθρώπων ἐμοί,   815
φονεῦcι πατρόc. ἆρά μοι καλῶc ἔχει;

LINE 807

ἐγγελάω   [ᾰ] laugh at, mock, jeer; [1× *El.*]

⁺φροῦδοc (2/3)   (contracted from πρὸ ὁδοῦ, farther on the road; S #124a) gone away, gone, away (understand ἐcτιν or
                               οἴχεται); > 'No, she has gone off exulting'

⁺ὡc   exclamatory: how (S #2682a, 2998)

⁺ἀπ-⁺⁺ώλεcαc   (ἀπόλλυμι, aor.¹ indic. act.) 'how have you destroyed me with your death!'

ἀπο-cπάω   (ἀποcπάcαc, aor.¹ ptc. act.) tear or drag away; sever, *rip out* (her emotions come through the confusing
                               hyperbatic structure of the sentence, which syntactically reads οἴχη γὰρ τῆc ἐμῆc ⁺φρενὸc ἀποcπάcαc [τῶν]
                               ⁺ἐλπίδων [ταύταc], αἵ μοι μόναι ἔτι παρῆcαν: Kells); > 'you've gone, *ripping out* from my heart/mind the only
                               hopes I still had left'; [1× *El.*]

LINE 810

cὲ . . . ταλαίνηc   The content of her hopes is structured in indirect discourse of accusative with infinitive: cὲ . . . ἥξειν ζῶντα
                               τιμωρόν; > 'that you would come alive one day as an avenger of our father and wretched me'

κἀμοῦ ταλαίνηc; καὶ   *enjambment*s indicating further her emotional upheaval
πατρόc; φονεῦcι πατρόc

LINE 813

⁺ἀπο-cτερέω   (ἀπεcτερημένη, pf. mid. ptc.) rob, bereave; pass: be robbed or in want of + genit.; > 'For I am alone, *de-
                               prived of* both you and our father'

δουλεύω   be a slave (με δουλεύειν accusative + infinitive following δεῖ: S #1985b); > 'now (it is necessary that
                               I . . .) = I must again be a slave'

ἔχθιcτοc (3)   (irregular superlative of ⁺ἐχθρόc: S #318) most hateful (with ἐμοί, dat. of disadvantage: S #1481; SS
                               84–85 §9); > 'among those *most hateful* of mortals to me'

ἆρά μοι καλῶc ἔχει   cf. 790, except that here ἔχει must be impersonal. μοι ethical dat. or dat. of feeling to denote the speaker's
                               interest (S #1486; SS 85§10); > 'aren't things good for me?'

ἀλλ' οὔ τι μὴν ἔγωγε τοῦ λοιποῦ χρόνου
ἔσομαι ξύνοικος, ἀλλὰ τῇδε πρὸς πύλῃ
παρεῖς' ἐμαυτὴν ἄφιλος αὐανῶ βίον.
πρὸς ταῦτα καινέτω τις, εἰ βαρύνεται,   820
τῶν ἔνδον ὄντων· ὡς χάρις μέν, ἢν κτάνῃ,
λύπη δ', ἐὰν ζῶ· τοῦ βίου δ' οὐδεὶς πόθος.

XO   ποῦ ποτε κεραυνοὶ Διός, ἢ ποῦ   στρ. ά
       φαέθων Ἅλιος, εἰ ταῦτ' ἐφορῶντες
       κρύπτουσιν ἔκηλοι ;   825
HΛ.   ἒ ἔ, αἰαῖ.
XO.   ὦ παῖ, τί δακρύεις;

LINE 817

†λοιποῦ †χρόνου	'from this time on, henceforth' (genit. of time)
πύλη, ἡ	[ῠ] gate, entrance, door; ἔσομαι, resolution of 1st anceps
†παρ-*εῖσα	(παρίημι, aor.² ptc. act.) 'letting myself fall'
ἄ-φιλος, ον	(ἀ privat., φίλος) without friends; resolution in 6th position ἄφιλος; [1× El.]
αὐαίνω	(fut. act.) dry, wither; [1× El.]

LINE 820

πρὸς ταῦτα	in regard to this, therefore, <u>in face of that</u>; see 383n
καίνω	(impv. pres. 3sg.) kill; [1× El.]
βαρύνω, ὕνῶ	[ῠ] torment; pass. <u>be vexed, annoyed</u>
τῶν †ἔνδον	supply ἀνθρώπων. Adv. with an article may be used to qualify a noun that is often omitted (S #1153e). Partit. genit. (S #1306, 1315; SS 58 §10. Cf. ἔνδον 155n.); > 'in face of that, let any *of those inside* kill me if he is annoyed [with me]'
†χάρις, –ιτος, ἡ	[ᾰ] favor, pleasure, gratification, gratitude (declension S #257)
ἢν (= ἐὰν) †*κτάνῃ	(κτείνω, aor.² subjv. act.) protasis of pres. general condition as is ἐὰν ζῶ (S #2295.1; S #2565). The apodoses are χάρις [ἐστί] and λύπη [ἐστί]; > 'it is a favor, *if someone kills* me, but pain if I live'
πόθος, ὁ	(ποθέω, love, yearn for) love, desire (LSJ II) (with τοῦ βίου as objective genit.: SS 53, S #1328); > 'there is no desire for life'

KOMMOS (Lyric Dialogue), LINES 823–870

This is a short lyric duet consisting of two strophic pairs between the Coryphaeus, who represents the Chorus, and Electra. The Coryphaeus tries to assuage Electra's grief over the news of Orestes' death by comparing it with a similar mythic situation, but Electra refuses to be comforted by the comparison.

FIRST STROPHE, Lines 823–836

LINE 823

κεραυνός, ὁ	thunderbolt, lightening (often weapon of divine justice); [1× El.]
φαέθω	(φάος, light) (pres. ptc. act.) shine; [1× El.]
Ἅλιος, ὁ	= †Ἥλιος, Sun >'blazing Sun' (the sun is thought to see everything); [1× El.]
ἐφ-†*οράω	(pres. ptc. act.) look at, observe (circumstantial ptc. expresses protasis of simple condition reflecting the tense in which the vb. itself would have stood, here in indic.: εἰ ἐφορῶσιν: S #2060, 2057; GMT #472, 841); > 'if *looking at* these things they complacently keep them hidden?'

ΗΛ.   φεῦ. ΧΟ. μηδὲν μέγ᾽ ἀύςῃς. ΗΛ. ἀπολεῖc.

           ΧΟ. πῶc;   830

ΗΛ.   εἰ τῶν φανερῶς οἰχομένων

        εἰς Ἀίδαν ἐλπίδ᾽ ὑποίσεις, κατ᾽ ἐμοῦ

           τακομέναc   835

        μᾶλλον ἐπεμβάcῃ.

ΧΟ.   οἶδα γὰρ ἄνακτ᾽ Ἀμφιάρεων χρυ-   ἀντ. α᾽

        cοδέτοιc ἔρκεcι κρυφθέντα γυναικῶν

        καὶ νῦν ὑπὸ γαίαc—

ΗΛ.   ἒ ἔ, ἰώ.   840

LINE 829

⁺μέγ᾽	= ⁺μέγᾰ (acc. neut. sg.) used as adv.: very much, exceedingly
ἀύω	(ἀύςῃς, aor.¹ subjv.) shout (μή with prohibitive subjv.: S #1800a; SS 219– 20 §6; GMT #259); [1× *El.*]
φᾰνερῶς (adv.)	(φᾰνερός visible) clearly, openly, manifestly; [1× Soph.]
ὑπο-⁺*φέρω	(ὑποίσεις, ind. fut. act.) <u>hold out</u>, suggest (fut. indic. is often used in the protasis to express a future condition. This is an emphatic form, stronger than the subjv., especially common when the condition contains a strong appeal to the feelings of the addressee or a threat or warning. Common in Tragedy [GMT #447]) > 'If you *shall hold* out hope for those who have clearly gone to Hades'); [1× Soph.]
ἐπ-εμ-⁺*βαίνω	(ἐπεμβάcῃ, indic. fut. dep. 2sg.) step upon, tread upon; trample upon (apodosis of future condition; > 'you will be *trampling* yet harder [μᾶλλον] on me as I waste away [τακομέναc = ⁺τηκομένης, genit. sg. fem.])'

FIRST ANTISTROPHE, Lines 837–848

LINE 837

Ἀμφιάρεως, ω	= Ἀμφιάραον; Argive hero and seer (acc. sg.: S #237–38. One of the Seven who fought in the expedition against Thebes, after being persuaded by Eriphyle, his wife, whom Polyneices bribed with a golden necklace. He was driven off during the attack, but the gods thought he was too good a man to be killed there, and had him swallowed up by earth instead. Amphiaraus retained his faculties in the Netherworld, where he rules. *Synizesis* of -εω-); [1× *El.*]
⁺κρυφθέντα	(κρύπτω, aor.¹ pass. ptc.) with Ἀμφιάρεων, participle after verb of knowing and perceiving, οἶδα (S #2106, 2592c; SS 260 §12, 318 §6)
χρῡσό-δετος, ον	bound with gold, set in gold; [1× Soph.]
ἕρκος, εος, τό	(ἔργω, εἴργω, shut in) enclosure (dat. of means. Kells: "plural for singular. Sophocles telescoped two meanings. For ἕρκεcι describes *both* the necklace that Eriphyle put on . . . and the 'snare' that the proceeding represented for Amphiaraus"); [1× *El.*]

ΧΟ.	πάμψυχος ἀνάσσει.	
ΗΛ.	φεῦ. ΧΟ. φεῦ δῆτ'· ὀλοὰ γὰρ— ΗΛ. Δάμαρ	
	ἦν. ΧΟ. ναί.	845
ΗΛ.	οἶδ' οἶδ'· ἐφάνη γὰρ μελέτωρ	
	ἀμφὶ τὸν ἐν πένθει· ἐμοὶ δ' οὔτις ἔτ' ἔσθ'· ὃς γὰρ ἔτ' ἦν,	
	φροῦδος ἀναρπασθείς.	

ΧΟ.	δειλαία δειλαίων κυρεῖς.	στρ. β'
ΗΛ.	κἀγὼ τοῦδ' ἴστωρ, ὑπερίστωρ,	850
	πανσύρτῳ παμμήνῳ πολλῶν	
	δεινῶν στυγνῶν τ' αἰῶνι.	

---

†γυναικῶν	the reference is to Eriphyle; the plural might be influenced by the plural of ἕρκεσι (SS 7 §4c); > 'For I know that the lord Amphiareus who was entombed through a woman's golden snare, now underground . . .'

LINE 843

πάμ-ψῡχος, ον	(πᾶς, ψυχή) in full possession of life, with spirit full of power; [1× Soph.]
ἀνάσσω	[ἄ] rule, hold sway (poetic verb mostly in pres.)
φεῦ †δῆτ'	alas indeed (S #2851, GP 277)
ὀλοός (3)	= ὀλόή (*†ὄλλῡμι, destroy) destructive, destroying; > 'Indeed, for the destructive . . .'; [1× El.]
δάμᾰρ, αρτος, ἡ	[ᾰ] (δαμάζω, make subject to) wife
†ναί (adv.)	yea, verily
μελέτωρ, ορος, ὁ	(μέλω, care) one who cares for, comforter, avenger (Amphiareus' son Alcmaeon, avenged his father by killing his mother); [1× Soph.]
†ἀμφί (+ acc.)	about; for, for the sake of
πένθος, εος, τό	grief, sorrow; misfortune; > 'an avenger appeared for *him in his sorrow*'
ἔστι	accented on the penult in existential use (S #187b); > 'but for me there *is* none'
ἀν-αρπάζω	(ἀναρπασθείς, aor.¹ ptc. pass.) snatch up; > 'for he whom I had, is gone, carried off'; (1× El.)

SECOND STROPHE, Lines 849–858

LINE 849

†κῠρεῖς	(poetic for τυγχάνεις) 'unhappy woman, *you meet with* unhappy circumstances (†δειλαίων)'; δειλαία δειλαίων polyptoton.
ἴστωρ, ορος, ὁ/ἡ	(*†οἶδα, know) one who knows (agent noun: S #839.3); [1× Soph.]
ὑπερ-ίστωρ, ορος, ὁ/ἡ	knowing but too well (with genit. Intensified repetition); [1× Soph.]
πάν-συρτος, ον	(πᾶς, σύρω) swept together from every side, accumulated; [1× Soph.]
πάμ-μηνος, ον	(πᾶς, μήν) through every month, through the livelong year (notice the alliteration of π); [1× Soph.]
στῠγνός (3)	hateful, abhorred; sad, gloomy
†αἰών, ῶνος, ὁ	period of existence; > 'I know this well, all too well, I, whose life through all the months that flow one into the other is one of many hateful afflictions'

ΧΟ.	εἴδομεν ἃ θροεῖc.	
ΗΛ.	μή μέ νυν μηκέτι	
	παραγάγῃc, ἵν' οὐ— ΧΟ. τί φήc;	855
ΗΛ.	πάρειcιν ἐλπίδων ἔτι κοινοτόκων	
	εὐπατριδᾶν ἀρωγαί.	
ΧΟ.	πᾶcιν θνατοῖc ἔφυ μόρος.	ἀντ. β'
ΗΛ.	ἦ καὶ χαλάργοιc ἐν ἁμίλλαιc	861
	οὕτωc, ὡc κείνῳ δυστάνῳ,	
	τμητοῖc ὁλκοῖc ἐγκῦρcαι;	
ΧΟ.	ἄcκοποc ἁ λώβα.	
ΗΛ.	πῶc γὰρ οὔκ; εἰ ξένοс	865
	ἄτερ ἐμᾶν χερῶν— ΧΟ. παπαῖ.	
ΗΛ.	κέκευθεν, οὔτε του τάφου ἀντιάcαc	
	οὔτε γόων παρ' ἡμῶν.	870

LINE 853

ἅ	relative pronoun; antecedent omitted: [ταῦτα] ἅ (S #2509)
θροέω	(θρόος, a confused noise) cry aloud; <u>speak, declare</u>; > 'we know what you are shouting about'
⁺μηκέτι (adv.)	(μή, ἔτι) no longer, no more, no further (notice the alliteration of μ)
παρ-άγω, -ήγαγον	(παραγάγῃc, aor.² subjv.) lead aside, divert (μή + prohibitive subjv.: S #1800a; SS 219–220 §6; GMT #259); > '*Do not divert* me any longer to where there are not . . .'
ἐλπίδων	genit. of definition or explanatory/appositional genit. (S. #1322; SS 53 §5); > 'consisting of hopes'
κοινό-τοκος, ον	(κοινόc, τεκεῖν) born of common parents; [1× *El.*]
εὐ-πᾰτρίδης, ου, ὁ	(εὖ, πᾰτήρ, genit. pl.) of a noble sire, of a noble family; > 'where there are no longer present aids (⁺ἀρωγαί) consisting of hopes that come *from noble ones* of the same stock'

SECOND ANTISTROPHE, Lines 860–870

LINE 860

⁺*ἔφυ	(φύω, aor.²); 'is a law of nature' (gnomic aorist expressing general truth: S #1931; GMT #154; SS 196–97 §17)
μόρος, ὁ	death; > 'death is the fate of all mortals'; [1× *El.*]
ἦ καί	interrogative ἦ usually followed by καί often introduces a suggested answer (GP 282–83)
χᾰλαργός (3)	Doric for χηλαργός (χηλή, horse hoof) with fleet hoofs; [1× Soph.]
ἅμιλλα, ἡ	contest; [1× *El.*]
τμητός (3)	(τέμνω cut) cut, shaped by cutting (here it clearly suggests cutting Orestes' body proper, see 747)
ὁλκός, ὁ	(ἕλκω, draw) that which draws, i.e., <u>dragging rein</u>; [1× *El.*]
ἐγ-*κῠρέω	(ἐγκῦρcαι, aor.¹ inf. act.) meet, to fall in with + dat.; > 'But to meet [death] thus, in a contest of swift hooves, such [as happened] to the unhappy one, by the raw-cutting, dragging reins?'; [1× Soph.]

LINE 864

ἄ-σκοπος, ον	(ἀ privat., σκοπέω) not to be seen: incredible
λώβη, ἡ	ill-usage (by word or deed), outrage, <u>mutilation, maiming</u>; Chorus' comment serves as apodosis to the following protasis; [1× *El.*]
ἄτερ (+ genit.)	without, apart from, away from

XP.　　　　　　ὑφ' ἡδονῆς τοι, φιλτάτη, διώκομαι
　　　　　　　τὸ κόσμιον μεθεῖcα cὺν τάχει μολεῖν.
　　　　　　　φέρω γὰρ ἡδονάc τε κἀνάπαυλαν ὧν
　　　　　　　πάροιθεν εἶχεc καὶ κατέcτενεc κακῶν.

κεύθω	cover up, hide, conceal (the perfect indicates a completed action the effects of which still continue into the present: S #1945); > 'lies buried.' (The present and perfect of the verb are used intransitively of the dead in Tragedy: Kamerbeek)
οὔτε . . . οὔτε	the protasis explains the apodosis: 'How not? If as an exile without my hands [tending to him] . . . he lies buried, having met with *no* rites of burial *or* lament from me.' The use of οὐ (οὔτε . . . οὔτε) rather than μή in the protasis comes from the explanatory content that El. regards as reality (SS 321–22 §4b; Finglass)
του	= τινός, any, some (indefinite pron. used here adj.: S #1266)
ἀντιάω	(ἀντιάσας, aor.¹ act. ptc.) meet with + genit.; as participle: 'having obtained' (LSJ I.1); [1× *El.*]

THIRD EPISODE, LINES 871–1057

The Third Episode divides into two parts: Part A: lines 871–937, and Part B, lines 938–1057.

Each part is subdivided into three sections:
Part A: Lines 871–937: (1) 871–891: After being sent to Agamemnon's grave Chrysothemis arrives with great excitement: she is convinced that she has proof that Orestes has arrived. (2) 892–919: Chrysothemis reports what she has seen on the tomb. (3) 920–937: In the ensuing conversation Electra convinces Chrysothemis of her error.

Part A: (1) Lines 871–891

LINE 871

⁺τοι	'you know,' 'I tell you' (according to GP 541.6, reveals "the speaker's emotional . . . state". Chr. wants El. to know of her joy: GP 537, 539. I.e.: 'I am so excited')
δῐώκω	pursue, go after; impel; mid.: 'impelled myself'
κόσμιος (3/2)	well ordered; τὸ κόσμιον order, <u>decorum</u> (substantival use of article with adjective. : S #1021, 1153a; SS 163 §1. Neuter expresses a general, abstract idea: S #1023); [1× Soph.]
⁺*μολεῖν	(βλώσκω, aor.² inf. act.) poetic verb occurring 89× in Sophocles, always in aor.²; dependent on διώκομαι; > 'My dearest, I am impelled by joy *to come* here quickly having put aside all decorum'
ἀνά-παυλα, ἡ	(ἀναπαύω, make cease) ease (from a thing), rest; [1× *El.*]
τε . . . καὶ	sometimes couples opposites, "and therefore rest from" (Kamerbeek)
ὧν	(a) the antecedent κακῶν is put into the relative clause and postponed to the end of the sentence; (b) the relative is attracted into the case of the antecedent: ἀνάπαυλαν <u>τούτων</u> <u>τῶν</u> <u>κακῶν</u> <u>ἃ</u> πάροιθεν εἶχες
πάροιθε(ν) (adv.)	formerly, erst, before
κατα-στένω	sigh over, lament; [1× *El.*]

ΗΛ.	πόθεν δ' ἄν εὕροις τῶν ἐμῶν cὺ πημάτων	875
	ἄρηξιν, οἷc ἴαcιc οὐκ ἔνεcτ' ἔτι;	
ΧΡ.	πάρεcτ' Ὀρέcτηc ἡμίν, ἴcθι τοῦτ' ἐμοῦ	
	κλύουc', ἐναργῶc, ὥcπερ εἰcορᾷc ἐμέ.	
ΗΛ.	ἀλλ' ἦ μέμηναc, ὦ τάλαινα, κἀπὶ τοῖc	
	cαυτῆc κακοῖcι κἀπὶ τοῖc ἐμοῖc γελᾷc;	880
ΧΡ.	μὰ τὴν πατρῴαν ἑcτίαν, ἀλλ' οὐχ ὕβρει	
	λέγω τάδ', ἀλλ' ἐκεῖνον ὡc παρόντα νῦν.	

LINE 875

πόθεν	whence
ἄν +*εὕροις	(εὑρίcκω, aor.²) potential opt. (S #1824). At times potential opt. is used to express irony (S #1826), here mixed with bitterness. To some the late placing of cύ suggests contempt; > 'And where *could **you** find* help for my sufferings?'
ἄρεξις, εως, ἡ	(ἀρήγω, help) help, succor; [1× *El.*]
ἴᾱcιc, εως, ἡ	(ἰάομαι, cure) cure, remedy; (1× *El.*)
+ἔν-+*εcτι	+ dat. (οἷc) > 'for which there is no more remedy'

LINE 877

ἡμίν	the -ι- is shortened even though the pronoun is emphatic (S #325f). Dat. of advantage (*commodi*) (S #1481; SS 84–85 §9); > 'Orestes is here for/with us'
+*ἴcθι	(+*οἶδα, pf. impv. act. 2sg.)
+κλύουcα	supplem. ptc. after vb. of knowing, +*ἴcθι, (S #2106; SS 260 §12e, 318 §6) in nominative agreement with the subject S #2108); >'*know* this, *hearing* it from me'
ἐναργῶc (adv.)	(ἐναργής, visible) distinctly, visibly; [1× Soph.]

LINE 879

ἀλλ' ἦ	'Why . . . ?' (GP 27.4: "starts "an objection in interrogative form, giving lively expression to a feeling of surprise or incredulity"")
μαίνω	(μέμηναc, pf. act. with pres. sense) be mad (usually poetic)
+γελάω	laugh; γελάω ἐπί τινι—laugh at, mock something; > 'Are you mocking both your suffering and mine?'
μά	[ᾰ] asseverative adv. + acc. of the deity or thing appealed to, by itself neither affirming nor negating (LSJ; S #2894)
ἑcτία, ἡ	(ἕζομαι, sit) hearth of a house (accusative used in oaths: S #1596b; SS 47 §19); > 'by our father's hearth' [1× *El.*]
ἀλλ'	as a strong adversative should be first in its clause, except when an oath or apostrophe precedes (GP 22–23, iii). The second ἀλλά is a simple repetition. While artistic repetition was considered stylistically effective, an accidental repetition was "a thing to be sedulously and artificially avoided" (GP lxii)
οὐχ +ὕβρει	[ῠ] 'I say this not in *hybris*/mockery'
ἐκεῖνον ὡc +παρ-+*όντα	Chr. reasserts her former message. The sense of λέγω is carried into this clause. Since λέγω regularly takes the infinitive or ὡc and ὅτι in indirect discourse, the use of a participle might suggest emphasis on Chr.'s insistence that Or. is alive and present (SS 318 §6; GMT #910, cf. Finglass on 676). The participial construction can come with or without ὡc. If it accompanies the participle it is often used to indicate the mental attitude of the subject of the main verb or another prominent person in the sentence (S #2120–2121); > 'I do not say this in mockery, but that both of us *have him here* (lit.: he is present for both of us). Cf. ἤγγειλαc 1341n

ΗΛ.   οἴμοι τάλαινα· καὶ τίνος βροτῶν λόγον
                τόνδ' εἰσακούσας' ὧδε πιστεύεις ἄγαν;

ΧΡ.   ἐγὼ μὲν ἐξ ἐμοῦ τε κοὐκ ἄλλου σαφῆ   885
                σημεῖ' ἰδοῦσα τῷδε πιστεύω λόγῳ.

ΗΛ.   τίν', ὦ τάλαιν', ἰδοῦσα πίστιν; ἐς τί μοι
                βλέψασα θάλπῃ τῷδ' ἀνηφαίστῳ πυρί;

ΧΡ.   πρός νυν θεῶν ἄκουσον, ὡς μαθοῦσά μου
                τὸ λοιπὸν ἢ φρονοῦσαν ἢ μώραν λέγῃς.   890

ΗΛ.   σὺ δ' οὖν λέγ', εἴ σοι τῷ λόγῳ τις ἡδονή.

LINE 883

⁺καί (adv.)	and (for stress. The query is an indignant comment on the preceding statement)
⁺ὧδε (adv.)	emphatic by anaphoric use, i.e., refers to what has immediately preceded: Chr.'s confidence (SS 155; S #1247)
⁺πιστεύω	believe, trust, put faith in; > 'from whom of men have you heard this story *in which you place too much* (ἄγαν) *belief?*'
μέν	either emphatic (Kamerbeek), i.e., emphasizes her confident belief, or antithetical (Kells), i.e., rejecting El.'s insinuation; > 'No, I . . .'
τε καί	see 873n: '(and) by me and not by anyone else'
σημεῖον, τό	(σῆμα, sign) mark, sign of token by which something is inferred; > 'I believe this story after having seen clear signs by my own eyes not [hearing] from anyone else'

LINE 887

πίστις, εως, ἡ	trust, that which gives trust, assurance, <u>proof</u>, proof of reliability; > ' What proof have you seen, poor girl?'
μοι	'tell me for my sake; 'I would like to know,' sets a scornful tone here; 'ethical dat.' or 'dat. of feeling' to denote the speaker's interest (S #1486; SS 85 §10)
⁺*βλέπω	(βλέψασα, aor.¹ act. ptc.) see (refers to Chr.'s ἰδοῦσα)
θάλπω	(pres. ind. pass.) warm, heat; metaphorically: inflame; [1× *El.*]
τῷδε	in anaphoric use, see ὧδε 884n
ἀν-ήφαιστος, ον	(ἀ privat. + Ἥφαιστος) without real fire (this is an emendation and unattested in Soph.; the codd. reading of ἀνηκέστῳ [1× *El.*]: incurable, desperate, fatal, is preferable)
πῦρ, πυρός, τό	fire (declension: S #285); > '(having looked at what =) what did you look at, I would like to know, that you are inflamed by this fire not from Hephaestus?'
⁺ὡς . . . ⁺*λέγῃς	final clause. subjv. after primary sequence of aor.¹ impv., ἄκουσον: S #2196; GMT #317. Impv. moods point to the future and thus considered as primary (S #1858a)
μου	ablatival genit., answers 'from where'; follows a verb of learning, ⁺*μαθοῦσα; (S #1391; SS 66–67 §28); > 'so that after having learned/heard *from me*, you can say then . . .'
τὸ ⁺λοιπόν	the remainder, the future
ἤ . . . ἤ	either . . . or
μῶρος (3)	stupid, silly, foolish; > 'whether I am sensible or addled'
δ'οὖν	permissive, used in drama according to GP 466.4: "to denote that the speaker waives any objection . . . to something being done, or contemplated, by another person . . . the tone is usually defiant." The following verb is usually in impv.; > 'All right, then, . . .'

XP.   καὶ δὴ λέγω coι πᾶν ὅcον κατειδόμην.
               ἐπεὶ γὰρ ἦλθον πατρὸc ἀρχαῖον τάφον,
               ὁρῶ κολώνηc ἐξ ἄκραc νεορρύτουc
               πηγὰc γάλακτοc καὶ περιcτεφῆ κύκλῳ   895
               πάντων ὅc' ἔcτιν ἀνθέων θήκην πατρόc.
               ἰδοῦcα δ' ἔcχον θαῦμα, καὶ περιcκοπῶ
               μή πού τιc ἡμῖν ἐγγὺc ἐγχρίμπτει βροτῶν.

Part A: (2) Lines 892–919

LINE 892

καὶ δή	'very well then' (GP 251: "in response to a definite command, often with word of command echoed")
καθ-⁺*ὁράω, -εῖδον	(κατειδόμην, aor.² mid.) look down; <u>see distinctly</u> (Kells: "Soph. not infrequently uses the middle of ὁρᾶν in the same sense as the active"); > 'exactly as I saw it'; [1× *El.*]
⁺γάρ (pcl.)	'the fact is that' (explanatory, see 32n)
ἀρχαῖος (3)	(ἀρχή, beginning) ancient, ancestral (containing the ashes of Ag.'s ancestors as well as his); [1× *El.*]
⁺τάφον	[ᾰ] the tomb consisted of a mound of earth beneath which there was a stone chamber where the dead were buried
κολώνη, ἡ	hill, mound, especially a sepulchral mound; [1× Soph.]
νεό-ρρῠτος, ον	(νέος, ῥέω) fresh flowing; [1× Soph.]

LINE 895

πηγή, ἡ	stream; [1× *El.*]
γάλᾰ, γάλακτος, τό	[ᾰ] milk (genit. of material: S #1323); > 'I saw rivulets of milk new- flowing from the top of the mound'; [1× Soph.]
περι-στεφής, ές	wreathed, crowned; [1× Soph.]
κύκλος, ὁ	ring, circle; [1× *El.*]
ἄνθος, εος, τό	flower; > 'and decked all around with every sort (ὅσα) of flower'; [1× *El.*]
θήκη, ἡ	(⁺*τίθημι) general term for sepulcher whatever the form (Jebb)
⁺*ἰδοῦσα δ'	repeats ὁρῶ from l. 894. Circumstantial participle denoting time (S #2060; SS 252–53 §4). Connective δέ (GP 162.I–165); > 'and when I saw [this] I was amazed'
θαῦμα, ατος, τό	wonder, marvel
περι-σκοπέω	look at from all sides, look about, watch and see (historical present for vividness: S #1883; SS 183 §3.1); [1× Soph.]
που (adv.)	somewhere
ἐγ-χρίμπτω	dash against, fall upon, attack; <u>approach</u> (περισκοπέω expresses apprehension with μή and fear clause. The fear can be present or past; μή therefore can be used with present or past of indicative: S #2224.a; GMT #369); > 'I looked around *lest* (someone of people =) *anyone was approaching* nearby; [1× Soph.]
ἐγγύς (adv.)	near; [1× *El.*]

ὡς δ' ἐν γαλήνῃ πάντ' ἐδερκόμην τόπον,
τύμβου προσεῖρπον ἆccον· ἐcχάτηc δ' ὁρῶ   **900**
πυρᾶc νεώρη βόcτρυχον τετμημένον·
κεὐθὐc τάλαιν' ὡc εἶδον, ἐμπαίει τί μοι
ψυχῇ cύνηθεc ὄμμα, φιλτάτου βροτῶν
πάντων Ὀρέcτου τοῦθ' ὁρᾶν τεκμήριον·

LINE 889

γαλήνη, ἡ	calm, stillness; [1× Soph.]
+*δέρκομαι	look, see, behold
τόπος, ὁ	place; [1× El.]
προσ-έρπω	(impf. indic.) creep, steal on, <u>draw near</u>; [1× El.]
ἆσσον (adv.)	(comparative of ἄγχι) nearer; [1× El.]
ἔσχᾰτος (3)	the farthest, uttermost, extreme
πῠρά, ἡ	funeral pyre (genit. of place, within which or at which an action happens: S #1448; SS 59 §11.ii: "on the edge of the mound")
νε-ωρής, ές	(νέος, ὥρα) new, fresh, late; [1× El.]
βόστρῠχος, ὁ	curl, lock of hair
τέμνω, τέτημαι	(τετμημένον, pf. pass. pct.) cut; > 'lock of hair just cut off'

LINE 902

ἐμπαίω	strike in; intransitive: <u>burst in upon</u> (historical present for vividness: S #1883; SS 183 §3.1; GMT #33); [1× Soph.]
συνηθής, ές	dwelling, living together; well acquainted, <u>familiar</u>; [1× El.]
+ὄμμα, ατος, τό	eye; image; illumination; poetic word; > 'as soon as I saw it, unhappy me, some familiar image struck my mind'
ὁρᾶν	Understand: '[I felt] that I saw.' The infinitive depends on the notion of her feeling implied in previous words (Kamerbeek)
φιλτάτου ... Ὀρέστου	for emphasis in a/b/b/a chiastic structure: φιλτάτου βροτῶν / πάντων Ὀρέστου

καὶ χερcὶ βαcτάcαcα δυcφημῶ μὲν οὔ,   905
χαρᾷ δὲ πίμπλημ' εὐθὺc ὄμμα δακρύων.
καὶ νῦν θ' ὁμοίωc καὶ τότ' ἐξεπίcταμαι
μή του τόδ' ἀγλάιcμα πλὴν κείνου μολεῖν.
τῷ γὰρ προcήκει πλήν γ' ἐμοῦ καὶ coῦ τόδε;
κἀγὼ μὲν οὐκ ἔδραcα, τοῦτ' ἐπίcταμαι,   910
οὐδ' αὖ cύ· πῶc γάρ; ἥ γε μηδὲ πρὸc θεοὺc
ἔξεcτ' ἀκλαύτῳ τῆcδ' ἀποcτῆναι cτέγηc.

LINE 905

⁺χερcί	dat. of means (S #1507; SS 88–89 §16); > 'with my hands'
⁺βαcτάζω	(aor.¹ ptc. act.) lift, lift up
δυcφημέω	utter an ill-omened word (οὔ at the end of a line is emphatic)
⁺χᾰρά, ἡ	joy, delight pleasure (dat. of means: S #1507; SS 88–89 §16)
πίμπλημι	fill
⁺δάκρυ, voc, τό	(= δάκρῠον, τό) tear (genit. of material: S #1323); > 'but at once my eye[s] filled [I filled in respect to my eye; ὄμμα acc. of respect] *with tears* of joy [with joy consisting *of tears*])'
νῦν θ' . . . καὶ τότ'	'both now and then'
ὁμοίωc (adv.)	(ὅμοιοc, like, resembling) in like manner, like, alike
ἐξ-επίcταμαι	know thoroughly (completive sense of ἐξ- 'thoroughly,' 'fully': S #1688.2; SS 111§9), lending emphasis to the following negative statement. Verbs of knowing take an accusative and infinitive structure: τόδ' ἀγλάιcμα . . . μή . . . μολεῖν (S #2106); > 'and I fully believe that . . .'; [1× *El.*]
ἀγλάιcμα, τό	ornament, pleasing gift; [1× *El.*]
του . . . κείνου	(= τινόc) ablatival genit. with verb of motion, 'from what source' (S #1391; SS 66 §26); > 'I fully believe that this pleasing gift came *from no one but him*'

LINE 909

⁺προc-⁺ήκει	impersonal with dat. (τῷ = τίνι) <u>beseems</u>, <u>belongs</u>, <u>befits</u>; > '*for to whom does this belong* besides me and you ?'
πῶc γάρ	elliptical interrogative formula indicating that something is impossible (S #2805b; GP 86); > 'how should that be?'
ἥ γε μηδέ	not οὐδε, because the causal relative clause has idea of classification ('of such a sort': S #2555b; SS 262 §1); > 'neither did you—for how could you?—*to whom it is not allowed . . .*'
⁺ἔξ-⁺*εcτι	+ inf. ἀποcτῆναι as subject + dat. (S #1984, 1985)
ἄ-κλαυτοc, ον	(κλαίω, weep) without tears, without lamentation (dat. of manner: S #1516; SS 90–92 §19. The punishment indicates that the restriction is specific to El. rather than to women at large); [1× *El.*]
ἀφ-⁺*ίcτημι, -έcτην	(ἀποcτῆναι, aor.² inf. act.) stand away, withdraw, keep off; > 'to go out of the house even to make offerings to the gods without (tears =) being punished'

ἀλλ᾽ οὐδὲ μὲν δὴ μητρὸς οὔθ᾽ ὁ νοῦς φιλεῖ
τοιαῦτα πράσσειν οὔτε δρῶς᾽ ἐλάνθαν᾽ ἄν·
ἀλλ᾽ ἔστ᾽ Ὀρέστου ταῦτα τἀπιτύμβια.   915
ἀλλ᾽, ὦ φίλη, θάρςυνε. τοῖς αὐτοῖςί τοι
οὐχ αὑτὸς αἰεὶ δαιμόνων παραςτατεῖ.
νῷν δ᾽ ἦν ὁ πρόςθε ςτυγνός· ἡ δὲ νῦν ἴςως
πολλῶν ὑπάρξει κῦρος ἡμέρα καλῶν.

ΗΛ.   φεῦ, τῆς ἀνοίας ὥς ς᾽ ἐποικτίρω πάλαι.   920

LINE 913

ἀλλ᾽ οὐδὲ μὲν δή	'but as for' (Jebb: "rejecting an alternative")
φιλεῖ	here in its 'philosophical' sense: "is accustomed"; > 'but as for our mother, her mind is not accustomed to do such things'
+*οὔτε +*δρῶς᾽ +*ἐλάνθαν᾽ ἄν	λανθάνω is supplemented by δρῶσα, which points to the main action while the ἐλάνθανε tells something about how the action occurred (S #2096a; GMT #887; SS 261 §12f). ἐλάνθαν᾽ ἄν is a potential indic. ἄν with the indic. of secondary tenses, generally imperfect and aorist, expresses past possibility, probability, or necessity (S #1784; GMT #198, 243–44); > 'nor could she have done it escaping [our] notice'
ἐπι-τύμβιος (3)	(ἐπι, τύμβος) at a tomb ('offerings at the tomb.' ἔςτι existential); > 'No, these are offerings at the tomb are from Orestes'; [1× *El.*]
θαρςύνω	[ῠ] be of good courage; [1× Soph.]
αὐτός	= ὁ αὐτός (S #1322) (ὁ αὐτός δαιμόνων: αὐτός in attributive position meaning 'same': S #1163, 1204.2, 1210. δαιμόνων is genit. of definition: SS 53 §5); lit.: 'the same one of the daimons' i.e., 'the same daimon/fortune'
παρα-ςτᾰτέω	stand by, <u>attend</u>; > 'the same fortune doesn't always *attend* the same people'; [1× *El.*]

LINE 918

ςτῠγνός (3)	<u>hateful</u>, abhorred; sad, gloomy (νῷν dual. dat. of possession: S #1476)
ἴςως (adv.)	perhaps; [1× *El.*]
ὑπ-άρχω	make a beginning (intransitive)
κῦρος, εος, τό	authority, validity (nom. without article serves as predicative to ἡμέρα. Note the emphatic two instances of *hyperbaton* of ἡ . . . ἡμέρα and πολλῶν . . . καλῶν that end Chr.'s speech); > 'the present day perhaps will begin as ratification of many good things'; [1× *El.*]

Part A (3), Lines 920–937

ἄνοια, ἡ	(ἄ-νοος, without understanding) lack of understanding (either genit. of cause: S #1405; SS 70–71 §34iii: "alas, how I have been pitying you *for your folly* all this while [πάλαι]." Or genit. after an exclamation, with comma following: SS 71–72 §35); > 'Alas *for your folly*! I pity you . . .'
+ἐπ-οικτίρω	have compassion for, pity

ΧΡ.	τί δ᾽ ἔστιν; οὐ πρὸς ἡδονὴν λέγω τάδε;
ΗΛ.	οὐκ οἶσθ᾽ ὅποι γῆς οὐδ᾽ ὅποι γνώμης φέρη.
ΧΡ.	πῶς δ᾽ οὐκ ἐγὼ κάτοιδ᾽ ἅ γ᾽ εἶδον ἐμφανῶς;
ΗΛ.	τέθνηκεν, ὦ τάλαινα· τἀκ κείνου δέ σοι
	σωτήρι᾽ ἔρρει· μηδὲν ἐς κεῖνόν γ᾽ ὅρα. 925
ΧΡ.	οἴμοι τάλαινα· τοῦ τάδ᾽ ἤκουσας βροτῶν;
ΗΛ.	τοῦ πλησίον παρόντος, ἡνίκ᾽ ὤλλυτο.
ΧΡ.	καὶ ποῦ 'στιν οὗτος; θαῦμά τοί μ᾽ ὑπέρχεται.
ΗΛ.	κατ᾽ οἶκον, ἡδὺς οὐδὲ μητρὶ δυσχερής.
ΧΡ.	οἴμοι τάλαινα· τοῦ γὰρ ἀνθρώπων ποτ᾽ ἦν 930
	τὰ πολλὰ πατρὸς πρὸς τάφον κτερίσματα;
ΗΛ.	οἶμαι μάλιστ᾽ ἔγωγε τοῦ τεθνηκότος
	μνημεῖ᾽ Ὀρέστου ταῦτα προσθεῖναί τινα.
ΧΡ.	ὦ δυστυχής· ἐγὼ δὲ σὺν χαρᾷ λόγους
	τοιούσδ᾽ ἔχους᾽ ἔσπευδον, οὐκ εἰδυῖ᾽ ἄρα 935
	ἵν᾽ ἦμεν ἄτης· ἀλλὰ νῦν, ὅθ᾽ ἱκόμην,
	τά τ᾽ ὄντα πρόσθεν ἄλλα θ᾽ εὑρίσκω κακά.

LINE 921

τί δ᾽ ἔστιν;	'What's the matter?' (conversational)
⁺πρὸς ⁺ἡδονήν	'to your pleasure' (for πρὸς with acc. of manner, see 369, 464, 1462, S #1608)
ὅποι	where, to what place (S #2498) (with genit. γῆς: 'where in the world?'; with genit. partit. of an abstract noun, ⁺γνώμης: SS 58 §10); > 'to what place in your mind, you are being carried'
κάτοιδα ... εἶδον	etymologically connected. κάτοιδα answers emphatically the preceding οἶσθα. 'Seeing' and 'knowing' are connected in Greek thought.
ἐμφανῶς (adv.)	(ἐμφανής appearing, manifest) visibly; [1× *El.*]
σωτήριος, ον	(σωτήρ, savior) saving, delivering; > 'the means of deliverance from him are gone/lost (ἔρρει) for you'
μηδὲν ...⁺*ὅρα	negated impv. (S #1835); > 'Don't look at all to him!'

LINE 926

πλήσιος (3)	(πέλας, near, close) near, hard by, close to (here an adv.: near)
τοῦ ... ⁺παρ-⁺*όντος	genit. as object of preceding ἤκουσας (S #1361); > *'from the man who was close by* when he perished'
ὑπ-⁺*έρχομαι	steal over; Kells: "really (τοι) wonder is stealing over me"
δυσ-χρής, ές	(δυσ-, χείρ) unpleasant, troublesome (μητρί, *apokoinou*, see p. 000. οὐδὲ ... δυσχερής: litotes: S #3032, for intensification); > 'not at all displeasing'; [1× *El.*]

LINE 930

κτερίσματα, τά	(κτερίζω, bury with due honors) funeral honors, obsequies (= κτέρεα) (here includes libations; in 434, it doesn't.) *hyperbaton*: τοῦ = τινός 'whose,' 'from whom'
μνημεῖον, τό	memorial
προσ-⁺*τί-θη-μι	(προσθεῖναι, aor.² inf. act.) <u>bestow</u>, add; > 'I think that someone *placed/bestowed* them [on the grave] as memorials of the dead Orestes'
σπεύδω	<u>hasten</u>; promote/further zealously

ΗΛ.	οὕτως ἔχει coι ταῦτ'· ἐὰν δ' ἐμοὶ πίθῃ,	
	τῆς νῦν παρούςης πημονῆς λύςεις βάρος.	
ΧΡ.	ἢ τοὺς θανόντας ἐξαναςτήςω ποτέ;	940
ΗΛ.	†οὐκ ἔςθ' ὅ γ' † εἶπον· οὐ γὰρ ὧδ' ἄφρων ἔφυν.	
ΧΡ.	τί γὰρ κελεύεις ὧν ἐγὼ φερέγγυος;	
ΗΛ.	τλῆναί ςε δρῶςαν ἂν ἐγὼ παραινέςω.	
ΧΡ.	ἀλλ' εἴ τις ὠφέλειά γ', οὐκ ἀπώςομαι.	
ΗΛ.	ὅρα, πόνου τοι χωρὶς οὐδὲν εὐτυχεῖ.	945

+ἄρα (pcl.) — really, truly (indicates realization of the truth of past event: GP 36.2); > 'not knowing in what a predicament we really were'

+ἵνα (relat. adv.) — where (S #2498; poetic) (with genit. of place); > lit.: "where of ruin we after all were," i.e., "not knowing in what sort of plight we really were" (Kells)

+ὅτε (adv.) — 'but now when/that I've come, I find our former troubles and others also'

Part B: Lines 938-1057. (1) 938–946 Electra prepares the ground to convince Chrysothemis to take part in the revenge. (2) 947–1016: Electra's speech explaining why the two of them should exact revenge all by themselves and Chrysothemis' refusal. (3) 1017–1057 the disagreement between the two sisters in the form of *stichomythia*.

Part B: (1) Lines 938–946

LINE 938

+*πείθω — (πίθῃ, aor.² mid. subjv. 2sg) mid.: obey, <u>listen to</u> (protasis of fut. more vivid condition, the apodosis is in fut. indicat, λύςεις: S #2297, 2321, 2323)

πημονή, ἡ — calamity, trouble

βάρος, εος, τό — weight, burden; > 'but if you listen to me, you'll lighten the weight of our present misery'

+ἤ (adv.) — introduces interrogative rhetorical sentence (GP 283.2)

ἐξ-αν-+*ίςτημι — (ἐξαναςτήςω, indic. fut. act.) make rise from; > 'What? Will I ever bring the dead to life?'; [1× El]

†οὐκ ἔςθ' ὅ γ† — 'that is not what I said' (Lloyd-Jones, following Kaibel). The relative pron., ὅ, lacks an antecedent, and is often emended to οὐκ ἐς τόδε εἶπον; > 'I did not speak with reference to that', or οὐ τοῦτό γ' εἶπον > 'I did not say this'

ἄ-φρων, ονος — senseless, witless, foolish; [1× Soph.]

+*ἔφυν — (aor.²) grew, was; > 'I am not such a fool'

κελεύω — urge on, exhort, bid, command

φερέγγυος (3) — (φέρω, ἐγγύη, surety) capable (only here with genit., usually with inf.); > 'why (γάρ), what of the things I'm capable of doing you command?'; [1× Soph.]

LINE 943

**τλάω, ἔτλην — (τλῆναι, inf. aor.², never found in pres.) endure, dare (understand κελεύω from previous line with acc. and inf.: ςε τλῆναι. δρῶςαν supplem. ptc. following vb. of enduring, τλῆναι: SS 260 §12a; S #2127; Campbell); > '[I bid] you to dare doing'

παρ-*αινέω — (παραινέςω, aor.¹ subjv.) advise, recommend, counsel (αἰνέω keeps a short vowel in the aor. and fut.: S #488b). Indefinite subjv., the reference not being to any particular thing, "but to any, or all": SS 225–56 §12; S #2545c); > 'whatever/what (ἄν = ἃ ἄν) I am going to advise'

ὠφέλεια, ἡ — help; profit, gain; > 'well, if there is any help [in it]'; [1× Soph.]

XP. ὁρῶ. ξυνοίcω πᾶν ὅcονπερ ἂν cθένω.

ΗΛ. ἄκουε δή νυν ᾗ βεβούλευμαι τελεῖν.
παρουcίαν μὲν οἶcθα καὶ cύ που φίλων
ὡc οὔτιc ἡμῖν ἐcτιν, ἀλλ᾽ Ἅιδηc λαβὼν
ἀπεcτέρηκε καὶ μόνα λελείμμεθον.   950
ἐγὼ δ᾽ ἕωc μὲν τὸν καcίγνητον βίῳ
θάλλοντ᾽ ἔτ᾽ εἰcήκουον, εἶχον ἐλπίδαc
φόνου ποτ᾽ αὐτὸν πράκτορ᾽ ἵξεcθαι πατρόc·

⁺ἀπ-ώcομαι	(⁺ἀπ-ωθέω); > 'I will not reject it'
⁺πόνοc, ὁ	pain, toil
χωρίc + genit.	without; > '(see, i.e.) remember, nothing truly (τοι) succeeds without pain'; [1× *El.*]

LINE 946

⁺cυμ-⁺*φέρω, -οίcω	gather, contribute, help
ὅcοc-περ, ὅcη-περ, ὅcον-περ	as much as, as many as
⁺cθένω	fut. more vivid condition (S #2297; GMT #444); > 'I shall help in everything as much as *I have strength for*'

Part B: (2) Lines 947–1016

⁺ᾗ	which way, <u>how</u> (S #346)
⁺βεβούλευμαι	the perfect tense emphasizes the decisiveness of her resolve; cf. at 385
⁺παρουcία, ἡ	presence (acc. of respect: S #1601c; SS 43 §14. φίλων subjective genit.: S #1330; SS 53 §4); > 'I suppose you know that as to the *presence/existence* of *our friends,* that we have no one'
Ἅιδηc	resolution in 9th position Ἅιδηc.

LINE 950

⁺μόνα ⁺λελείμμεθον	dual of the adj. and 1st pers.; > 'but Hades robbed us, having taken [them] away, *and we two are left alone*'
ἕωc (conj.)	as long as, until (referring to coextensive actions: S #2383 C)
θάλλω	bloom, flourish, swell, shoot out (ptc. in acc., θάλλοντα, required by verb of perception, εἰcήκουcον, in indirect discourse: S #2012); > 'so long as I still heard *that our brother was flourishing* in life'
πράκτωρ, οροc, ὁ	(πράccω) one who exacts punishment, avenger (acc. as the subject of the inf., ἵξεcθαι: S #1868a); [1× *El.*]
⁺*ἵξεcθαι	(inf. fut. dep.) come, arrive (εἶχον ἐλπίδαc = ἐλπίζω. Vbs. of hoping take fut. inf. in indirect discourse φόνου . . . πατρόc; note how the two words round the line); > 'I had hopes that *he would come* some day, an avenger of our father's murder'

νῦν δ' ἡνίκ' οὐκέτ' ἔcτιν, ἐc cὲ δὴ βλέπω,
ὅπωc τὸν αὐτόχειρα πατρῴου φόνου   **955**
ξὺν τῇδ' ἀδελφῇ μὴ κατοκνήcειc κτανεῖν
Αἴγιcθον· οὐδὲν γάρ cε δεῖ κρύπτειν μ' ἔτι.
ποῖ γὰρ μενεῖc ῥάθυμοc, ἐc τίν' ἐλπίδων
βλέψαc' ἔτ' ὀρθήν; ἢ πάρεcτι μὲν cτένειν
πλούτου πατρῴου κτῆcιν ἐcτερημένη,   **960**

LINE 954

⁺*ἔcτιν	'but now, when he *is* no more . . .'
⁺ὅπωc	opens object clause with μή with and fut. indic. for urgent exhortation (S #1920), following βλέπω as if it were verb of exhorting; > 'I look to you (δή emphasizes cέ) *that* you will not shrink from killing with your sister the agent of our father's murder'
αὐτό-χειρ, ρος, ὁ, ἡ	(αὐτός, χείρ) working with one's own hand, <u>agent</u>, murderer
κατ-οκνέω	shrink from doing (a thing); [1× Soph.]
⁺Αἴγιcθον	in powerfully emphatic *enjambment*; El. deliberately avoids mentioning matricide, although it is clear from 929 that Clyt. is on her mind; cf. also 604–5.
⁺κρύπτειν	acc., με, and inf., κρύπτειν, construction after δεῖ (S #1895b). El. does hide from Chr. that she means to kill their mother as well.

LINE 958

⁺ποῖ (adv.)	whither?; > 'to what end'
ῥάθυμοc, ον	[ᾰ] (ῥάδιος, θῡμός) lazy; > 'to what end will you remain inactive?' (1× Soph.)
⁺*μενεῖc	(μένω, fut.) some prefer the present μένειc because the waiting is already in process (Finglass).
⁺ὀρθήν	'having fixed your gaze to what hope that is still upright/unshaken?'
ἥ	dat. required by +πάρεcτι. Relative pron. whose antecedent is the subject of the former sentence: 'you to whom. . . .' πάρεcτι is repeated in 961 in an emphatic *anaphora*.
⁺cτένω	(cτενός, narrow) sigh, trans.: bemoan, lament, deplore, complain (only in pres. and impf.)
κτῆcιc, εωc, ἡ	(κτάομαι, acquire) possession, property (acc. after a passive vb.; cf. 114. genit. was expected as cτερέω takes acc. of person and genit. of thing: SS 39 §8)
cτερέω, ἐcτέρημαι	(ἐcτερημένη, pf. pass. ptc.) deprive, <u>rob</u>; > 'you who could (i.e., for whom after being robbed, it was possible to) complain of *being robbed* of the possession of your father's wealth'

πάρεστι δ' ἀλγεῖν ἐς τοσόνδε τοῦ χρόνου
ἄλεκτρα γηράσκουσαν ἀνυμέναιά τε.
καὶ τῶνδε μέντοι μηκέτ' ἐλπίςῃς ὅπως
τεύξῃ ποτ'· οὐ γὰρ ὧδ' ἄβουλός ἐςτ' ἀνὴρ
Αἴγιςθος ὥςτε ςόν ποτ' ἢ κἀμὸν γένος   965
βλαςτεῖν ἐᾶςαι, πημονὴν αὑτῷ ςαφῆ.
ἀλλ' ἢν ἐπίςπῃ τοῖς ἐμοῖς βουλεύμαςιν,

LINE 961

ἐς τοσόνδε χρόνου	'to this point of time'; cf. τοσόνδε ἐς ἥβης at 14
ἄ-λεκτρος, ον	(ἀ privat., λέκτρον, marriage bed) <u>without marriage bed</u>, <u>unwedded</u>
γηράσκω	grow old (inceptive/inchoative vb., points to a beginning of a process: S #526a). The acc. ptc., γηράκουσαν, is subject of the inf. ἀλγεῖν; [1× *El.*]
ἀν-ὑμέναιος, ον	(ἀ privat., ὑμεναῖος, wedding song) unwedded (ἄλεκτρα and ἀνυμέναια neuter plural internal acc. as adv. = ἀλγεῖν ἄλεκτρον and ἀνυμέναιον γῆρας: SS 41 §12. Resolution in 8th position: ἄν-ὔμ.); > 'You must feel pain at this point of time [i.e., of your life], growing old unmarried and unwedded'; [1× *El*]
καὶ . . . μέντοι	and however, <u>and of course</u> (S #2880) (GP 413: "sometimes introduces a new point or argument," as El. does here)
τῶνδε	refers to the ancestral possessions and above all to the marriage stressed in 965–96. The *hyperbaton* with τεύξῃ and the *enjambments* stress the loss of both.
ἐλπίζω	(ἐλπίς) hope (μή with prohibitive aorist subjv.: S #1800a; SS 220 §6; GMT #259); > 'No, no longer hope'
⁺*τεύξῃ, τεύξομαι	(τυγχάνω, fut. mid. 2sg.) + genit.: τῶνδε (ὅπως with fut. indic. denotes urgent exhortation: S #2213, and keeps strong modal sense, 'that', after a negated main verb μηκέτι ἐλπίςῃς: SS 314 §2); > 'No, no longer hope that *you will ever chance* upon them now'
ἄ-βουλος, ον	(ἀ privat., βουλή) fool, <u>ill advised</u>; Αἴγιςθος in emphatic *enjambment*.

LINE 965

⁺*βλαστεῖν	(βλαστάνω, aor.² act. inf.); see 546n
⁺*ἐᾶσαι	(ἐάω, aor.¹ inf. act.) ὥςτε with inf. for an anticipated or possible result (S #2251, 2254; GMT #582, 587); > 'Aegisthus is not so foolish *as ever to permit* children . . .'
αὑτῷ	= ἃ αὑτῷ ⁺ςαφῆ. dat. of disadvantage (S #1481; SS 84 §9); > 'as an obvious calamity for himself'
ἐφ-⁺*έπομαι	(ἐπί-ςπῃ, stem ςπ-; aor.² subjv. mid. 2sg.) comply with (ἢν = ἐάν with subjv, and fut. indic. in apodosis, οἴςῃ [φέρω] mid. 2sg., fut. more vivid condition S #2297, 2321, 2323); > 'if you comply with . . . you will win [carry for yourself]'
βούλευμα, ατος, τό	(βολεύω) plan, design

πρῶτον μὲν εὐcέβειαν ἐκ πατρὸς κάτω
θανόντος οἴcῃ τοῦ κασιγνήτου θ’ ἅμα·
ἔπειτα δ’, ὥσπερ ἐξέφυς, ἐλευθέρα   970
καλῇ τὸ λοιπὸν καὶ γάμων ἐπαξίων
τεύξῃ· φιλεῖ γὰρ πρὸς τὰ χρηστὰ πᾶς ὁρᾶν.
λόγων γε μὴν εὔκλειαν οὐχ ὁρᾷς ὅcην
cαυτῇ τε κἀμοὶ προcβαλεῖc πειcθεῖc’ ἐμοί;
τίc γάρ ποτ’ ἀcτῶν ἢ ξένων ἡμᾶc ἰδὼν   975
τοιοῖcδ’ ἐπαίνοιc οὐχὶ δεξιώcεται,

LINE 968

πρῶτον μέν . . . ἔπειτα δέ	first, in the first place . . . second, further . . .
†κἄcιγνήτου	'from our dead father below, and from our brother at the same time'
ἐκ-†*φύω	[ῠ] (ἐξέφυς, aor.²) intransitive: grow from, born from; > 'as you were born'
†*κἄλῇ	(καλέω, fut. mid. used as pass. only here. Cf. λησόμενον 1247n); > 'in the future (τὸ λοιπόν) you'll be called free'
γάμος, ὁ	[ᾰ] marriage, wedding (for the plural see γάμων 494n)
ἐπ-άξιος (2/3)	(†ἐπί, ἄξιος) worthy, deserving; > 'and you'll obtain a worthy marriage'; [1× El.]
φιλεῖ	Here in its 'philosophical' sense: is accustomed
χρηστός (3)	(χράομαι, use) useful, serviceable, good, favorable (τὰ χρηστά, a neuter used for persons; cf. 538, 1208: SS 14–15§10); > 'for everyone is accustomed to look toward *what is good* (i.e., a good woman)'

LINE 973

γε μήν	points to a new point (GP 349.3); > 'as to the renown on the lips of men'
εὔ-κλειᾰ, ἡ	good fame, renown (†λόγων subjective genit.: S #1330; SS 53 §4. The genit. plural is preferred to the codd. dat. sg., λόγῳ,: 'renown of/in words,' i.e., words telling of the renown)
προc-*βάλλω, -βαλῶ	(προcβαλεῖc, fut. indic.) add, attach; [1× El.]
†πειcθεῖσα	(πείθω, aor.¹ pass. ptc.) 'as to renown in words, don't you see how much (†ὅσην) you'll procure for yourself and me *if you listen to me*?'
ἀcτός, ὁ	(ἄcτυ) townsman, fellow citizen; [1× El.]
ἀcτῶν ἢ †ξένων	emphatic polar expression, which does not limit the praise to the *polis* alone.
ἔπ-αινος, ὁ	(ἐπί, αἶνος) approval, commendation; [1× El.]
δεξιόομαι	greet with the right hand; > 'won't greet us with the following words of praise'; [1× Soph.]

"Ἴδεσθε τώδε τὼ κασιγνήτω, φίλοι,
ὢ τὸν πατρῷον οἶκον ἐξεςωςάτην,
ὢ τοῖςιν ἐχθροῖς εὖ βεβηκόςιν ποτὲ
ψυχῆς ἀφειδήςαντε προὐςτήτην φόνου.   980
τούτω φιλεῖν χρή, τώδε χρὴ πάντας ςέβειν·
τώδ' ἔν θ' ἑορταῖς ἔν τε πανδήμῳ πόλει
τιμᾶν ἄπαντας οὕνεκ' ἀνδρείας χρεών."
τοιαῦτά τοι νὼ πᾶς τις ἐξερεῖ βροτῶν,
ζώςαιν θανούςαιν θ' ὥςτε μὴ 'κλιπεῖν κλέος.   985

LINE 977

τὼ κασιγνήτω ... ὢ	dual: 'the two sisters who'
ἐκ-⁺*ςῴζω, -έσωσα	(ἐξεσωσάτην, aor.¹ dual) utterly save, preserve from danger (completive sense of ἐκ- 'thoroughly,' 'fully': S #1688.2; SS 111§9)
⁺*εὖ βεβηκόςιν	(βαίνω, pf. ptc. act.) the perfect "is used as a stronger equivalent of εἰμί 'be', emphasizing the stability of the state reached": SS 198 §18); > 'enemies *firmly established*'
ἀ-φειδέω	(ἀφειδήσαντε, aor.¹ masc. dual forms of participles serve as feminine: SS 13 §9) be unsparing; > 'unsparing of their own lives'; [1× Soph.]
προ-⁺*ἵστημι, -έστην	(=προ-εστάτην, aor.² dual) + genit.: to place oneself in front of (with φόνου "be the author of slaughter": LSJ); > 'placed themselves as "champions of the murder"'(Kamerbeek)
ςέβω	worship, revere (τούτω ... τώδε stylistic variation (dual). πάντας subject of the infinitives φιλεῖν and ςέβειν; > everyone should love them both; everyone should honor them'; [1× *El.*]

LINE 982

ἑορτή, ἡ	festival; [1× *El.*]
πάν-δεμος, ον	(πᾶς, δῆμος) belonging to all the people (πανδήμῳ πόλει 'whole body of the city')
τιμάω	(inf. pres. act.) hold worthy, honor, respect (⁺ἄπαντας is the subject; [1× *El.*]
ἀνδρεία, ἡ	manliness, manly spirit (rare word in high poetic style before Eur.: Finglass, and an odd quality to ascribe to women); > 'on account of (⁺οὕνεκα) their manliness'; [1× Soph.]
⁺χρεών	copula (ἐστί) omitted after expression of necessity (S #944b)

LINE 984

⁺τοι	postpositive and enclitic pcl. with general reflection: 'you know,' 'be sure of it'
νώ	dual nom. and acc. of ἐγώ (S #325)
⁺ἐξ-⁺ερῶ	speak out, proclaim (fut. without any pres. in use. The vb. sometimes takes the acc. of the person spoken about); > 'be sure that everyone will proclaim such things about us (νώ)'
⁺*ζώςαιν ⁺*θανούςαιν θ'	(dual) temporal genit. absolute without its subject, which can be easily supplied from the context: 'we' (S #2058, 2070a, 2072)
⁺ἐκ-⁺*λείπω, -έλιπον	(ἐκλιπεῖν, aor.² inf.) intrans.: leave off, cease (LSJ II.4) (ὥςτε with inf. for an anticipated or possible result: S #2251, 2254; GMT #582, 587)
κλέος, τό	fame, glory, renown (only nom. and acc., sg. and pl.); > 'so that our fame will not (leave us =) die whether we are alive or dead'
⁺*πείσθητι	(πείθω, aor.² impv. pass.) 'obey' (Finglass points out that the aorist passive of this verb is "much rarer than the middle in classical and Hellenistic Greek," which would have drawn special attention of the spectators and gave further prominence to El.'s plea.)
ςυμ-πονέω	(pres. impv.) work with, help

ἀλλ᾽, ὦ φίλη, πείσθητι, cυμπόνει πατρί,
cύγκαμν᾽ ἀδελφῷ, παῦcον ἐκ κακῶν ἐμέ,
παῦcον δὲ cαυτήν, τοῦτο γιγνώcκουc᾽, ὅτι
ζῆν αἰcχρὸν αἰcχρῶc τοῖc καλῶc πεφυκόcιν.

XO. ἐν τοῖc τοιούτοιc ἐcτὶν ἡ προμηθία   990
καὶ τῷ λέγοντι καὶ κλύοντι cύμμαχοc.

XP. καὶ πρίν γε φωνεῖν, ὦ γυναῖκεc, εἰ φρενῶν
ἐτύγχαν᾽ αὕτη μὴ κακῶν, ἐcῴζετ᾽ ἂν
τὴν εὐλάβειαν, ὥcπερ οὐχὶ cῴζεται.

LINE 986

cυγ-κάμνω — labor, suffer with; [1× *El.*]

παῦcον . . . παῦcον — (παύω, aor.[1] impv.) 'stop!' (*anaphora*. El. tends to repeat this vb., cf. 796. The aor. points to the single occurrence versus the continuous aspect of cυμπόνει and cύγκαμνε): > 'free me from evil, and free yourself as well'

+*γιγνώcκουcα — (pres. act. ptc.); > 'realizing that to those noble by nature (+*πεφυκόcιν) it is shameful to live (+*ζῆν) shamefully'

+αἰcχρὸν αἰcχρῶc — play on different forms of the same word was greatly appreciated by the Greeks. Here each word has a different syntactic function: αἰcχρόν ἐcτι ζῆν αἰcχρῶc.

LINE 990

+προμήθια, ἡ — forethought, consideration

cύμ-μαχοc, ον — (cύν, μάχη) ally (supply τῷ before κλύοντι: SS 153 §21. Cf. μέλλοντα in 1498); > 'In such matters, foresight is *an ally* both to the one who speaks and to the one who listens.' A noncommittal statement; [1× *El.*]

+πρίν (conj.) — [ῐ] before (when subordinated to an affirmative clause, usually takes infinitive: S #2431, 2454, φωνεῖν); > 'Yes, and *before speaking*'

+*ἐτύγχανε — impf. indic. in protasis and apodosis (+*ἐcῴζετο ἄν) of contrary- to-fact condition. In a contrary-to-fact condition sometimes it is difficult to decide if the imperfect denotes present or past time (SS 280 §3a; S #2304; GMT #410). μή belongs to the entire sentence but its position emphasizes both the negation and the epithet κακῶν (Campbell); > 'if she (αὕτη = ἡ αὕτη) (had happened to have=) really had good sense, she would have preserved caution for herself), but she does not preserve [it]'

εὐλάβεια, ἡ — [ᾰ] discretion, caution

ποῖ γάρ ποτε βλέψαca τοιοῦτον θράcoc 995
αὐτή θ' ὁπλίζῃ κἄμ' ὑπηρετεῖν καλεῖc;
οὐκ εἰcορᾷc; γυνὴ μὲν οὐδ' ἀνὴρ ἔφυc,
cθένειc δ' ἔλαccον τῶν ἐναντίων χερί.
δαίμων δὲ τοῖc μὲν εὐτυχὴc καθ' ἡμέραν,
ἡμῖν δ' ἀπορρεῖ κἀπὶ μηδὲν ἔρχεται. 1000
τίc οὖν τοιοῦτον ἄνδρα βουλεύων ἑλεῖν
ἄλυποc ἄτηc ἐξαπαλλαχθήceται;
ὅρα κακῶc πράccοντε μὴ μείζω κακὰ
κτηcώμεθ', εἴ τιc τούcδ' ἀκούceται λόγουc.

LINE 995

ὁπλίζω — (pres. mid. 2sg) arm (αὐτή emphasizes the 2nd pers.); > 'What have *you* set your eyes on that *you've* armed yourself with such boldness . . . ?'; [1× *El.*]

ὑπηρετέω — serve, work for, help; > 'and call on me to help you?'

ἐλάσσον — neuter as adv. (ἐλάσσων, ον); in lesser degree (comparative of μικρός: S #319.6, with genit. of comparison, τῶν ἐναντίων: S #1069)

ἐν-αντίος (3) — opposing (substantival use of article with adj.: S #1021, 1153a; SS 163 §1 = enemy); > 'in power (χερί) you are less strong than [our] enemies'); [1× *El.*]

⁺δαίμων — τοῖc μὲν . . . ἡμῖν δέ, dat. of possession; > '*Their* luck, on the one hand . . ., *ours*, on the other . . .'

εὐ-τῠχής, ές — successful, lucky, fortunate

ἀπο-ρρέω — flow away from, run off like water; > 'drains away'; [1× *El.*]

καὶ ἐπὶ μηδὲν ἔρχεται — 'and comes to nothing'; μηδέν, not οὐδέν, to convey the idea of 'nothingness'

LINE 1001

τοιοῦτον — correption: -οι- shortened before the following diphthong; cf. 35, 1024, 1338

ἄ-λῠπος, ον — (ἀ privat., λύπη) without pain or grief; [1× *El.*]

ἐξ-απ-αλάσσω — (ἐξαπαλλαχθήσεται, fut. indic., pass.) free from (the pass. of the vb. does not differ semantically from the mid. The *three-word trimeter* marks a climax in the argument: Finglass. Cf. 13 on: κἀξεθρεψάμην. Note the accumulation of alphas); > 'Who then shall plan to kill such a man and *escape* unhurt by disaster?'; [1× Soph.]

⁺*πράσσω κακῶς — 'fare badly.' Masc. dual forms of participle serve usually as feminine (SS 13 §9). Pres. ptc. indicates continuous aspect with antecedent action (S #1872 a.1). SS 210 §32–33: "Take care that we, in an evil plight as we are, do not incur worse [μείζω = μείζωνα] evil"

κτάομαι — (κτησώμεθα, aor.¹ subjv.) acquire, procure, get for oneself (subjv. in fear clause in primary sequence, ὅρα: S #2221, 2223; GMT #365. Impv. moods point to the fut. and thus considered as primary: S #1858a; ὅρα implies the idea of fear; *enjambment*)

⁺*ἀκούσεται — (fut. dep.) acc. λόγους, with ἀκούω, points to the words and/or sound that is heard; genit. is used for the person whose words are heard (S #1361); for the fut. indic. in protasis, see ὑποίσεις 834n

λύει γὰρ ἡμᾶς οὐδὲν οὐδ' ἐπωφελεῖ 1005
βάξιν καλὴν λαβόντε δυσκλεῶς θανεῖν.
[οὐ γὰρ θανεῖν ἔχθιστον, ἀλλ' ὅταν θανεῖν
χρῄζων τις εἶτα μηδὲ τοῦτ' ἔχῃ λαβεῖν.]
ἀλλ' ἀντιάζω, πρὶν πανωλέθρους τὸ πᾶν
ἡμᾶς τ' ὀλέσθαι κἀξερημῶσαι γένος, 1010
κατάσχες ὀργήν. καὶ τὰ μὲν λελεγμένα
ἄρρητ' ἐγώ σοι κἀτελῆ φυλάξομαι,

LINE 1005

ἐπ-ωφελέω	aid, succor (with inf. +*θανεῖν)
βάξις, εως, ἡ	(βάζω, speak, say) saying, report, announcement; [1 × *El.*]
+*λαβόντε	(λαμβάνω, aor.² ptc.) masculine dual forms of participles serve as feminine (SS 13 §9); > 'it brings no relief or benefit to die ingloriously *after having acquired* a fine reputation'
δυσ-κλεῶς (adv.)	(δυσ-κλεής) ingloriously; [1× Soph.]
γάρ	explains δυσ-κλεῶς. Those, e.g., Finglass, who excise 1007–8 claim that Chr. is "concerned not with the manner of their death but with the fact of dying."
+χρῄζων	temporal ptc. (S #2060, 20161; SS 252–3 §4). Indefinite relative temporal clause with subjv., ὅταν . . . μηδὲ . . . ἔχῃ (SS 294 §4; GMT #462). ἔχω with an inf. (λαβεῖν) can mean 'can,' 'able to' (S 2000a); > 'for the worst thing is not to die, but *when one wishes to die*, yet (εἶτα) *is unable* to accomplish that.' Cf. +ὅτε 59n.

LINE 1009

ἀντιάζω	entreat, approach as suppliant; [1× Soph.]
πᾰν-ώλεθρος, ον (3)	(πᾶς, ὄλεθρος, ὄλλυμι) utterly ruined; [1 × *El.*]
+*ὀλέσθαι	(ὄλλυμι, aor.² inf. mid.) mid.: perish, come to an end
ἐξ-ερημόω	make utterly desolate, desert utterly (ἡμᾶς is probably subject of both infinitives. Kells suggests a supplied σέ subject of ἐξερημῶσαι: 'and you leave . . .'); > 'before we're totally destroyed and *leave our family completely desolate*, rein in your anger'; [1× Soph.]
+*λελεγμένα	(pf. ptc. pass.) things said, words
ἄρρ-ητος (2/3)	(ἀ privat., ῥηθῆναι, < ἐρῶ, say) that cannot be told, shocking
ἀ-τελής, ές	(ἀ privat., τέλος) without end, unaccomplished, ineffectual; [1× *El.*]
+φῠλάσσω	guard; mid.: keep in one's mind (σοι dat. of advantage: S #1481; SS 84–85 §9); > 'I for my part will guard your word unspoken and unrealized for your own good'

αὐτὴ δὲ νοῦν cχὲc ἀλλὰ τῷ χρόνῳ ποτέ,
cθένουcα μηδὲν τοῖc κρατοῦcιν εἰκαθεῖν.

ΧΟ. πείθου. προνοίαc οὐδὲν ἀνθρώποιc ἔφυ   1015
κέρδοc λαβεῖν ἄμεινον οὐδὲ νοῦ cοφοῦ.

ΗΛ. ἀπροcδόκητον οὐδὲν εἴρηκαc· καλῶc δ'
ἤδη c' ἀπορρίψουcαν ἀπηγγελλόμην.
ἀλλ' αὐτόχειρί μοι μόνῃ τε δραcτέον
τοὔργον τόδ'· οὐ γὰρ δὴ κενόν γ' ἀφήcομεν.   1020

LINE 1013

ἀλλὰ τῷ ⁺χρόνῳ	now at least, now at long last (GP 13.3)
⁺cθένουcα	time/causal participle (S #2060, 2061, 2064; SS 251–52 §3; conjunctive [i.e., coordinated with the existing principal verb] with εἰκαθεῖν. μηδέν negates the participle: SS 332 §8b)
τοῖc ⁺κρατοῦcι	'the rulers, those in power'; see τοῖc ⁺κρατοῦcι 396n
εἴκω, εἴκἄθον	(aor.² inf., poetic) yield, give way (depends on νοῦν cχέc; result clause without ὥcτε: S #2011a; SS 2382); > 'and you yourself have the sense at long last [so as you yield] to yield to those in power, since you have no strength'
⁺*πείθου	(pres. impv. mid. 2sg.) mid.: obey, listen to
πρόνοια, ἡ	foresight (the two genits. of comparison προνοίαc and νοῦ cοφοῦ bracket the statement); [1× *El.*]
⁺*λαβεῖν	with ἄμεινον, limiting or explanatory inf. (SS 240 §3, S #1712) > 'no better advantage to gain than …'
ἀμείνων, ον	better; comparative of ἀγαθόc (S #319, 319a)

Part B: (3) Lines 1017–1057

LINE 1017

ἀ-προc-δόκητοc, ον	unexpected; > 'you've said nothing unexpected' [1× Soph.]
⁺*οἶδα, ἤδη	(plupf.) know
ἀπο-ρρίπτω	throw away (supplementary participle in indirect discourse following verb of knowing, ἤδη: S 2106); [1× *El.*]
ἀπ-αγγέλλω	= ἃ ἀπηγγελλόμην; bring tidings, tell; > 'I knew quite well that you'd refuse what I proposed.' Does El. sound convincing here?; [1× *El.*]
αὐτό-χειρ, ροc, ὁ, ἡ	(αὐτόc, χείρ) working with one's own hand, agent, murderer
⁺*δραcτέον	'must be done' (verbal adj. with dat. of agent: S #1488); > '(it must be done by me, my own hand alone =) I have to this deed by my own hand and alone'
οὐ γὰρ δὴ … γε	certainly not (GP 243(2))
ἀφ-*ίημι	(ἀφήcομεν, fut. indic.) give up (*majestic plural* for impressive effect: S #1006; SS 6 §4); > 'I (we) certainly won't leave it (empty, futile =) undone'

XP.	φεῦ·
	εἴθ᾽ ὤφελες τοιάδε τὴν γνώμην πατρὸς
	θνῄσκοντος εἶναι· πᾶν γὰρ ἂν κατειργάςω.
ΗΛ.	ἀλλ᾽ ἦ φύςιν γε, τὸν δὲ νοῦν ἥςςων τότε.
XP.	ἄςκει τοιαύτη νοῦν δι᾽ αἰῶνος μένειν.
ΗΛ.	ὡς οὐχὶ ςυνδράςουςα νουθετεῖς τάδε.
XP.	εἰκὸς γὰρ ἐγχειροῦντα καὶ πράςςειν κακῶς.
ΗΛ.	ζηλῶ ςε τοῦ νοῦ, τῆς δὲ δειλίας ςτυγῶ.

(right margin) 1025

LINE 1021

εἴθ᾽ ὤφελες	fusion of two constructions: εἴθε [ἦσθα] and ὤφελες εἶναι (S #1780, 1781; GMT #734). Kells: "Would that such and such a thing had happened"
⁺γνώμην	acc. of respect (S #1608; SS 43 §14)
⁺πατρὸς ⁺*θνῄσκοντος	temporal genit. absolute (S #2070f) > 'If only you had been of such mind [of such nature (⁺τοιάδε) in respect to your mind] *when our father was murdered*'
κατ-εργάζομαι	(aor.¹ mid. 2sg.) effect, accomplish (ἄν with indic. for potential past action: S #1784; GMT #243–44); > 'you could have achieved anything'; [1 × *El.*]
ἦ	for ἦν 1sg. impf. of ⁺*εἰμί (S #768)
⁺φύσιν . . . τὸν ⁺νοῦν	accs. of respect (S #1608; SS 43 §14)
ἥσσων	(comparative of κακός) weaker, inferior (S #319.2) > 'by nature I was [the same] but in my understanding I was weaker then'; [1× *El.*]
⁺ἄσκει	(pres. impv. act.) with infinitive: practice
⁺τοιοῦτος, -αύτη, -οῦτο	such, of such kind, such as this (*correption*, cf. 35, 1001, 1338); > 'practice so as always to remain of *such* understanding (νοῦν acc. of respect)'

LINE 1025

συν-⁺*δράω	[ᾰ] (fut. ptc.) do together (circumstantial autonomous ptc. [i.e., expresses attendant or underlying circumstance: SS 250 §1, 251 §3], replaces finite verb συνδράσεις, hence the negation οὐ. SS 331 §8.b: "you give advice *as one not intending to share* the deed [i.e., 'implying that you will not . . .']")
νουθετέω	(νοῦς, τίθημι) bring to mind, warn, admonish, advise
ἐν-χειρέω	(ἐν, χείρ) take in hand, undertake (⁺εἰκός [ἐστι] 'it is likely' + inf., πράσσειν κακῶς and its subject ἐγχειροῦντα); > 'For, it is likely that one who *embarks upon/undertakes* it, should even (καί) fare badly'; Campbell: "the masculine gender of the participle and the present tense of the infinitive give generality to the expression"; [1× Soph.]
ζηλόω	(ζῆλος, emulation, envy) envy, admire, commend; [1× *El.*]
δειλία, ἡ	cowardice, timidity (τοῦ νοῦ and δειλίας genits. of cause after verbs of indicating emotion. SS 71 §34: "I admire you for your prudence, but loathe you for your cowardice")
στῠγέω	loathe, hate; [1× *El.*]

ΧΡ.	ἀνέξομαι κλύουσα χὥταν εὖ λέγῃς.	
ΗΛ.	ἀλλ' οὔ ποτ' ἐξ ἐμοῦ γε μὴ πάθῃς τόδε.	
ΧΡ.	μακρὸς τὸ κρῖναι ταῦτα χὠ λοιπὸς χρόνος.	1030
ΗΛ.	ἄπελθε· σοὶ γὰρ ὠφέλησις οὐκ ἔνι.	
ΧΡ.	ἔνεστιν· ἀλλὰ σοὶ μάθησις οὐ πάρα.	
ΗΛ.	ἐλθοῦσα μητρὶ ταῦτα πάντ' ἔξειπε σῇ.	
ΧΡ.	οὐδ' αὖ τοσοῦτον ἔχθος ἐχθαίρω c' ἐγώ.	
ΗΛ.	ἀλλ' οὖν ἐπίστω γ' οἷ μ' ἀτιμίας ἄγεις.	1035
ΧΡ.	ἀτιμίας μὲν οὔ, προμηθίας δὲ coῦ.	
ΗΛ.	τῷ cῷ δικαίῳ δῆτ' ἐπισπέσθαι με δεῖ;	
ΧΡ.	ὅταν γὰρ εὖ φρονῇς, τόθ' ἡγήcῃ cὺ νῷν.	

LINE 1028

ἀν-⁺*ἔχω   mid.: to endure, allow (with supplem. ptc. ⁺κλύουσα, after verb of enduring [SS 260 §12a]); > 'I will endure hearing [this]'

καὶ ὅταν εὖ ⁺λέγῃς   ἄν with subjv. in fut. indefinite temporal clause (S #2399, 1768; SS 294 §4); > 'also when you speak well of me'

⁺*πάθῃς   (πάσχω, aor.² subjv.) οὐ . . . μή with aor. subjv. for strong denial. Cf. ⁺*γιγνώσκω 43n; > 'you will never experience that [i.e., praise] from me'

⁺*κρῖναι   articular infinitive as epexegetic after an adjective (SS 248 §12; GMT #795); > 'the future is long enough to decide that'

ἀπ-⁺*έρχομαι   (ἄπελθε, aor.² impv.) go away; [1× El.]

ὠφέλησις, ἡ   (ὠφελέω) helping, aiding; advantage; [1× El.]

ἔνι   = ⁺ἔν-εστι + dat.; πάρα = ⁺πάρ-εστι (S #175b)

μάθησις, ἡ   (μαθεῖν) act of learning (the antithetical attitudes are reflected in the two -σις nouns: ὠφέλησις and μάθησις); > 'I do have (help) in me, but you are unable to learn'; [1 × El.]

LINE 1033

⁺ἐξ-*εῖπον   (aor.² act. impv.) tell of (σῇ emphatic at the end of the line and sentence)

ἔχθος, τό   hatred (with ⁺ἐχθαίρω cognate accusative: S #1564; SS 35 §2; double accusative: ἔχθος and σέ: S #1620, SS 41 §10) > 'On the contrary, I don't hate you as much as that'; [1× El.]

ἀλλ' οὖν . . . γε   well, at least (see 233n)

⁺ἐπίστω   = ἐπίστασο (pres. impv. mid.) know how; > 'Well, at least know. . .'

⁺οἷ   hither, how far (S #346. Often with genit.)

ἀ-τῑμία, ἡ   disgrace (genit. partitive of an abstract noun following οἷ: SS 58 §10. Cf. γνώμης following ὅποι at 922); > 'to what point of disgrace you are bringing me.' (The following genitives ἀτιμίας and προμηθίας are adopted from the previous line. coῦ objective genit.: S #1331; SS 53 §4); > 'not of dishonor but of concern for you'; [1 × El.]

LINE 1036

⁺δῆτα (pcl.)   really (emphatic: S #2851; GP 269–79)

ἐφ-⁺*έπομαι, -εσπόμην   (ἐπισπέσθαι, aor. stem σπ-, aor.² inf. mid.) comply with

⁺δίκαιος (3/2)   right, righteous, just (substantival use of article with adj.; i.e., attributive adjs. together with the article are often used as nouns: S #1021, 1153a; SS 163 §1. The neuter expresses a general abstract idea: S #1023)

⁺δεῖ   quasi-impersonal verb; i.e., its subject may be derived from the context (S #933b); 'is it necessary that I . . .'; > 'Really, do I have to comply with what is right in your eyes?'

ΗΛ.	ἦ δεινὸν εὖ λέγουcαν ἐξαμαρτάνειν.	
ΧΡ.	εἴρηκαc ὀρθῶc ᾧ cὺ πρόcκειcαι κακῷ.	1040
ΗΛ.	τί δ᾽; οὐ δοκῶ cοι ταῦτα cὺν δίκῃ λέγειν;	
ΧΡ.	ἀλλ᾽ ἔcτιν ἔνθα χἠ δίκη βλάβην φέρει.	
ΗΛ.	τούτοιc ἐγὼ ζῆν τοῖc νόμοιc οὐ βούλομαι.	
ΧΡ.	ἀλλ᾽ εἰ ποήcειc ταῦτ᾽, ἐπαινέcειc ἐμέ.	
ΗΛ.	καὶ μὴν ποήcω γ᾽ οὐδὲν ἐκπλαγεῖcά cε.	1045
ΧΡ.	καὶ τοῦτ᾽ ἀληθέc, οὐδὲ βουλεύcῃ πάλιν;	
ΗΛ.	βουλῆc γὰρ οὐδέν ἐcτιν ἔχθιον κακῆc.	
ΧΡ.	φρονεῖν ἔοικαc οὐδὲν ὧν ἐγὼ λέγω.	
ΗΛ.	πάλαι δέδοκται ταῦτα κοὐ νεωcτί μοι.	

ἡγέομαι	(ἡγήσῃ, aor.[1] subjv. 2sg.) lead (ὅταν +φρονῇς … ἡγήσῃ indefinite temporal clause for a single occurrence in the future. See ὅταν εὖ +λέγῃς 1028n); > 'Yes; when you think sensibly, you'll lead us both'; [1× El.]

LINE 1039

+ἦ	asseverative (prepositive) pcl.: in truth, in sooth, verily (S #2864)
ἐξ-*ἁμαρτάνω	mistake utterly (ἐξ), err greatly (the inf., ἐξαμαρτάνειν, is the subject of δεινόν [ἐcτί]); > 'It is really terrible when a person who speaks so well is so off the mark'; [1× El.]
+πρός-+κειμαι	be attached to (with dat.: κακῷ; the antecedent, κακῷ, is attracted into the case of the relative: ᾧ, should have been κακόν)
+ὀρθῶc (adv.)	(+ὀρθόc) <u>accurately</u>, truthfully; > 'You've described *accurately* the evil to which you are attached'
τί δ᾽	what?
+ἔνθᾰ (adv.)	when; > 'But there is/exists (ἔcτι) a time when even (καί) justice brings harm (+βλάβη)'

LINE 1043

ἐκ-*πλήccω	(ἐκπλαγεῖcα, aor.[2] pass. ptc.) strike out; aor. pass.: be panic-stricken (with acc. on analogy of a non-passive verb; e.g., φοβοῦμαι with acc.: SS 38 §8); > 'And indeed (καὶ μὴν) I *will* do it, not being alarmed/scared by you'; [1× El.]
ἀληθήc, έc	(ἀ privat., λήθω, escape notice) truthful, sincere; ; > 'Is that really so? Will you not consider/think again?'

LINE 1047

βουλή, ἡ	counsel, advice (genit. of comparison: S #1431; SS 69 §32); [1× El.]
ἐχθίων, ον	(irregular comparative of +ἐχθρόc); > 'For there is nothing more loathsome than bad advice'
+ἔοικαc	*You do not seem* to take account of anything I say'
+*δέδοκται	(δοκέω, pf. indic. mid.-pass.) with dat. of agent, μοι
νεωcτί (adv.)	(νέοc) lately, just now, recently (as opposed to +πάλαι); > '(These things have been decided by me =) I made up my mind long ago, not just now'; [1× Soph.]

ΧΡ.   [ΧΡ. ἄπειμι τοίνυν· οὔτε γὰρ cὺ τἄμ' ἔπη   1050
       τολμᾷc ἐπαινεῖν οὔτ' ἐγὼ τοὺc coὺc τρόπουc.

ΗΛ.   ἀλλ' εἴcιθ'. οὔ coι μὴ μεθέψομαί ποτε,
       οὐδ' ἢν cφόδρ' ἱμείρουcα τυγχάνηιc· ἐπεὶ
       πολλῆc ἀνοίαc καὶ τὸ θηρᾶcθαι κενά.]

ΧΡ.   ἀλλ' εἰ cεαυτῇ τυγχάνειc δοκοῦcά τι   1055
       φρονεῖν, φρόνει τοιαῦθ'· ὅταν γὰρ ἐν κακοῖc
       ἤδη βεβήκηιc, τἄμ' ἐπαινέcειc ἔπη.

Lloyd-Jones and Wilson excise lines 1050–1054 (1990: 92) and Dawe (1973: 191–92) places a lacuna after 1052 and gives 1053–57 to Chr. For a summary of views, see Finglass on lines. A playwright might not necessarily wish his characters to sound 'logical' or to avoid repetition in a heated conversation.

LINE 1050

ἄπ-ειμι — (ἀπό, εἶμι, S #773–76) go away; > 'I shall go'; [1× *El.*]

τολμάω — undergo, endure, venture, risk (followed by a complementary infinitive ἐπαινεῖν: SS 239 §4); > '. . . neither can you bring yourself to praise my words, nor can I (approve] your ways (†τρόπους)'

μεθ-†*ἕπω — (μεθέψομαι, fut. mid.) follow, search for (the mid. of this vb. is not found until the imperial period: Finglass. Notice that El. tends to use rare forms of verbs, see πείσθητι 996n. What impact could this have on the audience? οὐ μή with fut. indic. of 1st and 3rd pers. denotes negative prediction with strong denial: 'I will never follow you': S #2755b, GMT #294–95); [1× Soph.]

cφόδρα (adv.) — very much, exceedingly; [1× *El.*]

ἱμείρω — (ἵμερος, longing) long for, yearn for (supplem. ptc. ἱμείρουσα with τυγχάνω: S #2096a; GMT #887; SS 261 §12f. ἢν [= ἐάν] τυγχάνῃς, protasis of future more vivid condition: S #2297); > 'not even if you *you'd like me to* very much . . .'; [1 × *El.*]

ἄνοια, ἡ — (ἄ-νοος, without understanding) lack of understanding (genit. of definition: SS 55 §5)

θηράω — hunt, chase (articular inf. as nom. taking an object: κενά: SS 246 §11. The article makes the inf. more prominent as a noun: GMT #789. The preceding καί marks a descending climax. Difficult to translate: GP 293 IIA2); > 'since it is completely senseless *to chase* after nothing' or 'since *chasing* after nothing is completely senseless'; [1× *El.*]

LINE 1055

τυγχάνειc δοκοῦcα — supplemen. ptc. with τυγχάνω (S #2096a; GMT #887; SS 261 §12f). τυγχάνεις picks up from τυγχάνῃς of 1053 (Kells)

φρονεῖν, φρόνει — (φρόνει, pres. impv.) Repetition of words derived form the same root but with different endings is favored, but difficult to effect in translation; > 'If you (happen to think =) think you are showing any sense, then (think =) go ahead with this sort of sense'

ὅταν . . . †*βεβήκηιc — temporal clause; see ὅταν εὖ †λέγῃς 1028n. For the perfect †*βέβηκα, see 979n. SS 198 §18: "when *you are in a state* of misfortune"

XO.	τί τοὺς ἄνωθεν φρονιμωτάτους οἰωνοὺς	στρ. α'
	ἐσορώμενοι τροφᾶς κη-	
	δομένους ἀφ' ὧν τε βλάστω-	1060
	σιν ἀφ' ὧν τ' ὄνησιν εὕρω-	
	σι, τάδ' οὐκ ἐπ' ἴσας τελοῦμεν;	
	ἀλλ' οὐ τὰν Διὸς ἀστραπὰν	
	καὶ τὰν οὐρανίαν Θέμιν	
	δαρὸν οὐκ ἀπόνητοι.	1065

Chrysothemis exits through the palace doors (she will never reemerge). Electra remains as she was, close to the palace doors.

SECOND STASIMON, LINES 1058–1097

The second Choral song takes place after Chrysothemis enters the palace. Electra remains at the entrance to the palace as the Chorus sing and dance in the *orchestra*. The strong support the Chorus express for Electra here is very different from the caution they had recommended earlier, both in lines 990–991 and in their first encounter with Electra.

The stasimon consists of two strophic pairs with no epode. Both strophes begin with a comment of general application and turn to a specific situation in the antistrophe. Basing its argument on the conduct of birds toward their parents, the first strophic pair, 1058–1069, focuses on the correct forms of filial piety. Birds' care for their parents is contrasted with human negligence. Electra's devotion is thus praised. The second pair, 1070–1097, states in the beginning that no noble man consents to sully his name, and goes on to portray Electra's choice as right, although she lives a life of suffering.

FIRST STROPHE, Lines 1058–1069

LINE 1058

ἄνωθεν (adv.)	(ἄνω, upward) from above; [1× *El.*]
φρόνϊμος, ον	(φρονέω) sensible wise, prudent; [1× *El.*]
οἰωνός, ὁ	a (solitary) bird (especially a bird of prey); [1× *El.*]
κήδομαι	take care of, be concerned for (with genit. τροφᾶς = τροφῆς)
⁺*βλάστωσιν ... ⁺*εὕρωσι	(βλαστάνω, εὑρίσκω, aor.² subjv.) generalizing subjvs. in relative clause without ἄν, the reference "not being to any particular thing, but to any, or all" (SS 225–26 §12). Cf. ⁺*τέκῃ 771n
ὄνεσις, εως, ἡ	(ὀνίνημι, profit) profit, advantage; [1× *El.*]
ἀφ' ὧν ... ἀφ' ὧν	supply τούτων as antecedent. The repetition "lends urgency to the words" (Kamerbeek); > 'Why when we see the most wise birds above solicitous for the feeding [of those] *from whom* they sprang and *from whom* they benefited'
ἐπ' ⁺ἴσας	i.e., μοίρας, equal shares, equal portions/duties
⁺τελοῦμεν	(τελέω) 'do we not fulfill in equal measure?'

LINE 1063

ἀστρᾰπή, ἡ	lightning (before τὰν Διὸς ἀστραπάν and τὰν ... Θέμιν asseverative μά with acc. of divinity is understood: S #1596b, 2894); [1× *El.*]
οὐράνιος (3/2)	heavenly; [1× *El.*]
Θέμις, ἡ	goddess of law and order, Justice
δᾰρόν (adv.)	(Doric = δηρόν) all too long; [1× *El.*]
ἀ-πόνητος, ον	(ἀ privat., πονέω, toil) without trouble; > 'No, by the lightening of Zeus, and by heavenly Themis, trouble won't be long in coming'; [1× Soph.]

ὦ χθονία βροτοῖcι φάμα,
κατά μοι βόαcον οἰκτρὰν
ὄπα τοῖc ἔνερθ' Ἀτρείδαιc,
ἀχόρευτα φέρουc' ὀνείδη.

ὅτι cφὶν ἤδη τὰ μὲν ἐκ δόμων νοcεῖται,   ἀντ. α'
τὰ δὲ πρὸc τέκνων διπλῆ φύ-   1071
λοπιc οὐκέτ' ἐξιcοῦται
φιλοταcίῳ διαίτᾳ.
πρόδοτοc δὲ μόνα cαλεύει
ἁ παῖc, οἶτον ἀεὶ πατρὸc   1075
δειλαία cτενάχουc' ὅπωc
ἁ πάνδυρτοc ἀηδών,

LINE 1066

χθόνιος (3/2)	(⁺χθών) below the earth
⁺βροτοῖσι	ethical dat./of feeling, denoting the interest of the speaker (S #1486; SS 82–83 §6); 'on behalf of the mortals'
φάμα	(Doric) = ⁺φήμη
κατα-⁻*βοάω	(βόασον, aor.¹ impv. act.) cry down (*tmesis.* μοι ethical dat./of feeling; see 1066n; 'on my behalf'); [1× Soph.]
⁺οἰκτρός (3)	pitiable, lamentable
ὄψ, ὀπός, ἡ	voice, discourse, word; [1× Soph.]
ἔνερθε	from beneath; [1× *El.*]
Ἀτρείδης, ὁ	son of Atreus (–ιδης patronymic: S #845.4)
ἀ-χόρευτος, ον	(ἀ privat., χορεύω, dance) not attended by dance, joyless (for the Chorus, lack of dance is an indication of sadness); [1× Soph.]
ὄνειδος, τό	reproach, dishonor; > 'Oh rumor who goes beneath the earth, on behalf of mortals send down to Atreus' sons a pitiful cry, (on my behalf =) I pray you, carrying a joyless report of *dishonor*'; [1× *El.*]

FIRST ANTISTROPHE, Lines 1070–1081

LINE 1070

σφίν	[ῐ] dat. pl. of σφεῖς, 3rd pers. they; 'their' (dat. of possess.: S #1480; SS 83- 4)
τὰ ... ἐκ ⁺δόμων	the article makes into a noun a preposition and its case (S #1153c); >'the *tidings that come out of their house,*' i.e., 'what relates to their house.' The parallel is τὰ πρὸς ... ⁺τέκνων, '*things on the children's side*'
νοσέω	(νόσος, sickness) to be sick; [1× *El.*]
φύλοπις, ἡ	[ῠ] battle cry, battle; [1× Soph.]
φιλοτήσιος (3)	(φιλότης, friendship) of friendship, of love; [1× Soph.]
δίαιτα, ἡ	way of life; > 'that now their house is sick, and a double battle cry between the children is no longer moderated by loving behavior'; [1× *El.*]

LINE 1074

πρό-δοτος, ον	(προ-δίδωμι, betray) betrayed, abandoned
σᾰλεύω	move to and fro, roll or toss like a ship; [1× *El.*]
οἶτος, ὁ	ill fate, lot, doom
πάν-δυρτος, ον	poetic for πανόδυρτος (πᾶς, ὀδυρτός, mourned) all-lamentable, all- plaintive; [1× Soph.]

οὔτε τι τοῦ θανεῖν προμηθὴς
τό τε μὴ βλέπειν ἑτοίμα,
διδύμαν ἑλοῦς' Ἐρινύν.   **1080**
τίς ἂν εὔπατρις ὧδε βλάστοι;

οὐδεὶς τῶν ἀγαθῶν ⟨ἂν⟩   στρ. β'
ζῶν κακῶς εὔκλειαν αἰσχῦναι θέλοι
νώνυμος, ὦ παῖ παῖ·
ὡς καὶ σὺ πάγκλαυτον αἰ-   **1085**
ῶνα κλεινὸν εἵλου,
ἄκος καλὸν καθοπλίσα-
ca δύο φέρειν ⟨ἐν⟩ ἑνὶ λόγῳ,
cοφά τ' ἀρίcτα τε παῖc κεκλῆcθαι.

ἀηδών, ἡ, Attic ὁ,	[ᾰ] genit.: ἀηδόνος/ἀηδοῦς; (ἀείδω, sing) singer, songstress, i.e., the <u>nightingale</u>; > 'But the daughter betrayed, all alone tosses like a ship at sea, miserable forever lamenting the fate of her father, like the ever- plaintive *nightingale*'

LINE 1078

προ-μηθής, ές	(προ, μῆτις, wisdom) fore-thinking, cautious (with genit. of articular inf. τοῦ θανεῖν: S #2032; SS 248–49 §13; GMT #798); > '(*Does not consider=*) *Reckless* of death'; [1× Soph.]
ἑτοῖμος (3)	ready (τό ... μὴ ⁺βλέπειν not seeing [the light] equals ⁺θανεῖν, see 66n on δέρκομαι. For the articular infinitive, see τὸ κρῖναι 1030n); [1× *El.*]
οὔτε ... τε	'*both* reckless of death ... *and* ready to. ...' (LSJ 4)
⁺*ἑλοῦσα	(αἱρέω, aor² ptc. act. fem.) participle expresses condition's protasis: ἂν [μόνον] ἕλῃ διδύμαν Ἐρινύν; > 'reckless of death and ready not to see [the light], *if* [*only*] *she could overcome* the twin Erinys/Fury'
δίδῠμος (3)	[ῐ] twin; double ⁺Ἐρῖνυς refers to Clyt, and Aeg.; [1× *El.*]
εὔ-πᾰτρις, ιδος, ὁ/ἡ	(εὔ, πατήρ) nobly born, worthy of noble descent (now that Or. is thought to be dead, El. receives his epithet [162, 858]. ἂν βλάστοι potential optative); > 'Who could be born so noble?'; [1× Soph.]

SECOND STROPHE, Lines 1082–1089

LINE 1082

[ἂν]	deleted to restore strophic responsion
εὔ-κλειᾰ, ἡ	good fame, renown
νώνῠμος, ον	(νη-, ὄνυμα Aeolic for ὄνομα) without name, inglorious; > 'No one of the nobility (genit. partitive) wants to shame a good reputation by living *ingloriously*, my child, my child'; [1× Soph.]

LINE 1085

πάγ-κλαυτος, ον	(πᾶς, κλαίω, weep) all-lamented, most woeful; [1× *El.*]
⁺*εἵλου	(aor.² 2sg.) mid. of ⁺*αἱρέω: 'choose'; > 'Thus you have chosen a renowned life of tears'
ἄκος, τό	remedy; [1× *El.*]
καθ-οπλίζω	equip, array fully; [1× *El.*]
⁺*κεκλῆσθαι	(καλέω, perf. inf. pass.) final/consecutive inf. after vb. of choosing (SS 237–38 §2; GMT #770); > 'having armed a noble remedy *so as to be called* at once (ἑνὶ λόγῳ, in one word) wise and the best daughter'

ζῴης μοι καθύπερθεν

χειρὶ καὶ πλούτῳ τεῶν ἐχθρῶν ὅϲον   1091

νῦν ὑπόχειρ ναίειϲ·

ἐπεί ϲ' ἐφηύρηκα μοί-

ρᾳ μὲν οὐκ ἐν ἐϲθλᾷ

βεβῶϲαν, ἃ δὲ μέγιϲτ' ἔβλα-   1095

ϲτε νόμιμα, τῶνδε φερομέναν

ἄριϲτα τᾷ Ζηνὸϲ εὐϲεβείᾳ.

ἀντ. β'

SECOND ANTISTROPHE, Lines 1090–1097

LINE 1090

⁺*ζῴης	optative of wish without introductory particle (SS 232 §15; GMT 721–22). With dat. μοι, ethical/of feeling (S #1486; SS 82–83 §6); > '*May you live, I pray*'
καθ-ύπερθε(ν) (adv.)	[ῠ] + genit. (τέων ⁺ἐχθρῶν) above, over; [1× Soph.]
⁺χειρὶ καὶ ⁺πλούτῳ	dat. of means (S #1507a; SS 88–89 §16)
ὑπο-χείρ, ὁ/ἡ	under control/command; [1× Soph.]
⁺ναίω	dwell; > 'May you live, I pray, as much above your enemies in power and possessions, as now *you dwell* beneath them'

LINE 1092

ἐφ-⁺*ευρίσκω	(ἐφηύρηκα, pf. act.) detect, discover (ἐπεί opens causal clause of independent status: SS 304. σε . . . βεβῶσαν, see 979n)
μοῖρα, ἡ	fate; > 'I've found you placed/living in no happy fate'
νόμιμος (3)	substantival use of adjective without article (SS 163 §1). Neut. pl.: customs, laws; [1× *El.*]
⁺εὐσεβεία	Kamerbeek: "In a less emotional style: τὰ δὲ μέγιστα νόμιμα τὰ τοῦ Διὸς σέβουσαν, ἄριστα σ' ἐφηύρηκα φερομένην." τῶνδε, genit. of cause, is 'postcedent,' i.e., the relative clause precedes it (S #2541); > 'and yet with respect to the greatest laws that have arisen, (I've found you) winning the highest prize/noblest renown (ἄριστα) by your piety toward Zeus, on account of [your observance of] these (τῶνδε)'

OP.	ἆρ᾽, ὦ γυναῖκες, ὀρθά τ᾽ εἰσηκούσαμεν
	ὀρθῶς θ᾽ ὁδοιποροῦμεν ἔνθα χρῄζομεν;
XO.	τί δ᾽ ἐξερευνᾷς καὶ τί βουληθεὶς πάρει; 1100
OP.	Αἴγισθον ἔνθ᾽ ᾤκηκεν ἱστορῶ πάλαι.
XO.	ἀλλ᾽ εὖ θ᾽ ἱκάνεις χὠ φράσας ἀζήμιος.
OP.	τίς οὖν ἂν ὑμῶν τοῖς ἔσω φράσειεν ἂν
	ἡμῶν ποθεινὴν κοινόπουν παρουσίαν;

Orestes, Pylades, and at least two attendants enter through one of the side entrances. One attendant carries a small bronze urn. All the party are disguised as Phocians. The audience, having seen them at the start of the play, know who they are, but the Chorus do not.

FOURTH EPISODE, 1098–1383

The Fourth Episode is divided into two scenes: Scene A, lines 1098–1287, and Scene B, lines 1288–1383.
Scene A divides further into two: (1) lines 1098–1231: The news brought by the newcomers deepens Electra's misery. She sings a heart-wrenching lament over the urn that supposedly contains the ashes of her brother. This is one of the most memorable expressions of sorrow in Greek literature. Aulus Gellius (*Attic Nights* 6.5) tells a story about the actor Polus (4th century BCE) returning to the Athenian stage after the loss of his son, and reciting Electra's lament while holding the ashes of his own son. Electra's grief impels Orestes to reveal himself to her. (2) Lines 1232–1287: A joyful reunion sung in a duet between Electra and Orestes, in which Electra sings in a variety of lyric meters expressing her intense excitement, while Orestes mainly responds in spoken iambic trimeters, indicating his cool rationality (see Roisman 2000). In Scene B Electra, Orestes, and the Tutor converse as they prepare themselves for their revenge.

SCENE A: (1) Lines 1098–1231

LINE 1098

⁺ἆρα	interrogative pcl. indicating anxiety and impatience (LSJ 1; GP 46) which are further emphasized by the illogicality of the question: Or. wants to know if he is on the right path without telling the Chorus where he wants to go.
⁺ὀρθά	(neut. acc. pl.) adverbial acc. (SS 41 §12). The following adv. ὀρθῶς emphasizes the concern further.
ὁδοιπορέω	travel, journey; > 'Ladies, did we hear it right, are we traveling in the right way to where we need to go?'; [1× *El.*]
ἐξ-ερευνάω	search out, look for; > 'What are you looking for? And what do you want here [= and you are here wanting what]?' [1× *El.*]
ἱστορέω	learn by inquiry, question, inquire
οἰκέω, ᾤκηκα	(pf. indic. act.) inhabit; intransitive: live, dwell; > 'I've been asking all along about Aeg., where he has fixed his abode (pf., i.e., lives now)'; [1× *El.*]

LINE 1102

ἱκάνω	come (lengthened form of ἵκω, found in Epic and Lyric poetry, sometimes in Tragedy)
ἀ-ζήμιος, ον	(ἀ privat., ζημία, punishment) without loss, scot-free, without punishment; [1 × *El.*]
⁺*φράσας	(φράζω, aor.¹ ptc. act.) ὁ φράσας, articular substant. ptc. (S #2050–2052; S 257–58 §9; GMT #825); > 'the man who guided you deserves no blame'
τοῖς ἔσω	substantival use of article with an adverb (S #1153 e; SS 151 §19) 'to those inside'. ⁺*φράσειεν ἄν: aor.¹, potential optative for polite request: 'Could one of you report . . . ?' (S #1824; SS 231 §14)
ποθεινός (2/3)	(ποθέω) desired (ambiguous: desired by Clyt. and Aeg., but also by Or. [1× *El.*]
κοινό-πους, ὁ/ἡ	(κοινός, πούς) with common foot, of persons all together; [1× Soph.]
ἡμῶν . . . ⁺παρ-ουσίαν	ἡμῶν subjective genit. (S #1330; SS 53 §4); > 'of the desired presence of the two of us'

166

ΧΟ.	ἥδ᾽, εἰ τὸν ἄγχιστόν γε κηρύccειν χρεών.	1105
ΟΡ.	ἴθ᾽, ὦ γύναι, δήλωcον εἰcελθοῦc᾽ ὅτι	
	Φωκῆc ματεύουc᾽ ἄνδρεc Αἴγιcθόν τινεc.	
ΗΛ.	οἴμοι τάλαιν᾽, οὐ δή ποθ᾽ ἧc ἠκούcαμεν	
	φήμηc φέροντεc ἐμφανῆ τεκμήρια;	
ΟΡ.	οὐκ οἶδα τὴν cὴν κληδόν· ἀλλά μοι γέρων	1110
	ἐφεῖτ᾽ Ὀρέcτου Cτροφίοc ἀγγεῖλαι πέρι.	
ΗΛ.	τί δ᾽ ἔcτιν, ὦ ξέν᾽; ὥc μ᾽ ὑπέρχεται φόβοc.	
ΟΡ.	φέροντεc αὐτοῦ cμικρὰ λείψαν᾽ ἐν βραχεῖ	
	τεύχει θανόντοc, ὡc ὁρᾷc, κομίζομεν.	

LINE 1105

ἄγχιcτοc (2)	(superlative of ἄγχι, adv., near) nearest relative (for masc. gender see πάcχοντι 771n); [1 × *El.*]
κηρύccω	proclaim, announce
⁺χρεών	(indecl.) copula (ἐcτί) omitted after expression of necessity with inf. (S #944b); > 'This lady, if the closest relative is the one *who should announce it*'
⁺δήλωcον	(δηλόω, aor.¹ impv. act.) verb of declaring following by ὅτι introducing clause that is objectively factual. SS 313 §1: "go in and report that men from Phocis are looking for Aeg."
⁺*εἰcελθοῦcα	(εἰcέρχομαι, aor.² act. ptc.) 'having gone in declare that . . .'
⁺Φωκῆc . . . ἄνδρεc . . . τινεc	Does the *hyperbaton* bring "an off-hand, aloof effect?" as Kells suggests?
μᾰτεύω	seek, search after; [1× *El.*]

LINE 1108

οὐ δή	following by ποτε introduces in Soph. and Herodotus "a surprised or incredulous question" (GP 223ii; Finglass); " 'Surely not . . .?' 'You don't mean . . .?' "
ἧc . . . ⁺φήμηc	antecedent reserved for the main clause, which follows the relative clause (S #2541).
ἐμ-φᾰνήc, έc	(φαίνω) visible, manifest; > 'surely you are not bringing concrete proofs of the rumor we've heard?'
κληδών, όνοc, ἡ	rumor; reputation, glory; Why does Soph. have Or. use a synonym and not repeat his sister's noun φήμη?; [1× *El.*]
⁺ἐφ-*εῖτο	(ἐφίημι, aor.² ind. mid.) middle: command (with dat., μοι, that follows verbs of command: SS 83 §7)
πέρι	= περί, *anastrophe.*
Cτρόφιοc, ὁ	Strophius is a Phocian. Father of Pylades, to whose house El. sent Or. after Ag.'s murder. [1× *El.*]

LINE 1112

⁺ὥc	exclamatory: how (S #2682a)
ὑπ-έρχομαι	steal over, come upon; > 'What is it, stranger? How fear comes over me!'
⁺cμῑκρόc (3)	= μῑκρόc; small, little, trivial, insignificant
λείψᾰνον, τό	(⁺*λείπω) pl.: remnants, remains; [1× Soph.]
τεῦχοc, εοc, τό	a vessel of any kind
κομίζω	<u>bring</u>, provide (note the two instances of *hyperbaton*: φέροντεc . . . κομίζομεν and αὐτοῦ . . . θανόντοc); > 'He is dead, and as you see *we bring* the scanty remains, carrying them in a small urn'; [1× *El.*]

ΗΛ.	οἳ 'γὼ τάλαινα, τοῦτ' ἐκεῖν', ἤδη σαφές·	1115
	πρόχειρον ἄχθος, ὡς ἔοικε, δέρκομαι.	
ΟΡ.	εἴπερ τι κλαίεις τῶν Ὀρεστείων κακῶν,	
	τόδ' ἄγγος ἴσθι σῶμα τοὐκείνου στέγον.	
ΗΛ.	ὦ ξεῖνε, δός νυν πρὸς θεῶν, εἴπερ τόδε	
	κέκευθεν αὐτὸν τεῦχος, ἐς χεῖρας λαβεῖν,	1120
	ὅπως ἐμαυτὴν καὶ γένος τὸ πᾶν ὁμοῦ	
	ξὺν τῇδε κλαύσω κἀποδύρωμαι σποδῷ.	
ΟΡ.	δόθ', ἥτις ἐστί, προσφέροντες· οὐ γὰρ ὡς	
	ἐν δυσμενείᾳ γ' οὖσ' ἐπαιτεῖται τόδε,	
	ἀλλ' ἢ φίλων τις, ἢ πρὸς αἵματος φύσιν.	1125

LINE 1115

οἳ	exclamation of pain; here with nom. οἳ 'γὼ—*aphaeresis.*
τοῦτ' ἐκεῖν'	'that is it' (Finglass: "as an independent sense-unit is a colloquialism")
πρό-χειρος, ον	(πρό, χείρ) at hand, close; handy, ready
⁺ἄχθος, -εος, τό	<u>burden</u>, load of grief; > 'it seems I see a *burden* ready to be grasped'
ἄγγος, εος, τό	a vessel of any kind; [1× *El.*]
στέγω	(pres. ptc. act. neut.) hide, <u>conceal</u>, shroud; (τόδε ἄγγος . . . στέγον acc. and ptc. structure in indirect discourse following ἴσθι; S #2123, 2139); > 'If indeed (⁺εἴπερ) you weep about anything (τι) of the misfortunes of Or., *know that* this small urn *conceals his body*'; [1× *El.*]

LINE 1119

⁺*δός	(δίδωμι, aor.² impv.) give (answered by δόθ' [pl.] in 1123)
κεύθω	cover up, hide, <u>conceal</u>; > if this vessel really *holds him*'
ἀπο-δύρομαι	[ῡ] (pres. subjv.) lament bitterly (with aor. subjv., κλαύσω, final clause in primary sequence, δός. Impv. moods count as primary because they point to the fut.: S #2196, 1858a); > '*so that* with these ashes here I may weep and *bitterly lament for myself* and all my family together'; [1× Soph.]
τῇδε . . . ⁺σποδῷ	the slight *hyperbaton* "gives dignity and finality to her lines" (Kells)

LINE 1123

προσ-⁺*φέρω	bring to
δυσ-μένεια, ἡ	(δυσ-, μένος) ill will, enmity (ἐν δυσ-μενείᾳ, prep. + dat. denote situation in which the action takes place: SS 106 §8). ⁺*οὖσα (⁺*εἰμί, pres. ptc.); > 'Take it and give it [to her], whoever she is, for not as if she [being] were (in enmity =) a hostile person she asks or it'.
ἐπ-αιτέω	ask, solicit; [1× *El.*]
αἷμα, ατος, τό	blood (⁺φύσιν, acc. of respect/adverbial); > 'but as someone of his friends, or one of *his blood by nature.*'

ΗΛ.   ὦ φιλτάτου μνημεῖον ἀνθρώπων ἐμοὶ

ψυχῆς Ὀρέστου λοιπόν, ὥς ⟨ c' ⟩ ἀπ' ἐλπίδων

οὐχ ὧνπερ ἐξέπεμπον εἰcεδεξάμην.

νῦν μὲν γὰρ οὐδὲν ὄντα βαcτάζω χεροῖν,

δόμων δέ c', ὦ παῖ, λαμπρὸν ἐξέπεμψ' ἐγώ.   1130

ὡς ὤφελον πάροιθεν ἐκλιπεῖν βίον,

πρὶν ἐc ξένην cε γαῖαν ἐκπέμψαι χεροῖν

κλέψαcα ταῖνδε κἀναcώcαcθαι φόνου,

ὅπωc θανὼν ἔκειcο τῇ τόθ' ἡμέρᾳ,

τύμβου πατρῴου κοινὸν εἰληχὼc μέροc.   1135

LINE 1126

μνημεῖον, τό   memorial (it runs thus: ὦ μνημεῖον λοιπόν ψυχῆς Ὀρέστου, φιλτάτου ἀνθρώπων ἐμοὶ [ethical dat./of feeling]); > 'Oh last *memento* of Orestes' life, *for me* the dearest of men'

ἐκ-⁺*πέμπω   send out, send forth;

εἰc-⁺*δέχομαι   take into, admit; [1× *El.*]

οὐχ ὧνπερ   relative attraction to the antecedent ἐλπίδων (S #2532) for αἵσπερ. Kamerbeek: οὐχ "repeats the negative notion in ἀπό"; > 'how differently from the hopes with which I sent you away, have I received you back'

LINE 1131

πάροιθε(ν) (adv.)   formerly, erst, before

ὤφελον . . .⁺ἐκ-⁺*λιπεῖν   aor. inf. in unattainable wish for past time (S #1780, 1781; GMT #734). ὡς is less common than εἴθε; > 'For now I hold you as nothingness (you being nothing) in my two hands, but, my child, I sent you forth from home (⁺δόμων, genit. following ἐξέπεμψα) resplendent. *Would that I had died before that moment.*'

ξένος (3)   foreign

⁺κλέπτω   (κλέψαcα, aor.¹ act. ptc.) steal

ἀνα-⁺*σῴζω, -έσωσα   (ἀναcώcαcθαι, aor.¹ inf. mid.) rescue (πρίν with the two infs. 'before': S #2431); > 'before I *stole* you with these two hands and *sent* you to a foreign land and *saved* you from murder'; [1× *El.*]

ὅπως . . .⁺ἔκεισο   (κεῖμαι, impf. indic. 2sg.) secondary tenses of indic. are used in final clauses with ὅπως or ὡς to denote that the purpose depends upon some unaccomplished action or unfulfilled condition, and thus was not attained. In this case, El.'s death before sending Orestes away (GMT #333); > 'so that on that day (θανών, having died =) you'd have died and lain here'

*λαγχάνω   [χᾰ] (εἰληχώς, pf. act. ptc.) obtain by lot

μέρος, εος, τό   share, part; > 'and had your portion in common (⁺κοινόν, i.e., with the rest of family) in your father's grave'; [1× *El.*]

νῦν δ' ἐκτὸς οἴκων κἀπὶ γῆς ἄλλης φυγὰς
κακῶς ἀπώλου, σῆς κασιγνήτης δίχα·
κοὔτ' ἐν φίλαισι χερσὶν ἡ τάλαιν' ἐγὼ
λουτροῖς σ' ἐκόσμης' οὔτε παμφλέκτου πυρὸς
ἀνειλόμην, ὡς εἰκός, ἄθλιον βάρος,   1140
ἀλλ' ἐν ξένῃσι χερσὶ κηδευθεὶς τάλας
σμικρὸς προσήκεις ὄγκος ἐν σμικρῷ κύτει.
οἴμοι τάλαινα τῆς ἐμῆς πάλαι τροφῆς
ἀνωφελήτου, τὴν ἐγὼ θάμ' ἀμφὶ σοὶ
πόνῳ γλυκεῖ παρέσχον. οὔτε γάρ ποτε   1145
μητρὸς σύ γ' ἦσθα μᾶλλον ἢ κἀμοῦ φίλος,

LINE 1136

φῠγάς, αδος, ὁ	(⁺*φεύγω) fugitive, banished person
⁺*ἀπ-ώλου	(ἀπόλλῠμαι, aor.² mid. 2sg.) perish, die
δίχᾰ (+ genit.)	(-ῐ-) apart from
κοσμέω	(κόσμος, order) deck, adorn, <u>dress</u> (ἐν denotes the means: SS 107 §8); > 'but, I, alas, did not *dress* you and wash you *with loving hands*'
πάμ-φλεκτος, ον	(πᾶς, φλέγω, burn) all-consuming; all-blazing; [1× *El.*]
ἀν-⁺*αιρέω, - ειλόμην	(aor.²) take up, lift, bear away; [1× *El.*]
βάρος, εος, τό	weight, burden; > 'nor did I take up the sad burden, from the all- consuming fire as would have been fitting (ὡς εἰκός)'

LINE 1141

κηδεύω	(κηδευθείς, aor.¹ pass. ptc.) pay the last rites of the dead; > 'but you, miserable one, *had your last rites* from alien (ξένῃσι = ξέναισι) hands'; [1× *El.*]
ὄγκος, ὁ	bulk, weight (σμικρός ... ὄγκος oxymoron: 'small bulk'; [1× *El.*]
κύτος, εος, τό	[ῠ] a hollow vessel, urn (σμικρὸς ... σμικρῷ emphatic; *polyptoton*); > 'you've arrived as small bulk in a small urn'; [1× Soph.]

LINE 1143

⁺τροφῆς	genit. of cause used in exclamation (SS 71–72 §35, S #1407)
ἀν-ωφέλητος, ον	(ἀ privat., ὠφελέω, help) fruitless, worthless; > 'Oh miserable me for my fruitless nurture of you long ago'; [1 × *El.*]
θαμά (adv.)	often, ofttimes, frequently
τήν	= ἥν (the pronoun ὁ, ἡ, τό, originally demonstrative, appears occasionally in lyric and dialogue as a substitute for relative pronoun: SS 267 §6. Here probably to avoid immediate succession of two vowel sounds: ἀν-ωφέλητ<u>ου ἥν</u>)
γλῠκύς, εῖα,ύ	sweet; [1× *El.*]
παρ-⁺*έχω, -έσχον	(aor.²) render, provide (sometimes aorist refers to an action of long duration or consisting of repeated acts over a period of time. Here with emphasis on its termination, unlike the following imperfects: ἦσθα, προσηυδώμην, in which "she wishes to dwell on the former state with remembrance": SS 193 §13); [1× *El.*]
οὔτε γάρ ... φίλος	Kamerbeek: "you were not your mother's darling more than (by implication 'so much as') mine.' καί stresses ἐμοῦ"

οὔθ' οἱ κατ' οἶκον ἦσαν ἀλλ' ἐγὼ τροφός,
ἐγὼ δ' ἀδελφὴ coὶ προσηυδώμην ἀεί.
νῦν δ' ἐκλέλοιπε ταῦτ' ἐν ἡμέρᾳ μιᾷ
θανόντι cὺν coί. πάντα γὰρ cυναρπάcαc,   1150
θύελλ' ὅπωc, βέβηκαc. οἴχεται πατήρ·
τέθνηκ' ἐγὼ coί· φροῦδοc αὐτὸc εἶ θανών·
γελῶcι δ' ἐχθροί· μαίνεται δ' ὑφ' ἡδονῆc
μήτηρ ἀμήτωρ, ἧc ἐμοὶ cὺ πολλάκιc
φήμαc λάθρᾳ προὔπεμπεc ὡc φανούμενοc   1155

LINE 1147

οἱ κατ' οἶκον — substantival use of article with a prep. (S #1153 c; SS 151–152 §20): 'those in the house,' i.e., servants from among whom a 'nanny' (τρόφος) would have been provided.

προc-αυδάω — (impf. pass.) speak to, address (coί, dat. of agent with προσηυδώμην or dat. of possession with τροφή, or both; > 'but I was *your* nurse, always *called sister by you*'

cυν-αρπάζω — carry off; [1× *El.*]

θύελλα, ἡ — [ῠ] storm, whirlwind (+*βέβηκας; for the perfect, see 979n); > 'now with your death, in one day all this is ended, like a whirlwind you are gone having snatched up everything'; [1× *El.*]

LINE 1152

τέθνηκ' ἐγὼ coί — dat. of agent (S #1488; SS 85–86 §12). +*θνήσκω serves as pass. for +*κτείνω (LSJ 2); > *I've been killed by you; you yourself are dead and gone* (φροῦδος)'

μαίνω — be mad (usually poetic)

ἀμήτωρ, οροc — unmotherly (μήτηρ ἀμήτωρ, a well-known wordplay, which also prepares the stage for the upcoming 'justified' matricide); [1× Soph.]

ἧc — antecedent: μήτηρ. Either to be taken with λάθρᾳ 'without whose knowledge you often sent me messages that you in person would come as an avenger'; or as a subject of φήμας and objective genit. of +τιμωρός (LSJ I.2; S #1328; SS 52–53 §4); > 'about whom you often send me messages in secret, that you would come in person to punish'

πολλάκιc (adv.) — many times, <u>often</u>

λάθρᾳ (adv.) — secretly (with genit.: without one's knowledge); [1× *El.*]

προ-πέμπω — (= προ-έπεμπες (impf.) send beforehand; [1× *El.*]

+*φανούμενοc — (φαίνομαι, fut. mid. ptc.) ὡς with future participle explaining the content of the +φήμας; > 'that you would appear as an avenger'

τιμωρὸς αὐτός. ἀλλὰ ταῦθ' ὁ δυστυχὴς
δαίμων ὁ σός τε κἀμὸς ἐξαφείλετο,
ὅς σ' ὧδέ μοι προὔπεμψεν ἀντὶ φιλτάτης
μορφῆς σποδόν τε καὶ σκιὰν ἀνωφελῆ.
οἴμοι μοι.   **1160**
ὦ δέμας οἰκτρόν. φεῦ φεῦ.
ὦ δεινοτάτας, οἴμοι μοι,
πεμφθεὶς κελεύθους, φίλταθ', ὥς μ' ἀπώλεσας·
ἀπώλεσας δῆτ', ὦ κασίγνητον κάρα.
τοιγὰρ σὺ δέξαι μ' ἐς τὸ σὸν τόδε στέγος,   **1165**
τὴν μηδὲν ἐς τὸ μηδέν, ὡς σὺν σοὶ κάτω
ναίω τὸ λοιπόν. καὶ γὰρ ἡνίκ' ἦσθ' ἄνω,
ξὺν σοὶ μετεῖχον τῶν ἴσων· καὶ νῦν ποθῶ
τοῦ σοῦ θανοῦσα μὴ ἀπολείπεσθαι τάφου.
τοὺς γὰρ θανόντας οὐχ ὁρῶ λυπουμένους.   **1170**

LINE 1156

ἐξ-αφ-⁺*αιρέω, -εῖλον	(ἐξαφείλετο, aor.² mid.) mid: take away; > 'took them away' [1× Soph.]
προὔπεμψεν	= πρὸ ἔπεμψεν
μορφή, ἡ	shape, form, figure
σκῐά, ἡ	shade, shadow, phantom; [1× El.]
ἀν-ωφελής, ές	(ἀ privat., ὠφελέω) useless; > 'sent you to me in this way (as you are now) as ashes and useless shadow instead of your most beloved form; [1× Soph.]

LINE 1160

κέλευθος, ἡ	road, path; [1× El.]
ὦ … φίλτατε	voc. following a participial phrase ὦ πεμφθείς in apposition to it (SS 30 §10). δεινοτάτας … κελεύθους acc. of extent with verb of motion denoting area covered. SS 44 §15: "sent (implying 'traveling on') on a most dreadful journey (internal accusative)." I.e., from Crisa to Mycenae, coming back as dust.
⁺δῆτα (pcl.)	really, assuredly, in truth (S #2851) (echoes or endorses emphatically the speaker's own words: GP 277.3); > 'how you have destroyed me (⁺ἀπ-⁺*ώλεσας)! *Yes, you've destroyed me for sure*, dearest brother'
κασίγνητος (3)	<u>brotherly</u>, sisterly (κασίγνητον ⁺κάρα intense metonymy for 'dearest / my brother'; [1× El.]

LINE 1165

τοί-γαρ (pcl.)	so then, thus, therefore (usually first word in an iambic line GP 565–66)
στέγος, τό	=⁺στέγη, ἡ; house; > 'Therefore, receive me (⁺*δέξαι, aor.¹ impv. act.) into this [little] house of yours'; [1× El.]
τὴν μηδέν	μηδέν can be used indeclinably. τήν fem. article used for herself; > 'nothing [i.e., herself] to nothing'
⁺κάτω	below (the earth) as opposed to ⁺ἄνω above (the earth)
ὡς … ⁺ναίω	subjv. in final clause in primary sequence, δέξαι; see δός 1119n
μετ-⁺*έχω	partake of, have a share of + genit.; > 'I shared with you equally in all things (= τῶν ⁺ἴσων).' τῶν: all-inclusive article (Kells); [1× El.]
ποθέω	long for, yearn after (with complementary inf. ἀπο-⁺λείπεσθαι 'be wanting' with genit., τοῦ … ⁺τάφου. The latter embraces the line in emphatic *hyperbaton*). ⁺*θανοῦσα, conjunctive ptc. with μὴ ἀπολείπεσθαι, to be translated as an inf. (SS 250–51 §2); > 'and now I wish *to die* [and] not to be denied/wanting (of your grave =) a share in your grave.' μὴ ἀπολείπεσθαι—*synizesis*); [1× El.]

ΧΟ.	θνητοῦ πέφυκας πατρός, Ἠλέκτρα, φρόνει·
	θνητὸς δ' Ὀρέστης· ὥστε μὴ λίαν στένε·
	πᾶσιν γὰρ ἡμῖν τοῦτ' ὀφείλεται παθεῖν.
ΟΡ.	φεῦ φεῦ, τί λέξω; ποῖ λόγων ἀμηχανῶν
	ἔλθω; κρατεῖν γὰρ οὐκέτι γλώσσης σθένω.
ΗΛ.	τί δ' ἔσχες ἄλγος; πρὸς τί τοῦτ' εἰπὼν κυρεῖς;
ΟΡ.	ἢ σὸν τὸ κλεινὸν εἶδος Ἠλέκτρας τόδε;

1175

LINE 1171

λίαν (adv.) — too much

ὥστε μή . . . στένε — ὥστε in an independent clause has no effect on the mood of its verb, it can take a potential opt. or indic. with ἄν, a prohibitive subjv., an interrogative, or an imperative, as here (GMT #602); > 'so do not lament too much.'

⁺ὀφείλω — be under obligation

⁺*λέξω — (λέγω aor.¹ subjv) deliberative subjv. as the following ἔλθω (S #1805; SS 223–25 §12); > 'What shall I say?'

⁺ποῖ — whither? (with partitive genit. ⁺λόγων. SS 58 §10: "to what form of speech am I to come?")

ἀμηχανέω — (ἀμήχανος, without resources) (pres. act. ptc.) be at a loss (conjunctive participle, i.e., coordinate with the principal verb of the clause: SS 250–251 §2); ⁺λόγων goes with both ποῖ and ἀμηχανῶν (Kells); > 'being at a loss for words?'; [1× Soph.]

γλῶσσα, ἡ — tongue (genit. following ⁺κρατέω)

LINE 1176

⁺*ἔσχες — (ἔχω, aor.²) instantaneous aorist, see ἐπ-αράομαι (ἐπηράσω) 388n; > 'What is your trouble?'

⁺κῠρεῖς — (κυρέω is poetic for τυγχάνω) with supplem. ptc. ⁺εἰπών, that contains the main idea. When an aor. ptc. follows forms of τυγχάνω, λανθάνω, φθάνω in pres. or impf., it is not coincidental with the finite verb, but retains its own reference to past time (S #2096b; GMT #145, 146; SS 261 §12f); > Why *did you say* that?'

εἶδος, εος, τό — that which is seen, form (*hypallage*. ⁺κλεινόν is a transferred epithet; should be describing the genit. Ἠλέκτρας: [S #3023; SS 165 §4c] but goes with εἶδος); > 'Is this *the sight of the illustrious* El.?'; [1× *El.*]

ΗΛ.	τόδ' ἔcτ' ἐκεῖνο, καὶ μάλ' ἀθλίωc ἔχον.
ΟΡ.	οἴμοι ταλαίνηc ἆρα τῆcδε cυμφορᾶc.
ΗΛ.	οὐ δή ποτ', ὦ ξέν', ἀμφ' ἐμοὶ cτένειc τάδε; **1180**
ΟΡ.	ὦ cῶμ' ἀτίμωc κἀθέωc ἐφθαρμένον.
ΗΛ.	οὔτοι ποτ' ἄλλην ἢ 'μὲ δυcφημεῖc, ξένε.
ΟΡ.	φεῦ τῆc ἀνύμφου δυcμόρου τε cῆc τροφῆc.
ΗΛ.	τί δή ποτ', ὦ ξέν', ὧδ' ἐπιcκοπῶν cτένειc;
ΟΡ.	ὅc' οὐκ ἄρ' ᾔδη τῶν ἐμῶν ἐγὼ κακῶν. **1185**
ΗΛ.	ἐν τῷ διέγνωc τοῦτο τῶν εἰρημένων;
ΟΡ.	ὁρῶν cε πολλοῖc ἐμπρέπουcαν ἄλγεcιν.
ΗΛ.	καὶ μὴν ὁρᾷc γε παῦρα τῶν ἐμῶν κακῶν.

LINE 1178

⁺ἐκεῖνο	'this is it' (refers to εἶδος)
ἀθλίως (adv.)	miserably (ἀθλίως ἔχω 'fare miserably,' the subject is εἶδος); [1× *El.*]
⁺σύμφορα, ἡ	event, mishap, <u>misfortune</u> (for the genit., see ⁺τροφῆς 1143n; > 'Alas, then (ἄρα), for this unhappy misfortune.'
οὐ δὴ ποτ'	see οὐ δή, 1108n
⁺ἀμφί (+ dat.)	on account of, about, concerning, for the sake of
⁺στένεις τάδε	τάδε internal acc. treated as neuter substantive or adverbial acc. (S #1573, 1607; SS 39 §9, 42 §13) > 'that you sigh (*these sighs*) *in this way*'

LINE 1181

⁺ἀ-τίμως (adv.)	(⁺ἄ-τῑμος) without honor, in dishonored way; [1× *El.*]
ἀ-θέως (adv.)	(ἀ privat., θεός) in an ungodly way, unholy fashion, godless manner
*φθείρω, ἔφθαρμαι	(ἐφθαρμένον, 2nd pf. ptc.): be ruined
δυσφημέω	utter ill-omened word (the words are 'ill omened' because of ἀ-θέως); > 'There is none other than (ἄλλην ἢ) I that your ill-omened words describe' (Lloyd-Jones partially)
ἄ-νυμφος, ον	(ἀ privat., + νύμφη, bride) unwedded
δυσ-μόρος, ον	ill fated, ill starred (for genits., see ⁺τροφῆς 1143n)
ἐπι-σκοπέω	look upon/at, <u>gaze</u>; > 'Why, then (δή), stranger, do you sigh, *gazing* at me this way?'; [1× *El.*]

LINE 1185

⁺*ᾔδη	(οἶδα, plupf. 1sg.) 'how much (⁺ὅσα, i.e., how little) I knew of my own sorrows.'
δια-⁺*γιγνώσκω, - έγνων	(διέγνως, aor.² indic. 2sg.) discern, distinguish; [1× Soph.]
τῶν ⁺*εἰρημένων	(λέγω, pf. ptc. pass.) say (see τοῖς κρατοῦσι 1014n; partit. genit. describing τῷ [=⁺τίνι]: S #1306–7); > 'In what *of the things that have been said* did you discern this?'
ἐμ-πρέπω	be conspicuous for (supplemen. ptc. after verb of perceiving, ὁρῶν: S #2110–2112a; SS 260 §12c. oxymoron: ἐμπρέπω is usually connected with rich garments); > 'Seeing you *conspicuous for / in many sorrows*'; [1× Soph.]
καὶ μήν	and yet (a strong adversative: GP 357–58)

ΟΡ.	καὶ πῶς γένοιτ' ἂν τῶνδ' ἔτ' ἐχθίω βλέπειν;	
ΗΛ.	ὁθούνεκ' εἰμὶ τοῖς φονεῦσι σύντροφος.	1190
ΟΡ.	τοῖς τοῦ; πόθεν τοῦτ' ἐξεσήμηνας κακόν;	
ΗΛ.	τοῖς πατρός. εἶτα τοῖσδε δουλεύω βίᾳ.	
ΟΡ.	τίς γάρ σ' ἀνάγκη τῇδε προτρέπει βροτῶν;	
ΗΛ.	μήτηρ καλεῖται· μητρὶ δ' οὐδὲν ἐξισοῖ.	
ΟΡ.	τί δρῶσα; πότερα χερσίν, ἢ λύμῃ βίου;	1195
ΗΛ.	καὶ χερσὶ καὶ λύμαισι καὶ πᾶσιν κακοῖς.	
ΟΡ.	οὐδ' οὑπαρήξων οὐδ' ὁ κωλύσων πάρα;	

LINE 1189

⁺καί (conj.)	in an astonished question, see καί 385n; > 'And how'
⁺*γένοιτ' ἄν	potential optative, here close to a gnomic question (S #1824; SS 230 §14); > '*And* how can anything be more hateful to behold than this?'
ἐχθίων, ον	(irregular comparative of ⁺ἐχθρός) acc. pl. neut. (ἐχθίονα) with genit. of comparison τῶνδε (S #1431; SS 69–70 §32)
⁺*βλέπειν	'hateful *to behold*'; limiting/explanatory inf. with adj. (SS 239 §3b)
⁺ὁθούνεκα (conj.)	because
σύν-τροφος, ον	(< συν-τρέφω) living with; [1× *El.*]

LINE 1191

τοῖς τοῦ	= τοῖς φονεῦσι τίνος; answered by τοῖς [φονεῦσι] πατρός; > 'With whose murderers?' How can we explain Or.'s questions?
πόθεν	whence (= πόθεν ἐστὶ τοῦτο τὸ κακὸν ὃ ἐξεσήμηνας); > '*From where* is the evil that you hint at?'
ἐκ-*σημαίνω	(ἐξεσήμηνας, aor.¹ act.) hint at (instantaneous aor., see ἐπ-αράομαι [ἐπηράσω] 388n); [1× Soph.]
⁺εἶτα (adv.)	then (Jebb: "marks a further aggravation of her lot")
δουλεύω	be a slave (with τοῖσδε [φονεῦσι])
⁺βίᾳ	'perforce/by necessity'; (dat. of means: S #1507; SS 88–89 §16)
προ-τρέπω	drive to do a thing; > 'who of men subjects you to this constraint?'; [1× *El.*]

LINE 1195

πότερα . . . ἤ	introducing direct alternative question: 'whether . . . or' (S #2656). πότερα is frequently left untranslated in English. Resolution in 4th position: πότερα.
λύμη, ἡ	[ῠ] outrage, affront, disgrace, general maltreatment; > 'by violence, or by maltreatment in [daily] life?' Notice that we have never heard that El. was beaten.
ἐπ-αρήγω	οὑπαρήξων=ὁ ἐπαρήξων; come to help, aid; [1× Soph.]
κωλύω	[ῡ] prevent, hinder (articular substant. ptcs.: ὁ ἐπαρήξων and ὁ κωλύσων:S #2050–2052; SS 257–258 §9; GMT #825); [1× *El.*]
πάρα	= ⁺*πάρεστι (S #175b); > 'And *there is no one at hand* who will help you or stop her?'

ΗΛ.	οὐ δῆθ᾽· ὃς ἦν γάρ μοι cὺ προύθηκαc cποδόν.	
ΟΡ.	ὦ δύcποτμ᾽, ὡc ὁρῶν c᾽ ἐποικτίρω πάλαι.	
ΗΛ.	μόνοc βροτῶν νυν ἴcθ᾽ ἐποικτίραc ποτέ.	1200
ΟΡ.	μόνοc γὰρ ἥκω τοῖcι coῖc ἀλγῶν κακοῖc.	
ΗΛ.	οὐ δή ποθ᾽ ἡμῖν ξυγγενὴc ἥκειc ποθέν;	
ΟΡ.	ἐγὼ φράcαιμ᾽ ἄν, εἰ τὸ τῶνδ᾽ εὔνουν πάρα.	
ΗΛ.	ἀλλ᾽ ἐcτὶν εὔνουν, ὥcτε πρὸc πιcτὰc ἐρεῖc.	
ΟΡ.	μέθεc τόδ᾽ ἄγγοc νυν, ὅπωc τὸ πᾶν μάθηc.	1205
ΗΛ.	μὴ δῆτα πρὸc θεῶν τοῦτό μ᾽ ἐργάcῃ, ξένε.	
ΟΡ.	πιθοῦ λέγοντι κοὐχ ἁμαρτήcῃ ποτέ.	

LINE 1198

⁺οὐ δῆτα	'No!'; see 403n
ὃc ἦν	'he who was' (omitted antecedent: S #2509)
⁺προ-⁺τίθημι	= προ-έθηκαc (aor.¹) set before (the verb also denotes laying out the corpse.); > 'No, for *you have placed before* me the ashes of the one who was'
δύc-ποτμοc, ον	unlucky, ill starred; [1× *El.*]
⁺ὡc (conj.)	exclamatory: how (S #2682a, 2998)
⁺ἐπ-οικτίρω	be filled with pity (strong emotional verb repeated by El. in the following line in the same place in line. For the repetition, see 67n on πατρῷα/πατρῷον. It emphasizes El.'s bewilderment, and Or.'s callousness in not revealing himself.)
⁺πάλαι (adv.)	before; > 'How I've been filled with pity since I saw you'
⁺μόνοc	μόνοc ... μόνοc *anaphora*. The siblings repeat the words of each other. What does this *anaphora* effect?
⁺⁺ἴcθι ⁺ἐποικτίραc	verb of knowing with supplemen. ptc. (aor.¹) in indirect discourse (S #2106; SS 260 §12e); > 'pity [for me]')

LINE 1201

τοῖcι coῖc κακοῖc	Kells: "A quasi-instrumental dative"; > 'I alone have come feeling pain (⁺ἀλγῶν) *for your afflictions*'
οὐ δή ποθ᾽	see οὐ δή 1108n; 'Surely not ...?' 'You don't mean ...?'
cυγγενήc, έc	(cύν, ⁺⁺γενέcθαι) congenital, kin
⁺⁺φράcαιμ᾽ ἄν	(aor.¹ opt.) mixed condition: pres. indic. in protasis (πάρεcτι) with potential opt. in apodosis. Each clause has its proper force (GMT #503)
εὔνουc, ουν	(εὖ, νοῦc) well minded, <u>benevolent</u>, loyal (τῶνδε refers to the women of the Chorus, subjective genit.); > 'I would tell you, if a *benevolent* element/disposition is *present in these women*'
ὥcτε...⁺⁺ἐρεῖc	(λέγω, fut.) result clause with finite verb for actual result (S #2250, 2251, 2257; SS 311 §3; GMT #601); > 'Indeed there is, *so you will speak* to loyal women'

LINE 1205

⁺⁺μάθηc	(μανθάνω, aor.² subj.) final clause in primary sequence, μέθ-εc (μεθίημι, aor.² impv). See δόc 1119n (S #2196, 1858a; GMT #317); > 'Let go of this vessel, *so that you can learn* all'
πρὸc θεῶν	'By the gods!'; θεῶν—*synizesis*.
ἐργάζομαι	(ἐργάcῃ, aor.¹ subj.) work (+ double acc.; μὴ δῆτα ... ἐργάcῃ prohibitive subjv.: S #1800a; SS 220 §6; GMT #259); > 'No! By the gods, *do not do this to me*, stranger!'
⁺⁺πιθοῦ	(πείθω, aor.² impv. mid.) mid. and pass.: obey. The aorist is preferable to pres. impv. πείθου (as in 1015 where it implies mental process), because it is a single definite action. Cf. the aorist ⁺μέ-⁺θεc in 1205.
*ἁμαρτάνω	(ἁμαρτήcῃ, fut. indic. mid./dep.) go wrong; > 'and you will never go wrong.'

ΗΛ.   μὴ πρὸς γενείου μὴ 'ξέλῃ τὰ φίλτατα.

ΟΡ.   οὔ φημ' ἐάσειν. ΗΛ. ὢ τάλαιν' ἐγὼ ϲέθεν,
         Ὀρέϲτα, τῆϲ ϲῆϲ εἰ ϲτερήϲομαι ταφῆϲ.   **1210**

ΟΡ.   εὔφημα φώνει· πρὸς δίκηϲ γὰρ οὐ ϲτένειϲ.

ΗΛ.   πῶϲ τὸν θανόντ' ἀδελφὸν οὐ δίκῃ ϲτένω;

ΟΡ.   οὔ ϲοι προϲήκει τήνδε προϲφωνεῖν φάτιν.

ΗΛ.   οὕτως ἄτιμός εἰμι τοῦ τεθνηκότος;

ΟΡ.   ἄτιμος οὐδενὸϲ ϲύ· τοῦτο δ' οὐχὶ ϲόν.   **1215**

ΗΛ.   εἴπερ γ' Ὀρέϲτου ϲῶμα βαϲτάζω τόδε.

ΟΡ.   ἀλλ' οὐκ Ὀρέϲτου, πλὴν λόγῳ γ' ἠϲκημένον.

ΗΛ.   ποῦ δ' ἔϲτ' ἐκείνου τοῦ ταλαιπώρου τάφος;

LINE 1208

γένειον, τό   beard (touching the chin was customary in supplication. However, this appeal must be figurative, as it is unlikely that El. would withdraw one of her hands from the urn); [1× *El.*]

ἐξ-⁺*αιρέω, -εῖλον   (ἐξέλῃ, aor.² mid. subjv.) mid.: take away from (prohibitive subjv.: S #1800a; SS 220 §6; GMT #259); > 'No, by your beard, *don't take away* [from me] what's most precious to me!' [1× *El.*]

⁺*ἐάσειν   φημί requires infinitive. The finite verb and infinitive share the same subject: >'I say I will *not let* [you keep it]' (SS 316 §4). The division of a line between two speakers is called *antilabe,* which marks emotional agitation on the part of both siblings.

⁺ϲέθεν   old poetic form of ϲοῦ, genit. of ϲύ; genit. of exclamation/cause (S #1407; SS 72 §35: "unhappy am I *on your account,* Orestes, if I am robbed of your urn."). For the vocative, Ὀρέϲτα, see 6n.

ϲτερέω   deprive, rob; pass.: be derived, robbed

τἄφή, ἡ   (θάπτω, bury) burial. El. thinks she won't be able to bury Or.'s ashes; [1× *El.*]

LINE 1211

εὔ-φημος, ον   (εὖ, φήμη) abstaining from inauspicious words, i.e., being religiously silent

⁺φώνει   (pres. impv.) 'Utter only auspicious words! You do not lament with justice.' First clue to El. that Or. is alive, which she does not grasp.

⁺προϲ-ήκει (+ dat.) (ϲοι) beseems, belongs, befits (quasi-impersonal when the indefinite 'it' anticipates an infinitive as the subject: S # 933b; SS §5)

προϲ-φωνέω   speak; > 'it does not befit you to speak this way (to utter this speech')

⁺ἄ-τῖμος, ον   SS 54 §7: "compound adj. which includes a noun in its base may take a genit. in the same way as the noun itself"; > 'Am I so *without honor from the dead* (τοῦ τεθνηκότος)? You are not without honor from anyone (οὐδενός)'

LINE 1215

⁺εἴπερ γ'   '*Surely it is* (γε), if indeed this is the body of Orestes that I hold'

⁺ἠϲκημένον   (ἀϲκέω, pf. ptc. pass.) 'But it is not Orestes except as adorned with words' (LSJ i2).

τἄλαίπορος, ον   (⁺τάλας) suffering hardship, miserable; [1× *El.*]

OP.   οὐκ ἔςτι· τοῦ γὰρ ζῶντος οὐκ ἔςτιν τάφος.

ΗΛ.   πῶς εἶπας, ὦ παῖ;   OP.   ψεῦδος οὐδὲν ὧν λέγω.   **1220**

ΗΛ.   ἦ ζῇ γὰρ ἀνὴρ;   OP.   εἴπερ ἔμψυχός γ᾽ ἐγώ.

ΗΛ.   ἦ γὰρ ςὺ κεῖνος;   OP.   τήνδε προςβλέψαςά μου
         ςφραγῖδα πατρὸς ἔκμαθ᾽ εἰ ςαφῆ λέγω.

ΗΛ.   ὦ φίλτατον φῶς.   OP.   φίλτατον, ςυμμαρτυρῶ.

ΗΛ.   ὦ φθέγμ᾽, ἀφίκου;   OP.   μηκέτ᾽ ἄλλοθεν
              πύθῃ.   **1225**

ΗΛ.   ἔχω ςε χερςίν;   OP.   ὡς τὰ λοίπ᾽ ἔχοις ἀεί.

ΗΛ.   ὦ φίλταται γυναῖκες, ὦ πολίτιδες,
         ὁρᾶτ᾽ Ὀρέςτην τόνδε, μηχαναῖςι μὲν
         θανόντα, νῦν δὲ μηχαναῖς ςεςωμένον.

ΧΟ.   ὁρῶμεν, ὦ παῖ, κἀπὶ ςυμφοραῖςί μοι   **1230**
         γεγηθὸς ἔρπει δάκρυον ὀμμάτων ἄπο.

LINE 1219

τοῦ +*ζῶντος   (ζάω, pres. ptc. act.) articular substant. ptc. (S #2050–52; S 257–58 §9; GMT #825)

ψεῦδος, εος, τό   falsehood; > 'Nothing of what I say is a lie'; [1× *El.*]

ἦ   interrogative pcl.: in truth?

ἔμ-ψῡχος, ον   (ἐν, +ψῡχή) living; > 'If I am living, indeed'; [1× *El.*]

LINE 1222

προς-+*βλέπω   (προςβλέψαςα, aor.¹ act. ptc. f.) look at (circumstantial temporal ptc.: S #2055; SS 252–53 §4); [1× *El.*]

ςφραγίς, ῖδος, ἡ   signet ring; [1× *El.*]

ἐκ-+*μανθάνω   (ἔκμαθε, aor.² impv.) learn thoroughly; [1× *El.*]

ςυμ-μαρτῠρέω   bear witness with; > 'Dearest [light], *I do bear witness!*' [1× Soph.]

φθέγμα, ατος, τό   (φθέγγομαι, utter a sound) sound, voice; word

ἀφ-+*ικνέομαι   (ἐφίκου, aor.² indic.) arrive, come; >'Oh voice, have you come?'; [1× *El.*]

ἄλλοθεν (adv.)   (ἄλλος) from another place; [1× *El.*]

*πυνθάνομαι   [ᾰ] (πύθῃ, aor.² subjv.) <u>inquire</u>; hear, learn of (with genit. μή with prohibitive subjv.: S #1800a; SS 220 §6; GMT #259); > '*Do not inquire/ask* [about me] from another source'

LINE 1226

+*ἔχοις +ἀεί   opt. with ὡς (S #1814–15; SS 231–32 §15); > '*So may you always hold* me for the remainder of our days.'

πολῖτις, ιδος, ἡ   female citizen of the polis; [1× Soph.]

Ὀρέςτην τόνδε   the demonstrative pronoun sometimes is used to call attention to the presence of a person (SS 154 §23) > 'Orestes *here*'; cf. ἥδε . . . κείνη 665n

μηχᾰνή, ἡ   contrivance; [1 × *El.*]

+*ςεςωμένον   (ςῴζω, pf. pass. ptc.) 'dead by contrivance, and now saved (i.e., alive) by contrivance.' Note the positive spin on guile.

γηθέω   (γεγηθός, pf. act. ptc) be delighted, rejoice (*hypallage*; transferred epithet from μοι to δάκρυον.

ἕρπω   crawl, creep; glide

δάκρυον, τό   (= +δάκρυ) tear; > 'and a tear of joy for good fortune creeps from our eyes'; [1× *El.*]

ΗΛ.	ἰὼ γοναί,	στρ.
	γοναὶ ϲωμάτων ἐμοὶ φιλτάτων,	
	ἐμόλετ᾽ ἀρτίωϲ,	
	ἐφηύρετ᾽, ἤλθετ᾽, εἴδεθ᾽ οὓϲ ἐχρῄζετε.	1235
ΟΡ.	πάρεϲμεν· ἀλλὰ ϲῖγ᾽ ἔχουϲα πρόϲμενε.	
ΗΛ.	τί δ᾽ ἔϲτιν;	
ΟΡ.	ϲιγᾶν ἄμεινον, μή τιϲ ἔνδοθεν κλύῃ.	
ΗΛ.	μὰ τὰν Ἄρτεμιν τὰν ἀεὶ ἀδμήταν,	
	τόδε μὲν οὔποτ᾽ ἀξιώϲω τρέϲαι,	1240
	περιϲϲὸν ἄχθοϲ ἔνδον	
	γυναικῶν ὃ ναίει.	

SCENE A: (2) Lines 1232–1287
STROPHE, Lines 1232–1252

LINE 1232

γονή, ἡ	(⁺*γενέϲθαι, be, become), race, stock family (LSJ 2)
ϲωμάτων	refers to Ag. A 'sympathetic' plural influenced by the plural of γοναί (SS 7 §4); > 'O child—child of *the bodies* dearest to me.'
ἐφ-⁺*ευρίϲκω, -ηῦρον	(ἐφηύρετε, aor.² act.) detect, discover
ἐμόλετ᾽ . . . εἴδεϲθ᾽	the three vbs. ἐφηύρετ᾽, ἤλθετ᾽, εἴδεϲθ᾽, in *asyndeton* suggest high emotion (Finglass). The emphasis is on Orestes' coming: ἐμόλετε (βλώϲκω), ἐφηύρετε, ἤλθετε. For the rising tricolon of three successive actions with the last one as culminating one, see ἐκτρέφω 13n
⁺ἐχρῄζετε	'you've come [and] you've found, you've come [and] you've seen her whom you *longed for.*' οὓϲ masculine for feminine "by neutralization" (SS 12 §8, 8–10 §5) and in *majestic plural*.
ϲῖγα (adv.)	silently (an adverb with ἔχειν is often used as a periphrastic expression for an adj. with εἶναι or for a verb, i.e., = ϲιγᾶν (S #1438).
⁺πρόϲ-⁺*μενε	wait; > 'I am here (πάρεϲμεν *majestic plural*); but wait in silence.'

LINE 1237

ἔνδοθεν (adv.)	(⁺ἔνδον) from within
⁺κλύῃ	subjv. in fear clause in primary sequence [supply ἐϲτί] (S #2221, 2223; GMT #365); > 'It is better to be silent, *lest someone* indoors (from indoors) *should hear.*'
⁺Ἄρτεμιϲ, ιδοϲ, ἡ	Artemis (usually invoked in Tragedy by unmarried women, but see 626)
ἄ-δμητοϲ (3)	(ἀ privat., δαμάω tame) untamed, wild; [1× *El.*]
ἀξιόω	think/deem worthy (with limiting/explanatory inf.: SS 238–39; μέν *solitarium*, see μέν 61n, stresses the idea of the finite verb and infinitive.
*τρέω	(τρέϲαι, aor.¹ inf. act.) tremble, fear; [1× *El.*]
περιϲϲόϲ (3)	(περί, exceedingly) more than sufficient, superfluous (LSJ 3)
⁺γυναικῶν	genit. of definition, describes the content of the word attached to, ἄχθοϲ (SS 53 §5); > 'I will never think it worthy to tremble because of this superfluous *burden of women*, that dwells [inside]'

OP. ὅρα γε μὲν δὴ κἀν γυναιξὶν ὡς Ἄρης
     ἔνεστιν· εὖ δ' ἔξοισθα πειραθεῖσά που.

ΗΛ. ὀττοτοῖ ⟨ὀττοτοῖ⟩,   **1245**
     ἀνέφελον ἐνέβαλες οὔποτε καταλύσιμον,
     οὐδέ ποτε λησόμενον ἁμέτερον
     οἷον ἔφυ κακόν.   **1250**

OP. ἔξοιδα καὶ ταῦτ'· ἀλλ' ὅταν παρουσία
     φράζῃ, τότ' ἔργων τῶνδε μεμνῆσθαι χρεών.

ΗΛ. ὁ πᾶς ἐμοί   ἀντ.
     ὁ πᾶς ἂν πρέποι παρὼν ἐννέπειν
     τάδε δίκα χρόνος.   **1255**
     μόλις γὰρ ἔσχον νῦν ἐλεύθερον στόμα.

OP. ξύμφημι κἀγω· τοιγαροῦν σῴζου τόδε.
ΗΛ. τί δρῶσα;

LINE 1243

γε μὲν δή	strongly adversative: 'Yes, but see/mark . . .' (GP 396 [3])
⁺που (enclit. adv.)	frequently qualifies an expression = 'I suppose,' 'I think' (LSJ II); > 'from your own experience (⁺*πειραθεῖσα, πειράομαι, aor.¹ ptc. pass.), I think'
ἀ-νέφελος, ον	(ἀ privat., νεφέλη, cloud) cloudless, unveiled; [1× Soph.]
ἐμ-*βάλλω, -έβαλον	(ἐνέβαλες, aor.²) throw in; put in mind, <u>remind</u>; [1× El.]
κατα-λύσιμος, ον	[ῠ] (κατα-λύω, terminate) be made an end of, be resolved; [1× Soph.]

LINE 1247

⁺*λησόμενον	(λανθάνομαι or λήθομαι, fut. pass. ptc.) pass.: forget (fut. mid. used as pass. only here in Classical Greek: Kells. Cf. καλῇ 971n); > 'Alas, alas! You have reminded me of what (⁺οἷον) my sorrow (κακόν) was (⁺ἔφυ), never to be veiled, never to be resolved, never to be forgotten.'
ὅταν . . . ⁺φράζῃ	indefinite temporal clause for the future with subjv. and ἄν (S #2399, 1768; SS 294 §4)
*μιμνήσκω, μέμνημαι	(pf. inf. mid. pass.) mid.: remember, remind (+ genit. The inf. follows ⁺χρεών); > 'I know this too (καί), but when occasion/opportunity prompts/comes, then will be the moment *to recall* these deeds'.

ANTISTROPHE, Lines 1253–1272

LINE 1253

πρέπω	fit (often impersonal but here with noun subject; potential opt.: S #1824; SS 230 §14)
⁺ἐννέπω	poetic lengthening for ἐνέπω tell, speak (epexegetic inf. following πρέποι); > 'Every moment, every present moment would be rightfully fit *to tell* these things'
στόμα, τος, τό	<u>mouth</u>, speech, words, language
ξύμ-*φημι	agree; > 'I do agree. Therefore keep guarding this (i.e., ἐλεύθερον στόμα)'; [1× El.]
τοι-γαρ-οῦν (pcl.)	therefore (strongly emphatic, strengthened τοιγάρ: GP 568–69); [1× El.]

ΟΡ.	οὐ μή 'cτι καιρὸc μὴ μακρὰν βούλου λέγειν.	
ΗΛ.	τίc ἀνταξίαν coῦ γε πεφηνότοc	1260
	μεταβάλοιτ' ἂν ὧδε cιγᾶν λόγων;	
	ἐπεί cε νῦν ἀφράcτωc	
	ἀέλπτωc τ' ἐcεῖδον.	
ΟΡ.	τότ' εἶδεc, ὅτε θεοί μ' ἐπώτρυναν μολεῖν	
	⟨ x – ‿ – x – ‿ – x – ‿ – ⟩	
ΗΛ.	ἔφραcαc ὑπερτέραν	1265
	τᾶc πάροc ἔτι χάριτοc, εἴ cε θεὸc ἐπόρι cεν	
	ἁμέτερα πρὸc μέλαθρα· δαιμόνιον	
	αὐτὸ τίθημ' ἐγώ.	1270
ΟΡ.	τὰ μέν c' ὀκνῶ χαίρουcαν εἰργαθεῖν, τὰ δὲ	
	δέδοικα λίαν ἡδονῇ νικωμένην.	

LINE 1259

οὐ μή 'cτι ⁺καιρόc	'When it is not the right moment'
μᾰκράν (adv.)	(from fem. acc. of ⁺μᾰκρόc) 'at length'
ἀντ-άξιοc (3)	worthy, equivalent to (+ genit.); [1× Soph.]
μετα-*βάλλω, -έβαλον	(μεταβάλοιτ', aor.² mid. opt.) mid.: exchange (potential opt.: S #1824; SS 230 §14); [1 × *El.*]
⁺*πεφηνότοc	(φαίνω, pf. ptc. act.) genit. depending on ἀνταξίαν.
cιγή, ἡ	silence; > 'Who then could thus (as you order me) exchange speech for *silence* as the price of your appearance?'
ἀφράcτωc (adv.)	(ἀ privat., ⁺*φράζω) unexpectedly; [1× Soph.]
ἀέλπτωc (adv.)	(ἀ privat., ἔλπομαι, hope) beyond all hope; [1× Soph.]

LINE 1264

ἐπ-οτρύνω	excite, stir up, urge on. Does Or. feel guilty for not returning earlier?
ὑπέρτεροc (3)	comparative adjective of ὑπέρ; upper, higher; stronger, mightier
⁺πάροc (adv.)	before
πορίζω	bring, fetch (past condition with no implication as to non-fulfillment: SS 280 §2c); > 'You've told me of an even greater grace (ὑπερτέραν . . . ⁺χάριτοc, genit. of comparison) than the last [one], if a god *has brought* you to our house'; [1× *El.*]
μέλαθρον, τό	[ᾰ/ᾱ] rafter in a room, roof; pl.: house; [1× *El.*]
δαιμόνιοc (3)	divine; > 'I reckon (⁺*τίθημι) it was a god'; [1× *El.*]

LINE 1271

τά μέν . . . τὰ δέ	(adverbial, no noun to be understood) 'on the one hand . . . . on the other hand'
εἰργαθεῖν	(poetic aor.² inf. of εἴργω) hinder, prevent, check; [1× Soph.]
λίαν (adv.)	too much
νῑκάω	win over, overcome
δείδω, δέδοικα	(pf. with pres meaning) fear

ΗΛ.	ἰὼ χρόνῳ	ἐπ.
	μακρῷ φιλτάταν ὁδὸν ἐπαξιώ-	
	cαc ὧδέ μοι φανῆναι,	
	μή τί με, πολύπονον ὧδ᾽ ἰδών—	1275
OP.	τί μὴ ποήcω; ΗΛ. μή μ᾽ ἀποcτερήcῃc	
	τῶν cῶν προcώπων ἡδονὰν μεθέcθαι.	
OP.	ἦ κάρτα κἂν ἄλλοιcι θυμοίμην ἰδών.	
ΗΛ.	ξυναινεῖc; OP. τί μὴν οὔ;	1280
ΗΛ.	ὦ φίλ᾽, ἔκλυον	
	ἃν ἐγὼ οὐδ᾽ ἂν ἤλπιc᾽ αὐδάν.	
	⟨ἀλλ᾽ ὅμωc ἐπ⟩ έcχον ὀργὰν ἄναυδον	

EPODE. Lines 1273–1287

LINE 1273

ἐπ-αξιόω	(< ἄξιος, worthy) deem it right
⁺φιλτάταν ⁺ὁδόν	cognate/internal acc. with ⁺φανῆναι. SS 39–40 §9: "to make the most welcome journey and appear." "Sophocles made ample use," according to Morwood, of internal acc. and "its possibilities." Here he allies a noun, ὁδός, connected semantically but not formally to the vb. φαίνω, but omitting the verb of 'going,' which is implied; > 'Oh you who deemed it right after so long a time [to make] *a journey most dear* to me and appear like this, do not, having seen me like this full of suffering . . . '
τί μὴ ⁺ποιήσω	negative form of deliberative subjv.; > 'What am I not to do?'

LINE 1276

μή μ ⁺ἀπο-στερήσῃς	μή with prohibitive subjv. (S #1800a; SS 220 §6; GMT #259). With acc. of pers. (μέ) and acc. of thing (ἡδονάν); cf. κτῆσιν 960n
πρόσωπον, τό	face (appears 3× in plural in Soph, and 6× in singular, all of a single face: SS 5 §3)
⁺μέθεσθαι	(μεθ-*ίημι, aor.² inf. mid.) lose, forego (redundant epexegetic inf.); > 'Don't deprive me of the pleasure of your face, *so that I lose [it]*'
κάρτᾰ (adv.)	certainly, indeed, surely
θυμόω	be angry (fut. less vivid condition, opt. with ἄν in apodosis and aor.² ptc. ἰδών, as protasis instead of εἰ with a verb in aor.² opt.: GMT 472; S #2297); > 'I would certainly be angry if I saw this in another'; [1× *El.*]
συν-αινέω	agree or come to terms with a person

LINE 1280

ἐγὼ οὐδ᾽	*synizesis* at 1282 and 1287.
ἐλπίζω	(ἐλπίς) hope, expect (ἂν ἤλπισα potential indic. ἄν with the indic. of secondary tenses, generally impf. and aor., expresses past possibility, probability, or necessity: S #1784; GMT #198, 243–44. Sometimes ἄν is repeated to give prominence to particular words. Here it might be underscoring ἐγώ: S #1765); > 'a voice *I could not have hoped* [to hear].'
αὐδή, ἡ	human voice
ἀλλ᾽ ⁺ὅμως (adv.)	but still (S #2786)
ἄν-αυδος, ον	(ἀ privat., αὐδή) unutterable, without a voice, <u>silent</u>; > 'But still I held my passion *in silence* listening without a cry, unhappy as I am'; [1× *El.*]

οὐδὲ ϲὺν βοᾷ κλύουϲ’ ἁ τάλαινα.
νῦν δ’ ἔχω ϲε· προύφάνηϲ δὲ   **1285**
φιλτάταν ἔχων πρόϲοψιν,
ἃϲ ἐγὼ οὐδ’ ἂν ἐν κακοῖϲ λαθοίμαν.

ΟΡ.   τὰ μὲν περιϲϲεύοντα τῶν λόγων ἄφεϲ,
καὶ μήτε μήτηρ ὡϲ κακὴ δίδαϲκέ με
μήθ’ ὡϲ πατρῷαν κτῆϲιν Αἴγιϲθοϲ δόμων   **1290**
ἀντλεῖ, τὰ δ’ ἐκχεῖ, τὰ δὲ διαϲπείρει μάτην·
χρόνου γὰρ ἄν ϲοι καιρὸν ἐξείργοι λόγοϲ.

LINE 1284

προ-⁺φαίνω, -έφηνα	(προύφάνηϲ = προ-έφηνηϲ) show forth
πρόϲοψιϲ, ἡ	appearance, aspect; > 'you've appeared with your dearest countenance'; [1× *El.*]
⁺*ἂν … λαθοίμαν	(λανθάνομαι, aor.² opt. mid.) mid. and pass.: forget (with genit.: ἃϲ= ἧϲ. Potential opt.); > 'which I could never, even in my troubles, forget.'

SCENE B, Lines 1288–1383

LINE 1288

περιϲϲεύω	be over and above (τὰ περιϲϲεύοντα articular substant. ptc.: S #2050 52; SS 257–58 §9; GMT #825); [1× Soph]
ἀφ-⁺*ίημι	(ἄφηϲ, aor.² impv.) give up; > 'spare the superfluity of words'
⁺ὡϲ (conj.)	that (introduces indirect discourse where what is said is false or uncertain, or after negated verbs. The latter applies here: μήτε δίδαϲκε: S #3000; SS 314 §1)
κτῆϲιϲ, εωϲ, ἡ	(κτάομαι) possession, property
ἀντλέω	squander; (1× Soph.)
ἐκ-χέω	pour forth in vain, lavish, squander; [1× *El.*]
τὰ δέ	resolution in 6th position: τὰ δέ.
δια-ϲπείρω	scatter, spread about; > 'nor how Aeg. is draining our father's wealth from the household, or how he is squandering it or throwing it about'
ἐξείργω	shut out, hinder, block (potential opt.; ϲοι ethical dat., or of feeling indicating her interest but often not translatable: S #1486); > 'for the telling might block the opportune moment of time [for action]'; [1× Soph.]

ἃ δ' ἁρμόσει μοι τῷ παρόντι νῦν χρόνῳ
cήμαιν', ὅπου φανέντες ἢ κεκρυμμένοι
γελῶντας ἐχθροὺς παύcομεν τῇ νῦν ὁδῷ   1295
τούτῳ δ' ὅπως μήτηρ cε μὴ 'πιγνώcεται
φαιδρῷ προcώπῳ νῷν ἐπελθόντοιν δόμουc·
ἀλλ' ὡς ἐπ' ἄτῃ τῇ μάτην λελεγμένῃ
cτέναζ'· ὅταν γὰρ εὐτυχήcωμεν, τότε
χαίρειν παρέcται καὶ γελᾶν ἐλευθέρωc.   1300

ΗΛ.   ἀλλ', ὦ καcίγνηθ', ὧδ' ὅπωc καὶ cοὶ φίλον
καὶ τοὐμὸν ἔcται, τάcδ' ἐπεὶ τὰc ἡδονὰc
πρὸc cοῦ λαβοῦcα κοὐκ ἐμὰc ἐκτηcάμην.
κοὐδ' ἄν cε λυπήcαcα δεξαίμην βραχὺ
αὐτὴ μέγ' εὑρεῖν κέρδοc· οὐ γὰρ ἂν καλῶc   1305
ὑπηρετοίην τῷ παρόντι δαίμονι.

LINE 1293

ἁρμόζω — intransitive: fit (well), <u>suit</u> (ἃ antecedent omitted; happens especially with neuter relative: S #2511); [1× *El.*]

cημαίνω — signal; > 'But signal me (μοι) what will now suit the present moment'; *enjambment*; [1× *El.*]

ὅπου (adv.) — where

⁺γελῶντας — (γελάω) supplem. ptc. following vb. of stopping (S #2098; SS 260 §12a); > 'where through appearing (φανέντες < φαίνω) or hiding (κεκρυμμένοι < κρύπτω) we will stop the laughter of our enemies by our present expedition.'

LINE 1296

τούτῳ — Or. continues telling El. how to help him now: 'And by this . . .'

ἐπι-⁺⁺γιγνώσκω — <u>discover, detect</u> (*aphaeresis*; ὅπως with future denotes a warning or urgent exhortation. One could supply σκόπει or ὅρα ὅπως 'see that': S #1920, 2213; SS 289 §7, 308 §4); > 'so that our mother does not detect your state/you when the two of us (νῷν ἐπελθόντοιν, temporal genit. absolute dual for Or. and Pylades) enter the house by/because of your radiant face'; [1× *El.*]

φαιδρός (3) — beaming, radiant

στενάζω — lament (emphatic *enjambment*); > 'but lament as if over [my] ruin although falsely reported (⁺λελεγμένῃ ⁺μάτην)'; [1× *El.*]

⁺εὐ-τῠχήσωμεν — (εὐτυχέω, aor.² subjv.) protasis of relative future more vivid condition, with future ind. παρέσται in the apodosis (S #2297, 2323, 2565; GMT #529); > 'for when *we succeed*, then it will be possible (⁺παρέσται) to . . .'

LINE 1301

ὧδ' ὅπως . . . ἔσται — 'just so as pleases you, will be also (καί, adverbial: GP 324 2i) mine [conduct].'

κτάομαι — <u>acquire</u>, procure; > 'since I have acquired these pleasures received (⁺⁺λαβοῦσα, having received) from you, not as my own.'

⁺⁺δέχομαι — (δεξαίμην, aor.¹opt.) accept as mental reception. Here with inf., ⁺⁺εὑρεῖν, accompanied by a conditional participle, ⁺λῡπήσασα (Jebb). The idea could have been expressed by λυπῆσαι μέν . . . εὑρεῖν δέ following δεξαίμην (SS 251 §2); > 'I would not (accept =) agree to win a great benefit for myself, at the cost of vexing you even a little.'

ἀλλ' οἶcθα μὲν τἀνθένδε, πῶc γὰρ οὔ; κλυὼν
ὁθούνεκ' Αἴγιcθοc μὲν οὐ κατὰ cτέγαc,
μήτηρ δ' ἐν οἴκοιc· ἣν cὺ μὴ δείcῃc ποθ' ὡc
γέλωτι τοὐμὸν φαιδρὸν ὄψεται κάρα.   1310
μῖcόc τε γὰρ παλαιὸν ἐντέτηκέ μοι,
κἀπεί c' ἐcεῖδον, οὔ ποτ' ἐκλήξω χαρᾷ
δακρυρροοῦcα. πῶc γὰρ ἂν λήξαιμ' ἐγώ,
ἥτιc μιᾷ cε τῇδ' ὁδῷ θανόντα τε
καὶ ζῶντ' ἐcεῖδον; εἴργαcαι δέ μ' ἄcκοπα·   1315
ὥcτ', εἰ πατήρ μοι ζῶν ἵκοιτο, μηκέτ' ἂν
τέραc νομίζειν αὐτό, πιcτεύειν δ' ὁρᾶν.
ὅτ' οὖν τοιαύτην ἡμὶν ἐξήκειc ὁδόν,

ὑπηρετέω	(ὑπηρετοίην, opt.) serve, help (potential opt.); > 'for I would not be serving well the god (⁺δαίμων) who is with us now.'

LINE 1307

μέν	μέν *solitarium*, see μέν 61n, stresses the idea of the finite verb
ἐνθένδε (adv.)	thence (τἀνθένδε "what must be done next": Finglass); [1× *El.*]
⁺ὁθούνεκα (conj.)	because, that (analogous to ὅτι and ὡc introducing dependent sentence. Restricted to Tragedy especially Soph.: SS 313–14; S #2578; GMT #710)
δείδω	(δείσῃc, aor.¹ subjv.) μή with prohibitive subjv. (S #1800a; SS 220 §6; GMT #259)
ὡc . . . ⁺*ὄψεται	usually verb of fearing takes μή with subjv. in the fear clause (i.e., μὴ ἴδῃ, 'lest she may see'), but in Soph. one finds ὡc followed by the fut. indic. when the fear verb is negated (GMT #341; SS 292); > 'and do not fear that she will ever see. . . .' Cf. ὡc ἀτιμάσει 1426–27n.

LINE 1311

ἐν- ⁺τήκω, τέτηκα	(ἐντέτηκε, pf. act.) be melted, sink deep, <u>seep</u>; > 'For ancient hatred has seeped into me'; [1× Soph.]
ἐκλήγω	stop; [1× Soph.]
δακρυρροέω	melt into tears, <u>weep</u> (oxymoron with χαρᾷ; for ptc. δακρυρροοῦcα, see ⁺γελῶντας 1295n); > 'I will never stop *weeping* with joy'; [1× *El.*]
πῶc . . . ἐγώ, ἥτιc	potential optative > 'How indeed could I stop, I who . . .'
ἄ-cκοποc, ον	(ἀ privat., cκοπέω) not seeing; not to be seen: <u>incredible</u>
*ἐργάζομαι	(εἴργαcαι, pf. dep. 2sg.) work (+ double acc.); > 'you've done to me incredible things'

LINE 1316

τέραc, ατοc, τό	portent, sign
ἂν νομίζειν . . . πιcτεύειν	ὥcτε with inf. to denote a possible result with negative μή (S #2251, 2254; GMT #582, 587). The result clause is apodosis of less vivid condition, hence ἄν. ὁρᾶν, an inf. in indirect discourse depending on πιcτεύειν sharing the same subject (S #1972); > 'so that if my father should come back to life, I would not think it a prodigy, but believe I saw him'
ἡμίν	For the accent, see ἡμίν 17n
ἐξ-ήκω	arrived at; > 'since you've come to me on such a journey, command as your heart [moves you]'; [1× *El.*]

ἄρχ' αὐτὸς ὥς coι θυμός. ὡς ἐγὼ μόνη
οὐκ ἂν δυοῖν ἥμαρτον· ἢ γὰρ ἂν καλῶς   1320
ἔcωc' ἐμαυτήν, ἢ καλῶς ἀπωλόμην.

OP.   cιγᾶν ἐπῄνεc'· ὡc ἐπ' ἐξόδῳ κλύω
τῶν ἔνδοθεν χωροῦντοc. ΗΛ. εἴcιτ', ὦ ξένοι,
ἄλλωc τε καὶ φέροντες οἷ' ἂν οὔτε τις
δόμων ἀπώcαιτ' οὔτ' ἂν ἡcθείη λαβών.   1325

ΠΑ.   ὦ πλεῖcτα μῶροι καὶ φρενῶν τητώμενοι,
πότερα παρ' οὐδὲν τοῦ βίου κήδεcθ' ἔτι,

LINE 1319

*ἁμαρτάνω, ἥμαρτον	(aor.²) go wrong (contrary-to-fact condition for past time: S #2292.2); > 'For alone, *I'd have not gone wrong* in both things (δυοῖν, dual; i.e., I'd have achieved one of two things), either I'd have saved myself nobly, or died nobly'
⁺ἐπ-*αινέω	(ἐπῄνεσα, aor.¹) commend, <u>counsel</u> (αἰνέω keeps a short vowel in the aor. and fut.: S #488b. Instantaneous aorist, see ἐπηράσω 388n); >' I counsel to be silent'
ἔξ-οδος, ἡ	way out, exit, outlet (LSJ II, 1)
ἔνδοθεν (adv.)	(⁺ἔνδον) from within
⁺χωρέω	(χωροῦντος, pres. ptc.) go forth, advance, come (genit. following κλύω, supply τινός with χωροῦντος. τῶν ἔνδοθεν, genit. partit.); > 'for /as (ὡς) I hear someone of those inside coming out at the doors'

LINE 1324

ἄλλως τε καί . . .	both otherwise and . . . ; i.e., especially, above all (LSJ 3)
⁺*φέροντες	circumstantial causal participle (S #2064; SS 251 §3); > 'Go in, strangers, especially since you bring such objects as no one in the palace would reject, or be pleased to receive.'
⁺ἀπ-ωθέω	(ἀπώσαιτο, aor.¹ opt.) mid.: reject, disdain, repulse (potential optative)
ἥδομαι, ἥσθεν	(ἡσθείη, aor.¹ opt.) be pleased (potential optative); [1× *El.*]

LINE 1326

πλεῖστα (adv.)	(superlative < πολύς) exceedingly
μῶρος (3)	stupid, silly, foolish
τητάω	pass.: be in want, bereft, deprived; > 'deprived of wits'
πότερα . . . ἤ	whether . . . or (introduces direct alternative questions with πότερα; frequently left untranslated in English)
παρά (+ acc.)	in comparison with (παρ' οὐδέν 'compared with nothing,' i.e., 'of no account,' 'worth nothing')
παρ' οὐδὲν τοῦ βίου κήδεσθε	mixture of two constructions: πότερα παρ' οὐδὲν ἔτι [τίθεσθε] τὸν βίον: 'Do you deem your life worth nothing?' And πότερα οὐδὲν ἔτι κήδεσθε τοῦ βίου: 'Don't you care about your life anymore?' (Kamerbeek, Kells); > 'Don't you care for your lives at all anymore?'
κήδομαι	take care of, be concerned for (+ genit.: τοῦ βίου)

ἢ νοῦς ἔνεστιν οὔτις ὑμὶν ἐγγενής,
ὅτ᾽ οὐ παρ᾽ αὐτοῖς ἀλλ᾽ ἐν αὐτοῖσιν κακοῖς
τοῖσιν μεγίστοις ὄντες οὐ γιγνώσκετε;   1330
ἀλλ᾽ εἰ σταθμοῖσι τοῖσδε μὴ ᾽κύρουν ἐγὼ
πάλαι φυλάσσων, ἦν ἂν ἡμὶν ἐν δόμοις
τὰ δρώμεν᾽ ὑμῶν πρόσθεν ἢ τὰ σώματα·
νῦν δ᾽ εὐλάβειαν τῶνδε προὐθέμην ἐγώ.
καὶ νῦν ἀπαλλαχθέντε τῶν μακρῶν λόγων   1335
καὶ τῆς ἀπλήστου τῆσδε σὺν χαρᾷ βοῆς
εἴσω παρέλθεθ᾽, ὡς τὸ μὲν μέλλειν κακὸν
ἐν τοῖς τοιούτοις ἔστ᾽, ἀπηλλάχθαι δ᾽ ἀκμή.

LINE 1328

ἐγ-γενής, ές   (ἐν, γένος) inborn, native (see ἡμίν 17n for accent); > 'or is there no intelligence *born in you* . . . ?'

⁺*γιγνώσκω   know (verb of knowing with supplem. ptc. ὄντες, which represents the corresponding tense of the indic. in direct discourse: ἐστέ; S #2106; SS 260 §12.e; GMT #904); > 'since (ὅτε, not ὅτι, which does not elide) you don't *understand that you're* not merely on the threshold (παρ᾽) of the greatest evils, but right in the middle of them?'

LINE 1331

σταθμός, ὁ   doorpost; [1× *El.*]

⁺ἐκύρουν   (κυρέω, poetic for τυγχάνω) *aphaeresis.* Protasis of contrary-to-fact condition for the present time, the apodosis is also in imperfect: ἦν ἂν (GMT #410).

φυλάσσω   guard (supplem. ptc. following κῦρέω, completes the idea the main verb: S #2088; GMT #877, 884; SS 260 §12); > 'But if I had not been *keeping guard* at the doorposts here . . .'

⁺* τὰ δρώμενα   articular substantive participle (S #2050–2052; SS 257–58 §9; GMT #825). ἡμῖν dat. of disadvantage (S #1481; SS 84–85 §9); > 'your plans/doings would have been unluckily for us (to our disadvantage) in the house before your persons (lit.: bodies).' Cf. Or. bidding the Tutor to report to him τὸ δρώμενον in the palace at 40–41, and the Tutor's using the plural τῶν δρωμένων in 85, in a similar meaning to the one here.

νῦν δ᾽ . . . καὶ νῦν   νῦν in successive lines with different meanings: "but as it is . . . now" (Jebb)

εὐλάβεια, ἡ   [ἄ] discretion, caution (τῶνδε objective genit.: S #1328; SS 52–53 §4)

⁺προὐθέμην   (=προ-εθέμην, προ-τίθημι, aor.² mid.); > 'But as it is, I (exhibited caution =) took care in advance of these things myself'

LINE 1335

⁺ἀπ-αλάσσω   (ἀπαλλαχθέντε, aor.¹ ptc. pass. dual) intransitive: release, leave off, escape

ἄ-πληστος, ον   (ἀ privat., πίμπλημι) insatiate; > 'having done with your long speeches and insatiate cry of joy'; [1× Soph.]

παρ-⁺*ἔρχομαι   (παρέλθετε, aor.² impv. pl.) go; > 'go within (⁺εἴσω)'; [1× *El.*]

*μέλλω   be on the point of doing, to be always going to do (without doing), hence <u>delay</u>, put off, hesitate (τὸ μέλλειν articular inf.; see 265 note on πελει. τοιούτοις *correction.* Cf. 35, 1001, 1024, 1338); > 'for on the one hand, *delay* is bad in matters like this'

⁺ἀπηλλάχθαι   (ἀπ-αλάσσω, pf. inf. pass) to have done, cease with the connotation of 'make an end' (the perfect implies immediacy: Jebb, Finglass)

ἀκμή, ἡ   right point of anything, most fitting time (LSJ III); > 'it is the moment to make an end [of it] (ἀπηλλάχθαι)'

OP.   πῶς οὖν ἔχει τἀντεῦθεν εἰϲιόντι μοι;

ΠΑ.   καλῶϲ· ὑπάρχει γάρ ϲε μὴ γνῶναί τινα.   1340

OP.   ἤγγειλαϲ, ὡϲ ἔοικεν, ὡϲ τεθνηκότα.

ΠΑ.   εἷϲ τῶν ἐν Ἅιδου μάνθαν’ ἐνθάδ’ ὢν ἀνήρ.

OP.   χαίρουϲιν οὖν τούτοιϲιν; ἢ τίνεϲ λόγοι;

ΠΑ.   τελουμένων εἴποιμ’ ἄν· ὡϲ δὲ νῦν ἔχει
        καλῶϲ τὰ κείνων πάντα, καὶ τὰ μὴ καλῶϲ.   1345

ΗΛ.   τίϲ οὗτόϲ ἐϲτ’, ἀδελφέ; πρὸϲ θεῶν φράϲον.

OP.   οὐχὶ ξυνίηϲ; ΗΛ. οὐδέ γ’ †ἐϲ θυμὸν φέρω†.

OP.   οὐκ οἶϲθ’ ὅτῳ μ’ ἔδωκαϲ ἐϲ χεῖράϲ ποτε;

ΗΛ.   ποίῳ; τί φωνεῖϲ; OP. οὗ τὸ Φωκέων πέδον
        ὑπεξεπέμφθην ϲῇ προμηθίᾳ χεροῖν.   1350

LINE 1339

ἐντεῦθεν (adv.)   hence, thence (= τὰ ἐντεῦθεν. Jebb's and Kamerbeek's understanding "the next things" is preferable to Campbell's 'matters here'); > 'What comes next for me when I go in (⁺*εἰϲιόντι μοι)?'

ὑπ-άρχει   here impersonal with inf.: it is possible, the fact is (τινα subject of ⁺*γνῶναι [γιγνώϲκω, aor.² inf.] without indication of time. Possible to translate by future: Kamerbeek); > 'Well! *It is certain* that no one will recognize you' (ἀγγείλω, aor.¹ indic.) followed by supplem. ptc. in indirect discourse (S #2106). The ptc. in indirect discourse can come with or without ὡϲ (ὡϲ [με] τεθνηκότα). When ὡϲ accompanies the ptc. it is often used to indicate the mental attitude of the subject of the finite verb or another prominent person in the sentence. Here it might show Or.'s focus on his assumed death (S #2120–2121; SS 318 §6). Cf. ἐκεῖνον ὡϲ ⁺παρ-⁺*όντα 882n; > '*you've reported*, it seems, that *I am dead*.'

⁺*ἤγγειλαϲ

⁺εἷϲ, μία, ἕν   one (declension S #349)

τῶν ἐν Ἅιδου ⁺*μανθάνω   learn, study (supply ptc. ὤν to complete its meaning: SS 260 §12c)

ἐνθάδε (adv.)   here

τῶν ἐν Ἅιδου   The word on which the possessive genit. depends may be omitted after ἐν, thus 'in [the abodes] of Hades' (S #1302); > 'Know that here you are one of those in [the abodes] of Hades'

⁺τελουμένων   temporal genit. absolute without expressed subject occurs when it is easy to supply it from the context (SS 76 §42; S #2072a). The phrasing seems vague on purpose. εἴποιμ’ ἄν potential opt., the present and aorist opt. with ἄν are used for what will be (S #1828); > '*when things come to an end*, I will tell you, as things are, everything on their part (Clyt. and Aeg.) is good [for us], even what is not good [for them].'

LINE 1346

⁺ϲυν-⁺*ίημι   (ξυνίηϲ, pres. indic.) metaphorically: perceive, understand, <u>know</u> (οὐδέ γ’ 'no' 'not even': GP 156.i. ἐϲ θυμὸν φέρω does not appear elsewhere, but should not be suspected); > 'You don't *know*?—No, I [can't] bring [him] to mind'

ὅτῳ   = ᾧτινι (S #339)

πέδον, τό   (πούϲ foot) earth, ground

ὑπ-εκ-⁺*πέμπω   (ὑπεξεπέμφθην, aor.¹ pass.) to send away in secret (οὗ . . . χεροῖν [dual] —hyperbaton. οὗ, relative pronoun missing antecedent, or gathered from ποίῳ); > '[The man] by *whose* hands, through your planning, I was sent in secret to the land of the Phocians'; [1× Soph.]

ΗΛ.   ἢ κεῖνος οὗτος ὅν ποτ' ἐκ πολλῶν ἐγὼ
         μόνον προσηῦρον πιστὸν ἐν πατρὸς φόνῳ;

ΟΡ.   ὅδ' ἐστί. μή μ' ἔλεγχε πλείοσιν λόγοις.

ΗΛ.   ὦ φίλτατον φῶς, ὦ μόνος cωτὴρ δόμων
         Ἀγαμέμνονος, πῶς ἦλθες; ἦ cὺ κεῖνος εἶ,   1355
         ὃc τόνδε κἄμ' ἔcωcαc ἐκ πολλῶν πόνων;
         ὦ φίλταται μὲν χεῖρες, ἥδιστον δ' ἔχων
         ποδῶν ὑπηρέτημα, πῶς οὕτω πάλαι
         ξυνών μ' ἔληθεc οὐδ' ἔcαινεc, ἀλλά με
         λόγοιc ἀπώλυc, ἔργ' ἔχων ἥδιcτ' ἐμοί;   1360
         χαῖρ', ὦ πάτερ· πατέρα γὰρ εἰcορᾶν δοκῶ·
         χαῖρ'· ἴcθι δ' ὡc μάλιcτά c' ἀνθρώπων ἐγὼ
         ἤχθηρα κἀφίληc' ἐν ἡμέρᾳ μιᾷ.

LINE 1351

προc-⁺*εὑρίσκω, -ηῦρον   (aor.² indic.) find besides; [1× Soph.]

ἐλέγχω   cross-examine; [1× *El.*]

ὦ φίλτ. φῶc, ὦ μόνοc   nom. in exclamation in both parts, without making the second into voc. SS 23 §4: "Ah, sweetest (⁺ἥδιστον) light of day! Sole savior of the house of Agamemnon! how have you come?". ⁺Ἀγαμέμνονος, resolution, of 1st *anceps* in a trimeter is common with proper names. Cf. Ἀγαμέμνονος 2n.

LINE 1357

ὑπηρέτημα, ατος, τό   service rendered; >'you who have (ἔχων) the (sweetest service of feet =) sweetest feet to do your errands'; [1× Soph.]

λήθω   see ⁺*λανθάνω (ἔληθες, impf. act.) escape notice (with supplem, ptc. ⁺ξυνών [⁺σύνειμι] completing its meaning: S #2096a; GMT #887; SS 261 §12f); > 'how could you be with me for so long unrecognized (*eluding my notice*) . . . ?'

cαίνω   cheer, <u>greet</u>, please; > 'and not greet me'; [1× *El.*]

⁺ἀπ-⁺*όλλυμι   (ἀπώλυς, impf. indic. 2sg.) act.: destroy utterly; > 'but you were killing me with your words, although you had the sweetest (deeds =) reality for me'

LINE 1361

χαῖρε   Greetings! (πάτερ· πατέρα *polyptoton*. Play on different forms of the same word was greatly appreciated by the Greeks.)

⁺μάλιστα (adv.)   (superlative of μάλα, exceedingly) especially (with ὡς for heightened emphasis)

⁺ἐχθαίρω   (aor.¹ indic.) (ἔχθος, hatred) hate (κἀφίληc' = καὶ ἐφίληcα); > 'know that in one day *I* hated you and loved you exceedingly, more than any other man'

ΠΑ.   ἀρκεῖν δοκεῖ μοι· τοὺς γὰρ ἐν μέcῳ λόγουc —
           πολλαὶ κυκλοῦνται νύκτεc ἡμέραι τ᾽ ἴcαι,   **1365**
           αἵ ταῦτά cοι δείξουcιν, Ἠλέκτρα, cαφῆ.
           cφῷν δ᾽ ἐννέπω 'γὼ τοῖν παρεcτώτοιν ὅτι
           νῦν καιρὸc ἔρδειν· νῦν Κλυταιμήcτρα μόνη·
           νῦν οὔτιc ἀνδρῶν ἔνδον· εἰ δ᾽ ἐφέξετον,
           φροντίζεθ᾽ ὡc τούτοιc τε καὶ cοφωτέροιc   **1370**
           ἄλλοιcι τούτων πλείοcιν μαχούμενοι.

ΟΡ.   οὐκ ἂν μακρῶν ἔθ᾽ ἡμὶν οὐδὲν ἂν λόγων,
           Πυλάδη, τόδ᾽ εἴη τοὔργον, ἀλλ᾽ ὅcον τάχοc
           χωρεῖν ἔcω, πατρῷα προcκύcανθ᾽ ἕδη
           θεῶν, ὅcοιπερ πρόπυλα ναίουcιν τάδε.   **1375**

LINE 1364

⁺ἀρκεῖν δοκεῖ μοι	lit.: this seems enough to me = 'I think that is enough'
τοὺς γὰρ ἐν μέcῳ λόγους	The phrase ἐν ⁺μέcῳ ('in the middle') refers here to the period of time between the present and the moment in the past when Or. left Mycenae (Jebb, Finglass); > as for the (words =) story between the present and the past'
κυκλέω	<u>revolve</u>, circle; > 'many nights and the same number of days *revolve* around, which will show you these things clearly, Electra'; [1× *El.*]

LINE 1367

παρ-⁺*ίcτημι	(παρεcτώτοιν, pf. ptc. dual) make stand besides; pf.: stand besides (articular substant. ptc.: S #2050–2052; SS 257–58 §9; GMT #825; cφῷν also dual. The Tutor moves from El. to Or. and Pyl.); > 'I say *to you two who stand here* . . .'
ἔρδω	work, accomplish, do (νῦν . . . νῦν . . . νῦν the *anaphora* and *asyndeton* are greatly emphatic)
ἐπ-⁺*έχω	(ἐφέξετον, fut. dual); keep in, <u>hold back</u>
φροντίζω	<u>consider</u>, reckon, bear in mind (this verb does not usually take a participial construction in indirect discourse; when it does, the participle is in acc., or nom. with ὡς: ὡς μαχούμενοι: GMT #919); [1× *El.*]
⁺πλείων, ον	(comparison of ⁺πολύς) more (with genit. of comparison τούτων)
*μάχομαι, μαχοῦμαι	(μαχούμενοι, fut. dep. ptc.) > 'consider *that you will be fighting with* them (τούτοις: the domestics inside) and with others more numerous and skilled (cοφώτεροιc) than these'; [1× *El.*]

LINE 1372

τόδε εἴη τοὔργον	οὐδὲν ἔργον with genit. means "there is no need of" (Jebb, Finglass). (The phrase governs both the preceding μακρῶν λόγων and χωρεῖν in 1374. The opt. εἴη with ἄν for excitement: Finglass. Cf. ἂν μέλοιτο at 1436); > 'Pylades, *we do not* (οὐδέν) need any longer long words; our task is to go inside at once'
Πυλάδη	[ᾰ] resolution of 1st *anceps*: Πῠλάδη; see Ἀγ. 2n.
ὅcον ⁺τάχος	= ὡς τάχιστα as quickly as possible, at once
ἕδος, εος, τό	(ἕζομαι) seat, pedestal of a statue (*enallage*; SS 164–65 §4b). Here acc. for genit.: πατρῷα . . . ἕδη θεῶν = πατρῴων ἕδη θεῶν; > seats of my father's gods'; [1× *El.*]
προc-*κῠνέω	(προcκύcαντε, aor.¹ ptc. dual) render homage to; > 'after having rendered homage to'; (1× *El.*)
ὅcoc-περ, ὅcη-περ, ὅcον-περ	as many as
πρό-πῠλον, τό	(πρό, πύλη) portico, vestibule (resolution in position 6; [1× Soph.]

ΗΛ.　　　ἄναξ Ἄπολλον, ἵλεως αὐτοῖν κλύε,
　　　　　ἐμοῦ τε πρὸς τούτοισιν, ἥ σε πολλὰ δὴ
　　　　　ἀφ' ὧν ἔχοιμι λιπαρεῖ προὔςτην χερί.
　　　　　νῦν δ', ὦ Λύκει' Ἄπολλον, ἐξ οἵων ἔχω
　　　　　αἰτῶ, προπίτνω, λίccομαι, γενοῦ πρόφρων　　　　　　　　1380
　　　　　ἡμῖν ἀρωγὸς τῶνδε τῶν βουλευμάτων
　　　　　καὶ δεῖξον ἀνθρώποιcι τἀπιτίμια
　　　　　τῆc δυccεβείαc οἷα δωροῦνται θεοί.

Orestes, Pylades, and the Tutor enter the palace. Electra remains alone in front of the skēnē *and addresses the statue of Apollo*

LINE 1376

ἵλεως	propitious, <u>gracious</u>, kindly; > 'Lord Apollo hear them (αὐτοῖν dual. genit.) kindly, and [hear] me also'
πολλά (adv.)	many times
ἀφ' ὧν +*ἔχοιμι	Kells: "from what store I might have." Opt. of indefinite frequency for past time (Jebb).
λῑπᾰρής, ές	persisting, <u>insisting</u>, persevering, earnest
προ- +*ἵστημι	(προὔcτην = προ-έcτην, aor.²) approach, place oneself in front of (with acc. σε); > 'I who have *approached you* many times with insistent [praying] hand'

LINE 1379

ἐξ οἵων ἔχω	Kells (with Jebb and the Schol.): "on the basis of (i.e., 'at the price of') such possessions as I have." I.e., with no offerings at all, since she has none.
αἰτέω	ask, beg, request; Notice the following emphatic *asyndeton*.
προσ-πίτνω	(poetic for προσ-πίπτω); fall upon, embrace; prostrate, supplicate
λίσσομαι	beg, pray, entreat
+*γενοῦ	(γίγνομαι, aor.² impv. 2sg.) be
πρό-φρων, ονος, ὁ/ἡ	(+πρό, +φρήν) with forward mind, kindly, willing; [1× Soph.]
βούλευμα, ατος, τό	(βολεύω) plan, design (objective genit.); > (lit.: be a helper in this plans, =) help us in these plans'
+*δεῖξον	(δείκνῡμι, aor.¹ impv. act.) show, reveal
ἐπι-τίμιος, ον	(ἐπί, τιμή) as substantive: assessment of damages, penalty; [1× *El.*]
δυσσέβεια, ἡ	impiety; [1× *El.*]
δωρέομαι	give, present one with, bring a gift, <u>bestow</u> (ironic choice of a verb); > 'and show mortals what kind of wages/penalty gods *bestow* for impiety'

XO.	Ἴδεθ᾽ ὅπου προνέμεται	στρ. α´
	τὸ δυσέριστον αἷμα φυσῶν Ἄρης.	1385
	βεβᾶσιν ἄρτι δωμάτων ὑπόστεγοι	
	μετάδρομοι κακῶν πανουργημάτων	
	ἄφυκτοι κύνες,	
	ὥστ᾽ οὐ μακρὰν ἔτ᾽ ἀμμενεῖ	
	τοὐμὸν φρενῶν ὄνειρον αἰωρούμενον.	1390

Electra goes into the palace

THIRD STASIMON, LINES 1384–1397

The stasimon is comprised of a short strophic pair (1384–1390 = 1391–1397). The Chorus visualize the entry of the avengers as the arrival of inescapable hounds. The avengers are the embodiments of the spirits of the dead who demand the blood of their murderers.

STROPHE, Lines 1384–1390

LINE 1384

ὅπου (adv.)	where
προ-νέμω	mid.: gain ground, advance, spread; [1× Soph.]
δυσ-έριστος, ον	(δυσ-, ἐρίζω, quarrel) caused by evil strife; [1× Soph.]
αἷμα, ατος, τό	blood
φῡσάω	(φυσῶν, pres. ptc.) blow up, <u>pant</u>; > 'See where Ares advances panting with blood born of strife'; [1× *El.*]

LINE 1386

ἄρτῐ (adv.)	right now; [1× *El.*]
⁺*βαίνω	(βεβᾶσιν, 2nd pf. 3pl.) go (for the perfect, see εὖ βεβηκόσιν 979n)
ὑπό-στεγος, ον	(ὑπό, στεγή) under the roof, in the house; >'Right now they are beneath the house's roof; [1× *El.*]
μετά-δρομος, ον	(μέτα, δραμεῖν) pursuing, hunting; [1× Soph.]
πᾰνούργημα, ατος, τό	a knavish, roguish act, <u>crime</u> (κακῶν πανουργημάτων objective genit. with μετάδρομοι); > 'inescapable hounds pursuing evil crimes' [1× Soph.]
ἄ-φυκτος, ον	(ἀ privat., φυκτός) inescapable; [1× *El.*]
κύων, κυνός ὁ/ἡ	[ῠ] dog, hound; [1× *El.*)
μᾰκράν (adv.)	(from fem. acc. of ⁺μᾰκρός) 'at length'
ἀμμένω	= ἀνα-⁺*μένω (ἀμμενεῖ, fut. indic.) await, delay, tarry (ὥστε with finite verb for actual result: S #2250, 2551, 2257; SS 311 §3; GMT #601)
αἰωρέομαι	(αἰωρούμεννον, pres. pass. ptc.) pass. metaphorically: be in suspense; > *'so that* the vision of my mind *will not for long hover in suspense'*; [1× Soph.]

παράγεται γὰρ ἐνέρων   ἀντ. α'
δολιόπους ἀρωγὸς εἴcω cτέγας,
ἀρχαιόπλουτα πατρὸς εἰς ἐδώλια,
νεακόνητον αἷμα χειροῖν ἔχων·
ὁ Μαίας δὲ παῖς   1395
Ἑρμῆς cφ' ἄγει δόλον cκότῳ
κρύψας πρὸς αὐτὸ τέρμα κοὐκέτ' ἀμμένει.

ΗΛ.   ὦ φίλταται γυναῖκες, ἄνδρες αὐτίκα   cτρ.
                  τελοῦcι τοὔργον· ἀλλὰ cῖγα πρόcμενε.
ΧΟ.   πῶc δή; τί νῦν πράccουcιν; ΗΛ. ἡ μὲν ἐc τάφον
                  λέβητα κοcμεῖ, τὼ δ' ἐφέcτατον πέλαc.   1401

ANTISTROPHE, Lines 1391–1397

LINE 1391

παρ-άγω	lead aside, lead insidiously
ἔνεροι, οἱ	those beneath the earth, the dead; [1× Soph.]

δολιόπους, ὁ/ἡ, πουν, τό	(δόλιος, πούς) of stealthy foot; [1× Soph.]
ἀρχαιόπλουτος, ον	(ἀρχαῖος, πλοῦτος) rich from olden times; [1× Soph.]
ἐδώλιον, τό	(ἕδος) seat; [1× *El.*]
νεᾱκόνητος, ον	(νέος, ἀκόνη, whetstone) newly sharpened; > 'For the champion of those beneath the earth stealthily moves into the house, into the seats of his father's house rich of old, with *new-sharpened* death (αἷμα) in his hands'; [1× Soph.]

LINE 1395

cκότος, ὁ	darkness
τέρμα, ατος, τό	end, goal; > 'And Maia's son, Hermes, hiding his guile in darkness, leads him to the goal itself, and no longer delays.'

KOMMOS (Lyric Dialogue), LINES 1398–1441

The *kommos* is comprised of a strophic pair: 1398–1421 = 1422–1441. A lyric exchange between Electra, Chorus, Orestes, and Clytemnestra off-stage. The high point of this scene is the murder of Clytemnestra, followed by preparation for ensnaring Aegisthus.

STROPHE, LINES 1398–1421

LINE 1398

cῖγα (adv.)	silently
λέβης, ητος, ὁ	(λείβω, pour) cinerary urn; [1× *El.*]
κοcμέω	(κόσμος, order) order, deck, adorn
ἐφ-+*ἵστημι	(τὼ ἐφέcτατον, pf. indic. act. dual): stand by or over (articular substantive participle); > 'she is adorning the urn for burial, and those two stand near her'; [1× *El.*]

193

ΧΟ.	cὺ δ᾽ ἐκτὸc ᾖξαc πρὸc τί; ΗΛ. φρουρήcουc᾽ ὅπωc
	Αἴγιcθος ⟨ἡμᾶc⟩ μὴ λάθῃ μολὼν ἔcω.
ΚΛ.	αἰαῖ. ἰὼ cτέγαι
	φίλων ἐρῆμοι, τῶν δ᾽ ἀπολλύντων πλέαι.
ΗΛ.	βοᾷ τις ἔνδον. οὐκ ἀκούετ᾽, ὦ φίλαι;
ΧΟ.	ἤκους᾽ ἀνήκουστα δύc-
	τανος, ὥcτε φρῖξαι.
ΚΛ.	οἴμοι τάλαιν᾽. Αἴγιcθε, ποῦ ποτ᾽ ὢν κυρεῖς;
ΗΛ.	ἰδοὺ μάλ᾽ αὖ θροεῖ τις. ΚΛ. ὦ τέκνον
	τέκνον,
	οἴκτιρε τὴν τεκοῦcαν. ΗΛ. ἀλλ᾽ οὐκ ἐκ cέθεν

1405

1410

LINE 1402

⁺ἐκτός — outside

ἀίccω — [ῑ] (ᾖξας, aor.¹ act.) shoot, dart; > 'Why did you dart outside?'

φρουρέω — (φρουρήσουσα, fut. ptc.) keep watch, guard (final ptc. following vb. of coming [ᾖξα]:S #2065; SS 252 §3. ὅπως with aor.² subjv.,⁺⁺λάθῃ, opens an object clause after verb of effort, φρουρέω: S #2214.⁺⁺μολών [βλώσκω, aor.² ptc.] is supplem. ptc. following ⁺⁺λανθάνω: S #2096; SS 261 §12f); > 'in order to keep watch that Aeg. does not come in unobserved'; [1× El.]

ἐρῆμος (3/2) — deserted; [1× El.]

πλέος, α, ον — + genit.; full, filled

τῶν ἀπ-⁺⁺ολλύντων — (ἀπ-όλλυμι, pres. act. ptc.) articular substantive participle; > 'the house is empty of friends, but full of murderers.'

LINE 1406

ἀν-ήκουστος, ον — (ἀ privat., ἀκούω) unheard of (ἤκουσα ἀνήκουστα—word-play for emphasis in this crucial moment of the play); [1× Soph.]

δύστανος — = ⁺δύστηνος

φρίσσω — (φρῖξαι, aor.¹ inf. act.) shudder, horrify (ὥστε with inf. for intended result rather than an actual one: S #2251, 2254; GMT #582, 587); > 'so that made me shudder'; [1× El.]

⁺κῠρέω — (poetic for τυγχάνω) with supplementary participle ὤν, which states what the main action is (S #2096a; GMT #887; SS 261 §12f); > 'Aeg., where (do you happen to be =) are you?'

LINE 1409

θροέω — (θρόος, a confused noise) <u>cry aloud</u>; speak, declare

οἰκτείρω — pity

τὴν ⁺⁺τεκοῦσαν — (τίκτω, aor.² act. ptc.) articular substant. ptc. See ἡ τεκοῦσα 470n.

⁺ἐκ — = ὑπό with genit. of agent (⁺σέθεν see1209n)

γεννάω — (γεννήσας, aor.¹ ptc.) to beget (of the father); (ptc. in attributive position); > 'But he was not pitied by you, nor was his father who begot him'; [1× El.]

ᾤκτιρεθ' οὗτος οὐδ' ὁ γεννήσας πατήρ.

XO. ὦ πόλις, ὦ γενεὰ τάλαινα, νῦν σοι
μοῖρα καθημερία φθίνει φθίνει.

ΚΛ. ὤμοι πέπληγμαι. ΗΛ. παῖσον, εἰ σθένεις, διπλῆν.

ΚΛ. ὤμοι μάλ' αὖθις. ΗΛ. εἰ γὰρ Αἰγίσθῳ γ'
ὁμοῦ.   1416

XO. τελοῦσ' ἀραί· ζῶσιν οἱ
γᾶς ὑπαὶ κείμενοι.
παλίρρυτον γὰρ αἷμ' ὑπεξαιροῦσι τῶν
κτανόντων   1420
οἱ πάλαι θανόντες.

καὶ μὴν πάρεισιν οἵδε· φοινία δὲ χεὶρ   ἀντ.
στάζει θυηλῆς Ἄρεος, οὐδ' ἔχω ψέγειν.

ΗΛ. Ὀρέστα, πῶς κυρεῖ τάδ'; ΟΡ. ἐν δόμοισι μὲν
καλῶς, Ἀπόλλων εἰ καλῶς ἐθέσπισεν.   1425

LINE 1412

μοῖρα, ἡ   fate

καθ-ημέριος (3)   (= καθ' ἡμέραν) every day, daily, <u>from day to day</u>; [1× Soph.]

φθίνω   perish, waste away, decline, die; [1× El.]

*πλήσσω   (πέπληγμαι, pf. indic. pass.) strike; [1× El.]

παίω   (παῖσον, aor. act. impv.) hit, smite (with omitted internal object, leaving only the adjectival attribute
                                  διπλῆν: S #1272); > 'strike, if you have the strength, twice/a double blow; [1× El.]

ὁμοῦ (adv.)   (neut. genit. of ὁμός, joint) together, at once (εἰ γάρ opens an unattainable wish, here elliptical [no
                                  verb]); > 'if only Aeg. were [struck] too'

LINE 1417

ἀρά, ἡ   curse

οἱ *κείμενοι   articular substantive participle; > 'The curses are being realized; *those who lie* beneath the earth are living.'

πᾰλίρρῠτος, ον   flowing in retribution; [1× Soph.]

ὑπ-εξ-αιρέω   take away privily, remove secretly; [1× El.]

τῶν **κτανόντων   (κτείνω, aor.² act. ptc.) kill, slay (articular substantive participle); > 'those who perished long ago are in
                                  secret *draining from their killers* blood in return for blood.'

Orestes and Pylades emerge from the palace. Orestes is carrying a bloody sword.

<u>ANTISTROPHE</u>, Lines 1422–1441

LINE 1422

καὶ μήν   Look! (calls attention to something just heard or seen: GP 356 §7); > 'Look, they are here!'

στάζω   let drop, drip; [1× Soph.]

θῠηλή, ἡ   (θύω, to sacrifice) a sacrifice; > 'and a bloody hand drips with *a sacrifice* to Ares'; [1× Soph.]

ψέγω   find fault with (ἔχω can mean 'I can,' especially with inf. of vb. of saying: S #2000a); > 'and I can find no
                                  fault with it.'

HΛ. τέθνηκεν ἡ τάλαινα; ΟΡ. μηκέτ᾽ ἔκφοβοῦ
μητρῷον ὥc cε λῆμ᾽ ἀτιμάcει ποτέ.

HΛ. ⟨– ⏑ ⏑ – ⏑ x

x – ⏑ – x – ⏑ – x – ⏑ –

ΟΡ. x – ⏑ – x – ⏑ – x – ⏑ –⟩

ΧΟ. παύcαcθε, λεύccω γὰρ Αἴ-
γιcθον ἐκ προδήλου.

ΟΡ. ⟨x – ⏑ – x – ⏑ ⏑ – x – ⏑ –⟩

HΛ. ὦ παῖδεc, οὐκ ἄψορρον; ΟΡ. εἰcορᾶτε ποῦ   1430
τὸν ἄνδρ᾽; HΛ. ἐφ᾽ ἡμῖν οὗτοc ἐκ προαcτίου
χωρεῖ γεγηθὼc⟨– ⏑ – x – ⏑ –⟩.

⁺Ὀρέcτα   voc., see 6n; > 'Orestes, how are things?'
θεcπίζω   declare by oracle, prophesy (μέν *solitarium*, see 61n; notice the repetition of καλῶc); Is Orestes expressing doubt here, or rather confidence? Is the comment ironic?; [1× *El.*]

LINE 1426
ἐκ-φοβέω   to frighten
ἀ-τῑμάζω   (ἀ privat., τῑμή) disrespect (μηκέτι ἐκφοβοῦ ὡc ἀτιμάcει. Vb. of fearing takes usually μή with subjv. for the fear clause. I.e., μὴ cε ἀτιμάcῃ, 'lest her arrogance may disrespect you.' But in Soph. ὡc followed by the fut. indic. is also found when the fear verb is negated, as it is here μηκέτι ἐκφοβοῦ: GMT #341; SS 292); > '*do not fear any more that your* mother's arrogance *will disrespect* you again'; cf. ὡc ... ὄψεται 1309–10n; [1× *El.*]
μητρῷοc (3)   motherly; [1× *El.*]
λῆμα, τό   wish, will; in bad sense: <u>pride</u>, <u>arrogance</u>; [1× *El.*]

Since it is assumed that 1422–41 are antistrophic to 1398–421, it appears that three lines following 1427 have been lost; and an iambic line following 1429 and corresponding to 1409 has been lost; as well as the second half of the iambic 1431. The unfortunate losses do not, however, have an impact on the general sense.

⁺παύω   stop
πρό-δηλοc, ον   (πρό, δῆλοc) clear beforehand; ἐκ προδήλου 'manifestly'; [1× Soph.]

LINE 1430
ἄψορρον (adv.)   (ἄψ, backwards, back; ῥέω, flow) backward, back again
προ-άcτειον, τό   (πρό, ἄcτυ) outskirts of the city; [1× Soph.]
γηθέω   (γεγηθώc, pf. ptc. act.) be delighted, rejoice (supplem. ptc. sometimes accompanies a vb. of motion, χωρεῖ, to specify the manner of the coming, and contains the main idea: S#2099; GMT #895); > 'there he is, walking toward us *full of joy* from the outskirts of the city'

XO. βᾶτε κατ' ἀντιθύρων ὅσον τάχιστα,
  νῦν, τὰ πρὶν εὖ θέμενοι, τάδ' ὡς πάλιν —
OP. θάρσει· τελοῦμεν. ΗΛ. ἦ νοεῖς ἔπειγε νῦν. 1435
OP. καὶ δὴ βέβηκα. ΗΛ. τἀνθάδ' ἂν μέλοιτ' ἐμοί.
XO. δι' ὠτὸς ἂν παῦρά γ' ὡς
  ἠπίως ἐννέπειν
  πρὸς ἄνδρα τόνδε cυμφέροι, λαθραῖον ὡς
    ὀρούςη 1440
  πρὸς δίκας ἀγῶνα.

LINE 1433

⁺*βᾶτε	(βαίνω, aor.² impv. 2pl.) go
κατά (+ genit.)	down from
ἀντί-θυρον, τό	(ἀντί, θύρα) inner part of the house opposite the door, vestibule (κατ' ἀντυθύρων a rare use of κατά with genit. Kells suggests " 'go down from the vestibule,' i.e., retire from the vestibule into the inward parts of the house." The vestibule is thought as 'high,' i.e., exposed part of the palace); [1× Soph.]
τὰ πρὶν	substantival making power of the article with adverbs (S #1153e); > 'the earlier (things) business'
εὖ ⁺*θέμενοι	(τίθημι, aor.² ptc. mid.); > 'having settled the earlier business well, so now may you settle [= εὖ θῆσθε] this one in turn'
⁺ᾗ (adv.)	(dat. sg. fem. of relative pron.) which way, where, in/at what place
νοέω	think, mind, deem, <u>intend, mean</u>
ἐπείγω	hasten, hurry on; > 'hurry now to wherever you mean to go'; [1× El.]

LINE 1436

καὶ δή	'very well then' (GP 251: "in response to a definite command, often with word of command echoed"); > 'Very well then, I am on my way!'
ἐνθάδε (adv.)	here
ἂν ⁺μέλοιτο	The middle is used here like active (Kamerbeek). The opt. εἴη with ἄν for excitement (Finglass). Cf. ἂν εἴη 1372–73n; > 'I'll take care of matters here.'
⁺παῦρα	(acc. pl. neut.) internal object leaving only the adjectival attribute (S #1272)
ἠπίως	gently, mildly; ὡς ἠπίως 'as if kindly'; [1× Soph.]
ἂν ⁺cυμ-φέροι	potential opt.; > 'it might help to whisper as if kindly a few [words] in his ear'
λαθραῖος (2/3)	secret, hidden, stealthy; [1× El.]
ὀρούω	(ὀρούςῃ, aor.¹ act. subjv.) rush violently forward (potential opt., cυμφέροι, as main vb. takes a subjv. in dependent final clause: GMT #180); [1× El.]
⁺ἀγών, ῶνος, ὁ	contest, trial, struggle; > 'so that he may rush into the stealthy trial of justice.'

ΑΙΓΙΣΘΟΣ

τίς οἶδεν ὑμῶν ποῦ ποθ' οἱ Φωκῆς ξένοι,
οὕς φασ' Ὀρέστην ἡμὶν ἀγγεῖλαι βίον
λελοιπόθ' ἱππικοῖσιν ἐν ναυαγίοις;
σέ τοι, σὲ κρίνω, ναὶ σέ, τὴν ἐν τῷ πάρος   1445
χρόνῳ θρασεῖαν· ὡς μάλιστα σοὶ μέλειν
οἶμαι, μάλιστα δ' ἂν κατειδυῖαν φράσαι.

ΗΛ.   ἔξοιδα· πῶς γὰρ οὐχί; συμφορᾶς γὰρ ἂν
ἔξωθεν εἴην τῶν ἐμῶν γε φιλτάτων.

ΑΙ.   ποῦ δῆτ' ἂν εἶεν οἱ ξένοι; δίδασκέ με.   1450

ΗΛ.   ἔνδον· φίλης γὰρ προξένου κατήνυσαν.

EXODOS, LINES 1442–1510

Aegisthus enters and addresses himself to the Chorus and Electra. A recognition between Aegisthus and Orestes follows, and Aegisthus is marched off to his death.

LINE 1442

ποῦ (adv.)	where? > 'where the Phocian strangers are?'
+*φασί	(pres. indic. 3pl.) (φα-, φη-) φημί with acc. and inf. construction οὕς . . .+*ἀγγεῖλαι
ἡμίν	for accent, see 17n; > 'who they say have reported to us the that . . .+'
+*λελοιπότα	(λείπω, pf. ptc. act.) supplem. ptc. following vb. of saying ἀγγεῖλαι (S #2106; SS 318 §6)
ναυᾱγία, ἡ	shipwreck (nautical metaphor. Cf. 335); > 'Orestes lost his life in a chariot wreck.'

LINE 1445

κρίνω	judge
ναί	'yes' (asseverative pcl. in affirmative sentences) ; [1× El.]
+πάρος (adv.)	before
θρασύς, εῖα, ύ	bold; > 'you, you, I think, yes, you, so bold in former times, since I think it concerns you most especially'
+κατ-ειδυῖαν +φράσαι	(κατοῖδα, pf. act. ptc. fem.) acc. and inf. construction depending on οἶμαι; the infinitive reflects potential optative, hence ἄν; > 'since I think that *you are most likely to tell me from sure knowledge*'

LINE 1448

ἔξωθεν (adv.)	(ἔξω) from without; [1× Soph.]
ἂν . . . εἴην	potential opt.; > 'I know it well, of course, for otherwise I would be distant from the calamity of those dearest to me.'
ἂν εἶεν (οἱ ξένοι)	'Where may the strangers be/are likely to be?' I.e., "Where it is likely to turn out that they are?": GMT 238; (SS 230 §14ii)
πρό-ξενος, ὁ	host/hostess; [1× Soph.]
κατ-ἄνύω	arrive at a place, reach (with genit.); > 'They have come upon a friendly hostess'; [1× El.]

ΑΙ.	ἦ καὶ θανόντ᾽ ἤγγειλαν ὡς ἐτητύμως;
ΗΛ.	οὔκ, ἀλλὰ κἀπέδειξαν, οὐ λόγῳ μόνον.
ΑΙ.	πάρεστ᾽ ἄρ᾽ ἡμῖν ὥστε κἀμφανῆ μαθεῖν;
ΗΛ.	πάρεστι δῆτα καὶ μάλ᾽ ἄζηλος θέα.
ΑΙ.	ἦ πολλὰ χαίρειν μ᾽ εἶπας οὐκ εἰωθότως.
ΗΛ.	χαίροις ἄν, εἴ σοι χαρτὰ τυγχάνει τάδε.
ΑΙ.	οἴγειν πύλας ἄνωγα κἀναδεικνύναι
	πᾶσιν Μυκηναίοισιν Ἀργείοις θ᾽ ὁρᾶν,

1455

LINE 1452

ἐτητύμως (adv.)
: really (ὡς ἐτητύμως can connect either with θανόντ᾽ or ἤγγειλαν); > Kamerbeek: "did they actually (καί) report that he really died?"; [1× Soph.]

οὔκ
: ambiguous: for Aeg. it negates only the previous finite verb ἤγγειλαν; i.e., they did not only report but also showed. On another level, it denies the entire former sentence.

ἐπι-⁺*δείκνυμι
: (= καὶ ἐπέδειξαν) show forth; display; > 'they even (showed =) proved it, not by word alone'; [1× *El.*]

⁺πάρεστι (+ dat.)
: impersonal: it is in one's power (= ἔξεστι). Although Aeg. uses πάρεστι as an impersonal vb., the meaning of 'he is here' 'he is present' (πάρειμι), i.e., Orestes, is also there. El.'s repetition of the vb. in the next line plays further on the two meanings.

ἐμ-φᾰνής, ές
: (φαίνω) <u>visible</u>, manifest (usually ὥστε with inf., μαθεῖν, implies a possible or intended result or a tendency rather than actual fact, but here it seems redundant. The inf. can follow πάρεστι directly: GMT #588); 'Is it possible for me/(us) to learn (these things as *visible*, i.e.) this with my own eyes?'

LINE 1455

ἄ-ζηλος, ον
: unenviable, miserable; [1× *El.*]

θέα, ἡ
: sight; [1× *El.*]

ἦ (adv.)
: in truth, truly, verily

εἰωθότως (adv.)
: in the usual way; > 'indeed you are saying [things] that give me great pleasure, not in [your] usual way'; [1× Soph.]

χαρτός (3)
: delightful, gladdening; [1× *El.*]

⁺τυγχάνει
: 'then you may be pleased, if this really brings you pleasure.' (ὄντα [with τάδε] omitted. See τυγχάνω 46n)

LINE 1458

οἴγω
: open; [1× Soph.]

ἄνωγα
: I order; [1× *El.*]

ἀνα-⁺*δείκνυμι
: (= καὶ ἀναδεικνύναι, pres. inf. act.); make public (with ὁρᾶν limiting/ explanatory infinitive: SS 238–39 §3); [1× Soph.]

⁺πᾶσιν Μυκηναίοισιν Ἀργείοις θ᾽
: the townsfolk and the people of the neighboring district (Jebb). See also Ἄργος 4n

ὡς εἴ τις αὐτῶν ἐλπίσιν κεναῖς πάρος   1460
ἐξῆρετ' ἀνδρὸς τοῦδε, νῦν ὁρῶν νεκρὸν
στόμια δέχηται τἀμά, μηδὲ πρὸς βίαν
ἐμοῦ κολαστοῦ προστυχὼν φύσῃ φρένας.

ΗΛ.   καὶ δὴ τελεῖται τἀπ' ἐμοῦ· τῷ γὰρ χρόνῳ
νοῦν ἔσχον, ὥστε συμφέρειν τοῖς κρείσσοσιν.   1465

ΑΙ.   ὦ Ζεῦ, δέδορκα φάσμ' ἄνευ φθόνου μὲν οὐ
πεπτωκός· εἰ δ' ἔπεστι νέμεσις οὐ λέγω.

LINE 1460

ἐξ-αίρω	(ἐξῆρετο, impf. ind.) pass.: be raised (past condition with no implication as to fulfillment. εἰ with indicative ἐξῆρετο followed by two final subjunctives ὡς ... ⁺δέχηται, μηδέ φύσῃ; SS 279–80 §2b: "... in order that, if anyone of them previously was *buoyed up* with vain hopes ... he *may now be subject to my curb*"); [1× *El.*]
στόμιον, τό	bridle bit, bit (tools appear often in pl., because of their composite nature: SS 4–5 §3. στόμια resolution in 2nd position: στόμια); [1× *El.*]
πρὸς ⁺βίαν	= βιαίως. explained by ἐμοῦ κολαστοῦ προστυχών (Kamberbeek). See μηδὲν πρὸς ⁺ὀργήν 369n.
κολαστής, ὁ	punisher; [1× *El.*]
προσ-⁺*τυγχάνω	(προστυχών, aor.² ptc.) meet with (with genit. ἐμοῦ κολαστοῦ); [1× *El.*]
⁺*φύσῃ	(φύω, aor.¹ subjv.) with ⁺φρένας, acc. of manner; > '*nor may he become* wise against his will (πρὸς ⁺βίαν) through meeting me, his punisher.'

LINE 1464

καὶ δή	see 1436n
⁺τελεῖται	(τελέω, pres./fut. ind. mid.) Either the present tense, if El. is opening the doors as she speaks, or future tense indicating what she is about to do. (ἀπ' ἐμοῦ genit. of agent); > 'these things are/will be accomplished by me'
τῷ γὰρ ⁺χρόνῳ	'for at long last'
ὥστε συμφέρειν	ὥστε with inf. (outside indirect discourse) opens an result clause: it implies a possible or intended result or a tendency rather than actual result (S #2251, 2254; GMT #582, 587). Ironically echoes 1013–14. > 'for long last I've acquired the wisdom *so as to come to terms* with those who are more powerful.'
κρείσσων, ον	stronger (comparison of ἀγαθός: S #319.1. τοῖς κρείσσοσιν, substantival article with adj.: S #1021, 1153a; SS 163 §1); El. is echoing the words of Chr. in 340, 396, 1014. The spectators know, of ocourse, that she does not mean them, but they flatter Aeg.; [1× *El.*]

The ekkyklema is rolled out of the palace door, bearing the shrouded corpse of Clytemnestra. Orestes and Pylades emerge from the palace as the messengers who brought the news.

φθόνος, ὁ	ill will, envy, jealousy, grudge, malice; > 'O Zeus, I see a vision that has befallen, not without the ill will [of the gods]';
ἐπ-⁺*ειμι	be upon/at, attend; [1× *El.*]
νέμεσις, εως, ἡ	just or deserved anger; > 'but if righteous anger attends it, I say nothing [of it]'

χαλᾶτε πᾶν κάλυμμ' ἀπ' ὀφθαλμῶν, ὅπωϲ
τὸ ϲυγγενέϲ τοι κἀπ' ἐμοῦ θρήνων τύχῃ.

OP.   αὐτὸϲ ϲὺ βάϲταζ'. οὐκ ἐμὸν τόδ', ἀλλὰ ϲόν,   1470
τὸ ταῦθ' ὁρᾶν τε καὶ προϲηγορεῖν φίλωϲ.

AI.   ἀλλ' εὖ παραινεῖϲ, κἀπιπείϲομαι· ϲὺ δέ,
εἴ που κατ' οἶκον ἡ Κλυταιμήϲτρα, κάλει.

OP.   αὕτη πέλαϲ ϲοῦ· μηκέτ' ἄλλοϲε ϲκόπει.

AI.   οἴμοι, τί λεύϲϲω; OP. τίνα φοβῇ; τίν' ἀγνοεῖϲ;

AI.   τίνων ποτ' ἀνδρῶν ἐν μέϲοιϲ ἀρκυϲτάτοιϲ   1476
πέπτωχ' ὁ τλήμων; OP. οὐ γὰρ αἰϲθάνῃ πάλαι
ζῶν τοῖϲ θανοῦϲιν οὕνεκ' ἀνταυδᾷϲ ἴϲα;

LINE 1468

χᾰλάω   loose, loosen (the order is directed to Or. and Pyl.); [1× *El.*]
κάλυμμα, ατος, τό   (καλύπτω) covering; [1× *El.*]
ὀφθαλμός, ὁ   eye; [1× *El.*]
συγγενής, ές   (σύν, γενέσθαι) congenital, kin
ὅπως ... τύχῃ   (τυγχάνω, aor.² subjv.) Final clause following primary sequence, χάλατε; imperative moods count as primary because they point to the future (S #2196, 1858a); > '*so that kinship, at least* (τοι) *may receive* lamentations from my side as well'

LINE 1470

προσ-ηγορέω   (προσήγορος) address kindly, console; [1× Soph.]
οὐκ ἐμὸν ... ⁺*ὁρᾶν   τὸ ὁρᾶν is the subject, supply ἐστί. ταῦθ' refers to what is underneath the cover; > '*It is not mine, but yours to look upon this and address it lovingly.*'
*παρ-αινέω   advise, recommend, counsel
ἐπι-*πείθομαι   (κἀπιπείσομαι =καὶ ἐπιπείσομαι); comply with, obey; [1× Soph.]
σὺ δέ   Addressed to El.; > 'if Clyt. is somewhere in the house, call [her]'

LINE 1474

ἄλλοσε (adv.)   (⁺ἄλλος) in another place; [1× *El.*]
σκοπέω   look after (used only in pres. and impf.); [1× *El.*]
φοβέω   pass.: fear; > 'Whom/what are you afraid of?' Resolution in 6th position: τινα; [1× *El.*]
ἀγνοέω   not to know, not recognize; [1× *El.*]

LINE 1476

ἀρκύ-στᾰτον, τό   place in which the nets are set; > 'In the midst of what men's nets have I fallen, poor me!'; Is there a mythic allusion here to Clyt.'s ensnaring Ag. in a net in his bath when murdering him?; [1× Soph.]
οὕνεκα (conj.)   (= ὅτι) that (introducing dependent statement: S #2578e; SS 313–14 §1; GMT #710); [1× *El.*]
ἀντ-αυδάω   speak against, answer (*hapax legomenon*, a word occurring only once in the Greek corpus); > 'For have you not noticed that you, while still alive, *were* (answering =) *exchanging words* with the dead on equal terms?'

201

AI.   οἴμοι, ξυνῆκα τοὔπος· οὐ γὰρ ἔσθ' ὅπως

          ὅδ' οὐκ Ὀρέστης ἔσθ' ὁ προσφωνῶν ἐμέ.   **1480**

OP.   καὶ μάντις ὢν ἄριστος ἐσφάλλου πάλαι;

AI.   ὄλωλα δὴ δείλαιος. ἀλλά μοι πάρες

          κἂν cμικρὸν εἰπεῖν. ΗΛ. μὴ πέρα λέγειν ἔα,

          πρὸς θεῶν, ἀδελφέ, μηδὲ μηκύνειν λόγους.

          [τί γὰρ βροτῶν ἂν cὺν κακοῖς μεμειγμένων   **1485**

          θνήσκειν ὁ μέλλων τοῦ χρόνου κέρδος φέροι ;]

          ἀλλ' ὡς τάχιστα κτεῖνε καὶ κτανὼν πρόθες

          ταφεῦσιν ὧν τόνδ' εἰκός ἐστι τυγχάνειν,

          ἄποπτον ἡμῶν. ὡς ἐμοὶ τόδ' ἂν κακῶν

          μόνον γένοιτο τῶν πάλαι λυτήριον.   **1490**

LINE 1479

⁺ξυν-⁺*ῆκα   (συνίημι, aor.¹ act.); > 'I understand (your word, ⁺ἔπος =) what you're saying'

οὐ γὰρ ἔσθ' ὅπως   'it is not possible that' (ὅπως introduces a subordinated clause following verb of thinking, ξυν-ῆκα. In Soph. all examples follow negated main verb. Here: οὐκ ἐστι: SS 314)

προσ-⁺φωνέω   speak to, address; > 'that this man is not Or. who is speaking to me.' [1× El.]

*σφάλλω   trip up, deceive; > 'And (καί in sarcastic questions: GP 311, iI) although such a good prophet you were deceived for so long?'

LINE 1482

⁺πάρ-⁺*ες   (παρίημι, aor.² impv. 2sg.) allow

κἄν   = καὶ ἐάν with παρῇς ('allow'). ἄν is not to be connected with the infinitive εἰπεῖν (GMT #211); > 'yet, allow me to say one thing.'

πρὸς θεῶν   *synizesis.*

μηκύνω   [ῡ] lengthen, prolong; [1× El.]

LINE 1485

μίγνῡμι   mix (temporal genit. absolute: S #2070a; SS 76 §42. Lines 1485–86 are suspected by some, mostly on stylistic grounds: Finglass); > 'When mortals are involved with troubles'; [1× El.]

ὁ ⁺*μέλλων   substantival article with ptc. (S 1153b); > 'one who is about to die'

τί . . . ἂν . . . φέροι   *'what benefit can he who is about to die gain* from time' (i.e., from delay; τοῦ χρόνου genit. of explanation; S #1322; potential opt.)

LINE 1487

⁺*κτεῖνε καὶ κτανών   (pres. impv.; aor.² ptc.) > 'kill him, and after killing him . . .' (For etymological and semantic repetition, see 67n on πατρῴα/πατρῷον); El. is about to leave the stage while she is impressing on the audience her burning and unmitigated hatred.

τᾰφεύς, έως, ὁ   gravedigger; [1× El.]

⁺εἰκός ἐστι   with inf. (⁺*τυγχάνειν) and its subject in acc. (τόνδε); > 'expose (πρόθες) him to [such] gravediggers *as it is appropriate that this man meet with* (usually assumed: birds and dogs)'

ἄπ-οπτος, ον   seen at a distance; > 'far from our sight'; [1× El.]

ἄν . . . ⁺*γένοιτο   'since for me only this *could be* the release from my past sufferings' (potential opt.)

OP.	χωροῖс ἂν εἴсω сὺν τάχει· λόγων γὰρ οὐ	
	νῦν ἐcτιν ἀγών, ἀλλὰ сῆс ψυχῆc πέρι.	
AI.	τί δ’ ἐс δόμουс ἄγειс με; πῶc, τόδ’ εἰ καλὸν	
	τοὔργον, сκότου δεῖ, κοὐ πρόχειροc εἶ κτανεῖν;	
OP.	μὴ τάссε· χώρει δ’ ἔνθαπερ κατέκτανεc	1495
	πατέρα τὸν ἀμόν, ὡc ἂν ἐν ταὐτῷ θάνηc.	
AI.	ἦ πᾶс’ ἀνάγκη τήνδε τὴν cτέγην ἰδεῖν	
	τά τ’ ὄντα καὶ μέλλοντα Πελοπιδῶν κακά;	
OP.	τὰ γοῦν c’· ἐγώ cοι μάντιc εἰμὶ τῶνδ’ ἄκροc.	
AI.	ἀλλ’ οὐ πατρῴαν τὴν τέχνην ἐκόμπαсαc.	1500

LINE 1491

⁺χώροιс ἄν	2nd pers. opt. with ἄν can be sometimes a ‘polite’ command (as κλύοιс ἄν 637n), but here it is just a command or sarcastic politeness (SS 231 §14); > ‘Go inside quickly’
πέρι (prep.)	*anastrophe*; see παρά 34n.
πρό-χειροс, ον	(πρό, χείρ) close; ready; > ‘and why are you not ready to kill me?’
ἔνθᾰ-περ (adv.)	there where, where; [1× *El.*]
κατα-⁺*κτείνω, -έκτανον	(κατέκτανεс, aor.² act.) kill, slay, put to death
ὡς ἄν ... ⁺*θάνηс	(aor.² subjv.) final clause in 1st sequence, χώρει. ὡς with subjunctive sometimes takes ἄν in positive clauses (S #2201); > ‘go where you killed my father, *so that you may die* in the same place.’

LINE 1497

ἦ πᾶс’ ἀνάγκη	‘*Is it really necessary* that this house see . . . ?’ (with inf. ⁺*ἰδεῖν and its subject τήνδε τὴν cτέγην)
τὰ ⁺*ὄντα καὶ ⁺*μέλλοντα	τά is understood with μέλλοντα as well (SS 153 §21). Cf. κλύοντι at 991.
γοῦν (pcl.)	(γε οὖν) at least (limitative: GP 450–454. Frequent in answers); > ‘yours, at least (τὰ . . . σά, i.e., κακά). I am your consummate prophet of these’; [1× *El.*]
κομπάζω	brag; > ‘you cannot boast about this art as inherited from your father’; [1× *El.*]

OP.   πόλλ' ἀντιφωνεῖς, ἡ δ' ὁδὸς βραδύνεται.
       ἀλλ' ἔρφ'. ΑΙ. ὑφηγοῦ. ΟΡ. coὶ βαδιστέον
           πάροc.

ΑΙ.   ἡ μὴ φύγω ce; ΟΡ. μὴ μὲν οὖν καθ' ἡδονὴν
       θάνῃc· φυλάξαι δεῖ με τοῦτό coι πικρόν.
       χρῆν δ' εὐθὺc εἶναι τήνδε τοῖc πᾶcιν δίκην,   1505
       ὅcτιc πέρα πράccειν γε τῶν νόμων θέλοι,
       κτείνειν· τὸ γὰρ πανοῦργον οὐκ ἂν ἦν πολύ.

ΧΟ.   ὦ cπέρμ' Ἀτρέωc, ὡc πολλὰ παθὸν
       δι' ἐλευθερίαc μόλιc ἐξῆλθεc
       τῇ νῦν ὁρμῇ τελεωθέν.   1510

LINE 1501

ἀντι-φωνέω   reply; [1× El.]

βρᾰδύνω   delay; > 'the journey is delayed'; [1× El.]

ἕρπω   crawl, creep; glide

ὑφ-ηγέομαι   guide, lead the way; (1× Soph.)

βᾰδιστέον   (βαδίζω, go) must go (with dat. of agent coί: S #1488a); > 'You need to go first'

μὴ ⁺*φύγω   (φεύγω, aor.² subjv.) supply φοβεῖς, followed by fear clause in subjv. (S #2220b); > 'Lest I escape you?'

μὴ . . . ⁺*θάνῃς   = ἵνα μὴ . . . θάνῃc (aor.² subjv.) final clause; > 'No, so that you may not die as you please'

⁺φῠλάξαι   (aor.¹ inf. act.) inf. required by *δεῖ, with acc. με as subject; > 'it is necessary that *I make sure* that this (i.e., death) is bitter for you.'

LINE 1505

⁺χρῆν   (= χρὴ + ἦν, impf.) when χρῆν is used alone, the denial of the action of the inf., here εἶναι, is always implied (GMT #419). Jebb: "The imperf. χρῆν with εἶναι, implies that though it ought to be so, it is not."

⁺*θέλοι   opt. without ἄν indicates the generality of the statement; > 'This punishment should be instantaneous upon all, *whoever likes* to act outside the laws—death.'

⁺*κτείνειν   rather than ⁺*θνήσκειν. Or. speaks from the point of view of the executioner.

παν-οῦργος, ον   (πᾶν, ἔργον) ready to do anything; mostly in a bad sense: villainous; > 'for then there would be little *crime*'; [1× El.]

LINE 1508

cπέρμα, ατος, τό   (cπείρω) metaphorically: offspring, issue; [1× El.]

⁺*πάθον   (πάσχω, aor.² ptc.) suffer, experience

ἐλευθερία, ἡ   freedom (SS 103: "after much suffering, with the spirit of freedom you have at last reached the end crowned by this present enterprise." Morwood also maintains: ". . . the phrase with διά indicates the route followed . . . and not the end reached . . . hence the Chorus must be referring by δι' ἐλευθερίαc to the attitude of independence and resolution that led Orestes and Electra to their present consummation."); [1× Soph.]

ὁρμή, ἡ   attack, onset, enterprise; [1× El.]

τελεωθέν   Kamerbeek: "'confirmed' [in the possession of your royal rights]"

IRREGULAR (AND UNPREDICTABLE) PRINCIPAL PARTS

A

ἀγγέλω, ἀγγελῶ, ἤγγειλα, ἤγγελκα, ἤγγελμαι, ἠγγέλθην   *announce*

ἄγω, ἄξω, ἤγαγον, (ἀγαγ-), ἦχα, ἦγμαι, ἤχθην ⟨ἀχθ-)   *lead*

αἰνέω,   usually in compounds with ἐπί, παρά, etc. -αινέσω, -ήνεσα, -ήνεκα, ἤνεμαι,
   -ήνεθην   *praise*

αἱρέω, αἱρήσω, εἷλον (ἑλ-), ᾕρηκα, ᾕρμαι, ᾑρέσθην   *take*, mid.: *choose*

αἴρω, ἀρῶ, ἦρα, ἦρκα, ἦρμαι, ἤρθην, ἀρθήσομαι   *raise*

αἰσθάνομαι, αἰσθήσομαι, αἰσθήσομαι, ᾐσθόμην, ᾔσθμαι   *perceive or apprehend by
   senses, hear*

αἰσχύνω, αἰσχυνῶ, ᾔσχυνα, ᾐσχύνθην   *disgrace*; mid.:   *feel ashamed*

ἀκούω, ἀκούσομαι, ἤκουσα,   (plpf. ἀκήκοα/ἠκηκόη), ἠκούσθην   *hear*

ἁλίσκομαι, ἁλώσομαι, ἑάλων/ἥλων, ἑάλωκα/ἥλωκα   *be captured*

ἁμαρτάνω [ᾰ] ἁμαρτήσομαι, ἥμαρτον, ἡμάρτηκα, ἡμάρτημαι, ἡμάρτην   *err*

ἀραρίσκω, ἦρσα, aor.² ἤραρον, transitive and intransitive, pf.² ἄρᾱρα, ἤρθην   *fit, join*

ἀρέσκω, ἀρέσω, ἤρεσα   *please*

ἄρχω, ἄρξω, ἦρξα, ἦρχα, ἦργμαι, ἤρχθην   *begin, rule*

ἀπόλλῡμι, ἀπολῶ, ἀπώλεσα, ἀπωλόμην (aor.² mid.), ἀπολώλεκα/ἀπόλωλα   *destroy*

B

βαίνω, βήσομαι, ἔβην, βέβηκα   *come, go*

βάλλω, βαλῶ, ἔβαλον, βέβληκα, βέβλημαι, ἐβλήθην   *throw, hit*

βλαστάνω, ἔβλαστον, βεβλάστηκα (ἐβλάστηκα)   *bud, sprout*

βλέπω, βλέψομαι, ἔβλεψα   *see*

βλώσκω, μολοῦμαι, ἔμολον, μέμβλωκα   *go*

βοάω, βοήσομαι, ἐβόησα   *shout*

Γ

γίγνομαι, γενήσομαι, ἐγενόμην, γέγονα (*I am*; pf. ptc. γεγώς), γεγένημαι, (late: ἐγενήθην)
  become, be

γιγνώσκω, γνώσομαι, ἔγνων, ἔγνωκα, ἔγνωσμαι, ἐγνώσθην *know*

Δ

δείκνυμι, δεικνύω, δείξω, ἔδειξα, δέδειχα, δέδειγμαι, ἐδείχθην *show, reveal*

δέρκομαι, aor.² ἔδρακον, pf. δέδορκα as pres.; pass. aor.¹ ἐδέρχηθν (in Tragedy),
  aor.² ἐδράκην *saw*

δέχομαι, δέξομαι, ἐδεξάμην, δέδεγμαι, -εδέχθην *receive, await*

δέω, δήσω, ἐδέησα, δεδέηκα, δεδέημαι, ἐδεήθην need, lack, mid.: *ask*; impersonal: δεῖ, (ἔδει
  impf.) δεήσει, ἐδέησε *it is necessary*

διδάσκω, διδάξω, ἐδίδαξα, δεδίδαχα, δεδίδαγμαι, ἐδιδάχθην *teach, explain*

δίδωμι, δώσω, ἔδωκα (aor. pl.) ἔδομεν, δέδωκα, δέδομαι, ἐδόθην *give*

δοκέω, δόξω, ἔδοξα, δέδογμαι, -εδόχθην *think, seem*

δράω, δράσω, ἔδρασα, δέδρακα, δέδραμαι, ἐδράσθην *do, accomplish*

E

ἐάω (impf. εἴων), ἐάσω, εἴασα, εἴακα, εἴαμα, εἰάθην *permit, allow, let alone*

ἐθέλω, ἐθελήσω, ἐθέλησα, ἐθέληκα *wish, be willing*

εἴκω, no pres. in use, εἴξω, ἔοικα, *resemble, appear* (impersonal: ἔοικε, *it seems*)

εἶμι   (S #773) (*will*) *go*

εἰμί, ἔσομαι, ἦν *be*

εἶπον,   see λέγω

ἕπομαι (impf. εἱπόμην), ἕψομαι, ἑσπόμην (aor. stem σπ-) *follow*

ἐργάζομαι augments to ἠ-and εἰ-, reduplicated to εἰ: ἐγαζόμην, ἐργάσομαι, ἠργάσαμην,
  εἴργασμαι, ἠργάσθην, ἐργασθήσομαι *work*

εὑρίσκω, εὑρήσω, ηὗρον/εὗρον, ηὕρηκα/εὕρηκα, εὕρημαι, εὑρέθην *find*

ἔρχομαι, ἐλεύσομαι, ἦλθον, ἐλήλυθα *come, go*

ἐφ-ίημι, -ήσω, -ῆκα, -εῖκα, -εῖμαι, -εἵθην *send against, let go, loosen*

ἔχω (impf. εἶχον), ἕξω and σχήσω, ἔσχον (aor. stem σχ-), ἔσχηκα, -ἔσχημαι, ἐσχέθην *have*

Z

ζάω, ζήσω/ζήσομαι, ἔζησα, ἔζηκα *live*

H

ἥδομαι, ἡσθήσομαι, ἥσθεν   *be pleased*

Θ

θέλω, see ἐθέλω
θνήσκω, ἀπο-θανοῦμαι, ἀπ-έθανον, *be killed* τέθνηκα *I am dead*
θύω, θύσω, ἔθυσα, τέθυκα, τέθυμαι, ἐτύθην   *sacrifice*

I

ἵημι, -ἥσω, -ἧκα, εἶκα, -εἷμαι, -εἵθην   *send*
ἵστημι, στήσω, ἔστησα and ἔστην, ἕστηκα (plpf. εἱστήκη, fut. pf. ἑστήξω), ἕσταμαι, ἐστάθην
    stand, make stand, cause to stand
ἱκνέομαι, ἵξομαι, ἱκόμην   *come, arrive*

K

καλέω, καλῶ, ἐκάλεσα, κέκληκα, κέκλημαι, ἐκλήθην   *call*
κάμνω, καμοῦμαι, ἔκαμον, κέκμηκα   *labor, be weary, be sick*
κλαίω, κλαιήσω/ κλᾱήσω (κλαύσομαι shall suffer for it), ἔκλαυσα   *weep*
κρίνω, κρινῶ, ἔκρῑνα, κέκρικα, κέκριμαι, ἐκρίθην   *judge*
κτείνω, κτενῶ, ἔκτεινα, -έκτονα   *kill*
κυλίνδω, ἐκύλῑσα, κατα-κεκύλῑσμαι, ἐκυλίσθην [ῑ], ἐκ-κυλῑστήσομαι   *roll*
κῠνέω, κυνήσομαι, ἔκυσα   *kiss;* poetic: προσκυνέω   *render homage to*
κῠρέω/κύρω, κύρσω, ἔκυρσα   *meet, happen to*

Λ

λαγχάνω, λήξομαι, aor.[2] ἔλαχον, pf.[2] εἴληχα, εἴληγμαι, ἐλήχθην   *obtain by lot*
λαμβάνω, λήψομαι, ἔλαβον, εἴληφα, εἴλημμαι, ἐλήφθην   *take, receive*
λανθάνω, λήσω, ἔλαθον, λέληθα   *escape notice, lie hidden*
λέγω, λέξω and ἐρῶ, ἔλεξα and εἶπον, εἴρηκα, λέλεγμαι and εἴρημαι, ἐλέχθην and
ἐρρήθην   *say, proclaim*
λείπω, λείψω, ἔλιπον, λέλοιπα, λέλειμμαι, ἐλείφθην   *leave*

M

μανθάνω, μαθήσομαι, ἔμαθον, μεμάθηκα   *learn by inquiry*

μάχομαι, μαχοῦμαι, ἐμαχεσάμην, μεμάχημαι   *fight*

μέλλω, μελλήσω, ἐμέλλησα   *be at the point of doing, intend, be about to*

μένω, μενῶ, ἔμεινα, μεμένηκα   *remain*

μιμνήσκω, -μνήσω, -έμνησα, μέμνημαι, ἐμνήσθην   *remind*; mid.: *remember*

N

νέμω, νεμῶ, ἔνειμα, νενέμηκα, νενέμημαι, ἐνεμήθην   *distribute*

νομίζω, νομιῶ, ἐνόμισα, νενόμικα, νενόμισμαι, ἐνομίσθην   *believe, think*

O

οἶδα, plupf. ᾔδη, εἴσομαι   *know*

οἶμαι = οἴομαι, impf. ᾤμην, οὐήσομαι, ᾠήθην   *think, suppose*

ὄλ-λῡμι   see under ἀπόλλῡμι

ὁράω (impf. ἑώρων), ὄψομαι, εἶδον (aor. stem ἰδ-), ἑόρακα/ἑώρακα, ἑώραμαι/ὦμμαι,
   ὤφθην   *see*

Π

πάσχω, πείσομαι, ἔπαθον, πέπονθα   *suffer, experience*

πείθω, πείσω, ἔπεισα (aor.² ἔπιθον), πέπεικα/πέποιθα (*trust*), πέπεισμαι, ἐπείσθην *persuade*,
   mid.: *obey*

πέμπω, πέμψω, ἔπεμψα, πέπομφα, πέπεμμαι, ἐπέμφθην   *send*

πειράομαι, πειράσομαι, ἐπειρασάμην, πεπείραμαι, ἐπειράθην   *try, attempt*

πήγνῡμι, πήξω, ἔπηξα, pf.² πέπηγα *am fixed*, aor.² pass.: ἀπάγην   *fix, make fast*

πίπτω, πεσοῦμαι, ἔπεσον, πέπτωκα   *fall*

πλήσσω, -πλήξω, -έπληξα, pf.² πέπληγα, πέπληγμαι, aor.² ἐπλήγην but in compound -επλάγην,
   πληγήσομαι   *strike*

ποθέω, ποθήσω or ποθέσομαι, ἐπόθησα   *desire, miss*

πράσσω, πράξω, ἔπραξα, πέπραχα/πέπραγα, πέπραγμαι, ἐπράχθην   *do*

πυνθάνομαι, πεύσομαι, ἐπυθόμην, πέπυσμαι   *learn, inquire*

Σ

σημαίνω, σημανῶ, ἐσήμηνα, σεσήμασμαι, ἐσημάνθην   *show*

σπείρω, σπερῶ, ἔσπειρα, ἔσπαρμαι, ἐσπάρην   *sow*

στέλλω, στελῶ, ἔστειλα, -έσταλκα, ἔσταλμαι, ἐστάλην   *send*

σφάλλω, σφαλῶ, ἔσφηλα, ἔσφαλμαι, aor.² pass.: ἐσφάλην, σφαλήσομαι   *trip up, deceive*

σῴζω, σώσω, ἔσωσα, σέσωκα, σέσωμαι, ἐσώθην   *save, keep*

Τ

τάττω, τάξω, ἔταξα, τέταχα, τέταγμαι, ἐτάχθην   *arrange*

τέμνω, τεμῶ, ἔτεμον, -τέτμηκα, τέτμημαι, ἐτμήθην   *cut*

τήκω, τήξω, ἔτηξα, pf.² τέτηκα 'am melted.' aor.² pass. as intransitive: ἐτάκην 'melted,' *melt*

τίκτω, τέξομαι, ἔτεκον, τέτοκα   *bring forth, bear, beget*

τίθημι, θήσω, ἔθηκα (pl. ἔθεμεν), τέθηκα, τέτειμαι, ἐτέθην   *put*

τίνω, τείσω, ἔτεισα, τέτεικα, -τέτεισμαι, -ετείσθην   *pay, expiate*

*τλάω, not found in pres., τλήσομαι, ἐτάλασσα Epic aor.² ἔτλην, τέτληκα usually as pres. pf.²
τέτλαμεν *endure*

τρέω, ἔτρεσα   *tremble*

τυγχάνω, τεύξομαι, ἔτυχον, τετύχηκα   *happen, hit, obtain*

Χ

χαίρω, χαιρήσω, κεχάρηκα, ἐχάρην   *rejoice*

χράομαι, χρήσομαι, ἐχρησάμην, κέχρημαι, ἐχρήσθην   *use*

Φ

φαίνω, φανῶ, ἔφηνα, πέφαγκα/πέφηνα, πέφασμαι, ἀφάνθην/ἐφάνην   *show*

φέρω, οἴσω, ἤνεγκον/ἤνεγκα, ἐνήνοχα, ἐνήνεγμαι, ἠνέχθην   *carry, bear*

φεύγω, φεύξομαι/φευξοῦμαι, ἔφυγον, πέφευγα   *flee, run away*

φημί, φήσω, ἔφησα   *say*

φθείρω, φθερῶ, ἔφθειρα, ἔφθαρκα, and ἔφθορα, ἔφθαρμαι, ἐφθάρην *corrupt, destroy,* pf.²
   be ruined

φράζω, φράσω, ἔφρασα, πέφρακα, πέφρασμαι, ἐφράστην   *tell, declare,* mid.:   *devise, plan*

φύω, φύσω, ἔφυσα/ἔφυν, πέφυκα   *produce* aor.² *grew, was;* pf. *be by nature*

APPENDIX A
METRICAL ANALYSIS

⌣̲ means that the first of the two lines in question has a short in this position and the second a long.

⌢̄ means that the first of the two lines has a long in this position and the second a short.

⌣⌣̲ means that the first of the two lines in question has two shorts and the second a long.

⌣⌣̄ means that the first of the two lines in question has a long and the second two shorts.

⌣⌣ (no space between the two marks for a short) resolution, i.e., two short syllables standing for a long one.

For the various meters see "Meter and Prosody."

PARODOS 121–250

121–36 (first strophe) = 137–52 (first antistrophe)

– – – – – ⌣ ⌣ –	121 ~ 137 choriambic dimeter
– – – – – ⌣ ⌣ –	122 ~ 138 choriambic dimeter
– – – ⌣ ⌣ – ⌣ – – –	123 ~139 glyconic, spondee, or catalectic iamb
– ⌣ ⌣ – ⌣ ⌣ – ⌣ ⌣ – ⌣ ⌣	124 ~ 140 dactylic tetrameter
– ⌣ ⌣ – ⌣ ⌣ – ⌣ ⌣ – ⌣ ⌣	125 ~ 141 dactylic tetrameter
⌣ – ⌣ –/⌣ ⌣ ⌣ ⌣/– ⌣ – ⌣ ⌣⌣ ⌣ –	126 ~ 142 iambic trimeter
⌣ – – – ⌣ – ⌣ – –	127 ~ 143 syncopated iambic trimeter catalectic
– ⌣⌣ – – – –	129 ~145 dactylic trimeter
– ⌣ ⌣ – ⌣ ⌣ – ⌣ ⌣ – ⌣ ⌣	130 ~ 146 dactylic tetrameter
– ⌣ ⌣ – ⌣ ⌣ – ⌣ ⌣ – ⌣ ⌣	131 ~ 147 dactylic tetrameter
– ⌣ ⌣ – ⌣ ⌣ – ⌣ ⌣ – ⌣ ⌣	132 ~ 148 dactylic tetrameter
– ⌣ ⌣ – ⌣ ⌣ – ⌣ ⌣ – ⌣ ⌣	133 ~ 149 dactylic tetrameter
– – – – – ⌣ ⌣ – ⌣ ⌣ – ⌣ ⌣ – ⌣ ⌣	134 ~ 150 dactylic hexameter
⌣/ – – ⌣ – ⌣ – –	135 ~ 151 iambic dimeter catalectic
– – ⌣ – –	136 ~ 152 iambic penthemimer

153–72 (second strophe) = 173–92 (second antistrophe)

– – – – –	153 ~ 173 contracted hemiepes
⏑⏑ ⏑⏑ – ⏑ –	154 ~ 174 lecythion
⏑ / – ⏑⏑ – – – ⏑ – ⏑ – –	155 ~ 175 syncopated iambic trimeter catalectic or iambic monometer, ithyphallic
– ⏑⏑ – – – ⏑ – ⏑ – ⏑	156 ~ 176 syncopated iambic trimeter catalectic or iambic monometer, ithyphallic
– – – ⏑͝⏑ – ⏞– – ⏞– – ⏑⏑ – ⏑͝	157 ~ 177 dactylic hexameter
⏑͞ – ⏑ – ⏑ – –	159 ~ 179 iambic dimeter catalectic
– ⏑⏑ ⏑ – – –	160 ~ 180 iambic dimeter catalectic or iamb, spondee
– ⏑⏑ ⏑ – – –	161 ~ 181 iambic dimeter catalectic or iamb, spondee
– ⏑⏑ – ⏑⏑ – ⏑⏑ – ⏑⏑	162 ~ 182 dactylic tetrameter
– ⏑⏑ ⏑ ⏞– – ⏑ – ⏑ ⏞– – ⏑ – –	164 ~ 184 iambic trimeter catalectic
– ⏑⏑ ⏑ ⏑⏑ ⏑ ⏑ ⏞– – ⏑ – ⏑ – –	165 ~ 185 iambic trimeter catalectic
⏑ ⏞– – ⏑ – – ⏑ – ⏑ – –	166 ~ 186 syncopated iambic trimeter catalectic or iamb ithyphallic
– ⏑⏑ – ⏑⏑ – ⏑⏑ – ⏑⏑	168 ~ 187 dactylic tetrameter
– ⏑⏑ – ⏑⏑ – ⏑⏑ – ⏑⏑	167 ~ 187 dactylic tetrameter
– ⏑⏑ – ⏑⏑ – ⏑⏑ – ⏑⏑	169 ~ 189 dactylic tetrameter
– ⏑⏑ – ⏑⏑ – ⏑⏑ – ⏑⏑	170 ~ 190 dactylic tetrameter
⏑ – – – ⏑ –	171 ~ 191 syncopated iambic dimeter
⏑ – – – ⏑ – ⏑ – –	172 ~ 192 syncopated iambic trimeter catalectic

193–212 (third strophe) = 213–32 (third antistrophe)

– – – – – – –	193 ~ 213 paroemiac
– – – – – – – –	194 ~ 214 anapestic dimeter
⏑⏑ – – – – – – –	195 ~ 215 anapestic dimeter
⏑͝⏑ – – – – – –	196 ~ 216 paroemiac
⏑⏑ – ⏑⏑ – ⏑⏑ – – –	197 ~ 217 anapestic dimeter
– – – – ⏑͝⏑ – – –	198 ~ 218 anapestic dimeter
– – ⏞– – ⏑⏑ – ⏑⏑ –	199 ~ 219 anapestic dimeter
– ⏑ – ⏑ – ⏑͞	200 ~ 220 ithyphallic
– – – – – ⏑͝⏑ – ⏑͝⏑	201 ~ 221 anapestic dimeter
– – – – – –	202 ~ 222 paroemiac
– – – – – – – –	203 ~ 223 anapestic dimeter
– – – –	204 ~ 224 anapestic monometer
⏑͞ ⏑⏑ ⏑⏑ –	205 ~ 225 dochmiac
⏑⏑ – ⏞– – ⏑⏑ – ⏞– –	206 ~ 226 anapestic dimeter
– ⏑⏑ ⏑ – – ⏑ –	207 ~ 227 syncopated iambic dimeter

⏑⏑–⏑–⏑⏒	208 ~ 228 lecythion
⏒⏑⏑⏑⏑⏑–⏑–	209 ~ 229 iambic dimeter
⏒⏑⏑⏑⏑⏑–⏑–	210 ~ 230 iambic dimeter
–⏑⏑–⏑⏑–⏑⏑–⏑⏑	211 ~ 231 dactylic tetrameter
⏒⏑⏑⏑–⏑–⏑⏒	212 ~ 232 iambic dimeter catalectic

233–50 (epode)

– – – – – – –	233 paroemiac
– – – – – – –	234 paroemiac
– – – – – – –	235 paroemiac
–⏑⏑–⏑⏑–⏑⏑–⏑⏑	236 dactylic tetrameter
–⏑⏑–⏑⏑–⏑⏑–⏑⏑	237 dactylic tetrameter
–⏑⏑–– – – –	238 dactylic tetrameter
– – – – – – – –	239 anapestic dimeter
– – – – – – – –	240 anapestic dimeter
– – – – – –⏑⏑	241 anapestic dimeter
– – – – – –⏑⏑	242 anapestic dimeter
–⏑⏑–⏑–	243 dochmiac
–⏑⏑–⏑– –⏑⏑–⏑–	245 dochmiac dimeter
–⏑–⏑–	246 hypodochmius
–⏑–⏑–	247 hypodochmius
– – –⏑⏑–⏑–	248 glyconic
– –⏑– –	249 iambic penthemimer
⏑– – –⏑–⏑– –	250 syncopated iambic trimeter catalectic

FIRST STASIMON 472–515

472–86 (strophe) = 488–501 (antistrophe)

– – –⏑⏑– –⏑⏑– –	472 ~ 489 choriambic hendecasyllable OR asclepiadean
– – –⏑⏑–⏑–	473 ~ 490 glyconic
–⏑–⏑– –	475 ~ 491 ithyphallic
⏑–⏑–⏑⏑⏑–⏑–⏑–	476 ~ 492 iambic trimeter
⏑–⏑– –⏑–⏑–	477 ~ 493 syncopated iambic trimeter
⏑–⏑–⏑	479 ~ 495 contracted iambic dimeter
–⏑⏑–⏑–⏒	480 ~ 496 aristophanean
–⏑–⏑–⏑–	481 ~ 497 lecythion
– –⏑–– –⏑–	482 ~ 498 iambic dimeter
– – – –⏑–	483 ~ 499a syncopated iambic dimeter

– – ◡ – – – ◡ –	484 ~ 499b iambic dimeter
◡̲ – – – ◡ ◡̲	485 ~ 500 syncopated iambic dimeter
– – ◡ ◡ – ◡ – –̄ – ◡ – – –	486 ~ 501 telesilleus and syncopated iambic dimeter

504–515 (epode)

– ◡◡◡ ◡ – – –	504 iambo-dochmiac
◡ ◡◡◡ ◡ – – –	505 iambo-dochmiac
– ◡◡◡ ◡ – – –	506 iambo-dochmiac
– ◡ –	507 cretic
– ◡◡◡ ◡ – – –	508 iambo-dochmiac
– ◡◡◡ ◡ – – –	509 iambo-dochmiac
– – – ◡ –	510 dochmiac
– – – – – –	511 molossus dimeter
– – ◡ – – –	512 iambo-dochmiac
– ◡ –	513 cretic
◡ ◡◡◡ – – – –	514 iambo-dochmiac
◡ ◡◡◡ ◡ – – –	515 iambo-dochmiac

KOMMOS (LYRIC DIALOGUE) 823–70

823–36 (first strophe) = 837–48 (second antistrophe)

– ◡◡◡ ◡ – – ◡ ◡ – –	
◡ ◡ – – ◡ ◡ – – ◡ ◡ – –	823–24 ~ 837 = 38 iamb, 3 choriambs, adoneum
– – ◡ ◡ – –	825 ~ 839 reizianum
◡ ◡ – –	826 ~ 840 ionic monometer
– – ◡ ◡ – –	828 ~ 841 reizianum
– – – ◡ ◡ – – ◡ ◡ – –	830 ~845 pherecratean augmented by choriamb
– – ◡ ◡ – – ◡ ◡ –	
– ◡ ◡ – – ◡ ◡ – – ◡ ◡ –	
– ◡ ◡ – – ◡ ◡ – – –	831–835 ~ 846–848 telesilleus with choriambic expansion, ending in molossus (OR perhaps: with dragged ending)

849–58 (second strophe) = 859–70 (second antistrophe)

– ◡ – – ◡ – ◡ –	849 ~ 860 cretic, hypodochmius
– – – – – ◡◡◡ – –	850 ~ 861 anapestic dimeter
– – – – – – – –	851 ~ 862 anapestic dimeter
– – – – – – ◡̲	852 ~ 863 anapestic dimeter catalectic

– ⏑⏑ – ⏑ –	853 ~ 864 dochmiac
– ⏑ – – ⏑/–	854 ~ 865 hypodochmiac
⏑⏑ – ⏑ – ⏑ –	855 ~ 866 lecythion
⏑ – ⏑ – ⏑ – ⏑⏑ – ⏑⏑ –	856 ~ 869 iambelegus
– ⏑⏑ – ⏑ – –	857 ~ 870 aristophanean

SECOND STASIMON 1058–97

1058–69 (first strophe) = 1070–81 (first antistrophe)

⏑ – ⏑ – – ⏑⏑ – ⏑ – ⏑ – –	1058 ~ 1070 iamb, choriambic enneasyllable
⏑⏑ – ⏑ – ⏑ – –	1059 ~ 1071 anacreontic
⏑⏑ – ⏑ – ⏑ – –	1060 ~ 1072 anacreontic
⏑⏑ – ⏑ – ⏑ – –	1061 ~ 1073 anacreontic
⏑⏑ – ⏑⏑ – ⏑ – ⏒	1062 ~ 1074 ionic
– – – ⏑⏑ – ⏑ –	1063 ~ 1075 glyconic
– – – ⏑⏑ – ⏑ –	1064 ~ 1076 glyconic
– ⏒ – ⏑⏑ – –	1065 ~ 1077 pherecratean
– ⏑⏑ – ⏑ – ⏑ – –	1066 ~ 1078 choriambic enneasyllable
⏑⏑ – ⏑ – ⏑ – –	1067 ~ 1079 anacreontic
⏑⏑ – ⏑ – ⏑ – –	1068 ~ 1080 anacreontic
⏑⏑ – ⏑⏑ – ⏑ – –	1069 ~ 1081 ionic

1082–89 (second strophe) = 1090–1097 (second antistrophe)

– – – ⏑⏑ – –	1082 ~ 1090 pherecratean
– ⏑ – – – ⏑ – – – ⏑ –	1083 ~ 1091 syncopated iambic trimeter
– ⏑⏑ – – –	1084 ~ 1092 dodrans
–/⏑ – ⏑ – – ⏑ –	1085 ~ 1093 syncopated iambic dimeter
– ⏑ – ⏑ – –	1086 ~ 1094 ithyphallic
⏑ – ⏑ ⏓̄ – ⏑ –	1087 ~ 1095 iambic dimeter
⏑ ⏑⏑ – ⏑⏑⏑ –	1088 ~ 1096 iambic dimeter
⏑ – ⏑ – – ⏑ – ⏑ – –	1089 ~ 1097 syncopated iambic trimeter catalectic

RECOGNITION DUET 1232–87

1232–52 (strophe) = 1253–72 (antistrophe)

⏑ – ⏑ –	1232 ~ 1253 iambic monometer
⏑ – – ⏑ – ⏑ – – ⏑ –	1233 ~ 1254 dochmiac dimeter

⏑ ⏖ – ⏑ –	1234 ~ 1255 dochmiac
	(1235–36 ~ 1256–57 iambic trimeters)
⏑ – ⏓	1237 ~ 1258 bacchiac
	(1238 ~ 1259 iambic trimeter)
⏒ – – ⏑ – – ⏑ ⏑ – ⏒ –	1239 ~ 1260 dochmiac dimeter
⏑ ⏖ – ⏑ – ⏑ – ⏑ –	1240 ~ 1261 dochmiac dimeter
⏑ – ⏑ – ⏑ – –	1241 ~ 1262 iambic dimeter catalectic
⏑ – – ⏑ – –	1242 ~ 1263 bacchiac dimeter
	(1243–44 ~ 1264 + lost line iambic trimeters)
– ⏑ ⏗ – ⏑ –	1245 ~ 1265 cretic dimeter
⏒ ⏖ ⏖ ⏖ ⏖ – ⏖ ⏖ ⏖ ⏖	1246 ~ 1267 dochmiac dimeter
– ⏑ ⏖ – ⏑ ⏖ – ⏑ ⏖	1247 ~ 1269 cretic trimeter
– ⏖ – ⏑ ⏒	1250 ~ 1270 dochmiac
	(1251–52 ~ 1271–72 iambic trimeters)

1273–87 (epode)

⏑ – ⏑ –	1273 iambic monometer
⏑ – – ⏑ – ⏑ ⏖ – ⏑ –	
– – ⏑ – ⏑ – –	1274 dochmiac dimeter, iambic dimeter catalectic
– ⏖ ⏑ ⏖ ⏑ – ⏑ –	1275 iambic dimeter
⏑ – ⏑ – ⏑ – – ⏑ – –	1276 iambic trimeter catalectic
– – ⏑ – ⏑ – – ⏑ – –	1277 iambic trimeter catalectic
– – ⏑ – ⏑ – – ⏑ – – ⏑ –	1279 iambic trimeter
⏑ – ⏑ – –	1280 bacchiac dimeter
– ⏑ ⏑ ⏑ ⏑	1281 trochaic monometer
– ⏑ – ⏑ – –	1282 trochaic dimeter
– ⏑ – ⏑ – ⏑ – – ⏑ ⏑	1283 syncopated trochaic trimeter
– ⏑ – ⏑ – ⏑ – – ⏑ ⏑	1284 syncopated trochaic trimeter
– ⏑ – ⏑ – ⏑ ⏑	1285 trochaic dimeter
– ⏑ – ⏑ – ⏑ ⏑	1286 trochaic dimeter
– ⏑ – ⏑ – ⏑ – –	1287 trochaic trimeter catalectic

THIRD STASIMON 1384–97

1384–90 (strophe) = 1391–97 (antistrophe)

⏖ ⏑ ⏖ ⏑ –	1384 ~ 1391 cretic dimeter
⏑ ⏖ – – ⏑ – ⏑ – ⏑ –	1385 ~ 1392 dochmiac dimeter
⏒ – ⏑ – ⏑ – ⏑ – ⏑ –	1386 ~ 1393 iambic trimeter

ᵕ ᵕᵕ – ᵕ – ᵕ – – ᵕ –   1387 ~ 1394 dochmiac dimeter
ᵕ – – ᵕ –   1388 ~ 1395 dochmiac
– – ᵕ – ᵕ – ᵕ –   1389 ~ 1396 iambic dimeter
– – ᵕ – ᵕ – ᵕ – ᵛ̄. – ᵕ ᵛ̆   1390 ~ 1397 iambic trimeter

KOMMOS (LYRIC DIALOGUE) 1398–1441

1398–1421 (strophe) = 1422–41 (antistrophe)

                        (1398–1403 ~ 1422–27 6 iambic trimeters)

– ᵕᵕ – ᵕ –   1404 ~ (line lost) dochmiac OR dodrans

                        (1405–6 ~ 2 lines lost) 2 iambic trimeters

– – ᵕ – – ᵕ –   1407 ~ 1428 iambic dimeter catalectic
– ᵕ – ᵕ – –   1408 ~ 1429 ithyphallic

                        (1409–12 ~ lost line, 1430–32) 4 iambic trimeters

– ᵕᵕ – ᵕᵕ – ᵕ – ᵕ – ᵛ̄   13 ~ 1433 dactylic dimeter and ithyphallic
– ᵕᵕ – ᵕᵕ – ᵕ – ᵕ –   1414 ~ 1434 dactylic dimeter and hypodochmiac

                        (1415–16 ~ 1435–36) 2 iambic trimeters

ᵕ – ᵕ – – ᵕ –   1417 ~ 1437 syncopated iambic dimeter
– ᵕ – – ᵕ –   1418 ~ 1439 syncopated iambic dimeter
ᵕ – ᵕ – ᵕ – ᵕ – ᵛ̄ – ᵕ – ᵕ – –   1420 ~ 1440 iambic tetrameter catalectic
– ᵕ – ᵕ – ᵛ̄   1421 ~ 1441 ithyphallic *or* syncopated iambic dimeter
                                        catalectic

APPENDIX B
LEXICAL ANALYSIS

I.

The occurrence of each word in the play (except prepositions, conjunctions, particles, etc.) is documented in the notes, whether it is its sole occurrence in the play or in the extant Sophoclean corpus (not including fragments). In this appendix I offer a Lexical Table of the entire play. It includes separate word counts for all the parts of the play, enabling a comparison of the incidence of *hapax*-words in various sections of the play and in the entire Sophoclean corpus. This kind of analysis is not typically found in Classical scholarship. However, we do know from Aristotle that usage of common (*kyrioi*) and uncommon (rarely used, *xenikoi*) words was a critical consideration in ancient times for assessment of the style's register, as it is today. Aristotle claims that a composition overburdened with uncommon words (loan words, metaphors, etc.) would suffer from a lack of clarity, while being limited to ordinary or common words would result in a banal, platitudinous, or dull style. Aristotle therefore suggests a moderate mix of common and uncommon words to render the style pleasant and to maintain clarity (*Poetics* 1458a–b).[1] Furthermore, he recommends a stricter regulation of the use of unfamiliar and uncommon words in iambic poetry, because the iambic meter is largely an imitation of ordinary speech, which calls for immediate intelligibility.

Scrutiny of the Lexical Table below clearly demonstrates that in Sophocles' *Electra*, recitative and singing parts are richer in *hapax*-words than the spoken parts. The latter mainly accord with Aristotle's recommendation that iambic poetry mostly use words common to ordinary conversation. (This will of course explain to the students why they might need to look up more words when reading lyric passages.)

The lexical overview is intended mainly to help students wishing to undertake further research of lexical usages. To draw fully fledged conclusions about the significance of the occurrences of common or uncommon words, a student would need to study not only *Electra* but all the extant Sophoclean plays as well. This kind of lexical research is rather technical, but engaging in such an endeavor can provide a wealth of insights.

---

1. See also discussion in Larkin (1971), 56–71.

Scholarship in Greek tragedy has sporadically engaged with word usage. In the case of the disputed authorship of the *Rhesus*, for instance, some scholars who claim it was not composed by Euripides point out that it contains a high percentage of words that are not used elsewhere in extant tragedy or in classical Greek literature.[2] However, this phenomenon has primarily been used as evidence for disputing Euripides' authorship. One could ask whether the presence of uncommon words is actually because the main characters in the play are non-Greek, and whether Euripides wished to emphasize their foreign identity by giving them a more bombastic vocabulary. Is it possible that because *Rhesus* might have been a prosatyric play, the playwright wanted it to be distinct from a play in a trilogy?[3] Another example of a higher incidence of rare word usage is found in Hecuba's *agōn* with Helen in *Trojan Women*. Euripides gives Hecuba eleven rare words that appear only there, or in a few other places in extant tragedy, while Helen has only one such word. Without further study of word occurrences, it is impossible to know whether this use of non-common vocabulary makes Hecuba sound more old-fashioned and thus in some way more authoritative, or just underscores her non-Greekness in contrast to Helen.[4]

The study of word usage could be profitable in gaining more insights into characterization. For example, are some *hapax*-words used more frequently by certain characters? If so, what features did the tragedian mean to underscore in these characters? Do rare and bombastic words elevate the style for the purpose of excitement, aloofness, or some other emotional effect? Taking stock and renegotiating our relationship with the text is always a good idea, and the significance of this kind of approach can be assessed only by testing it.

II.

The following Lexical Tables provide word counts and word percentages for each integral part of this play. To demonstrate what can be gleaned from the examination of this table, and how we can connect the usage of words with content, I offer the following examples, which include two cases of spoken parts, and one of a choral ode.

The first eighty-five lines of the prologue, which form a dialogue between the Tutor and Orestes, attract attention because of having a significantly higher percentage of *hapax*-words

---

2. Liapis (2012), liii–lviii. It is noteworthy that when the percentage frequency of *hapax*-words of the *Rhesus* was compared to that of Euripides' undisputedly genuine plays, it was calculated not by number of words, but by number of lines.

3. For seeing the *Rhesus* as a pro-satyric play, see Roisman 2018; *Rhesus* is surpassed only by the *Cyclops in hapax*-words: 2.81% to 3.1%, which is undisputedly by Euripides.

4. Eu. *TW*, Hecuba: ἐξεμαργώθης (992), κατακλύζω (995), ἐγκαθυβρίζειν (997), ἀνολολύζω (1000), δοριπετής (1003), ἀγωνία (1003), ἀνταγωνιστής (1006), ἀκουσίως (1011), συνεκκλέπτω (1018), κατάπτυστος (1024), ἀποσκυθίζω (1026). Helen has one word that is attested only once more in Euripides but not in any other extant tragedy: θεοπόνητος (953).

than any other spoken part in the play: 8.8% appear only once in this play, and 4.7% appear only once in extant Sophocles. The average percentage of *hapax*-words in other spoken parts in *Electra* and extant Sophocles is 6.9% and 3.4% respectively. However, the overall percentage of rare words both in the first eighty-five lines and in overall spoken parts (i.e., in iambic trimeter) is still lower than the percentages of uncommon words in the recitative or sung parts: 10.8% and 8% in *Electra* and extant Sophocles respectively. How can we explain this higher ratio of *hapax*-words in the prologue? Did Sophocles wish to have a grand opening? Is this type of speech a characteristic of the Tutor and Orestes? After all, the prologue is crucial for rendering a play clear and accessible, and the use of nonordinary words stands in the way of clarity. To reach a conclusion, one needs to analyze other lines delivered by both the Tutor and Orestes, and see whether they contain the high percentage of uncommon words spotted in the Prologue.

At the other end of the spectrum of uncommon word usage we find the Fourth Episode, in which the spoken lines offer only an average of 4.1% of *hapax*-words in *Electra* and 1.5% in extant Sophocles. Because this is one of the lowest percentages of uncommon words in iambic trimeter, it requires some explanation. Does the high percentage of stichomythic verses (5.9% of all the verses in the episode) play a role in the low count of uncommon words? It might be interesting for a student to compare the usage of common and uncommon words in stichomythic passages, and attempt to find explanations for the relatively low number of uncommon words in these passages. Could it be because stichomythic language tends to be restricted, mundane, and easily accessible?

In the sung part of the play, the Second Stasimon (472–515) stands out. The Chorus sing after hearing from Chrysothemis that there are freshly poured libations and a freshly cut lock of hair on Agamemnon's previously untended grave. Of the choral ode's words, 25.2% occur only once in the entire extant Sophoclean corpus, the highest percentage of *hapax*-words of any sung part of the play (8% in average). Is the extremely elevated diction meant to suggest the Chorus' newly gained confidence that Justice will soon overtake Clytemnestra and Aegisthus? If not, what could the explanation be?

The following Lexical Table offered opens a window to many other questions that students can pursue.

LEXICAL TABLES

Abbreviations: 1× *El.* = words occurring only once in the play *Electra.*

1× Soph. = words occurring only once in the extant Sophoclean corpus (not including fragments)

PROLOGUE
<u>Lines 1–120</u>

ll. 1–85 (*dialogue*)	489 words	1× *El.*: 43 wds = 8.8%	1× Soph. 23 wds = 4.7%
ll. 86–120 (El.'s recitative)	170 words	1× *El.*: 19 wds = 11.7%	1× Soph. 17 wds = 10%
total	**659 words**	1× *El.*: 62 wds = 9.5%	1× Soph. 40 wds = 6%

PARODOS
<u>Lines 121–250</u>

total (song)	**556 words**	1× *El.*: 72 wds = 12.9%	1× Soph. 30 wds = 5.4%

FIRST EPISODE
<u>Lines 251–471</u>

total (dialogue)	**1380 words**	1× *El.*: 82 wds = 5.9%	1× Soph. 31 wds = 2.25%

FIRST STASIMON
<u>Lines 472–515</u>

total (song)	**123 words**	1× *El.*: 10 wds = 8.1%	1× Soph. 31 wds = 25.2%

SECOND EPISODE
<u>Lines 516–822</u>

ll. 516–659 (dialogue)	913 words	1× *El.*: 54 wds = 5.9%	1× Soph. 13 wds = 1.4%
ll. 660–822 (dialogue)	925 words	1× *El.*: 84 wds = 9%	1× Soph. 44 wds = 4.7%
total	**1838 words**	1× *El.*: 138 wds = 7.5%	1× Soph. 57 wds= 3.1%

KOMMOS (Lyric Dialogue)
<u>Lines 823–870</u>

total (song)	**150 words**	1× *El.*: 14 wds = 9.3%	1× Soph. 10 wds = 6.6%

THIRD EPISODE
<u>Lines 871–1057</u>

ll. 871–937	419 words	1× *El.*: 26 wds = 6.2%	1× Soph. 10 wds = 2.3%
ll. 938–1057	723 words	1× *El.*: 35 wds = 4.8%	1× Soph. 14 wds = 1.9%
total	1142 words	1× *El.*: 61 wds = 5.3%	1× Soph. 24 wds = 2.1%

SECOND STASIMON
<u>Lines 1058–1097</u>

total (song)	164 words	1× *El.*: 19 wds = 11.5%	1× Soph. 11 wds = 6.7%

FOURTH EPISODE
<u>Lines 1098–1383</u>

ll. 1098–1231	822 words	1× *El.*: 47 wds = 5.7%	1× Soph. 14 wds = 1.7%
ll. 1232–1287	235 words	1× *El.*: 11 wds = 4.6%	1× Soph. 4 wds = 1.7%
ll. 1288–1383	685 words	1× *El.*: 15 wds = 2.1%	1× Soph. 8 wds = 1.1%
total	1742 words	1× *El.*: 73 wds = 4.1%	1× Soph. 26 wds = 1.5%

THIRD STASIMON
<u>Lines 1384–1397</u>

total (song)	56 words	1× *El.*: 6 wds = 10.7%	1× Soph. 9 wds = 16%

KOMMOS (Partially Lyric Dialogue)
<u>Lines 1398–1441</u>

total (partially song)	224 words	1× *El.*: 16 wds = 7.1%	1× Soph. 8 wds = 3.5%

EXODOS
<u>Lines 1442–1510</u>

total (dialogue)	453 words	1× *El.*: 34 wds = 7.5%	1× Soph. 11 wds = 2.4%Play's
Total play's words:	8487	1× *El.*: 587 wds = 6.9 %	1× Soph. 288 wds = 3.4%

Averages of uncommon words for spoken and sung passages:

Spoken passages*:   7044 wds   g1× *El.* 431 wds = 6.1%   1× Soph. 172 wds = 2.4%

*iambic trimeter included in choral odes or lyric dialogue is not included in the count.

Song (and   1443 wds   1× *El.* 156 wds = 10.8%   1× Soph. 116 wds = 8%
recitative):

GLOSSARY

Because of their frequency in the play, it is highly recommended that the student memorize the following words upon their first occurrence.

A

ἄγᾱν (adv.)	*very, much, very much; too much*
*ἀγγέλω	*announce*
ἄγω	[ᾰ] *draw, hold*
ἀγών, ῶνος, ὁ	*place of contest, contest*
ἀδελφή, ἡ (ᾰ)	*daughter of the same mother, sister*
ἀδελφός, ὁ (ᾰ)	*son of the same mother, brother*
ἀεί (adv.)	(the ᾰ/ᾱ) *ever, always*
ἄθλιος (2/3)	*wretched*
αἰαῖ	*interjection of grief; alas*
Ἀίδης, Ἀίδᾱο, ὁ	*Hades, the god of the Netherworld*
αἰεί	*see ἀεί*
αἰκία, ἡ	[ῑ] *injurious treatment, outrage*
αἰκῶς (adv.)	*poetic = ἀεικῶς (ἀεικής) unseemly, shamefully*
*αἱρέω	*take away, seize, overpower, overcome; mid.: choose*
*αἰσθάνομαι	*perceive or apprehend by senses, hear; + acc. / genit.*
αἰσχρός (2/3)	*shameful, disgraceful*
αἰών, ῶνος, ὁ	*period of existence*
*ἀκούω	*hear, listen; +acc. for words, sound, etc., that one hears; + genit.* *for the person whose words are heard*
ἄκρος (3)	*at the end, topmost*
ἀλγέω	*suffer pain, grieve, be troubled, distressed*
ἄλγος, εος, τό	*pain, sorrow, grief, distress*
ἀλλά (conj.)	*but; (neut. pl. of ἄλλος with changed accent); with commands* *and exhortations; well*

ἀλλὰ νῦν	*now at least, now at long last*
ἄλλος, η, ο	*other* (of several)
ἅμα (adv.)	*at the same time*
ἀμφί (prep.)	+acc. *about; for, for the sake of;* + dat. *on account of, about concerning, for the sake of*
ἀνάγκη, ἡ	*constraint, necessity*
ἄναξ, ακτος, ὁ	*lord, king*
ἄνευ (prep.)	+ genit.; *without*
ἀνήρ, ἀνδρός, ὁ	*man*
ἀν-*ίημι	*let go*
ἀντί (prep.)	+ genit.; *instead of; for the sake of; because of*
ἄνω (adv.)	*upward, up*
ἄξιος (3)	*worthy, befitting, deserving*
ἀπ-αλάσσω	*set free, release;* in pass. sometimes: *to have done*
ἄ-πᾶς, ἄπᾶσα, ἄπαν	(ἅμα, πᾶς, strengthened for πᾶς) *quite all, all together*
ἄπ-*ειμι	(ἀπό, εἰμί) *be away, be absent*
ἀπό (prep.)	+ genit.; *from, after, by, because, as a result of*
ἀπ-*όλλῡμι	act.: *destroy utterly;* mid.: ἀπ-όλλῡμαι *perish, die, cease to exist*
ἀπο-στερέω	*rob, bereave;* pass: *robbed or in want of* + genit.
ἀπ-ωθέω, -ωσα	mid.: *reject, disdain, repulse*
ἄρα	(postpositive pcl.) *then, therefore* (connective, confirmatory and inferential marking the immediate succession of events and thoughts, adding lively feeling of interest)
ἆρα	interrog. pcl. indicating anxiety and impatience
ἆρα μή	= μῶν; interrog. pcl. expecting the answer 'no'; *'You don't [think] that . . . , do you?*
⁺Ἀργεῖος (3)	*of or from Argos, Argive*
Ἄρης, ὁ	*Ares, god of war/warlike frenzy*
ἀρκέω	*be strong, avail; aid, assist* (+ dat.); impersonal: ἀρκεῖ μοί = *it is enough for me;* ἀρκεῖν δοκεῖ = *it seems enough, seems good*
Ἄρτεμις, ιδος, ἡ	*Artemis*
⁺ἀρτίως (adv.)	*just now, exactly*
*ἄρχω	*be first* whether of time: *begin,* or of place or station: *govern, command, rule* + genit.
ἀρωγός, ὁ	*helper*
ἀσκέω	*adorn, fashion, decorate;* + inf.: *practice, train*
ἀστήρ, -έρος, ὁ	*star*
ἄτη, ἡ	*state of infatuation or the ruin arising from it*
ἄ-τῑμος, ον	*without honor, dishonored*

αὖ (adv.)   of time: *again, anew, once more*; pcl. (postpositive) adversa-
tive: *on the other hand, again*

αὐτός, αὐτή, αὐτό   (intensive pron.) *–self*; in oblique cases pers. pron. of 3rd pers.

ἄχθος, -εος, τό   *weight, burden, load of grief*

Β

*βαίνω   *go*

βαστάζω   *lift, lift up, clasp*

βίᾱ, ἡ   *violent force, might*

βίος, ὁ   *life*

βλάβη, ἡ   [ă] *harm, damage*

*βλαστάνω   *bud, sprout, burst forth*

*βλέπω   *see*

*βλώσκω, ἔμολον   *come, go*; (tenses formed from root μόλω); poetic verb

*βοάω   *shout*

βοή, ἡ   *cry, shout, outcry*

βουλεύω   *take counsel, consider, determine*

βραχύς, εῖα, ύ   *short, brief*; ἐν βραχεῖ *shortly, briefly*

βροτός, ὁ   *mortal person*; (poetically opposed to ἀθάνατος or θεός; as adj.:
mortal)

Γ

γάρ   (postpositive conj.) *for*; introduces a reason for the preceding
statement, explanatory; *the fact is that*

γε   *at least*; postpositive enclitic pcl., used to emphasize a word;
sometimes attached to the word: ἔμοιγε *to me at least*; in conversation to be transl.: 'yes'

γε μέντοι (pcl.)   *all the same, and yet, however*

γελάω   *laugh*; γελάω ἐπί τινι—*laugh at, mock over something*

γένος, ους, τό   *race, stock, kin*

γέρων, ον   *old, aged*

γῆ, ἡ   *earth, land*

*γίγνομαι   *become, be*

*γιγνώσκω   *know*

γνωμή, ἡ   *mind, judgment*

γονεύς, έος, ὁ   *begetter, father*; mostly in pl.: *parents*

γόος, ὁ   *weeping, wailing, groaning*; often in the plural

γῠνή, γυναικός, ἡ   *woman*

Δ

δαίμων, ονος, ὁ	god; fate
δάκρυ, υος, τό	tear (= δάκρυον, τό)
δακρύω	weep, shed tears
*δεῖ	it is necessary
*δέω	need, lack + genit.; mid.: ask
*δείκνῦμι	show, reveal
δείλαιος (3)	(lengthened form of δειλός, miserable, wretched) wretched, sorry, paltry
δεινός (3)	fearful, terrible, shrewd
δέμας, τό	bodily frame, living/dead body; used in nom/acc.
*δέρκομαι	see, look, behold
*δέχομαι	receive; accept (mental reception, i.e., agree)
δή (pcl.)	postpositive; of course, indeed, quite (adds explicitness (voilà), marks something as immediately present and clear to the mind); ἦ δή "expresses lively surprise" (S #2865)
δηλόω	make known, disclose, reveal
δῆτα (pcl.)	(emphatic) assuredly, really, in truth
διά (prep.)	through; in Sophocles with genit., rarely with acc.
*δῐδάσκω	teach, explain
*δίδωμι	give
δίκαιος (3/2)	right, righteous, just
δίκη, ἡ	order, right; atonement, satisfaction, penalty, retribution
διπλοῦς, ῆ, οῦν	twofold; pl.: both, two
δοκέω	form an opinion, think, imagine; intransitive: seem, appear
δόλος, ὁ	cunning, trickery, deceit
δόμος, ὁ	house, chamber
*δράω	do, accomplish
δρόμος, ὁ	course, race; lap
δυσ-μενής, ές	bearing ill will, hostile
δύστηνος (2)	wretched, unhappy, unfortunate (sometimes without moral connotation)
δυσ-τυχής, ές	unlucky, unfortunate
δῶμα, ατος, τό	house

E

*ἐάω	[ᾱ] permit, let, suffer, allow, let alone
ἔγωγε	emphatic for ἐγώ

*ἐθέλω	= θέλω; *wish, be willing, desire*
εἰ δ' οὖν	*but if so-and-so does happen*
εἰκός	*like truth, likely, probable, reasonable;* ὡς εἰκός *as is proper*
*εἰμί, ἔσομαι, ἦν	*be*
εἴπερ	*if indeed, if at all events* (expresses concessive meaning, especially when the truth of the statement is implicitly denied or doubted)
εἶπον	*said* (aor.[2]· εἴπω, εἴποιμι, εἰπέ, εἰπεῖν, εἰπών); defective verb for pres. ⁺λέγω
εἰς/ἐς (prep.)	+acc.; *into; up to, until, toward, to*
εἷς, μία, ἕν	*one*
⁺εἰσ-*ἀκούω	*hear, listen*
εἴσ-*ειμι	*go in, go into*
εἰσ-*έρχομαι	*come into, enter; technical term of entering a race*
εἰσ-*οράω	*look at/upon, behold; pay attention*
εἴσω	*to, within, into;* + genit. (improper prep., i.e., an adv. used as a prep. but incapable of forming compounds)
εἶτα (adv.)	*then*
εἴ-τε . . . εἴ-τε	*either . . . or, whether . . . or*
ἐκ, ἐξ (prep.)	+ genit. (ἐξ before a vowel); *out of, from, after, as the result of;* = ὑπό + genit. of agent: *by*
ἐκεῖνος (3)	(demons. pron.) *the person there, that person/thing* (usually with reference to what has gone before)
ἐκ-*λείπω	*leave out, pass over; intransitive: leave off, cease*
ἐκ-*πέμπω	*send out, send forth*
ἐκτός	*without, outside, out of beyond* +gen. (improper prep., i.e., an adv. used as a prep. but incapable of forming compounds)
ἐλεύθερος (3)	*free*
ἐλπίς, ίδος, ἡ	*hope*
ἐν (prep.)	+ dat. *in, at*
ἔνδον (adv. and prep.)	+ genit.; *within*
ἐν-*ειμι	*be within, be in or among; impersonal:* ἔνεστι τινί *it is in one's power, one may or one can*
ἔνθᾰ	*where* (correl. relative adv. taking the place of οὗ); *when*
ἐννέπω	*poetic lengthening for* ἐνέπω *tell, speak*
ἐξ	*see* ἐκ
ἐξ-ερῶ	*speak out, proclaim; fut. without any pres. in use*
ἔξ-εστι	(ἐξ-ειμι) *it is allowed, possible, in one's power;* ἐξόν = *it being possible or with inf. as its subject*

ἐξ-ῑσόω	*make equal, level;* pass.: *be equal, be match for*
ἔοικα	*be like; seem* (+ inf.); *it seems* (impersonal)
ἐξ-*εῖπον	(aor.² act. indic.) *tell of* + double acc.; in use of ἐξ-αγορεύω, ⁺ἐξ-ερῶ
ἐξ-*ἔρχομαι	*come out of*
ἐξ-ερῶ	*speak out, proclaim;* fut. without any pres. in use
ἔξ-*οιδα	(pf. with pres. sense) *know thoroughly well, know well*
ἔοικα, ας, ε, etc.	pf. with present sense of εἴκω to *seem likely, seem;* ἔοικε *it seems;* ὡς ἔοικε *as it seems, as is fitting*
ἐπ-*αινέω,	*approve, sanction, commend*
ἔπειτα (adv.)	(ἐπί, εἶτα) *then, thereafter, thereupon*
ἐπί (prep.)	+ acc.: *to, toward, for;* + dat.: *on, by, in addition to, for, over*
ἐπίστᾰμαι	*know how (to do), be able (to do)*
ἐπ-οικτίρω	*have compassion for, pity*
ἕπομαι	*follow*
ἔπος, εος, τό	*word*
Ἐρῑνύς, ύος, ἡ	*Erinys, Fury*
ἔρρω	*come to ruin, perish, disappear*
ἔργον, τό	*deed, action, work*
*ἔρχομαι	*come, go*
ἐρῶ	*will say, proclaim, tell, announce, order* (φημί, λέγω, and ἀγορεύω used as pres. and εἶπον as aor.²)
ἐσθλός (3)	(poetic adj.) *good* (ἀγαθός); (of persons) *brave, noble;* morally: *faithful*
ἔσω	see εἴσω
ἔτι (adv.)	generally: *yet, still, besides*
εὐθύς (adv.)	*straightaway, at once*
εὐνή, ἡ	*bed;* often pl.; figuratively *resting place*
*εὑρίσκω	*find; win*
εὐσέβεια, ἡ	*reverence toward the gods, piety; respect, devotion*
εὐ-τὔχέω	(εὖ, τύχη, chance, fortune) *be lucky, be well off, succeed*
ἐχθαίρω	(ἔχθος, hatred) *hate*
*ἔχω	*have, hold ; be able to;* in verse ἔχω is often used as κατέχω, *hold back, curb; keep away from* + genit.
ἐχθρός (3)	*hating, hostile, hated, hateful;* as substantive = *enemy*
ἐφ-*ίη-μι	*permit, allow;* mid.: *command;* impf. often used in oracular responses and with verbs of command; + genit.: *aim at, long, desire*

Z

*ζάω	*live*
Ζεύς, Διός, ὁ	(Διϝός, S #285.12) *Zeus*

Η

ἤ (conj.)	disjunctive: *or*; comparative: *than*; interrog. in indirect question
ἤ . . . ἤ	*either . . . or*
ἦ (adv.)	(a) strengthens or confirms: *in truth, truly, verily*; (b) in interrog. sentence
ᾗ (adv.)	(dat. sg. fem. of relative pron.) *which way, where, in/at what place*
ἦ δή	see δή
ἦ-τοι (conj.)	*indeed, surely, verily* (= ἦ τοι)
ἤδη (adv.)	*already, by this time, now, immediately, in the past*
ἡδονή, ἡ	*delight, enjoyment, pleasure*
ἡδύς, ἡδεῖα, ἡδύ	*sweet, pleasant, welcome*
ἥκιστα (adv.)	*least*; in reply to a question: *not at all, <u>no</u>* (emphatic)
ἥκω	*have come, have arrived* (like οἴχομαι, a pres. with pf. sense)
ἥλιος, ὁ	*sun*
ἡμέρα, ἡ	*day*; καθ᾽ ἡμέραν *every day*
ἡνίκα (adv.)	*at the time when*
ἤτοι (conj.)	*or else*

Θ

θαρσέω	*be of good courage*
θάρσος, τό = θράσος [ᾰ]	*confidence, courage, overboldness, rashness, insolence*
θέλω	= *ἐθέλω.*
θέμις, θέμιστος, ἡ	*law, right* (agreed-upon common consent or prescription); θέμις ἐστί [*this*] *is right*
θεός, ὁ	*god*
*θνήσκω	*die; be killed*
θνητός (2/3)	*mortal*; θνητοί = *mortals*
θρῆνος, ὁ	*lamenting, funeral song, dirge*
θῦμος, ὁ	*breath; soul; desire; temper; spirit, courage*
*θύω	*sacrifice*

I

*ἱκνέομαι	(with - ῑ-; lengthened form of ἵκω, *come, reach*) *come, arrive*; poetic in pres., *come as a suppliant, beseech, entreat*
ἱππικός (3)	*of a horse* or *horses*
ἴσος (3)	*equal in size, strength,* or *number* + dat.
*ἵστημι	*cause to stand, set* (transitive forms are in the pres., impf., fut., and aor.[1] act.)
ἰώ	(ῐ) *Oh!*

K

καί (adv.)	*also, even*; usually stresses the idea in the word that follows
καί (conj.)	*and; actually*
καιρός, ὁ	*right point of anything, right time for action, critical moment, opportunity*
καί-τοι (pcl.)	adversative: *and yet, although*; rarely continuative: *and so then, and further*
κακός (3)	*bad, ill omened*
*κᾰλέω	*call, call by name*
κᾰλός (3)	*beautiful, good, noble*
κάρᾱ, τό	[ᾰ] *head*; poetic for κεφαλή
κᾰσίγνητος, ὁ/ἡ	*brother/sister*, adj. ος, η, ον
κατά (prep.)	+ acc.: *over, throughout, among all along*; + genit.: *down from*
κατ-*έχω	*hold, withhold, come from high sea to shore, reach destination safely*
κατ-*οῖδα	*know well, be assured of* (*κατ-είδω)
κάτω (adv.)	*down, below*; οἱ κάτω θεοί = *the gods below*; οἱ κάτω = *the dead*
κεῖμαι	*lie down, be situated, be placed/laid*
κεῖνος (3)	see ἐκεῖνος
κενός (3)	*empty, destitute, vain, futile, mean*
κέρδος, εος, τό	*gain, profit*
κλαίω	*weep, lament, wail*
κλεινός (3)	*renowned*
κλέπτω	*steal, accomplish by stealth; cozen, cheat, deceive*
κλύω	*hear, give ear, listen to* + genit.
κοινός (3/2)	*shared in common, kindred*
κόνις, εως, ἡ	*dust*
κόρη, ἡ	*girl; daughter*
κρᾰτέω	*rule, be master, lord*

κράτος, εος, τό	strength, might, power, mastery, victory
κρυπτός (3)	hidden, secret, concealed, secluded
κρύπτω	hide
*κτείνω	kill, slay
κῠρέω	(poetic for τυγχάνω) hit the mark

Λ

*λαγχάνω	obtain by lot; + partit. genit.: become possessed of a thing
*λαμβάνω	take, receive
λαμπρός (3)	bright, brilliant, radiant
*λανθάνω	act.: escape notice; mid. and pass.: forget, lose the memory of + genit.
*λέγω	say, proclaim
*λείπω	leave
λεύσσω	look; (poetic verb; pres. and impf. only)
λήγω	cease from + genit.
λήθω, λήθομαι	collateral forms of ⁺λανθάνω
λόγος, ου, ὁ	word, story, tale, fiction
λοιπός (3)	remaining, surviving; last; τὸ λοιπόν = the remainder, the future; τοῦ λοιποῦ (supply χρόνου) for the rest of the time, henceforward; τὰ λοιπά the rest, for the future
λούτρον, τό	bath, washing (of the corpse); poetic word libations
Λύκειος, ον	belonging to a wolf (λύκος) (an epithet of Apollo, 'Lycean' sometimes refers to Apollo's role as wolf-slayer, i.e., protector of flocks, sometimes to his role as god of light, <*λύκη, morning light)
λῡπέω	give pain, pain, distress, annoy
λύπη ἡ	[ῡ] pain of body or mind, grief, distress, suffering
λῠτήριος (3)	+ genit.: losing, delivering, setting free from; substantivized: atonement
λύω	[ῡ] loosen

M

μᾰκρός (3)	long, large
μάλιστα (adv.)	(superlative of μάλα, exceedingly) yes (emphatic), of course, especially
μᾶλλον (adv.)	(comparison of μάλα) more, more strongly, rather
μάντῐς, εως, ὁ	(μαίνομαι) a diviner, soothsayer, seer, prophet; (as fem.) a prophetess

*μανθάνω	learn, study
μάτην (adv.)	[ă] in vain, falsely, at random, pointlessly
μέγας, μεγάλη, μέγα	big, large, great
μέγιστος (3)	biggest, greatest, closest; superlative of μέγας, μεγάλη, μέγα
μεθ-*ίημι,	set loose, let go; + acc.· throw; mid.: loose, forego
μείζων, μεῖζον	bigger, greater; comparison of μέγας, μεγάλη, μέγα
*μέλλω	be on the point of doing; + pres./fut. inf. forms the periphrastic future; pres. inf. usually expressing will; be on the point of doing; to be always going to do (without doing), hence: delay, put off, hesitate
μέλω	be an object of care; impersonal use + dat.: it is a care (to me)
μέν	surely, certainly, indeed; μέν solitarium (i.e., with no δέ clause) emphatic, stressing and affirming
*μένω	remain
μέσος (3)	middle
μήτηρ, μητρός, ἡ	mother
μῑκρός (3)	small, little, trivial, insignificant
μῖσος, εος, τό	hate, hatred, grudge
μόλῐς (adv.)	with difficulty, hardly, scarcely, only just
μόνος (3)	alone, forsaken, only
μοῦνος	Ion. for μόνος
Μῠκηναῖος (3)	Mycenaean

N

ναίω	dwell
νομίζω	hold as custom or usage, practice as custom
νόμος, ὁ	custom, convention, law
νοῦς, ὁ	mind, thought
νύξ, νυκτός, ἡ	night
νῦν (adv.)	now, at present, as things are

Ξ

ξένος, ὁ	host, guest-friend; stranger
ξυν- see συν-	
ξυν-ίημι	see συν-ίημι, metaphorically: perceive, understand, know

O

ὅ-δε, ἥ-δε, τό-δε	(demon. pron.) this (points out what is present or before one)
ὁδός, ἡ	road, way, journey, wayfaring

ὁθούνεκα (conj.)	*because, that* (causal, but analogously to ὅτι introduces dependent sentence after verbs of 'saying'; restricted to Tragedy.)
οἷ (relative adv.)	*to which place, whither*
*οἶδα	*see with the mind's eye; know* (old pf. used as pres.)
οἶκος, ὁ	*house, abode, dwelling; home*
οἰκτρός (3)	*pitiable, lamentable*
οἷος, οἵα, οἷον	*such as, of which sort*
*οἴχομαι	*come, go, be gone*
ὀκνέω	*hesitate, hold back, shrink from doing* (physically or morally)
*ὄλ-λῡμι,	*destroy, ruin;* mid.: *perish, come to an end*
ὅμαιμος, ὁ/ἡ	*of the same blood, kinswoman*
ὄμμα, ατος, τό	*eye; light; illumination;* poetic word
ὁμοῦ (adv.)	*together, at once*
ὅμως (adv.)	*nevertheless, still;* ἀλλ' ὅμως = *but still*
ὄνειρον, τό	*dream*
ὁπόταν	= ὁπότε + ἄν; *when, as long as, whenever*
ὅπως (conj.)	with purpose clause: *so that;* comparative: *as;* time: *when*
*ὁράω	(aor. stem ἰδ-) *see*
ὀργή, ἡ	*natural impulse, temperament, disposition, anger, wrath passion*
ὀρθός (3)	*straight, erect, upright; right, true,*
ὀρθῶς (adv.)	*rightly, truthfully, justly*
ὄρνις, ὄρνιθος, ὁ/ἡ	*bird; omen*
ὅς, ἥ, ὅ	(relative pron.) *who, that*
ὅσος (3)	*how much, as great, as many*
ὅστις, ἥτις, ὅ τι	(indefinite/general relative pron.) *whoever, any one who, whatever, anything which*
ὅτε (adv.)	*when* (ὅταν = ὅτε + ἄν, temporal clauses referring indefinitely to the fut. take subjv. with ἄν, or opt. without ἄν); ὅταν περ = *just as soon as; since*
ὅτι (conj.)	*that* (introduces indirect discourse after phrases/verbs of 'saying' and 'thinking.' So do οὕνεκα, ὁθούνεκα, ὡς, ὅπως)
οὐ δῆτα	*indeed/certainly not!* (in emphatic negative answers)
οὐκ-έτι, μη-κέτι (adv.)	*no longer, no more, no further*
οὔκουν (adv.)	(= οὐκ οὖν) *and so not? not therefore? not then?* (often with 2nd pers. fut. indic., or opt. with ἄν, at an opening of a speech)
οὖν (conj.)	*so now, therefore, then, in fact, at all events* (inferential: marks transition to a new thought)
οὕνεκα	*on account of for the sake of* + genit., usually postpositive; (improper prep., i.e., an adv. used as a prep. but cannot form compounds); conj. introducing dependent statement = ὅτι

οὖς, ὠτός, τό	ear, handle
οὔ-τις, οὔ-τινος	no one, nobody
οὔ-τοι (adv.)	indeed not
οὗτος, αὕτη, τοῦτο	(demon. pron.) this, that (designates the nearer of two things, place, time, thought); opposed to ἐκεῖνος
οὕτως (adv.)	so, thus, in this manner
ὀφείλω	be under obligation

Π

παῖς, παιδός, ὁ/ἡ	child
πάλαι (adv.)	long ago, formerly, before
παλαιός (3)	old in years, old in date, ancient
πάλιν (adv.)	again, once more, in turn
παρά (prep.)	+ genit.: from; + acc.: running along, beside; in comparison with; παρ᾽ οὐδέν compared with nothing, i.e., of no account, worth nothing; + dat. by the side of
πάρ-*ειμι	be by, be present / near; πάρεστι + dat.; impersonal: it is in one's power
παρ-*ίημι	let drop beside, let fall, give up, slacken, disregard, pass by, allow
πάρος (adv.)	before
παρ-ουσία, ἡ	presence
πᾶς, πᾶσα, πᾶν	all, every, everything
*πάσχω	suffer, experience, be affected by anything (whether good or bad)
πατήρ, πατρός, ὁ	father
πατρῷος (3)	of one's father
παῦρος (3)	little, small, short
παύω	stop
*πείθω	persuade (πείσω, ἔπεισα, πέπεικα); 2 pf. πέποιθα :trust, believe, rely; have confidence in; πέπεισμαι, ἐπείσθην, πεισθήσομαι pf. and aor.² mid. and pass.: obey
*πειράομαι	try, attempt
πέλᾰς	near, hard by, close (improper prep., i.e., cannot form compounds., + genit. and also + dat.); adv.: near, by
*πέμπω	send
πέρ	(postpositive and enclit. pcl.) much, very, just, even (adds force to the word to which it is annexed)
πέρᾱ	beyond measure, across, over, further, excessively; (improper prep., i.e., cannot form compounds)

πῆμα, ατος, τό	*misery, calamity, suffering*
πικρός (2/3)	*bitter, harsh, cruel*
*πίπτω	*fall*
πιστεύω	*believe, trust, put faith in*
πιστός (3)	*reliable, faithful, loyal*
πλήν (prep.)	+ genit. *except, save;* (adv.) *besides, unless, save, except*
πλέον (comparative adv.)	(⁺πολύς, πολλή, πολύ, *much*) *more*
πλοῦτος, ὁ	*wealth, riches*
ποῖ	*whither?; to what end? sometimes* + genit.
ποῖος (3)	(interrog. adj.) *of what sort*
πολύς, πολλή, πολύ	*much;* πολλά (adv.) *many times*
πολύ-πονος (2)	*much-suffering; causing much pain, painful*
πόνος, ὁ	*pain, toil*
*πόρω	*bring, pass, contrive*
πότερον/ πότερα . . . ἤ	*whether . . . or* (introduces direct alternative questions with πότερον/πότερα frequently left untranslated in English)
που (enclit. adv.)	*frequently qualifies an expression* (οἶσθα) = 'I suppose'
ποῦ (interrog. adv.)	*where?*
πούς, ποδός, ὁ	*foot*
πρᾶγμα, ατος, τό	*deed, matter*
*πράσσω	*do, achieve, effect, bring about bring to pass*
πρέπω	*be like, resemble;* quasi impersonal: *it beseems*
πρίν (conj.)	[ῐ] *before, erst, formerly* (when subordinated to an affirmative clause usually takes inf.)
πρό (prep.)	+ genit.: *before, in front of*
πρό-δοτος (2)	*betrayed, abandoned*
προμήθια, ἡ	*forethought, consideration*
πρός (prep.)	+ genit.: *from, at the hand of* (with verbs of having, receiving, etc.); + genit. of agent: *by* is common in poetry; + dat.: *agreeable, becoming, be on the side of, hard by, near, at; in addition to*
προσ-ήκω	*have come/arrived; be near, be at hand;* impersonal + dat.: *beseems, belongs, befits*
πρόσθε(ν)(adv.)	*before, formerly, long ago, previously*
προς-⁺κείμαι	+ dat.: *lie with, lie near, placed near; be attached to*
προσ-*μένω	+ acc.: *wait for, await*
πρόσ-πολος (2)	*servant, attendant*
προ-*τίθημι	*place, set before; lay out a dead body;* mid.: *exhibit*
πρῶτον (adv.)	*first*
πρῶτος (3)	*first, foremost, front*

πῶλος, ὁ	*foal*, whether a *colt* or *filly*
πως (adv.)	*somehow, in any way*
πῶς (adv.)	*how?*

Σ

σαφής, ές	*clear, distinct, plain*
σέθεν	*old poetic form of* σοῦ, *genit. of* σύ
σθένω	*have power, be strong*
σμῑκρός (3)	= μῑκρός
σοφός (3)	*clever, wise, prudent, skilled*
σποδός, ἡ	*ashes*
στέγη, ἡ	*house*; lit.: *roof*
στενάχω	[ᾰ] (lengthened for στένω) transitive: *bemoan, bewail, lament*
στένω	(στενός, narrow) *sigh*; transitive: *bemoan, lament, deplore, complain*; only in pres. and impf.
στέφω	*crown, wreathe, honor*
στρατός, ὁ	*army, people, crowd*
συμ-φέρω	*gather, contribute, help*
συμφορά, ἡ	*bringing together, event, mishap, misfortune, calamity*
σύν (prep.)	+ dat.: *with*; (adv.) *together, at once, jointly; besides, moreover*
συν-είδω	*share in the knowledge*; (σύνοιδα, pf. with present sense)
σύν-*ειμι	*associate, live with*
συν-ίημι	metaphorically: *perceive, understand, know*
*σῴζω	*save, keep, keep alive*
σῶμα, ατος, τό	*body, dead body*

T

τάλᾱς, τάλαινᾰ, τάλᾰν	(*τλάω, suffer) *suffering, wretched, enduring;*
τανῦν (adv.)	= τὰ νῦν; *now, at present*
*τάττω	*arrange, form, array, order, dictate* pass.: *be posted, stationed*
τάχος, εος, τό	*swiftness, speed;* ἐν τάχει *quickly*
τᾰφος, ὁ	*grave, tomb; rites of burial*
τέκνον, τό	*child*
τεκμήριον, τό	*proof, sign*
τελέω	*accomplish, finish*
τήκω	*pine, melt away* (pf. act. is used intransitively = pres. pass);
*τίκτω	*bring forth, bear, beget*

*τίθημι	place, put, set
τιμωρός, ὁ	avenger
τίς, τί	[ῐ] (interrog. pron.) who? which? what?
τὶς, τι	(indefinite pron.) anyone, anything
τλήμων, ονος, ὁ/ἡ	suffering, enduring, wretched, miserable; bold, daring, reckless, rash
τοι	postpositive and enclitic particle of inference: therefore, accordingly; strengthening an assertion: in truth, verily
τοιοῦτος, τοιαύτη, τοιοῦτο(ν)	(demon. pron.) such (in quality)
τοιόσδε, τοιάδε, τοιόνδε	such (in quality)
τοιοῦτος, -αύτη, -οῦτο	such, of such kind, nature, quality, such as this
τοσόσ-δε, τοσή-δε, τοσόν-δε	so great; demon. pron. τόσος (3) with stronger demon. sense
τοσόνδε (adv.)	so very, so much, to such a degree
τότε (adv.)	at that time, then, next
τρόπος, ὁ	way, mode
τροφή, ἡ	nourishment, food, rearing, nursing
*τύγχάνω	happens to be, meet, hit, obtain, chance, fall with, hit upon (+ genit.)
τύμβος, ὁ	tomb, grave
τύχη, ἡ	fate, good/bad luck, chance, accident; fatal accident/chance

Υ

ὑβρίζω	outrage, insult, maltreat
ὕβρις, εος, ἡ	[ῠ] outrage

Φ

*φαίνω	bring to light, show, make known, reveal, disclose; aor.[2] fut. pass./intrans.: appear
φάσμα, ατος, τό	apparition, phantom
φά-τις, εως, ἡ	(oracular) speech, rumor, report, story
φέρε	come, now, well (used like ἄγε, as an adv.)
*φέρω	bring, carry, bear; endure
*φεύγω	flee, run away
φήμη, ἡ	(Doric = φάμα) voice, rumor, message
*φημί	say, say yes
φθίω/φθίνω	decline, decay, wane

φιλέω	love, treat affectionately, welcome; + inf.: be wont to, use to, tend to
φίλη, ἡ	near and dear, friend
φίλος, ὁ	near and dear, friend
φίλος (2/3)	loved, near and dear (poetic adj. with active sense: loving)
φόβος, ὁ	fear, terror, fright, dismay
φοίνιος (2/3)	bloody (poetic for φόνιος)
φονεύς, έως, ὁ	murderer, slayer
φόνος, ὁ	murder, slaughter; homicide; (plural refers to one deed)
φορέω	constantly bear; frequentative of φέρω, implying repeated or habitual action
*φράζω	tell, declare, pronounce (stronger than λέγω); devise, plan; mid.: devise, consider, plan for (a person)
φρήν, φρενός, ἡ	midriff; mind (often in plural)
φρονέω	to be so minded towards, have certain thoughts for/toward (+ dat. and acc.); think, have an understanding
φῠλάσσω	guard; mid.: keep in one's mind
φύσις, εως, ἡ	[ῠ] nature, inborn quality; natural origin
*φύω	bring forth, produce; aor.² grew, was; pf. be by nature
φροῦδος (2/3)	gone away
φωνέω	speak loud or clearly
Φωκεύς, έως, ὁ	Phocian (from Phocis, a region in northern Greece that includes Delphi)
φῶς, φωτός, τό	= φάος, εος, τό light, daylight (usually signifies life versus the darkness of the Otherworld)

X

*χαίρω	rejoice; impv. is a common form of greeting either at meeting or parting: hail or farewell
χᾰρά, ἡ	joy, delight pleasure
χάρις, –ιτος, ἡ	[ᾰ] favor, pleasure, gratification, gratitude; χάριν + genit.: for the sake of, on account of (acc. sg. as a postpositive improper prep., i.e., an adv. used as a prep. but cannot form compounds)
χείρ, χειρός, ἡ	hand; metaphorically: force, power
χθών, χθονός, ἡ	the earth, ground, land, country
χράομαι	+ dat.: use, avail oneself of
χρεών	(indecl.) which must be, necessary
χρήζω	desire, long for; want, have need for, like

χρόνος, ὁ	*time*
χρή	*it is necessary* (indecl. noun, 'necessity,' with ἐστί supplied)
χωρέω	*go forward, advance, go, come*

Ψ

ψῡχή, ἡ	*breath, soul, life*

Ω

ὧδε (adv.)	*in this way, thus; so very, so exceedingly; hither*
ὡς (conj.)	causal: *inasmuch as, since, seeing that* (= ὅτι); temporal: *after, when* (= ἐπεί); indicating purpose: *in order that; so that* (= ὅπως); restrictive *as, for as for*; introduces indirect discourse (= ὅτι): *that*
ὡς	relat adv.: *as*; with comparative force *as*; heightens superlative: *as much, as possible*; exclamatory: *how*; in wishes: *if only*
ὥς	adv. of manner: *just so, thus*; demon. (with an accent) = οὕτως: *thus*
ὥσπερ (conj.)	*just as, as* (introduces comparative clause of quality)
ὥστε (conj.)	*so that, so as to*; (ὡς + connective τέ that has lost its meaning; opens result clause with finite verb or inf.)

241

BIBLIOGRAPHY

Battezzato, L. 2014. "Meter and Rhythm." In *Encyclopedia of Greek Tragedy*, ed. H.M. Roisman. Chichester, UK, and Hoboken, NJ: Wiley-Blackwell: Vol. II: 5822–839.

Blundell, M.W. 1989. *Helping Friends and Harming Enemies*. Cambridge: Cambridge University Press.

Burnett, A.P. 1998. *Revenge in Attic and Later Tragedy*. Berkeley, Los Angeles, and London: University of California Press.

Buxton, R.G.A. 1984. "Sophocles." *Greece & Rome. New Surveys in the Classics*, no. 16. Oxford; New York: Published for the Classical Association at the Clarendon Press.

Campbell, L. 1881. *Sophocles*. Vol. II. Oxford: Oxford University Press.

Conacher, D.J. 1967. *Euripidean Drama: Myth, Theme and Structure*. Toronto: University of Toronto Press.

Csapo, E., and W.J. Slater. 1995. *The Context of Ancient Drama*. Ann Arbor: University of Michigan Press.

Davies, M., and P.J. Finglass. 2014. *Stesichorus: The Poems*. Cambridge: Cambridge University Press.

Dawe, R.D. 1973. *Studies on the Text of Sophocles I: The Manuscripts and the Text*. Leiden: Brill.

Dawe, R.D. 1975. *Sophoclis Tragoediae*. Tom. I. Leipzig: BSB Teubner.

Denniston, J.D. 1954. (2nd ed.) Rev. by K.J. Dover. *The Greek Particles*. Oxford: Oxford University Press. First published 1934.

Devine, A.M., and L.D. Stephens. 1980. "Rules for Resolution: The Zielinskian Canon." *TAPHA* 110: 64–79.

Diggle, J. 1996. "Sophocles, *Ichneutae* (fr. 314 Radt)." *ZPE* 112: 3–17.

Dugdale, E. 2014a. "Features of Greek Tragedy." In *Encyclopedia of Greek Tragedy*, ed. H.M. Roisman. Chichester, UK, and Hoboken, NJ: Wiley-Blackwell. Vol. I: 507–13.

Dugdale, E. 2014b. "Sophocles: *Electra*." In *Encyclopedia of Greek Tragedy*, ed. H.M. Roisman. Chichester, UK, and Hoboken, NJ: Wiley-Blackwell. Vol. III: 1278–86.

Easterling, P.E. 1987. "Women in Tragic Space." *BICS* 34: 15–26.

Esposito, S. 1996. "The Changing Roles of the Sophoclean Chorus." *Arion* 4: 85–114.

Finglass, P.J. 2005. "Is There a *Polis* in Sophocles' *Electra*?" *Phoenix* 59: 199–209.

Finglass, P.J. 2007. *Electra,* Sophocles. Cambridge, UK, and New York: Cambridge University Press.

Fitton Brown, A.D. 1956. "Notes on Sophocles' *Electra*." *CQ* 6: 38–39.

Goodwin, W.W. 1893. *The Moods and Tenses of the Greek Verb.* Boston: Ginn.

Griffin, J. 1999a. "Sophocles and the Democratic City." In Griffin 1999b: 73–94.

Griffin, J. (ed.) 1999b. *Sophocles Revisited: Essays Presented to Sir Hugh Lloyd-Jones.* Oxford: Oxford University Press.

Haslam, M. 1975. "The Authenticity of Euripides, *Phoenissai* 1–2 and Sophocles, *Electra* 1." *GRBS* 16: 140–75.

Hartigan, K.V. 1996. "Resolution without Victory/Victory without Resolution: The Identification Scene in Sophocles' *Electra*." In Sophocles' *"Electra" in Performance,* ed. F.D. Dunn. Stuttgart: M and P, 82–92.

Jebb, R.C. 1894. *Sophocles: "Electra."* Cambridge: Cambridge University Press; repr. London: Bristol Classical Press, 2004.

Kaimio, M. 2014. "Titles of Tragedies." In *Encyclopedia of Greek Tragedy,* ed. H.M. Roisman. Malden, MA, and Oxford: Wiley-Blackwell. Vol. III: 1398–400.

Kamerbeek, J.C. 1974. *The Plays of Sophocles, Part V: The "Electra."* Leiden: Brill.

Kells, J.H. 1973. *Sophocles: "Electra."* Cambridge: Cambridge University Press.

Knox, B.M.W. (1964) 1983. *The Heroic Temper: Studies in Sophoclean Tragedy.* Berkeley and Los Angeles: University of California Press.

Knox, B.M.W. 1982. "Sophocles and the *Polis.*" In *Sophocle.* Entretiens *Hardt* 29: 1–27.

Larkin, M. 1971. *Language in the Philosophy of Aristotle.* The Hague and Paris: Mouton.

Lefkowitz, M. 2014. "Sophocles: Literary Biography." In *Encyclopedia of Greek Tragedy,* ed. H.M. Roisman. Malden, MA, and Oxford: Wiley-Blackwell: Vol. III: 1290–95.

Ley, G. 2006. (Rev. ed.) *A Short Introduction to the Ancient Greek Theater.* Chicago and London: University of Chicago Press.

Ley, G. 2014. "Chorus." In *Encyclopedia of Greek Tragedy,* ed. H.M. Roisman. Malden, MA, and Oxford: Wiley-Blackwell. Vol. I: 220–24.

Liapis, V. 2012. *A Commentary on the "Rhesus" Attributed to Euripides.* Oxford and New York: Oxford University Press.

Liddell, H.G. and R. Scott. 1968. *A Greek-English Lexicon.* With a Supplement. Revised and augmented throughout by H. S. Jones with the assistance of R. McKenzie and with the co-operation of many scholars. 9th edition of 1940. Oxford: Clarendon Press.

Lloyd, M. 1999. "The Tragic Aorist." *CQ* n.s. 49: 24–45.

Lloyd, M. 2005. *Sophocles: "Electra."* London: Duckworth.

Lloyd-Jones, H., and N.G. Wilson. 1990. *Sophoclea: Studies on the Text of Sophocles.* Oxford: Oxford University Press.

Lloyd-Jones, H. and N.G. Wilson. 1997. *Sophocles: Second Thoughts.* Göttingen: Vandenhoeck und Ruprech.

MacLeod, L. 2001. *Dolos and Dike in Sophocles' "Elektra."* Leiden: Brill.

March, J. 2001. *Sophocles: "Electra."* Warminster, UK: Aris and Phillips.

Marcovich, M. 1984. *Three-Word Trimeter in Greek Tragedy.* Königstein.Ts., Germany: A. Hain.

Moorhouse, A.C. 1982. *The Syntax of Sophocles.* Leiden: Brill.

Pelliccia, H. 2009. "Sophocles: '*Electra*' by P.J. Finglass." *CR* 59.1: 34–38.

Prag, A.J.N.W. 1985. *The "Oresteia": Iconographic and Narrative Tradition.* Warminster: Aris and Phillips.

Pickard-Cambridge, A. 1988. *The Dramatic Festivals of Athens,* 2nd ed. Rev. by J. Gould and D.M. Lewis. Oxford: Clarendon Press.

Roisman, H.M. 2000. "Meter and Meaning." *New England Classical Journal (NECJ)* 27: 182–99.

Roisman, H.M. 2005. *Sophocles: "Philoctetes."* London: Duckworth.

Roisman, H.M. (2008) 2017. (2nd printing with updates.) *Sophocles: Electra; Translation with Notes, Introduction, Interpretative Essay and Afterlife.* Newburyport, MA: Focus Publishing/Hackett.

Roisman, H.M. 2017. "Euripides' Electra." In *A Companion to Euripides,* ed. L.K. McClure. Chichester: John Wiley & Sons, 166–81.

Roisman, H.M. 2018. "The *Rhesus*—A Prosatyric Play." *Hermes* 146.4 (2018): 432–446.

Roisman, H.M., and C.A.E. Luschnig. 2011. *Euripides "Electra": A Commentary.* Norman: University of Oklahoma Press.

Sale, W. 1973. *Electra,* by Sophocles. Englewood Cliffs, NJ: Prentice-Hall.

Segal, C. 1966. "The *Electra* of Sophocles." *TAPhA* 97: 473–545.

Sheppard, J.T. 1927. "Electra: A Defense of Sophocles." *CR* 41: 2–9.

Smyth, H.W. 1956. *Greek Grammar.* Rev. by G. M. Messing. Cambridge, MA: Harvard University Press.

Sutton, D.F. 1980. *The Greek Satyr Play.* Meisenheim am Glan: Anton Hain.

Swift, L. 2015. "Stesichorus on Stage." In *Stesichorus in Context,* ed. P.J. Finglass and A. Kelly. Cambridge: Cambridge University Press, 125–44.

Taplin, O. 1978. *Greek Tragedy in Action.* Berkeley and Los Angeles: University of California Press.

West, M.L. 1978. Review of Dawe's first edition (1975), *Gnomon* 50: 236–43.

West, M.L. 1982. *Greek Metre.* Oxford: Clarendon Press.

West, M.L. 1984. "Tragica VII." *BICS* 31: 171–96.

Whitman, C.H. 1951. *Sophocles: A Study of Heroic Humanism.* Cambridge, MA: Harvard University Press.

Wiles, D. 1997. *Tragedy in Athens: Performance Space and Theatrical Meaning.* Cambridge: Cambridge University Press.

Wilson, P. 2000. *The Athenian Institution of the* Khoregia: *The Chorus, the City and the Stage.* Cambridge: Cambridge University Press.

Winnington-Ingram, R.P. 1980. *Sophocles: An Interpretation.* Cambridge: Cambridge University Press.

Winnington-Ingram, R.P. 2003. "Euripides: *Poiētēs Sophos.*" In *Euripides,* ed. J. Mossman. Oxford: Oxford University Press, 47–63 (= *Arethusa* 2 [1969] 127–42).

Woodard, T. 1966a. "The *Electra* of Sophocles." In *Sophocles: A Collection of Essays,* ed. T. Woodard. Englewood Cliffs, NJ: Prentice Hall, 125–45.

Woodard, T. (ed.) 1966b. *Sophocles: A Collection of Critical Essays.* Englewood Cliffs, NJ: Prentice Hall.